THE PASSING SUMMER

A South African Pilgrimage in the Politics of Love

Also by Michael Cassidy

Bursting the Wineskins
Chasing the Wind

THE PASSING SUMMER

A South African Pilgrimage in the Politics of Love

Michael Cassidy

Hodder & Stoughton

LONDON SYDNEY AUCKLAND TORONTO

British Library Cataloguing in Publication Data

Cassidy, Michael
  The passing summer: a South African pilgrimage in
  the politics of love.
  1. South Africa. Christian theology
  I. Title
  261.7

  ISBN 0-340-42627-6

*Published by Hodder and Stoughton Ltd, Mill
Road, Dunton Green, Sevenoaks, Kent TN13 2YA. Editorial Office: 47
Bedford Square, London EC1B 3DP. Photoset by Rowland Phototypesetting
Ltd, Bury St Edmunds, Suffolk. Printed in Great Britain by Richard Clay
Ltd, Bungay, Suffolk.*

The harvest is past,
the summer has ended,
and we are not saved.
(Jeremiah 8:20)

For my friends and colleagues in African Enterprise

. . . all of whom long for a 'new day' in the
Beloved Country,
and pray that the summer is not past . . .

Contents

Appendices

Foreword

Anybody who writes a book on South Africa at this critical stage of her history takes a risk: the risk of challenging the people of South Africa. He also takes the even greater risk of being proved wrong by subsequent events.

In this book Michael Cassidy dares to be vulnerable by exposing himself to judgement at the bar of history. His courage, which is to be envied, is based on the unshakeable belief that the word of God is true for all times and is a sure basis for a secure and lasting future. He leaves no one comfortable. South Africans of all hues of political persuasion are challenged, in fact shaken, when they are made to see many of their long-cherished and selfish visions destroyed one after another. In this lies the greatness of this book.

In our country there is a very narrow understanding of patriotism. A patriot is understood to be one who does not disturb the status quo, one who joins those who do not like to see real change in our country. In fact a patriot is taken to be one who is prepared to take up arms or lose his life to oppose any such change. Michael Cassidy is not such a patriot. He is a patriot of a different mould, a patriot *par excellence* who articulates the will of God with a prophetic sharpness both to people in high places and to ordinary people. One of his favourite texts is 2 Chronicles 7:14 – 'If my people will humble themselves and pray, then will I hear from heaven and forgive their sin and will heal their land.'

This book is an appeal, a loud cry, to the people of South Africa: 'Time is running out.' If we do not heed the warning we may be too late to redeem the situation. In the words of Martin Luther King (Jnr) quoted in this book: 'It is indeed possible to be too late in history with the right answers.'

The various options or scenarios facing our country are put before us and analysed in a crystal-clear way. Many of these options cannot stand this acid test and disintegrate before our eyes. The attitudes, fears, prejudices and idiosyncrasies of the people which are responsible in no small way for the difficulties we face are also brought to the surface for all to see. No racial group has been spared and with amazing objectivity we are shown ourselves as if in a mirror. This is the kind of therapy we need as a people and I trust that as many people as possible will read this book and be helped thereby. Indeed in the words of Professor Sampie Terreblanche: 'The key to the future may lie in the death of the myths of the past.'

Referring to the crisis of hope facing many of us, Michael Cassidy writes: 'The trouble is that too many of us in this land have built prisons for ourselves and have occupied them so long and become so accustomed to their walls that we have accepted the notion that we must be incarcerated for life. This makes us abandon the hope of ever getting the place right and seeing our dreams of better things fulfilled.'

This book makes no apology for offering only one solution to the problems of our land – *the Christian solution*.

This is seen in the politics of love. As Michael says: 'Love is the most neglected yet most necessary political virtue, especially in South Africa, where every other form of politics has been tried and found wanting. In fact to labour for such love in the social arena is to labour for the kingdom of God in some measure at least in the here and now.'

The author also opens a window on the outside world by emphasising the global significance of our national crisis. In the words of Richard Neuhaus: 'The debate about the future of South Africa is in many ways a debate about the future of our life together on this small earth – about relations between rich and poor, between races and ideologies, indeed about the meaning of freedom, peace and justice in a deeply disordered world. Much of the debate is about oddities, wrongs, fears peculiar to South African society. But those who have ears to hear should be left with no doubt that South Africans talking about themselves are in fact talking about all of us, the kind of people we sometimes hope, and sometimes fear, we may really be!'

May this contribution by Michael Cassidy to save South
Africa be earnestly embraced by readers and blessed by God!
PULA! MOJALEFA!
LET IT RAIN! Mojalefa (Michael's Sotho name)

Rev. Mmutlanyane Stanley Mogoba
Presiding Bishop of the Methodist Church of Southern
Africa

Preface

I am a South African, so I love my land. I am also a Christian, so I love my Lord (much more, actually, than I love my land, though the two loves need not be antithetical). I am also an evangelist, so I love preaching the gospel of Jesus Christ. My purest delight comes, therefore, when I can bring my three loves together and preach the gospel of my Lord to the land of my birth.

However, as all the world knows, something has gone wrong, terribly wrong, with this land of my birth. As far as my own life and calling are concerned, I find that the South African crisis has made normal evangelising very difficult, and in some cases impossible. Sometimes I feel like a harvester who heads down to his fields only to find that the grain is on fire, the labourers fighting and the cattle stampeding. Suddenly normal harvesting is impossible. Something prior to that needs to be done. The fire must be put out, the labourers reconciled and the cattle pacified. Then the harvester can get on normally with his work.

In other words, in South Africa today so serious is our downward spiral towards national tragedy that there is a major Christian agenda to face along with whatever other work each of us is called to do: to resolve our extremely dangerous socio-political crisis. This must of course involve politicians, social scientists, economists, and so on. But in my judgement it most especially involves, certainly in this context, the Christian church.

The fact is that seventy-eight per cent of South Africans profess to be Christian. Theoretically, at least, they profess an allegiance transcending nation, tribe, language and party. Surely, then, if that allegiance were faithfully activated and those supra-national Christian links from left to right of the political spectrum were faithfully nurtured and activated, a way forward could be found. But instead we find genuine Christians on every side of the South African conflict and in dozens of different opposing camps. In many ways, therefore, our political problem is really a religious and theological one, and to miss this is to miss a crucial component in the whole drama. It also means overlooking where clues to the future may be found.

This makes South Africa not only 'the workshop of the world' – politically, socially and economically – but a test case for the workability and relevance of the Christian faith in polarised contexts anywhere.

The question is, 'Can and will the church make a difference?' But the prior question is, 'What can and should the church do?' This raises the issue of how the church anywhere should relate to the socio-political issues raised by the various contexts in which it lives.

Because of the difficulty and complexity of our South African arena, this question has pressed in on me and others with ever-deepening and often confusing intensity. The result has been to make me pause, take stock, do some new homework and struggle with the issue in new ways. To be sure, it can't be evaded. Thus has this task and this book thrust itself upon me.

Reflecting on how to tackle this volume, I concluded there was only one contribution I could bring, and only one story and one struggle I could meaningfully write about – and that was my own. My own birth, history and destiny have cast me for good or ill into this place and given me exposure to many of the more interesting actors upon this strange stage. And this exposure is integral to my own current struggles with how Christians relate to their surrounding society.

So I'm going to tell my story. Not as an autobiography, mind you. I am taking only one thread of experience and thought (*i.e.* the gospel and how it addresses the socio-political issue) and following it personally.

I hasten to add that I do not have all the answers. I am indeed, with many others, a fellow struggler along the way towards new light. But I hope that what is shared in these pages will shed some light on the path, not only for other South African strugglers, but also for Christians in other parts of the world in their own contexts. Perhaps they will find points of similarity or identification with what I and their Christian brothers and sisters are working through in this particular corner of God's multidimensional harvest field. Indeed, if the South African church and nation can in the years ahead find under God a way through, then there will emerge from this unlikely place a message which will bless, encourage and inspire the world.

My aim is to address the thinking Christian layperson, rather than the secular political analyst or the professional theologian. I want to try to illuminate this context and its inner dynamics meaningfully and relevantly for the person in the pew who shares my struggles.

In a real sense, fellow South African Christians are my special and primary focus, and for them I pray that clear minds, hearts and wills may be moved towards those paths of national healing which God has for us at this late hour in our history. But I sincerely hope that readers in the wider world who eavesdrop on this discussion will find here not only grist for the mill in their praying for South Africa but also truths and principles valid for their own situations.

A last point. In writing about a thoroughly alienated and polarised context, one might be tempted to plug one group's particular line or try to please one particular constituency. I have, however, vigorously resisted this. I have simply written about how I personally see this situation and our Christian responsibility in it. A particular hope, however, is that I will at least be able to manifest Christian integrity and a sincere attempt at biblical faithfulness in the conclusions reached.

One editorial point: at a few places in the text I have changed the names of people where protecting their identity seemed advisable.

May God bless and prosper what we now send forth, not only for the sake of South Africa but for the sake of his kingdom everywhere.

Michael Cassidy   Pietermaritzburg, April 1988

Acknowledgements

My first debt of gratitude in this project must go to those people, too many to enumerate, who have lifted the writing of this volume to the Lord in intercession. This has meant more than words can express.

Special gratitude must go to Nellis Du Preez, an indefatigable personal assistant, friend and counsellor, and to my research assistants Lonni Jackson and John Young, who came over from the United States to help me diligently and ably over so many months.

On the editorial side, monumental and invaluable help was given me by Derryn Hurry and Anthea Garman. Without their labours, encouragement, insights and prayers this book would not have seen the light of day.

Useful reflections and counsel at various points also came from Hugh Wetmore, David Richardson, Frank Chikane, Philip le Feuvre, Ron Sider, Coretta Scott King, Vincent Harding, Michael Nuttall and Alan Paton.

Others who read sections of the book and gave most helpful counsel include Andrew Mohibidu, David Bosch, Wessel Dirksen, Mbulelo Hina, Bill Winter, Harry Oppenheimer, John Tooke, Mmutlanyane Mogoba, Don Jacobs, Zig Aske, David Hewitson, Paul Birch, Lutando Charlie, Koos Venter, Nicky Grieshaber, Peter Kerchhoff, David Geerdts and Abiel Thipanyane. Of course, for all the views herein, plus any errors of facts or figures, I remain personally responsible. They are mine, and not necessarily those of African Enterprise or the National Initiative for Reconciliation or anyone else.

Huge typing and word processing labours were sacrificially done by Lois Stephenson and Colleen Smith, whom I cannot thank enough. I am likewise deeply indebted to Edward England, my agent in London, to David Wavre, of Hodder & Stoughton, and to David Mackinder, my copy-editor, who painstakingly piloted the project through its final stages.

Finally, I must express very particular appreciation to four most special people – my wife Carol, and my children, Cathy, Debbie and Martin. Not only have they made many sacrifices in family time to enable me to complete this project, but they have encouraged me with patience, love and prayers all along the line – and that means the world to me.

I mustn't forget to mention the marvellous places of retreat, quiet and sanctuary for writing which were graciously given me through 1987 by Alastair and Pearl Gilson, Lynn and Derryn Hurry, Geoff and Dawn Beghin, Jack and Betty Badham and the Everglades staff. How much I owe them all!

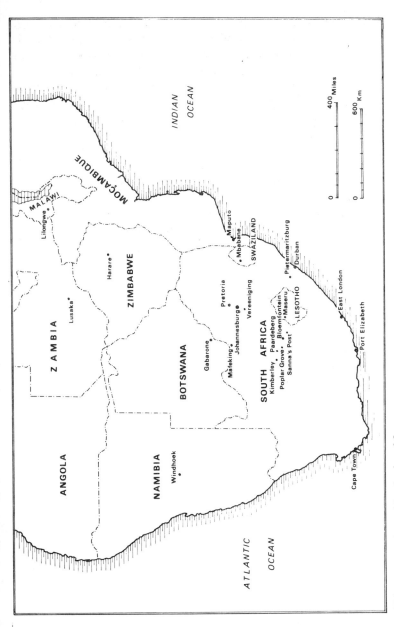

[Places mentioned in the book]

Part One

NATION AFLAME
(South Africa in crisis)

1   The Passing Summer

One gets quite tired of saying things which are first mocked at and then adopted, sometimes, alas, too late.

Winston Churchill

There is such a thing in history as being too late with the right answers.

Martin Luther King

The harvest is past,
the summer has ended,
and we are not saved.

Jeremiah 8:20

BURNING LAND

I woke early at home in Pietermaritzburg on the Sunday morning of 8 June 1986, with my head in a whirl. Was it not too late now for South Africa to be saved? Had its summer-time of opportunity for peaceful change not passed?

A myriad of thoughts relating to the previous days tumbled and churned through my mind as I struggled to make sense of it all. From President Kaunda of Zambia to Cape Town. From Parliament and its protected precincts to a nation on fire. What to make of it?

The country was burning. People were dying daily. Cars and houses were alight.

In dozens of townships across the nation the police and the military were in confrontation with young black activists. Black factions were in collision with each other. Black hearts were aflame with political passion and pent-up rage. Bottled-up frustration was pouring from every pore of South Africa's black community. They were screaming to the world and to their rulers: 'Enough is enough!'

The air reeked of revolution. It felt like the lid of the whole South African cauldron was finally about to blow. Many blacks were smelling victory and felt liberation was finally in sight. Another few puffs of smoke in Soweto or Langa or KwaMashu, and the whole apartheid edifice would come tumbling down.

Whites for their part had never felt more anxious and afraid. Thousands were wondering when the township rage would spill over into their hitherto protected suburbs. Fear was suddenly a new and daily companion to many who had never known its dread clutches before. Gun shops were also doing a roaring trade.

The Government response seemed to be to screw the lid down ever more tightly, with one tough measure upon another. In Johannesburg the previous week, I had picked up *Business Day* – a consequential daily – and noted its editorial comment: 'South Africa's past is – irrevocably – past.'[1] 'At least', I had thought to myself, 'we can be thankful for a relatively free press' – probably the freest in Africa. Little did I realise then that we were enjoying the last few days of such freedom.

As I lay in bed in those early Sunday-morning hours, it was not only what I heard and saw in South Africa that was on my mind, but what I had experienced in Lusaka, the capital of Zambia, a few days previously.

A VISIT TO LUSAKA

Never before had I been met at an airport by the President's men, whisked into a VIP lounge, had my customs formalities handled for me, and then been driven in a flag-flying government limousine to an exclusive hotel as a guest of the President (but then I'd heard that President Kaunda was a most gracious man).

Two good friends, Robin and Gareth, were with me. Over breakfast next morning, and before our meeting with the President, we met with the two senior African leaders of the

Evangelical Fellowship of Zambia, which had invited our African Enterprise team to conduct a city-wide evangelistic campaign to Lusaka in 1988 or 1989.

These two evangelical leaders, James and Titus, were fine men, gracious, godly and Christ-centred. I was thankful Africa had such Christian leaders.

But from all accounts they were lucky to be alive.

Lusaka under attack

Just a few days previously they had heard the huge noise outside their offices of a high-powered, low-flying plane. They rushed out to see two bombers flying 'very low and slow – just above tree-top height'. Seeing the face of a white pilot, they suddenly gasped: 'These can't be Zambian planes!'

No sooner had the thought formed than the two men were mesmerised by a car racing by and firing a sort of smoke signal up towards the plane – at which point, to their astonishment, they saw 'huge silver things drop out from the planes'.

'Bombs!', they yelled, incredulous, as they fled into the house. Several shattering explosions followed just outside, culminating in the screaming acceleration of the planes as they raced from the scene of their attack.

Someone had bombed Lusaka. Who? It was mind-boggling.

James and Titus had escaped death by only a few metres.

'We went outside,' said the two Christian leaders, 'concluding quickly that this must have been a South African attempt to blow up the ANC [African National Congress]. But they got the wrong place completely. ANC offices are far from there. Instead they had mistakenly targeted a United Nations transit camp with about twenty Moçambicans and Angolans in it. But even this they missed, the bombs falling wide of the mark and injuring a few children instead, and a couple of young girls, one pregnant, who was hit by shrapnel. Two people died, one Zambian, one Namibian, and about ten were injured.'

The men wore quizzical looks of futility, lips pursed, eyes

questioning. Robin, Gareth and I just stared, not knowing what to say.

'You know, brothers,' said one of the men very quietly, 'you people in South Africa must face the fact that change is coming. And the church, the Lord's people, must prayerfully see where you all fit in, and help people prepare for change. You must also try to minimise confrontation. You all need to speak with a prophetic voice.'

It was quite a challenge.

An audience with President Kaunda

State House, Lusaka, was built originally for the British Colonial Governor: it has grace, spaciousness and an air about it.

The President's aides gave us a warm welcome and then ushered us towards an open door. 'We hope you won't mind saying something to the press,' said a senior aide, almost in a casual aside.

I nearly flipped. We thought we were coming on a confidential, private visit. However, there was no time even to verbalise these panicked thoughts, for we were now already in a room jam-packed with tape-recorders, TV cameras and journalists all poised with pad and pen.

After we'd faced an initial bout of wide-ranging questions, President Kaunda, immaculate in safari-suit and clutching the legendary white handkerchief, entered the room and the questioning continued. Thereafter, having negotiated the ordeal, we were on our own with one of Africa's more famous men.

Kenneth Kaunda, one saw at once, was a gentleman and a Christian. This emerged quickly in the way he responded to our questions about how he viewed the South African situation. Kaunda made many significant comments and some striking political observations.

Kaunda's viewpoint

First, he said, the major tragedy of South Africa, as it had been in Angola, Moçambique and old Rhodesia, is one of missing opportunities to do something while there is still time.

Kaunda told us how he had offered his services in Rhodesia to Prime Minister Winston Field, to act as a bridge between the white Government and the black nationalists. 'But this was declined. And the gap widened.' Later he said he had counselled the British to deal with the brewing UDI situation before it got out of hand. He sent similar signals to Ian Smith. They were disregarded and forty-five thousand people lost their lives in a drawn-out bush war. Likewise, he had sent a senior aide to Salazar in Portugal saying, 'You fear communism. But if you fail to deal in time with the black nationalists in Angola and Moçambique, you'll definitely deal with black communists.' Salazar apparently thought this a joke.

So too Kenneth Kaunda had said in 1969 to the South African Prime Minister John Vorster: '*You* can change the situation. Act while you have time.' Then in 1975 he told him again about Soweto, 'You are sitting on a volcano,' to which Vorster had replied: 'Mr President, you don't know what you are talking about.'

'In 1972,' said Kaunda, 'I told a press conference there will be an explosion in fifteen years [*i.e.* 1987] unless South Africa moves quickly. I would love to have been proved wrong. But I wasn't. So I say to Mr Botha that he should deal now with leading black nationalists or South Africa will be destined later to deal with black communists.

'Another of South Africa's problems relates to perceptions,' he continued, as he went on to talk about Nelson Mandela and Mr Oliver Tambo, President of the African National Congress, in terms which would be novel to those of us who are average white South Africans. 'Mr Mandela and Mr Tambo are perceived as extremists. Yet in time they will be seen as moderates. But then it will be too late.

'I meet Mr Tambo often, and we pray and say grace at the table. He's a decent human being. And even now neither Mandela nor Tambo say they want to drive the whites into the sea.

'And only last year the ANC reaffirmed its commitment to non-racialism. And when they met in the bush with your businessmen, it was Mr Tambo who said: "The way we're

sitting is confrontational. Let's mix up and be round a table."
Then he said grace.

'Can you not deal with a man like that? By meeting you can
iron out differences, surely?

'The British said Kenyatta in jail was "the leader of darkness". Later they said he was a "world statesman". In Zambia
the British called me "the black mamba". But I have not been
one!' said the President chortling. 'The problem is perceptions. If your perceptions are wrong, your responses will be
wrong.'

Kaunda went on: 'The Boers fought the Boer War and then
founded the Broederbond. And Africans know why. It was to
gain Afrikaner freedom. How can the Afrikaner not see now
that Africans have the same aspirations and are equally
assured of victory?'

The possibility of a regional summit

We then asked the President whether he himself would be
willing to be an honest broker in seeking to bring about a
regional summit or some connection between alienated
groups in Southern Africa.

'Every summit must have a purpose and a worthwhile
agenda,' he replied. 'If I felt we could establish such a purpose
and agree on such an agenda, and if I felt something could
come from it between P W Botha and the Frontline States, I
would be willing to help. We took a chance in meeting
with Vorster and would be willing to take such chances
again.'

'Would the process of unbanning the ANC and the release
of Mandela be an adequate agenda?' one of us asked. The
President nodded in affirmation.

'Could we convey this to leadership in Cape Town?' we
asked. Indeed.

'Mandela must be released and allowed to consult with his
colleagues,' said Kaunda. 'He and Mr Tambo will sooner
or later be required back there to control and guide the
people. To talk about this process would be a worthy agenda.
Certainly you can convey this to Cape Town.'

It was quite a thought. It fitted too with our reconciling purposes in making the trip in the first place.

We ended this first session with prayer.

The ANC and Chief Buthelezi

Later, over lunch, I asked Kaunda if he had ever been to South Africa. Huge laughter. 'I was there once long ago – in 1958. I was locked up for twenty-four hours at Jan Smuts airport and not even allowed accommodation at a hotel. So I didn't really see your country!' (I thought of Gandhi's experience in South Africa. We do have a knack of getting it wrong with emerging key figures!)

I then put a very South African question to the President.

'What about the communist threat in Southern Africa?'

'Black nationalists', said Kaunda, 'have often sought help from the West in their struggles for freedom, but generally it was not forthcoming. Many then turned to the Soviets. The tragedy is that the ideology which makes the weapons will often follow the weapons unless political conflicts and struggles for freedom are peacefully resolved round a table.'

'And the ANC?' I asked. 'Don't communists predominate in it? I would see that as very problematic.'

'No way. They are in an absolute minority. The communist wing could never overwhelm the nationalist wing.' (I secretly wondered if this was not wishful thinking, but noted that this view accorded with the considered conclusion of the *Economist*, a relatively conservative and usually reliable magazine, which estimated the ANC was two-thirds nationalist and one-third communist.)

'And Mr President, what about Chief Mangosothu Buthelezi?'

President Kaunda said he saw him as a very important factor in the equation.

I was obviously also aware that the ANC were very down on Buthelezi, yet I knew him as a man of great consequence for the future, though struggling (in integrity, I believe) like so many other South Africans, to cope with the legacies of history and with the impossibles of the situation.

Our time with Kaunda ended with him personally serving coffee to each of us.

'He always does it himself,' said an admiring aide.

Back at the hotel, it didn't take us long to decide that rather than all returning home immediately, we should go to Cape Town.

A few phone calls, and the deed was done.

A VISIT TO CAPE TOWN

Our hours in Cape Town the following evening and the day after that were filled with parliamentary encounters. Each person we met was a Christian, and we opened each discussion with prayer.

Was there no way to thaw the seemingly intractable relationships between black and white leaders? Could Kaunda not be a facilitator?

We saw that the prevailing view in Cape Town was that 'politically it was impossible'.

But could we not make even any modest beginnings to get talks about talks, especially with a facilitator like Kaunda?

Seemingly not.

I found this exasperating, especially when one government leader said, 'We are in a situation where hours count,' and another prophesied, 'The next two weeks will determine the next two decades.' Yet political factors seemed destined endlessly to prevent *any* really bold, quantum leap out of the log-jam, either now or at any time. And opportunities, as Kaunda had said, would be lost ever more irrevocably and finally.

Robin, Gareth and I felt floored – but then we were not politicians. Besides, we were very small fry.

That much we knew. Yet Jesus had used nobodies before: that was some comfort.

Prisoners of history

Robin, Gareth and I convened a little prayer breakfast early the next morning with three MPs (two Afrikaner Nationalists and one Progressive Federal Party (PFP) member). We went immediately to prayer, even before eating.

The two Afrikaners were not only in crisis, they were in tears. The dreadful, deteriorating situation was not lost on them. Their faith too was in collision with so much that was happening.

Now here was a paradox! Two men, both part of the system and both with integrity too – deep, godly, Christian men. Both feeling God had put them there for his purposes – maybe as Nehemiahs and cupbearers to the king (Neh 1), or as seemingly collaborationist Obadiahs at the court of Ahab, but in league with the confrontationist Elijah (1 Kings 18).

The idea would be unthinkable in Lusaka and in a thousand South African townships. Christians in such a place? Impossible! But it's true. God has many of his people in the South African political establishment. Each of course with their own histories, and sometimes still the prisoners of those histories.

Faith, hope and despair

As we talked and shared about Lusaka and the present crisis, the heart of the South African tragedy stared us in the face. One of the men asked if there was any thought I had from the scriptures.

At the very top of head and heart was the matter of time. Had it run out or not for South Africa? Is the summer nearly over – or completely over, as the people of Judah had lamented just before Babylonian judgement, 'The harvest is past, the summer has ended, and we are not saved' (Jer 8:20)? Was it too late for answers?

We looked first at Jeremiah 18:7–12. The context is God's impending judgement on rebellious, apostate, oppressive Judah. The divine word seems to be that there is still a little time for the nation to repent, and if it does so, judgement, even at that late hour, would be averted.

But the story is different in Jeremiah 27. There time has fully run out. The die of judgement is cast. Nebuchadnezzar's armies will not now be stopped. They will advance by God's permissive will to inflict judgement on Judah – the sacking of

Jerusalem, the destruction of the Temple and the taking of most of Judah into a seventy-year captivity in Babylon. If repentance came not from God's pleas through the prophets, it would come now under the duress of judgement.

Yet still there is some good news. Even when delivering a massive historical spanking, God still has his good plans for us, to give us a future and a hope.

A later passage reads:

> For I know the plans I have for you, says the Lord, plans for welfare and not for evil, to give you a future and a hope. Then you will call upon me and come and pray to me, and I will hear you. You will seek me and find me; when you seek me with all your heart, I will be found by you, says the Lord, and I will restore your fortunes and gather you from all the nations and all the places where I have driven you, says the Lord, and I will bring you back to the place from which I sent you into exile. (Jer 29:11–14, RSV)

So we are locked into faith and hope regardless. We can never give way to despair. It is the only option closed to the Christian.

With these thoughts in our minds, the three of us and our parliamentary friends then went to prayer.

'Oh God, in wrath, remember mercy.'

A desperate situation looms

From our breakfast we went out to Cape Town University to get the counsel and reflections of Professor John Reid, deputy Vice-Chancellor of the University.

John Reid is one of South Africa's special people – cool, calm, collected, brilliant and Christian. Beyond academia, building relationships is his special spiritual commitment.

'Well, John, what do you think?' we asked as we shared the experiences of the last few days. He made several points.

'The Government has chosen force. This makes life very complicated for all of us.

'However, there is a "security" word abroad that armed ANC militants plan a massive incursion on 16 June (Soweto

Day) to put white suburbs to the torch. But who knows how accurate this story is?

'An equally major threat is seemingly coming from the extreme right wing. The rumour is that with 16 June approaching, many AWB people [*Afrikanerweerstandsbeweging*, or Afrikaner Resistance Movement, an extreme right-wing political movement] are spoiling for a fight and are planning really to get stuck in if any blacks menace the white suburbs. Part of our job in reconciliation, therefore, is to speak not only to black leaders but to the white revolutionaries in the Orange Free State and Transvaal.' (I resolved there and then to ring a top Dutch Reformed Church leader and ask him to contact the AWB leader, Eugene Terreblanche, and plead with him and his people to 'cool it' on 16 June. This was duly carried out the next day, and the message conveyed.)

'Even if this is so,' Reid went on, 'the President has become overly concerned with the extreme right wing at the expense of facing the root cause of black anger and pain.'

Reid concluded this tale of woe with a twinkling smile which showed a man of faith rising above all the doom and gloom. 'Our job now,' he said, 'is to do faithfully, each one of us, what is to hand. For you that means going now to share all you can with all and any who have leverage. There is a specially desperate need for the authorities to get *accurate* information about what's really happening at grass roots in the country and with leaders beyond our borders.'

Emergency measures

As Robin left for overseas, Gareth and I, spurred by John Reid's almost fatherly advice, began work on trying to see three of the most senior cabinet ministers.

With the first one we had a fruitful time of discussion. My impression once more was of a fine man, but a prisoner of personal history and political circumstance. Even so, he was not uninterested in Kaunda's thoughts – although, he added, 'I am not in the market for Kaunda's tears.'

Maybe so, I thought. But then someone must weep for us.

Then we met Nationalist MP Wynand Malan and Progressive Federal Party MP Graham McIntosh, at the Houses
of Parliament, where the atmosphere was electric. A bit like
the House of Commons on 2 September 1939, as war was
about to be declared, I imagined.

With parliamentary bells ringing stridently like fire alarms,
I saw the Minister of Law and Order, Louis le Grange,
striding towards the House of Assembly for the emergency
debate on the deteriorating situation and the proposed
emergency legislation. If he did not have the world on his
shoulders, he certainly had South Africa on his shoulders –
and it looked heavier. President P W Botha also hurried by.
Seeing him now, obviously agitated and trying to look on top,
I felt sorry for him. He too, was a prisoner of history.

That day we failed to get through to the other two cabinet
ministers we had wanted to see.

Anyway, what Gareth and I saw and heard that evening in
Parliament cast us to the ground. My journal, written later
that night on a 'red-eye special' flight home to Durban caught
my mood:

> Listened to a bit of debate in the Assembly and in the House
> of Representatives (Coloured) re the two draconian security
> measures before Parliament. My gloom deepened and I left
> disconsolate and overwhelmed in spirit. 'Parliamentary parlour
> games', say some, and they are right. And the longer they run the
> more doomed we are to judgement and tragedy. I recollect that
> last time I was in Parliament, I also became disconsolate . . . Oh
> SA! Oh SA! If only you knew the things that belong to your
> peace. Says the Lord: 'How often I would have gathered you –
> but you would not!'

At Cape Town Airport I had picked up the *Cape Argus*
newspaper dated 6 June 1986. I noted two items of news. The
first was explanatory of the parliamentary debate earlier that
evening:

> The security measures at the centre of the controversy are the
> Public Safety Amendment Bill and the Internal Security Amend-
> ment Bill. The first seeks to grant the Minister of Law and Order

the power to declare 'areas of unrest' for periods of up to three months, renewable on the authority of the State President.

In such declared areas the Minister would have the authority to frame regulations which in his opinion were necessary to prevent or curb unrest. They would give the security forces emergency powers similar to those which could be granted in terms of a state of emergency.

The Minister of Law and Order, Mr Louis le Grange, has already said that the media would be restricted in unrest areas. The security forces would also be granted an indemnity against legal action in carrying out their duties in such areas.

The Internal Security Amendment Bill provides for the police to detain up to 180 days without trial people whose removal from society would, in their opinion, contribute to preventing or quelling unrest or violence.[2]

If such powers were approved, I thought, South Africa would be plunged to new depths of restriction.

The second item of news shook me just as much. The Government had announced a ban on all meetings in Soweto on 16 June, the tenth anniversary of the great uprising in 1976.

'I don't believe it,' I said to myself. 'One can't stop people mourning or remembering. Besides it will only intensify rage and frustration to unprecedented levels.'

For me it was another sort of blow – because four of us (black and white Christian leaders) had been planning to meet with the Law and Order Minister, Louis le Grange the following Monday evening, to plead with him on just that point – not to ban meetings on Soweto Day. 'Don't screw the lid down more,' was to have been our plea. Now the screws were well in, and the lid pressed down tighter than ever.

'Lord, have mercy'

I hired a car in Durban and sped away into the night.

En route home to Pietermaritzburg, which is eighty-six kilometres from Durban, I began to pray: 'Lord, have mercy, please, upon our land. Grant us a little more time before you decree your judgement. Keep summer on the go a little longer.'

But in my heart, deep down, I felt that autumn leaves were falling everywhere. And soon we would be well into 'the winter of our discontent'.

Unless, that is, we could as a nation discern the times, and act.

2   The Long Week

A week is a long time in politics.

Harold Wilson

We must work the works of him who sent me, while it is day; night comes, when no one can work.

John 9:4, RSV

. . . the time is short.

1 Corinthians 7:29

Some weeks drag by; others race by. But now and then a week grabs you by the throat, stands you on your head, and makes you think and re-think a thousand things.

Such a week was the one following the Lusaka-Cape Town exercise. It was the week leading up to not only the tenth anniversary of the Soweto uprising in 1976, but also to the imposition of a full State of Emergency in South Africa.

All over the country there was deep concern that black people should not in any way be denied the right to grieve on 16 June, for there is more danger in repression than in expression.

I had discussed this with several black Christian leaders in Durban and Soweto. Two very senior black churchmen had agreed to come to Cape Town to join the PFP MP Mr Graham McIntosh and myself in making representation to the Law and Order Minister Louis le Grange.

SUNDAY: 8 JUNE 1986

The interview was set for Sunday night, 8 June. We were to meet the man holding the awesome power and responsibility for the South African law enforcement apparatus.

During the day, a call from one of the two black leaders coming to Cape Town informed me he had had to go at the last minute to his daughter's school, which was in riotous turmoil. It was left therefore for Mmutlanyane Mogoba, then the General Secretary and now the President of the Methodist Church of South Africa, to speak alone on behalf of the black masses of South Africa.

'Mike,' he had said, 'in the black community talking to such people [as Le Grange] is often totally unacceptable. But my gospel requires me to see such people if there is anything positive to be achieved.'

Encounter with Le Grange

At 9:30 that night Graham, Mmutlanyane and I passed edgy security guards and blinding searchlights into the drive of Le Grange's personal residence.

South Africa's senior law enforcement officer met us at the door. 'I'm sorry I kept you waiting,' he apologised, 'but my wife has not been at all well, and I had to take her down to the hospital for something. I'm a bit concerned about her.'

So here we were, coming in on normal domesticity and humanness – an anxious husband, an unwell wife, the smell of coffee in the kitchen. It was hard to believe we were in the presence of the awesome personal power behind South Africa's state security machine.

Graham, who must have confronted Le Grange many times across the floor in Parliament, opened our time in prayer and then, surprisingly affably for an opposition MP, introduced the purpose of our errand.

Introductions over, Graham asked Rev. Mogoba to share his heart.

Listening to Mmutlanyane, I grasped afresh that South African blacks, and especially black Christians, are in many ways incredible. Their capacity to bear pain, to tolerate indignity, to forgive, to dredge up new goodwill from who knows where and still be gracious never ceases to amaze me.

Mogoba could not by anybody's remotest definition be called anything other than a truly authentic, credible South African black. Yet here, in the presence of this man who in black eyes was behind all the abominated detentions, he could with gentle dignity and quiet assurance open his comments saying, 'Mr Minister, thank you for letting us see you tonight. We are concerned for you as a person working under so much pressure. So we have felt the need to come and agonise with you and affirm you as a human being with your great responsibilities.'

I listened, taking verbatim notes.

He went on, 'But we are also deeply concerned and really worried over South Africa and its future. In fact we are baffled by the statements made by the authorities and by their actions. As far as the police go, the situation is even more worrying because their behaviour is very unbecoming and they are now seen by our people as the enemy.

'However, there is the wider problem, and 16 June must be seen as part of that larger context. You see, Mr Minister, because of what your Government has done, our people have lost hope in the future. Your Government has brought some reforms, for which we have been grateful. But the timing is all wrong. Little reforms coming too late and bit by bit, piecemeal, don't help.

'And the Mandela issue. If you had released him two years ago you would have had a breakthrough. Release him in a few years time and it will be a non-event. You will have lost the opportunity to change things.'

I thought to myself, 'Here once again is Kaunda's line: time running out, the summer quickly passing.'

Le Grange sat attentive and respectful.

'Mr Minister,' continued Mogoba, 'you and your Government have got to face the problem of black perceptions in the townships.

'The people do not perceive the Government as seriously caring for them as people or as understanding them and their feelings in any way.

'For example, as regards Soweto Day, in black culture it is important for people to come together and remember. The issue is not just our need to commemorate, but the problem of a ban on *all* meetings. It is very painful.

'These present actions are very complicating. They jeopardise the whole future. They put blacks and whites into a trap of confrontation. The result is that unless something very major happens now, it will not be possible to talk in the future.'

Le Grange's eyes seemed to grow wider. Graham and I listened, equally transfixed. Mogoba was speaking a prophetic word with the gentle firmness of his Lord.

'However,' he concluded, 'the gospel of Jesus Christ is wonderful and is our hope, even now. I myself met the Lord in solitary confinement on Robben Island. I was there for three years for my political views. Then Jesus met me, even though I had no Bible! It was also there he called me into the ministry. Jesus then took away all my bitterness to whites which had been consuming me. I can now be angry with whites but never bitter. Experiences like this therefore give me hope.'

The Big Man was now visibly moved. (My experience is that even the toughest Afrikaners have a gentle and soft side to them. They are a people of feeling – in spite of the popular caricature.)

Le Grange warmly thanked this eloquent and gracious black spokesman for his remarks, and then expressed marvel at Mogoba's spiritual experience on Robben Island, adding enigmatically and with emotion, 'Yes, it is very strange the things through which God speaks.'

To Graham and me, spectators to this dialogue, the incongruity of this encounter between the prisoner and the police chief was not lost on us. It was the sort of thing only Jesus would organise.

Le Grange then began to speak, and launched into what was a pretty straight-down-the-line statement of 'the Government view'.

'Yes, the situation is very serious. And we are not without some effort at a Christian understanding of it. In fact, we are probably the only cabinet in the world which could come together with our wives and our dominee [pastor] for a prayer meeting. We may be a lot of so-and-so's, but we do embrace some of these Christian values. We try to find our strength where we should.'

Le Grange's opening statement would madden many Christians, both black and white, who would denounce it as reprehensible hypocrisy, yet I sensed sincerity. We were close to the heart of the Afrikaner paradox.

Le Grange now proceeded to make a series of points.

1.   The measures instituted by the Government to cope with the unrest of the last two years had been only partially successful. For political, social and economic reasons, the situation refused to normalise. Unrest must be brought to an end, although they realised final answers didn't lie in strong-arm methods.

2.   In the last ten days they had very carefully examined the security situation, and though previous 16 June days had been reasonably manageable, this one reflected a changed set-up, with every organisation from Lusaka to the small towns of South Africa getting involved in bringing this to an unprecedented climax. His information indicated that there would be a huge increase in acts of terror, mass demonstrations and even of irresponsible people planning violence in the white suburbs.

3.   The Government has had to act, though this is very unpopular, to bring these destructive forces to a standstill so that they can get on with the job of reform which the country 'urgently needs'. If the Government didn't act on the security issue many whites would pull back from reform.

4.   As to 16 June, his hope was that blacks would commemorate the day in *bona fide* church services.

Mmutlanyane, Graham and I responded to these points by conceding the validity of some but stressing that the *real* unrest was in people's hearts and could not be stilled by military or police force. People have aspirations, and the situation cried frantically for political, not military, solutions. Moreover, it is the system itself which is to blame for the rage and destructive violence now endemic in the country. Political unrest would not end through screwing the lid down but through meaningful political change. Nor should we be surprised, given the fact that all meaningful political outlets are denied to blacks, that they should use funerals, church services and days such as 16 June in a political way.

Le Grange told us he would take our thoughts next morning to the State Security Council.

Our mission for that night was now over. We closed our time with prayer for Le Grange, his personal needs and his public responsibilities. After these closing prayers, Le Grange showed us out to the car – personally opening the door for Mogoba and saying, 'I still can't believe what happened to you on Robben Island!'

It had indeed been a strange and perplexing encounter, though not, we prayed, without value, for here were widely differing South African viewpoints in interaction. Hearing the other side is not a South African forte, but it had happened that night.

MONDAY: 9 JUNE 1986

A dark Cape Monday dawned inauspiciously the next morning on 9 June.

After a meeting with military personnel, at which we urged restraint on 16 June, I headed out to the burning, convulsed squatter-camp-cum-shantytown of Crossroads with business-man David Christie and Christian intercessor Els van Wyk.

The place was virtually in a state of civil war. Two factions – 'Comrades' (black political militants) and '*Witdoeke*' or 'White Caps' (black vigilantes incensed at the Comrades' militancy) – were by now notorious to the public of the Western Cape. Somewhere, in the shadows in between, lay the police.

Crossroads

We arrived in Crossroads about 10:30 a.m., just before the main violence broke out.

Smoke was rising hundreds of feet into the air as the Zolani Community Centre and Clinic, which had sheltered over two thousand refugees the chilly night before, was put to the torch.

As we headed to the SACLA Clinic (launched by Dr Ivan Toms in 1980 after the 1979 South African Christian Leadership Assembly, or SACLA), we found the tension in the atmosphere so thick you could cut it with a knife.

Every adult male we saw was armed with a lethal weapon – knives, machetes, or deadly Heath-Robinson contraptions – and all were moving purposefully, as if headed for some hellish rendezvous.

The events of the day proved this to be the case. The *Cape Argus*, which I purchased later, unfolded the story.

> The Zolani Clinic and relief centre in Nyanga East were severely damaged by fire today as battles broke out between Crossroads groups. Police said the confrontation involved up to 11 000 men. Latest reports said the centre operated by St John Ambulance and housing 2 200 people – mainly women and children – was burning fiercely and there was little hope of saving it.
>
> At 11.15 a.m. police reported that Witdoeke had broken through police lines and were engaging the Comrades. Police mounted an operation against the occupants of a house near KTC from which repeated gunfire was heard. The violence appeared to have started at 10.30 a.m. after about 3 000 Witdoeke and 8 000 Comrades confronted one another in open veld.
>
> A police spokesman said security forces were moved into the area in an attempt to separate the groups and tear gas was used. But these measures were fruitless.[1]

Into this situation David, Els and I wended our precarious way, helpless to do much about the big picture, but feeling we should at least go and identify in Christ's love with the SACLA Clinic folk, with whom we had some links.

Though fear hovered everywhere like a witch's blanket, I felt a curious calm.

SACLA Clinic

As we arrived at the Clinic – an unobtrusive prefab squeezed cheek-by-jowl between pitiful little makeshift shacks –

ambulances were coming and going, bringing in the wounded from the battlefield, as it were.

Nurse Dorcas Cyster, one of our colleagues in the National Initiative for Reconciliation (NIR) reflects on the day we visited: 'I was that day treating refugees from an earlier vigilante ambush several days earlier. As I neared the community centre building, it became clear that more bloodshed and burning would occur very soon . . . My commitment to impartial service to the injured was severely challenged that day as I bandaged wounds and splinted fractured limbs under the critical eyes of "Witdoeke" leaders. As the warm blood covered my hands and the groans filled my ears, I fought to keep back my anger toward all who fostered such senseless injury.'

Dr Di Hewitson, a sensitive and dedicated doctor and deeply committed Christian, looked exhausted and pressed beyond measure as she came out of her little cubbyhole office to meet us.

'Oh, come in,' she said. 'How wonderful you've come! It couldn't have been at a better time. We feel so desperate and discouraged.'

She went on to explain that one of the excruciating pressures they faced was that the SACLA Clinic was physically located in what had now become a Witdoeke area, while many of the Clinic's workers lived in the Comrades area. Therefore, as they came to work, they were accused of going to tend to the wounds of the enemy. In terms of local politics, this was tantamount to treason and could cost you your life.

We ended our time with Di Hewitson in a period of deep prayer for her and her colleagues and all others seeking to witness, care and help in Christ's name in such a place.

Peacemakers

The skies had cleared as we stepped out of the SACLA Clinic.

Wandering around some of the shacks and talking to a few anxious women holding babies, I was profoundly gripped by the utter awfulness and extreme peril of the place in which our nation had landed itself.

My spirit literally heaved within me, and a profound

conviction settled in my soul, 'This kind comes not out but by prayer and fasting. O God, *only* you can resolve all this. And without the power of prevailing prayer our land will never be healed or saved.'

However, the Lord needs his people not just in prayer but in active peacemaking in such polarised contexts.

One such is the Rev. John Freeth, a Cape Town Anglican minister, and an NIR leader in the Western Cape. In those very days, unbeknown to me, John was in Crossroads, boots and all.

John later told me about that time: 'The basic division was and is between older and younger blacks. The older, more conservative ones – the Witdoeke – have learnt to live in some measure with apartheid, while the younger ones, the Comrades, are hell-bent on overthrowing it completely. This puts them on collision course.'

John's involvement in Crossroads that week led him and other Christians right into the cross-fire, both metaphorically and literally, in an attempt to secure an understanding between Witdoeke and Comrade protagonists.

'Our group of fifteen went in but were twice repulsed by police tear gas. Then three of us, Syd Luckett, Joe Seremane and I, finally made it on a third attempt and were able to walk through all the burning to meet with about seventy Witdoeke.

'We started with prayer – all of them removing their hats as we did. We felt a deep sense of God's grip on things, even in all the chaos. I'm not sure we achieved anything dramatic, but the level of hostility was somewhat reduced.'

Perhaps David, Els and I might have seen modest John and his brave band as we drove on into the battlefield that day, but as we rounded one corner we found ourselves faced by an army of thousands of stick-waving blacks marching militantly towards us and spanning the entire road.

It would have been folly to proceed, so we did one of the century's more expeditious U-turns, retraced our tracks, and finally headed, heavy-hearted, back to town.

The armies we left behind were soon locked in combat. At the end of the day the unofficial toll was twenty-one dead with thirty-three wounded; there were 1 500 shacks destroyed in the area and 'between 55 000 and 70 000 homeless'.[2]

By evening, when my plane took off for Port Elizabeth, I could see a pall of smoke hanging over Crossroads. I'm told it reduced even ground-visibility there to a hundred yards.

No one else in South Africa could see much further.

Port Elizabeth

I arrived in Port Elizabeth to be whisked from the airport by Neil Pagard, an African Enterprise colleague, to a meeting sponsored by the NIR in a church in Walmer, a white suburb near the airport.

The waiting congregation, though mainly white, nevertheless had a significant sprinkling of blacks who had most graciously come in from some of the townships for the meeting.

Everyone looked troubled and burdened about the situation.

I was thankful there were still so many whites like these around South Africa who desperately wanted to see change, justice and healing in our land through the power of Christ. But they were for the most part paralysed as to what to do; the whole thing seemed to have got so out of hand.

Beyond that, one could not but marvel also that there were still blacks, at such a time as this, who were willing to identify in Christ with their white brothers and sisters and struggle to find a way forward.

'Things which cannot be shaken'

That night Neil and I stayed with a Methodist minister, George Irvine, one of the Eastern Cape's most faithful Christian witnesses. (George and the Anglican bishop, Bruce Evans, had at considerable cost to themselves and their families stood for justice with more credibility than any other white church leaders in the area. And their faithful voices reached throughout the land.)

George was not very happy as we chatted late that night.

'Things are getting bad here,' he said. 'First of all it's very tough on some of the clergy and people caught between the

Comrades and the police. The threats are deadly against any black minister if he gives Christian burial to the charred remains of a suspected collaborator or 'sell-out' who has been necklaced.

'The other day one of our ministers buried a man who'd been shot for being a suspected collaborator. But some activists dug up both coffin and victim and burnt them. This kind of thing puts many of our pastors at a desperate place.'

Neil and I shuddered as the mental picture of this horror sank in. Here was the in-between trauma that I had encountered the day before in Crossroads.

George went on: 'Then economically also things are getting very rugged. For example, we have about a hundred businesses each month going bankrupt in the Eastern Cape. Politically, the gap is wider than ever. In places like New Brighton [a black township on the edge of Port Elizabeth] an alternative government under street committees is in place. These are working well, and the blacks have organised themselves very capably. Government operatives and black police daren't go in there. Some of the people are saying openly: "We are free already. We've got two countries in South Africa. One country has unbanned the ANC and is living under its authority already. And the other has not."'

Then George gave a twinkling Irish smile, and the man of faith shone through, 'But you know, all this tremendous shaking is good, because it forces us to look beyond all the temporal things being shaken to all the "eternal things which cannot be shaken". But let us not think that this insight can absolve us from working not only for costly reconciliation but also for justice.'

The point was well taken.

TUESDAY: 10 JUNE 1986

In order to express our concern for reconciliation and understanding, we went next morning to meet and pray with Mr Ben Olivier, the mayor of the city, and a very worried man, whom we encouraged to continue his tentative initiatives and contacts with blacks.

New Brighton

From the mayor we travelled into New Brighton, the black township on the edge of Port Elizabeth, to our friend, the Rev. de Villiers Soga, a man of enormous energy, dedication and zeal, both for his people and for his Lord.

As Neil and I drove in, we were moved by the friendly waves and smiles from the many children who called out 'Mojalefa' – my Sesotho name, which they had discovered a couple of weeks previously when, along with other local speakers, I had addressed a rally of 40 000 at their Dan Qeqe Stadium.

De Villiers Soga

De Villiers Soga, the local chairman of IDAMASA (Inter-denominational African Ministers Association of Southern Africa), was very discouraged and sombre that day as he served us coffee in his home.

'I now feel we can get to peace only via revolution,' he lamented. 'One of our problems is that white Christians who are living in a fool's paradise are not showing concern for the suffering we are going through.'

A telling blow, I thought, considering my own privileged and protected living in a secure white ghetto, the majority of whose citizens were living light years away from the New Brightons of this world – effectively on another political planet.

De Villiers went on to tell us how every street of the township had its own street committee. 'And there is a remarkable drop in crime,' he added, 'because our own disciplinary units are taking weapons from people and requiring all the shebeens [African drinking bars] to close at 9 p.m. Liquor sales are way down. Government police have fled, and we are running the place.'

It was hard to know what to think of it all. Nor could one visualise such a situation being tolerated indefinitely by Pretoria. Where would it all end?

We prayed with De Villiers and his family and went out to the car, where more children rushed up with their astonishing cries of 'Mojalefa!' to shake us both by the hand.

We then went to meet with another black leader, one of the leaders of the UDF (United Democratic Front) in the Eastern Cape, whose name had recently been mentioned to us and whom we'll call Mr Jabavu. (Where he stood ideologically we didn't know.)

'Mr Jabavu'

A jovial, bearded man with alert and penetrating eyes and an effusive personality, Mr Jabavu met us and took us to his office.

'Sit down, please,' he said, pointing us to two chairs squeezed into a tiny, dilapidated office at the head of an unpretentious and dingy staircase.

There we questioned him about his reading of the situation.

One of our hopes was that we might get him and the mayor and some other white leaders into dialogue.

He made several points simply, concisely and in quick succession.

1. The problem of the Eastern Cape is a problem of mis-understanding between the people, the police and the SADF (South African Defence Force). This could be resolved only if real negotiation could open up and whites would truly listen to black grievances.
2. Blacks are obliged in the South African situation to fight for their rights. No self-respecting people could do otherwise.
3. The Eastern Cape is traditionally an ANC area.
4. Blacks know the churches have a key role to play. 'We speak like the churches against hatred and we know we cannot say the whites must go. We all belong here. But we must all have equal rights.'

It seemed reasonable enough.

I asked him to tell us more about himself, for we knew nothing about him. 'Well,' he drawled with a big smile that lit his face up like a Christmas tree and which said there was more to his story than met the eye, 'I was in prison on Robben Island from 1963 to 1981, "for furthering the aims of the ANC". My last daughter was two months old when I was arrested and when I came out she was eighteen and doing matric. Four of my children grew up while I was in prison.'

As a parent, my heart skipped an emotional beat in grasping vainly to imagine the extent of trauma which such an experience would induce, yet the man seemed void of bitterness.

'If you were on Robben Island, did you get to know Mandela?' Neil enquired.

'Oh yes, I know him well,' said Mr Jabavu. 'He is a man of the people, both black and white. He is not anti-white. In fact from the time he was in the ANC Youth League, he believed in non-racialism and worked for it. He just wants a free South Africa for all people. That's why he worked with Z K Matthews and others to draw up the Freedom Charter.'

Mr Jabavu was referring to the populist manifesto drawn up at Kliptown (now part of Soweto) in 1955 by the African National Congress and its affiliates when they were legal organisations. Its slogan – 'South Africa belongs to all its peoples, black and white' – has become holy writ for almost all blacks who know it. And, although its economic line, proposing the transfer of universal wealth, banks and monopoly industry to the ownership 'of the people as a whole', sticks in the gullet of free marketeers, few could have much quarrel with its line on human rights. (See Appendix 2.)

Of course Neil and I didn't get into all this with Jabavu that warm Port Elizabeth morning as we heard him speak of the Freedom Charter. Maybe there would be another time to ask the tougher questions.

As we sat with Mr Jabavu that morning in his little office and reflected on the woes of the Eastern Cape, we ended by sharing our testimonies of Jesus Christ with him and having prayer. I suspect this startled him, but my conviction has always been that in ministry with leaders one should always seek to share Christ with them, whoever they are, and then encourage them to draw on his resources and wisdom for their responsible work.

Four days later this fellow struggler within South Africa's entangling web was back in jail.

At the time of going to press, nearly three years later, he remains incarcerated.

Joza

Neil and I now left Port Elizabeth and drove the scenic ninety miles to Grahamstown during a balmy and exquisitely beautiful afternoon.

It was hard to reconcile the poignant beauty of the land with its ugly political face; and Joza township, on the edge of the famous university city, had a sullen, eerie stillness to it as we drove in.

That night in Joza we met over dinner with Bishop Sigqibo Dwane, another black church leader.

Like all black church leaders, Bishop Dwane was struggling with many things. These ranged from the difficulties of normal pastoring to the problems of boycotting school children, angry frustrated parents, gaping gaps between white and black clergy, and especially massive unemployment.

'You know, seventy per cent of our township is unemployed. Port Elizabeth used to be our place of economic hope and salvation. But now PE is an economic disaster-area with sixty per cent unemployment. It can't take our people. I know one white builder who last year earnt R5 000 a month and employed many blacks. This year he's "on the dole" from his church so he can feed his family.

'Frankly, I find dealing with chronic unemployment the most desperate and soul-destroying thing. Especially when there is no hope of it all turning round.'

As Sigqibo said this, I reflected also that many whites from Port Elizabeth were either leaving the country or moving up to the Reef. Ford Motors also seemed on the way out, their huge factory employing thousands of blacks was now winding down.

I remembered that a notice in a Port Elizabeth hotel had chuckled its sinister exhortation: 'Will the last person in PE please turn out the lights and feed the dolphins!' (referring to PE's huge, famous and much-loved aquarium).

There was, of course, no instruction for the blacks who couldn't leave.

Dwane continued: 'I know some say that if you turn away from violence as a means of change, you must press for sanctions. One fact, however, is that increasing unemployment,

as we experience it here first hand, breeds more frustration, which spawns more violence. It's a vicious
circle.'

The Bishop paused in what had become a fairly passionate
though unorthodox discourse as far as many black church
leaders are concerned, then he added, 'And what if black
majority rule comes when the economy has collapsed? Liberated blacks would then in frustration have to tumble out the
black government because there would be no food. The
thing's a nightmare. This is where this system has finally
landed us.'

One area in which it did seem we could help the Bishop
practically related to the many bored and frustrated youths in
the township. We undertook to get a bus-load of them up to
our African Enterprise Centre in Pietermaritzburg to help
train them for a positive contribution in their community.
This happened, later on, with wonderfully rewarding
consequences.

WEDNESDAY: 11 JUNE 1986

After staying overnight in the home of Bishop Bill Burnett
and his wife Sheila, Neil and I burst from the starting-blocks
early the next morning, to be on hand in King William's
Town, some ninety miles further on.

Zwelitsha

After a high school meeting we went to two clergy meetings –
one with the black clergy, who had gathered in the nearby
township of Zwelitsha, the other a luncheon with white clergy
in the centre of town.

Zwelitsha, effectively a black suburb of King William's
Town, is, by one of those political aberrations only South
Africa could conjure up, part of another country, the home-
land Republic of Ciskei.

A huddled little group of black clergy awaited us.

'How are you?' I asked as I was introduced to one. 'Positive,' he replied, grinning widely, thereby rebuking my faithless spirit and some of the negativism spawned by all we had seen and heard in the previous few days.

The major lament of these men was the separation between them and the white ministers in the town. It was so painful for one of them that he said he wanted to cry or stamp or yell. (When in heaven's name will white South African Christians get their act together and stop betraying the gospel like this?)

Later, over lunch with the white clergy, I put this challenge to them. The chairman, Johann Neethling, was clearly with me. His look of frustration spoke volumes as he caught my eye. That unabated frustration led him a couple of months later to leave the country. At that time he would have joined the fifty or so other whites *per day* who were leaving for pastures new in Australia, Canada or New Zealand.

But in fairness, it must be said that not all South African whites are segregationist and isolationist. Thousands are not. And Neil and I met with a sample of them in a large public rally that night. Many, like Ian and Wendy Fleming, our hosts that night, were saying in all humility and with chastened spirits, 'Lord have mercy on us and on our land. Show us where we've all gone wrong and help us to fix it.'

THURSDAY: 12 JUNE 1986

We were also encouraged the next morning by the (then) President of the Methodist Church, Ernest Baartman, a powerful black leader whom we met in East London, where the atmosphere was again very electric and tense.

'What is happening now is terrible,' said Ernest, 'and it works both ways. For example, I find when speaking to crowds of blacks that one wants to feel heard and be seen as relevant, so one says what they want to hear. This gets one cheered, but it can be a contradiction of the cross and the word of God. The real message of the Lord is generally directly opposite to where we all are!'

The sword falls

As Ernest and his colleague Paul Welsh were encouraging us in terms of NIR's reconciliation endeavours, a messenger of bad tidings arrived to confirm to us that all the black street and block committee leaders in nearby Duncan Village and Mdantsane, East London's major black township, were being 'picked up and detained'. 'All the moderates too,' said our messenger.

With heaviness beyond the telling enveloping him like a shroud, Ernest quietly reflected, 'This will leave the mob leaderless.'

But the full import of this news only reached me later in the day as I alighted at Durban airport en route home. The sword of Damocles had now fallen. South Africa had just been placed under the strictest and most stringent State of Emergency in all its history. It was Thursday 12 June 1986.

Soon it became known that a thousand people had been detained. The number seemed mind-boggling, but we knew nothing yet. It would climb to over 29 000 before the end of the year – 25 631 under the State of Emergency regulations, 3 512 under the Internal Security Act. An average of eighty-one per day.[3]

Draconian measures

With the press muzzled and South Africa now for the first time denied access to the full facts of daily news, a very solemn State President Botha said to a hushed and shocked Parliament that same day, 'The Government is well aware of the fact that stricter security action will elicit strong criticism and even punitive measures from the outside world.

'However . . . no responsible Government can allow the indefinite disruption of normal political and economic activities in its country by extra-parliamentary and violent actions . . .'

President Botha went on to say he had hoped the Government could deal with the continuing instances of unrest 'without subjecting the country to the inconvenience of a

State of Emergency. In fact, the Government possesses intelligence information regarding plans made by radical and revolutionary elements for the coming days which pose real danger for all population groups in the country.'[4]

The draconian terms of the Emergency quickly became known. They included the following:

* The security forces may enter any premises without a warrant and seize anything they deem necessary; arrest any person whose detention is deemed necessary; interrogate any person arrested or detained.
* No civil or criminal proceedings may be instituted against the State, the State President, cabinet members or force members acting 'in good faith'.
* The Commissioner of Police may ban comment on news in connection with any conduct of the force or any member of the force.
* It is an offence for any person to make, write, print or record any subversive statement.[5]

Incredibly, part of the definition of a subversive statement was 'one which contains anything which is calculated to have the effect or is likely to have the effect . . . of engendering or aggravating feelings of hostility in the public or any section of the public or any person or category of persons towards any section of the public or person or category of persons'.[6]

One didn't know whether to chuckle or choke. I chose to chuckle. 'Darling,' I said to my wife, 'please don't engender or aggravate in me any feelings of hostility or you will be locked up for subversion!'

SOWETO DAY: MONDAY 16 JUNE

The almost tangible fear and apprehension which gripped the country on the evening of Sunday 15 June, the day before Soweto Day, was something few who lived through those days will ever forget.

Blacks were fearful of what the massive display of military might would mean in their already emotionally pulverised townships; whites feared that a black invasion of the white suburbs to put them to the torch might yet happen.

For many Christians, prayer was the only resource which seemed to have any availing relevance.

16 June dawned with a sullen silence over the land.

I had resolved, whatever happened, to go into the black township outside Pietermaritzburg and identify with blacks generally in their pain and with my own black colleagues from African Enterprise in particular.

Knowing anything could happen, my wife Carol said to me, 'I think only one of us should go.' I agreed, sensing intuitively her unverbalised thoughts.

For some of my other white colleagues in African Enterprise, the decision to go into the black township of Edendale on 16 June had been more of a battle. Afterwards, quadraplegic Allan Peckham, our accountant, wrote movingly about his struggle: 'I tried to reason through it – lists of fors and againsts. Was the fact that we had been invited sufficient reason for going? Was it just being heroic? Or worse, provocative? Irresponsible? But didn't my colleagues need the encouragement we could give by going? Should we not live out our caring? My reasonings seemed to loop back on themselves and criss-cross in confusion.' Finally, Allan went. 'It didn't in the end seem to matter whether I lived or died. In a sense I had died already.'

Other colleagues went through similar struggles. Each of us knew in some measure what Allan had felt. Confessed Jack Garratt, 'It affected my sleep in those days. The thought of going into that township on 16 June really scared me.'

For myself, driving down the almost deserted freeway from my home to town on Monday 16 June was something I, likewise, will long remember. I felt the city had never been so disturbingly quiet.

It was the silence of suppression.

'O South Africa, South Africa!'

In town I met up with some of my colleagues and we went out to Edendale.

For whites, the garaged cars that day constituted an implicit confession of fear and retreat from danger. For blacks, the deserted streets, which met our surprised eyes as our AE Combi got to Edendale, were signals of sullen protest, churning anger and deepening despair.

We pressed on past intermittent clusters of Casspir armoured vehicles gathered every few blocks along the road. The sight which met our eyes as we arrived at the church was pathetic. Not the 'bulging-at-the-seams', buoyant crowds of blacks one normally encountered, but a huddled little flock of scarcely more than a dozen. The remnant of a people hurting and temporarily broken. Their eyes said that force and might had for the moment won. But who knew what whirlwinds were being stored up in them, and in other hearts hidden within those shuttered homes?

Anyway, we prayed and sang and praised and preached and dreamt. And it was all most movingly appreciated. Each white, unbelievably, felt loved, welcomed and forgiven.

I recollected that on 16 June 1976, ten years previously, when Soweto 'blew', I was opening a preaching mission in Rosebank Union Church in Johannesburg. My theme as Soweto burnt and raged and wept, was 'O South Africa, South Africa! Would that even today you knew the things that make for peace!' (Luke 19:41–44, RSV). Yes, the summer was passing even then.

And now, ten years later, was it past forever, with our Lord now weeping over us, 'How often would I have gathered you together, South Africa, as a hen gathers her brood under her wings, and you would not'?

'Gathered you together'? Somehow 'together' seemed not to be our word in South Africa. Our word, our idolised word – our ideologised word – was 'Apart'.

Such seemed to be our fateful choice.

I was in a mental whirl until I finally pulled into the drive at Namirembe, my home, after the huddled little happening in the Edendale church on 16 June 1986.

'I need to stop and reflect,' I said to myself. 'Do some homework. Consult with others. Read. Pray. Seek the Lord. Think it all through again from the very beginning . . . Maybe even write a book.'

Part Two

PILGRIM WITH A PROBLEM
(Personal struggles with applying the gospel)

3   Family and Volk

I can trace my ancestry back to a protoplasmal primordial atomic globule. Consequently my family pride is something inconceivable.

Gilbert and Sullivan, *The Mikado*

Nations, like men, have their infancy.

Viscount Bolingbroke (1678–1757)

Listen to me, you who pursue righteousness
    and who seek the Lord:
Look to the rock from which you were cut
    and to the quarry from which you were hewn . . .

Isaiah 51:1

For me in mid-1986, as the South African drama unfolded further, going back to the beginning to think things through from scratch meant going back to my roots, to my family history. It meant looking, as in the ancient exhortation of Isaiah, to the rock whence I was cut and to the quarry whence I was hewn!

In fact this exercise had already been pressed upon me in the middle of the boiling cauldron of 1985 when President P W Botha had asked me with some scepticism during a not very auspicious encounter whether I was a South African. Opposition to the country's system seemingly raised such questions in his mind.

Yet I knew then that I love my land, though (as I said in the preface to these pages) not as much as I love my Lord. Perhaps that was where the conflict came.

But my love is in fact profoundly real, being born as it is out of an interplay of mighty forces which, though coming to a head in the mid 1980s, have nevertheless been here incipiently from the earliest history of this nation.

And this kaleidoscope of relationships which interweaves both family and volk[1] is true of most South African families. Indeed the land has forged all of us in its own unique furnace and engendered in us mysterious emotions which bring both divisive collision and united commitment.

SETTING THE STAGE

South Africa has had a long history. The stage was not set in a moment.

By the end of the seventeenth century and the early years of the eighteenth century, the elements of what was to become one of the most complex societies in the world were beginning to come together.

England was colonising North America, and at the same time competing with Holland and France for trade in India and the East.

In Southern Africa, the groups commonly termed Hottentots and Bushmen roamed at will, hunting game and fighting each other. African tribes from central and East Africa were migrating southwards to settle in Southern Africa along with those indigenous Africans who had probably lived here from as early as the fourteenth or fifteenth centuries. By 1988 this African population of South Africa would number some twenty-five million.

For their part, whites made their appearance, as every South African schoolchild knows, in 1652, when the Dutch East India Company established a refreshment station at the Cape, and Cape Town became the halfway house between East and West. The Dutch settlers, in due course, imported slaves from East and West Africa, Madagascar and later Malaya. From this amalgam, with an admixture of European blood, emerged in due course the Cape coloured population of South Africa. By 1988 they would number two and a half million.

The Dutch East India Company and its Dutch settlers also introduced the first elements of Christian piety, which was to take root deep in the fibre of South African life. They believed that they were accomplishing the divine will by advancing the interests of the Company.

As one writer observes, 'A kind of partnership had, it seemed, grown up between the Company and the Almighty and there were occasions indeed in which the Company seemed ready to step in and act as spokesman when the Almighty seemed unduly reticent.'[2] For example, Jan van Riebeeck (the leader of the first Dutch settlers at the Cape) ordained that anyone absent from daily prayer should forfeit six days' drink ration, while anyone absenting himself three times from daily prayer should work in chains at the public works for a year! Van Riebeeck left the Cape in 1662. The Company records show that he left behind thirty-nine freemen, fifteen wives and twenty-two children, whose descendants, amalgamated with other migrant groups from continental Europe, would form the Afrikaners. In 1988 they would number three and a half million.

THE WHITE POPULATION GROWS

Van Riebeeck's successor, Simon van der Stel, expanded the settlers' area of control beyond the village of Cape Town, and the little white population grew as other small contingents of Dutch and Germans arrived. But more immigrants were needed. Strangely enough it was Louis XIV, the Sun-King of France, who helped out in 1685 by withdrawing freedom of worship from the Huguenots or French Protestants.

All Protestant ministers who did not wish to return to the Catholic faith had to leave France within fifteen days. Within a few months fifty thousand families left France. They went all over the world. And during the seven months from December 1687, seven vessels, loaded with the Pilgrim Fathers of the South, sailed round the Cape of Good Hope. With them came the deep, sincere and strict faith of John Calvin. It was a faith destined to gain a permanent hold, for the Huguenots now reinforced the Reformed faith already present in the Dutch settlers.

A hundred years later the Dutch East India Company was

bankrupt. But by this time it mattered little to the tough, independent and religious settlers of the Cape. They had, they said, 'no other fatherland'. South Africa was theirs.

THE ARRIVAL OF THE BRITISH

Or was it? For in June 1795 nine British warships sailed into the Cape of Good Hope. In September, the castle fort of Cape Town surrendered. The British had indeed arrived. And with a flourish. The inception of their relationship with the Afrikaners was hardly auspicious, even though they had come partly at the request of the now exiled ruler of Holland, the Dutch Prince of Orange.[3]

The point was that after the French Revolutionary armies had invaded Holland in 1795, Britain, by arrangement with the Prince of Orange, occupied the Cape for the first time. However, when the Treaty of Amiens (1802) provided that the Cape be restored to the Dutch, it was to the Dutch Government, not the Dutch East India Company that it was handed over. But when Napoleon renewed the war against Britain, the British Government felt it would endanger her trade with the East if the Cape were to remain in the hands of an ally of France. She therefore reoccupied the Cape in 1806. In 1815 this was ratified by the Congress of Vienna.[4]

ROOTS

In any event, by 1988 South Africa's English-speaking population, which had its beginnings in these early British occupations, would number some two and a half million, and they would still find themselves to a measure strangers from Afrikaner culture.

Yet they shouldn't really. For if I think of my own children, Cathy, Debbie and Martin, and the rock from which *they* are cut, I see their roots deep in both the soil and the soul of this mysterious land.

Their earliest South African roots spring up from my wife's side. Carol's father's ancestors were the Bams of Schwerin in

the Prussian Grand-Duchy of Mecklenburg on the Baltic Sea.
Old J A Bam came out to South Africa in 1725, seventy-three
years after Van Riebeeck, aboard the *East Indiaman Geer-
truider* and bearing the grand-rank of Lance Corporal. Eight
years later he sought and secured discharge and set up as a
baker. In this he prospered sufficiently well to take up a
trading concession in wine and brandy!

Although settler life in the Cape Colony was tough and
demanding, the family flourished, multiplied, intermarried
with other settler stock, and rose in the world. Cross-
pollination of national backgrounds pressed on apace with,
for example, German, English, Dutch, and French Huguenot
intermarriage. One of old J.A.'s descendants even won a
place in the Colonial Cape Parliament and was later knighted
to be Sir Pieter Bam MP.

Carol's mother's family also came from Mecklenburg in
Prussia in the mid 1700s. They were Schoemans who married
into the Dutch Esterhyses, Trichardts (relatives of Louis
Trichardt, the Voortrekker), Van Heerdens and Moolmans,
and also into the Swedish Pietersens and finally into the
French Huguenot clan of du Plessis. All these names are
profoundly interwoven into South African life and history.

Noenkie Bam, Carol's mother, christened Wilhelmina,
spoke both English and Afrikaans in the home, and had Carol
christened in the Dutch Reformed Church. Carol possesses
not a drop of English blood in her veins.

THE PRINGLES OF THE VALLEY

800 kms away in the Eastern Cape, near what is now Port
Elizabeth, two Bam sisters, Kathleen and Elise, married two
Pringles, nicknamed Sandy and Rob Roy respectively, descendants of the famous Thomas Pringle, one of the main
leaders of the 1820 settlers who had landed in Algoa Bay. The
Pringle party were part of a mass influx of some fifty thousand
British settlers who emigrated to South Africa due to unemployment in Britain following the Napoleonic wars. The
ever-increasing British settler population now created one of

the longstanding complications of South Africa's life as they stood so often in 'interface' with the Boers.

In his celebrated *Narrative*, a comprehensive diary of the adventure, Thomas Pringle tells of the day they arrived on a ridge overlooking the valley in which they were to settle near the modern town of Bedford:

> 'And now, mynheer,' said the Dutch field-cornet who commanded our escort, 'daar leg uwe veld,' – 'there lies your country'. Looking in the direction where he pointed, we beheld extending to the northward, a beautiful vale, about six or seven miles in length, and varying from one to two in breadth.

He adds a few days later:

> Descending into the middle of the valley, we unyoked the wagons, and pitched our tents in a grove of mimosa trees on the margin of the river; and the next day our armed escort, with the train of shattered vehicles, set out on their return homeward, leaving us in our wild domain to our own courage and resources on the 29th June 1820.[5]

THE FAITH OF THE ENGLISH

If Holland's Calvinistic and Reformed faith had taken root among the Afrikaners in the Western Cape, it was inevitable that Scotland's rather different Presbyterianism, as well as England's Methodism and Anglicanism, would take root in the burgeoning English settler communities of the Eastern Cape.

It was fun to go one day with Carol, her cousin Colin Pringle, his wife Glen, and our respective children, to the acacia tree spot where Thomas and his party had their first service in the valley. This is how his narrative tells it:

> The day was bright and still, and the voice of psalms rose with a sweet and touching solemnity among those wild mountains where the praise of the true God had never, in all human probability, been sung before. The words of the hymns were appropriate to our situation, and affected some of our congregation very sensibly.[6]

A RELIGIOUS CLASH

The picture Thomas Pringle paints illumines further the basically religious and Christian roots of this land.

Here in the Eastern Cape were people of faith, but it was a faith nurtured more by the Scottish and English reformers and the British-cum-American liberal tradition than by the more austere tradition of the Synod of Dort (1618–1619) on which the religious life of the Afrikaner was based.[7]

In any event, it seemed that a religious clash of both principle and precept was inevitable between Boer and Briton.

It came then, as it continues in measure now, on the issue of race.

Only eight years after Thomas Pringle and his party had their first little service under the acacia tree, the issue came to a head with the passing in 1828, largely as a result of the persistency of Dr Philip of the London Missionary Society, of the much resented and famous 'Fiftieth Ordinance'. This established the principle of equality in the eyes of the law for 'all free persons of colour'.

The ruling met with loathing from the frontiersmen. Anna Steenkamp, a Boer woman, wrote in her diary of 'the un-biblical policy of equality between black and white'.

Not only was there the religious cleavage, but there had also been Kaffir wars, as the frontier wars between white settlers and blacks were called, and the British Government had refused to satisfy the land-hunger of the farmers by annexing for them more African land. Discontent built up.

THE GREAT TREK

Inevitably it all had to come to a head. In 1836 a large group of Boers decided to leave the colony and trek into the hinter-land. 'We quit this colony', wrote Piet Retief, one of the leaders, 'under the full assurance that the English Government will allow us to govern ourselves without its inter-ference.' Said Anna Steenkamp, 'We withdrew in order to preserve our doctrines in purity.' During the decade 1838–46,

some ten thousand men, women and children left the Cape
Colony with only their wagons, a few possessions, their
firearms and their faith.

Eric Walker, the South African historian, writes: 'The
Great Trek was more than a matter of mere belly-need. It was
unprecedented in South African history by reason of its
organization, its size and its spirit.'[8]

It was in effect a prayer-meeting on the march. However,
its main significance as a political, cultural and religious event
lay in the fact that in a very real sense it gave birth to the
modern Afrikaner nation. It gave special stimulus to the rise
of Afrikaner nationalism and later the Nationalist Party. It
changed the course of South African history by withdrawing
much of the Afrikaner influence from the Cape, thereby
leaving British ideas and institutions to gain a fuller hold in
that part of South Africa.[9]

THE BOER WAR

If the first major coming to a head of the Boer–British
collision was the Great Trek, the second was the Boer War,
some sixty years later (1899–1901) – at which point my own
family, as against my wife's, comes more into the act.

In the year the war broke out, my paternal grandfather,
Stewart Cassidy, was captaining a Union Castle liner, as he
had been doing for years, round the Cape of Good Hope.
His life and contact with South Africa was intermittent, as
would be expected of a British naval captain. Even so, a
plaque in the Seaman's Mission in Cape Town permanently
remembers him and honours his qualities as 'ever those of
a Christian Gentleman'. (That made me feel good when I
first saw it.)

Far from intermittent, however, was the experience and
contact of my grandfather on my mother's side, Edward
Reading. As a British captain in the Royal Canadian Cavalry
when the Boer War seemed imminent, he came out in 1898.
Of special importance to me was the fact that his soul was
conquered by the beauty, challenge and people of South
Africa, which now became the land of his adoption.

TRAGEDY STRIKES

But the war, he knew, and so he taught me, was a tragedy.

It had been brought on, of course, as everyone knows, mainly by the Empire-building expansionism of the British – as typified in men such as Cecil Rhodes, Leander Starr Jameson and Alfred Lord Milner.

The discovery of diamonds at Kimberley in 1870 and gold on the Witwatersrand in 1886 had wrenched South Africa out of her agricultural rut and plunged her into the convulsive and acquisitive dynamics of boom fever.

Within a few years of these discoveries there were more foreigners or Uitlanders than Boers in the Transvaal, which had become the new home the trek-Boers had carved out for themselves in the South African hinterland. The construction of a railway from the Cape to Lourenco Marques in Moçambique gave further impetus to the spectacular economic developments.

However, even before the mineral discoveries, the world scramble for Africa had been under way. The Berlin Conference of 1884 had arranged for the peaceful partition of Africa among the European powers. Rhodes and Co. were in effect just part of Britain's expansionist endeavours as sanctioned by the Berlin Conference. His dreams, however, of an Africa painted 'red' (for the British Empire) from Cape to Cairo presumably went somewhat beyond what the Conference had in mind!

Now, as South African Africans looked on helplessly, and as Afrikaner breasts became rightly anxious about British motives, Paul Kruger, President of the Transvaal Republic, presented himself as a formidable stumbling-block to the ambitions of Rhodes.

And he had good grounds to be suspicious. After all, by now Rhodes had secured from the Matabele Chief, Lobengula, the mining rights to the area later to be called Rhodesia. To Lobengula the cession meant usufruct; to Rhodes, inevitably, it meant possession. Rhodesia was thus 'secured' by Rhodes for a thousand Martini-Henry rifles, a hundred thousand rounds of ammunition, twelve hundred pounds per annum, and a steam-boat on the Zambesi. Lobengula at the time thought it was a good deal; Rhodes knew it was!

KRUGER AND RHODES COLLIDE

But in the Transvaal Paul Kruger was not to be so easily taken in by the charming and wily Rhodes. Rhodes knew the patriarchal old President would not come round in debate. He decided to annex the Transvaal by a sudden stroke. The raid on Johannesburg, led by Dr Jameson, was an ill-conceived and abortive catastrophe. It turned Afrikaners throughout the subcontinent even more against the British, who were now held to be utterly untrustworthy. Kruger saw them as interested in little except money and political conquest. Relationships between Britain and the Boer Republics now deteriorated hopelessly. Neither side seemed able to extricate itself. In 1899, less than a year before the dawn of the twentieth century, Boers and British went to war.[10]

W A de Klerk, in his classic study *The Puritans in Africa*, observes that the outbreak of war on 11 October 1899 was

> the denouement of the personal tragedies of Rhodes and Kruger. The tragedy of Rhodes was that of a man who dreamt deeply, constructed vastly, but had insufficient understanding of the traditional world of Kruger. He was a man who tried to force the time to fit his vision. The tragedy of Kruger, on the other hand, was that of a man of heroic virtues who had insufficient understanding of the world of Rhodes and the modern forces of which he was a part. He resolutely turned the clock back in order to maintain his tradition intact. What they shared was the common ground, the soil of the land itself.[11]

In a sense both men finally lost the land they loved. And all who were part of their struggles both at the time and subsequently were the losers too. We might try to retrieve the consequences of decisions taken by others in those far-off times, but all of us are prisoners of history and the consequences live on.

But the human spirit's capacity to rise from enmity and bitterness to magnanimity and forgiveness is one of the imponderable and mysterious grounds for hope in our situation, even now. I said earlier that South Africa conquered my grandfather Edward Reading's soul. And curiously it was the Boer War which was the improbable matrix out of which this conquest came.

OUR FAMILY'S GRANDFATHERS CLASH

Though later very unhappy about Britain's role in the Boer War, my grandfather's experiences were, I suppose, typical of those of many British troops. His diaries are peppered with cryptic, soldierly entries and laments. Thus on 18 February 1900, as the battle of Paardeburg in the Orange River Colony got under way: 'Marched the clock round all night – about 23 miles. Arrived at Paardeburg 6 a.m. and breakfasted. Firing commenced between enemy entrenched at bend of Modder River.'[12]

In his classic book *The Boer War*, Thomas Pakenham describes how the Boer general Cronje had allowed himself to be surrounded at Paardeburg by British troops and adds, 'He had found a steel noose and put his head in it.'[13] My grandfather was part of this surrounding noose of steel. That the Boer General was surrounded was a source of enormous concern to other Boer generals, notably the brilliant Christiaan de Wet, who set out for the rescue.

And now again, from another side, our family gets further into the story. For within de Wet's commando was Commandant A J Bester, great-grandfather of my brother-in-law Tony (also called A J Bester, and married to my sister, Judy. Tony's first South African ancestor, curiously enough, had also come from Prussia in about 1712.).

The plot within our own family was now thickening. Grandparents on two sides of our present family were closing in on each other in battle! (Neither could have foreseen that their offspring would finally intermarry!)

When the three-hundred-strong commando with old A J Bester in it were no less than fifteen miles away from Paardeburg, they heard the 'firing' of which my grandfather's diary speaks.

However, they were not in fact able to affect the final outcome of the battle, which was the surrender of Cronje and four thousand Boers a few days later.

THE BRITISH MISCALCULATE

On 13 March, after further battles at Koedoes Rand, Poplar Grove (which the intrepid President Kruger visited on 7 March to rally the burghers) and Driefontein, the British columns rode into Bloemfontein, which surrendered without further struggle, grandfather finding it 'a nice city, very clean and quite pretty'. It was in fact to become a centre in subsequent months of much Boer misery.

As is well known, Lord Roberts and the British, amidst the fearful typhoid epidemic which soon broke out, here made a major miscalculation in thinking that Boer resistance was virtually spent and that the war would quickly be over. Like many down to this present day, especially in overseas government lobbies, as Pakenham observes, 'Roberts had no insight into South Africa, knew nothing of the tenacity of Afrikaner nationalism and the extraordinary resilience of the Boer – hunter and hunted, fighting animal and political animal.'[14]

Then there was Milner's idea. Both he and the irrepressible Rudyard Kipling, who had turned up in South Africa, put it that they would 'crush the Afrikaner idea once and for all' and 'extinguish the irreconcilable enemy'. This was as faulty and self-deceiving a miscalculation then as it is now, nearly ninety years later. In fact the Afrikaner was even then forging in the crucible of war a nationalism which, though finally losing the war, was nevertheless destined to win the peace.

MOLLY CRAUFURD

In a subsequent battle with the Boers at Sanna's Post, near Bloemfontein, a battle in which A J Bester was also probably involved, grandfather Reading was badly wounded in the knee. Exactly what happened then history does not relate. But in many ways our family history was profoundly affected and determined by that one bullet.

This wound, which nearly resulted in the loss of grandfather's leg, and which terminated his cavalry career, landed him in hospital.

There he was nursed by Sister Molly Craufurd, fresh from the relief of Mafeking, where she, Lord Baden-Powell and the British garrison had held out against the legendary Boer siege of that little Northern Cape hamlet for over seven months.

Molly Craufurd was to become my grandmother. Her influence on me was one I will always treasure, especially her sympathetic presentation to me of the Boer cause and her lament over British culpability in the war.

Bloemfontein and her experience there as a nurse in the hospital and in the concentration camps was a decisive crucible for her subsequent commitments to Afrikaner and English reconciliation. It was this commitment for which I most especially remember her.

MAFEKING

How Molly Craufurd got to Mafeking is intriguing in itself. Her sister Helen had answered an employment advert from Cape Town and come out to South Africa from England. Molly, concerned for her with the care of an elder sister, and seeing their mother had died, followed her out to the Cape.

Work on the great railway to the north had reached Mafeking, and when the war broke out and the siege began Molly and Helen found themselves there with a certain, as yet unknown, Colonel Baden-Powell in charge of the British garrison.

Though having had only the most modest nursing training, Molly was asked by Baden-Powell to take charge of the children's hospital. Her remarkable diary of the siege was later published in England and makes astonishing reading.

She and her sister became pillars of practical care and positive morale as they tended the wounded and coped with the daily perils while Baden-Powell with his legendary resourcefulness led the defence of Mafeking.

Perhaps it was from her faith, attested to by regular diary references to the much appreciated 'Sabbath services', that my grandmother derived her professional and humane commitment to nurse as and wherever there was need, whether on the British or Boer side. Thus in February 1900, while my grandfather was gearing up for the battle of Paardeburg over in the Orange River Colony, she could write: 'My patients have been a mixture of English and Dutch, some from the town, but more from the women's laager.'[15]

Towards the end of the siege of Mafeking she rushed out under very heavy fire, with her sister, to tend the wounded of both sides. Says her diary: 'Shall I ever forget that run? Bullets seemed to come from all round, whizzing near us, and our legs seemed as if they would not move fast enough!'[16]

J Emerson Neilly, a war correspondent with the *Pall Mall Gazette* of London, later wrote his eye-witness account of that day:

> The pluckiest acts of the afternoon were done by two young ladies – Mrs Buchan and Miss Craufurd. They are sisters. In the morning the Boers seized the women's hospital, near the laager on an exposed part of the veldt – of which the ladies had charge. One dead Boer and four wounded ones were brought in, and the ladies looked after the latter. At three o'clock I saw the two girls cross the veldt under a hot fire, carrying tea to the fort and the beleaguered ones . . . These ladies were *the* heroines of the siege. They volunteered early for hospital work, and all through the trouble did splendid service, both in the hospital wards and the convalescent home of which Miss Craufurd had charge until the women's hospital was established. They have both been mentioned in despatches, and if any honours can be given to ladies for services during the beleaguerment, they are before all others deserving of being made recipients.[17]

The London *Daily Telegraph* wrote a few days later: 'The day's fighting was replete with interesting incidents. The work done by Miss Craufurd, matron of the Children's Hospital, and Mrs Buchan could not be surpassed for gallantry and devotion by anything in the war.'[18]

CAPTURED BY THE BOERS

This episode, for which Lord Kitchener later personally decorated my grandmother with the Royal Red Cross (the women's equivalent of the Victoria Cross) for highest bravery, in fact resulted in her capture by the Boers. They were, however, only too happy to avail themselves of her medical care. Says her diary:

> A Boer commander (we think this was Commandant Eloff) came over and said that Colonel Hore and Captain Singleton, with other officers, were their prisoners, and he was sending over their own wounded to us, if we would admit them. Of course we could do nothing else, so we, with our hospital, were 'commandeered'. Four wounded were brought in then, and more later.[19]

An African servant, seeing the Boer burghers and Aunt Helen, the British lady, together, cried out in bewildered consternation, 'Missis, Missis, what are you doing with the Dutch?'

FROM SIEGE TO CONCENTRATION CAMP

Commandant Eloff, my grandmother's captor, was in fact captured himself later that same day and taken to Baden-Powell's headquarters, where the British Commander greeted him pleasantly, 'Good evening, Eloff, you're just in time for dinner!'

Two days later the columns of Colonels Mahon and Plumer entered Mafeking. After 217 days, Mafeking had been relieved. The British Empire, as one writer put it, 'went on an emotional spree bordering on delirium'.[20]

After a brief spell back in England, my grandmother was called back to Bloemfontein by Lord Baden-Powell to nurse in the South African Constabulary (SAC) camps. Looking back on this, my mother recently told me: 'The war was still dragging on in its desultory and tragic way when mother was eventually put in charge of a Concentration Camp (outside

Bloemfontein) for Boer women and children who were dying like flies under canvas in the bitter winter cold. She had the chance later of seeing Emily Hobhouse and pointing out to her her distress and indignation over the British cruelty of forcefully removing these people from their farm homes under the pretext that they were sheltering and harbouring the Boer soldiers. This cruelty, I recognise, has never been forgotten in the subsequent relations between Afrikaner and British in this country.'[21]

In fact so traumatised was my grandmother by the deaths of several Boer children she was trying to nurse back to health, that fifty years later, in 1951, when she was dying, she called out some of their names.

Interestingly enough, to keep the family's Boer War links all properly connected, it is worth noting that the great-grandmother of Tony Bester, my brother-in-law, was in fact in one of these Bloemfontein concentration camps and was reputedly the Boer spokeswoman. With my own grand-mother being in charge of the Bloemfontein camp for a while, it is possible they knew each other. What one wouldn't give for a record of that encounter!

THE WAR STAGGERS TO AN END

As for old Commandant Bester, while grandmother and grandfather were edging romantically towards engagement and no doubt exchanging tales in Bloemfontein of Sanna's Post and Mafeking *etc.*, he for his part was quite possibly bouncing across the Eastern and then the Western Cape with General Smuts' commando in an epic two-thousand-mile ride, said by some to be both the most daring and the most brilliant manoeuvre of the war.

Certainly in Smuts' Cape commando was Boer Com-mander Deneys Reitz, later to become an intimate friend of my grandparents and, by extension, a person of influence in my own life.

Reitz describes how the commando came on the sea near Port Elizabeth:

Few of the men had ever seen a bigger stretch of water than the dam on their parent's farm. Mounted on their horses they looked in wonder on the Atlantic, then, like Greek soldiers, rushed forward in a body, crying 'The sea!', each wanting to be the first on the beach.[22]

As they were all frolicking, shouting and laughing in the waves – some even yet on their horses – a coloured fisherman called out 'What are you doing? Where are you going?'

'To England,' Reitz replied. 'We are crossing tonight to capture London.'

'My God, baas, don't do it,' yelled the distraught fisherman, 'the water is over your head and you will all be drowned!'[23]

While there near Port Elizabeth with Smuts, Deneys Reitz heard that men from General Maritz's commando had a few days previously at Lamberts Bay taken a few potshots from the shore at a British cruiser anchored off shore, thus earning for themselves the distinction of having conducted the only naval battle of the Boer War![24]

Later on, their frolics behind them and much of the North Western Cape again under Boer control, news reached Smuts and his commando that they should proceed to the north for peace talks at Vereeniging on the northern banks of the Great Vaal River.

The Boer War had now staggered to its dreadful conclusion. It had taken three desperate, catastrophic and tragic years for half a million British troops, at the height of British imperial power, to subdue a Boer army of less than fifty thousand. Afrikaner casualties were 28 000 dead in British concentration camps (mainly women and children), 32 000 captured, and 3 800 killed on the battlefield. Two thirds of all Afrikaners who died in the war were under sixteen. It had cost the British 21 942 casualties and £250 million to subdue the Boers. How much, asked one London newspaper, would it cost to govern them?[25] One young captain in a British unit commented with deep concern and anguish of conscience: 'We can't exterminate the Dutch or seriously reduce their numbers. We can however do enough to make hatred of

England and thirst for revenge the first duty of every
Dutchman.'[26]

Commenting further on Boer reactions as British troops
burnt down their farmhouses in the scorched-earth policy of
Lord Kitchener, the captain wrote: 'Their talk is invariably,
and without so far a single exception, to the same effect: "We
will never give in and God sooner or later will see us
through."' The words were prophetic. Added the British
captain after an orgy of burning Boer farms ('six to a dozen in
a day'), 'all the suffering we can inflict only serves to harden
their resolution'[27] – and, be it noted in passing, that same
resolution is at work in 1988.

When it finally came to the Peace Treaty at Vereeniging in
May 1901, old A J Bester was one of six *'bitter-einders'*
present who refused to sign. 'But has the bitter end not
come?', asked Boer Generals De la Rey, Smuts, Louis Botha
and others.

Says Pakenham:

> Twenty-one thousand 'bitter-einders' finally emerged from their
> hiding-places (over twice as many as British Intelligence had
> bargained for). There was the same brief ritual as in previous
> surrenders: their rifles thrown in heaps (mostly captured British
> Lee Enfields, by this stage of the war); then prayers uttered by
> the commandants. Then they trekked off to the concentration
> camps to look for their families. Their discipline and morale –
> they held their heads high, like men who have won a moral
> victory – were conspicuous. Their time would come.[28]

Molly Craufurd, Mafeking nurse, and Edward Reading,
Canadian Cavalryman, who had both been through it all,
were married in 1903 in Cape Town. Family and volk were
indeed intertwining irrevocably. All of which, I would
suppose, does in fact make me a South African.

Our family story, of course, is not unique. Thousands of
other South African families have a similar tale to tell. But
what we must observe is that out of all this long European
settler cross-pollination in our family and in thousands of
others, an authentic, white South Africanism was struggling
to be born, though scarcely cognisant that blacks within the
occupied subcontinent needed somehow to be included.

But even a comprehensive and deep white South African-ism, let alone one embracing blacks, has proved strangely elusive and in the view of many has yet to come forth.

In any event, when my grandparents finally told me their own extraordinary story, which later included a deep friendship with the legendary Boer Commander Deneys Reitz (as related in a later chapter), it was to put into my young soul at a tender age the conviction that war, alienation, vendetta and bitterness were not the way: forgiveness and reconciliation were.

Beyond that, the perils of pride on both sides stand forth to warn all who follow later, and especially all who live now. The exhortation of William Gladstone in 1879 still enshrines the wisdom of the ages: 'Look back over the pages of history; consider the feelings with which we now regard wars that our forefathers in their time supported . . . see how powerful and deadly are the fascinations of passion and of pride.'[29]

4 Conviction, Conversion and Confusion

It is not easy to describe my religious development during
these years, for my heart and mind were a battlefield of the
most diverse influences.

W A Visser t'Hooft

Do not conform any longer to the pattern of this world, but
be transformed by the renewing of your mind.

Romans 12:2

CONVICTIONS AND INFLUENCES

I was not very far along in my young life when several
influences playing upon me, not least my grandparents' Boer
War and post-Boer War experience, brought me to the
conviction that people and relationships mattered, and that
somehow in South Africa this principle was massively
threatened. This latter conviction also alerted me to the fact
that beyond goodwill and hard work in personal relationships, the political process was the way to get things set
right in South Africa so that English–Afrikaner alienation
and black–white racism could be removed and love of all for
all take its place.

Then came Christian conversion at Cambridge, after a
good church-school grounding at Michaelhouse in Natal, and
the pendulum now started to swing away from the line of my
initial conviction. I now believed that the transforming power
of Christ in the human heart by conversion was the only thing
which mattered, because it was only God's power which was

capable of giving people, whether English or Afrikaans, black or white, the capacity for love, plus the necessary inner resources for interracial love and mutual acceptance.

But then I began to discover with shock to my young, innocent faith, that seemingly deeply committed and converted people were often also thorough racists and the worst propagators of segregationist politics.

This ushered in a state of confusion. Was South Africa's need *either* conversion *or* politics – or both or neither or something else quite different? This was the question.

The influences which generated in me the conviction that relationships and people mattered, that we had got this wrong in South Africa, and that the political process was important were not overtly or self-consciously Christian. They just seemed to be expressing a logical consequence of basic humanness. To be concerned about people was a corollary of the way God had created all of us in his image. To treat people differently on the basis of race was not only to deny one's own humanity and theirs, but also to deny the creative act of God that embraces every human being.

This was certainly the view of my parents, and I recollect the pride I felt in hearing someone say of my father, who was then senior mechanical and electrical engineer in Basutoland (now Lesotho), that he was 'very fair with all who worked under him – whether white or black – a man of total justice'. To him people were people. My mother also taught music to both black and white pupils, and often commented how much better the blacks were than the whites! And of course in colonial Basutoland I was constantly meeting highly capable blacks whom my parents knew, like Mr Mohasi, the best vet in town, who looked after my dog, Dingo, and my horse, Punch!

Patrick Duncan

Someone else who also greatly loved South Africa, and especially its black peoples, was Patrick Duncan, who lived next door to us in Maseru. He was the son of Sir Patrick

Duncan, who had been Governor-General of South Africa under Smuts.

Pat was also possessed, as I have said elsewhere, of

passionate political commitments to justice and a fair shake for all. He abominated apartheid and all its ways, but he equally abominated anything to do with violence. Mahatma Gandhi and his philosophy of Satyagraha was his guiding star. I became a childhood convert. Discrimination was wrong. Justice was right. Apartheid would doom South Africa. I was glad and proud when Pat joined Peter Brown and Alan Paton in founding the South African Liberal Party.[1]

Pat was, however, overcome with grief and distress when in 1948 the Nationalist Party came to power. I didn't understand all about the 1948 election, being only a child of eleven, but walking across a hill-side Pat told me it was a tragic and fateful happening. We had as a nation gone down a wrong road and would regret it. I of course believed him.

By 1953, Pat's views on apartheid had consolidated into an intense antipathy. 'Any system that can produce cruelties on this scale must be a bad system,' he said.

For him this conclusion had several consequences. First he resigned from the Basutoland Colonial Service so he could get actively involved in South African politics. Then he began to write and pamphleteer. Then he engaged in active defiance in the spirit of his mentor, Mahatma Gandhi. This of course landed him in trouble with the authorities.

He was later to speak one of the truest prophetic words ever to come out of South Africa: 'Mark my words, apartheid is a word that is destined to mobilise the world.'

Pat, whose strategy had moved from somewhat abortive efforts at defiance through to ever-angrier journalism in *Contact*, the Liberal Party newspaper of the 1960s, was hounded into hiding by the Special Branch and later into flight from the country. By the time he escaped in 1964, he had in despair and disillusionment turned to violence and been banned. In sadness we parted political company, though without terminating our deep friendship. My father said to me one evening, 'The tragedy with this country is that it turns basically peaceloving people like Pat into law-breakers.'

Alan Paton and other prophets

Another haunting word which registered with me was Alan Paton's prognosis made to us schoolboys at Michaelhouse in the early 1950s, that the fruits of apartheid would finally be black hatred on an unimaginable scale, which would come to a head just when whites would begin thinking of change and reform. In the words of old Msimangu as he spoke at the end of *Cry the Beloved Country* about belated white repentance: 'I have one great fear in my heart, that one day when they turn to loving they will find we are turned to hating.'[2]

His prophecies and political posture in due course earned him – though he was probably the most honoured South African in the wider world – the removal of his passport. The Rev. Trevor Huddleston, whom I was soon to meet in England, had his home raided just a couple of days after he got the manuscript of *Naught for Your Comfort* off to his overseas publisher.

Albert Luthuli banned, Z K Matthews ignored, and Walter Sisulu and others imprisoned: thus were our prophets greeted. In fact the fate of our prophets, both secular and sacred, now as then, is to whistle in the dark to a deaf audience.

CONVERSION AND REINTERPRETATION

Convinced that Pat Duncan and Alan Paton and all these political people were on the right track, in October 1955 I headed off to the heady halls of Cambridge University.

Here another sort of adventure was to burst like a tempestuous torrent upon my questing mind and soul. My sense of bliss was complete. Life was opening up. My world was widening. And I was an undergraduate at what I felt sure was the best university in the world!

It was within hours of moving into my digs at 45 Newnham Road that I received a visit from a most delightful and friendly man who introduced himself as Chris Wilson of the Cambridge Inter-Collegiate Christian Union, or CICCU for short. He asked if there was anything he could do to help me get settled in and handed me a printed invitation to the Freshers' Sermon to be conducted by the Rev. Maurice Wood. My room-mate, Alasdair Macaulay, also a South African from Michaelhouse, received a similar invitation and retaliated by proposing to join the Heretics Club and going along to a lecture on Buddhism by Mr Christmas Humphries! Quite unaware of my own spiritual bankruptcy, I resolved to try to convert him, at which he threatened to join the Nudist Association! (Later, thankfully, the Hound of Heaven laid his loving grip upon him.)

In those weeks I was also called on with increasing regularity by other CICCU men. One of these, Robert Footner, an Anglican and a law student, invited me one Sunday morning to communion at the Round Church.

After the communion service, Robert and I found ourselves with twenty minutes to kill before the College dining room opened for breakfast. Robert invited me up to his room. He closed the door rather firmly and we both sat down. I later discovered that his chief goal that morning was to head off my announced intentions of joining the CICCU until I knew a bit more of what real Christianity was all about!

In his first question he asked me how I had enjoyed the communion service. I replied that it had been a good experience, but not perhaps as meaningful as it should or could be. I noted that Rome was not built in a day, and that if I pressed on with determination my faith would one day come to mean something to me.

Robert did not appear impressed with this line. He then asked me straight out: 'Michael, do you know Christ?' I was flabbergasted, annoyed and embarrassed. I made a few rather lame comments about going to church, and all that, and not being quite sure what he meant. His next question was equally abrupt. 'Michael, have you ever surrendered your life to Christ?' If I had missed the import or meaning of the first question, I could scarcely mistake that of the second.

I knew immediately that he had struck at my weakest point. I knew also that he had asked me the one question I did not want to be asked. I knew in my heart of hearts that I had done everything possible in the religious life but that. I also knew that was the one step I had resisted through all my teenage years. I had not been willing to give my life to God, mainly because I was persuaded that if I did so, God would see to it that he made my life a misery. He would take all life's sparkle away and would at the very least send me into the ministry and at the worst lock me up in a monastery!

However, Robert's love, concern and sincerity carried the day. I knew he had something, and I liked what he had. I began to think that if what he said was not true I had nothing to lose by responding to it. However, if it was true, it was the heart of the universe and I had everything to gain by embracing it. It all clicked together as he shared Revelation 3:20 about Jesus knocking at the door of our hearts. *If we opened* to him, he *would* come in. It seemed too marvellous to be true. I resolved there and then to take the plunge. We knelt in a simple act of prayer, and I invited Christ into my life.

That very same day I became aware of his presence. It has never left me since – not ever. Ecstatically, I knew life could never be the same again. The following Sunday I went to church and on a billboard outside I saw the text of 2 Corinthians 5:17, 'If any man be in Christ, he is a new creature: old things are passed away; behold, all things are become new.' I remember being overwhelmed at the thought that even the apostle Paul had found what I had just found!

Almost immediately I reinterpreted the entire nature of the problems in South Africa. Although I still strongly believed myself called to teaching at that stage, rather than anything political, I nevertheless experienced almost immediately a sense also of spiritual calling to South Africa. I had no idea of its shape or form, except that my life was being redirected.

Within three weeks of my conversion a little book came into my hands entitled *The Cambridge Seven* by John Pollock. It was the story of a group of Cambridge men, headed by the great cricketer C T Studd, who went out to China and gave their lives for the evangelisation of that country. At the end of the book this sentence appears: 'Theirs is a story of ordinary men, and thus may be repeated.'[3] The sentence hit me with the force of a sledge-hammer. 'The story of ordinary men . . .' Surely I was an ordinary man. And if the story could be repeated through ordinary men, then perhaps I could form part of such a repetition. I was challenged at the depths of my being.

At this time (*i.e.* late 1955 and half-way through my first term at Cambridge) an event of profound importance for my own life took place. Dr Billy Graham visited Cambridge for a mission. Coming when it did, the mission grounded me in my faith and consolidated my recent commitment to Christ. Dr Graham's message took root deep in my soul, and overnight I had another hero. I recall attending a Christian Union tea-party given for Dr Graham. There were literally hundreds of students present. Dr Graham moved slowly round the room, shaking hands with every ninth or tenth student. I remember being both excited and overwhelmed when he shook hands with me! I never ever dreamt that later he would become a good personal friend.

Stranger stirrings now began to move within me. My newly developed prayer list suddenly had a previously unimaginable entry in it; 'Revival in South Africa.' I was beginning to question whether anything could be wrought through politics. Revival was the answer.

Even so, South Africa and its needs never left me. But now the gospel – not dear Pat and the Liberal Party – was the answer. My diary was peppered with revealing entries: 'Thurs. Jan. 19, 1956. We are going to get Senator Edgar Brookes to speak to us. He also believes that Christianity is the only answer for South Africa.'

On 7 February 1956 I recorded having a South African political journalist plus ten friends for a tea and coffee evening: 'Very interesting but frustrating in that one can *never* get any satisfactory answers. In fact there is *no* political answer, a fact brought home to me very forcibly by such a discussion as tonight's.'

Beyond all this, evangelising others now became my daily passion. Thus I bewailed a friend who was 'too blind to see the remedy in Jesus', while another 'maddened me with his superior attitude to Christ', making me resolute to 'show him much more love and patience'.

The thought of preaching was captivating. Thus a later

entry about a Bible study led by John Stott exults: 'Absolutely terrific. How I long for the day when I can clearly expound God's Word!'

CONFUSION

Inevitably, of course, I couldn't make a totally clean jump to the view that political involvement was out and evangelism in. Thus it was that intimate friends such as Michael Nuttall (now Bishop of Natal) and stirring visitors to the University such as Father Trevor Huddleston stressed the need to keep both things in tension.

I recollect several of us, including Michael Nuttall and John Reeves (the son of Bishop Ambrose Reeves of Johannesburg), breakfasting at an uncomfortably early hour with Trevor Huddleston. He was in the University just after the sensational publication of *Naught for Your Comfort* to speak on 'Apartheid – A Challenge to Christian Conscience.'

I went with some suspicion and reservation, but found the man thoroughly impressive, godly and deeply spiritual.

And of course soon thereafter I read his book.

Indeed, it had naught for my comfort, either politically or theologically. In fact it was all a bit confusing to such a young disciple, though I could not and would not deny the validity of his case.

Naught for your comfort

Early in his book Huddleston spoke of Alexandra township, where there was 'a crisis – and one which has within it the seeds of a great tragedy. Only, like so many other crises in our country, it is unknown to most white citizens of Johannesburg . . .'[4]

I remembered that Pat the politician said things like that.

Now I was hearing it from Huddleston the priest.

He punched home the point by speaking of the dehumanising effects of apartheid for blacks.

'I pray God', he went on,

I may never forget nor weary in fighting against it, for it seems to me that as a Christian, and above all as a priest, my manward task is always and everywhere the same: to recognise in my brother more than my brother: more even than the personality and the manhood that are his: my task is to recognise Christ Himself. And I cannot, therefore, stand aside when it is He whom men treat contemptuously in the streets of the city.

'I was in prison, and ye visited me not . . .'[5]

But now Huddleston shattered this poor and bewildered young convert – all hot with the view that South Africans merely needed to be converted to Christ – by pointing out categorically that it was in fact professed Christians in South Africa who were propagating the system I had already come to loathe. The challenge before white South African Christians, he said, was to ask the question 'Who is my neighbour?'[6]

What gripped Huddleston was the absence in white Christians of any sense of urgency about the need to grapple with this problem. In fact they seemed not to see the problem. Then he added: 'It is not that white Christians are bad: very far from it. It is simply that they fail to see the relevance of their faith to social problems.'[7]

The problem with this, argued the intrepid Anglican priest, was that it had the potential to affect adversely the church's whole credibility, witness and capacity to be God's instrument of love to all people.

Huddleston's parting shots in *Naught for Your Comfort* called for Christians to bring together their faith and their political concerns:

if the Church refuses to accept responsibility in the political sphere as well as in the strictly theological sphere, then she is guilty of betraying the very foundation of her faith: the Incarnation. It is when the Church has so abdicated her position of political trust that the State, freed from any absolute higher than itself, has assumed a totalitarian shape and a dictatorial attitude. That is a matter of history, not of opinion.[8]

And the basis for working the marriage of the personal and social dimensions of faith is love, not the sentimental thing, but love as a searching, revolutionary and passionate force which will not live comfortably with injustice.[9]

Thus there are historical consequences if Christians fail, because God is not mocked. If people persist 'in violating fundamental human rights, rights based upon the Nature of Man and the Nature of God, [they] will have to take the consequences of [their] persistence'.[10]

Who's right and who's wrong?

Huddleston's book hit not only me but the whole of Cambridge and indeed all of England like a bombshell. Furious debate went on inside the church and outside it. Huddleston stuck to his guns.

Alexander Steward of South Africa House now wrote a reply entitled *You Are Wrong Father Huddleston*, and labelled him 'an unreliable observer'. It was in its way an eloquent and undoubtedly sincere statement from a likeable man.

It pleaded with all the vigour of one profoundly convinced for a recognition that 'the dignity of the individual' was 'implicit in Apartheid'.[11]

He claimed for South Africans generally, and I don't doubt it was true for him, 'a natural and uncomplex good-will towards the Black man'.[12] The only problem is that 'the intentions and motives of the South African people, and particularly the National Party, have been twisted and distorted beyond recognition'.[13]

And this was his line when he came to speak at Cambridge, a meeting at which my room-mate Alasdair Macaulay first tried his hand at heckling. 'Oh, come now Mr Steward!', he blurted out, leaving me lost in wonder at his courage.

The sincerity of Steward came through, along with all the standard arguments for apartheid, plus a catalogue of Government achievements in housing, money spent on education *etc.* But there was something wrong . . . something terribly wrong. What was it?

The answer, for me at least, came at the end of Steward's address when Eric Walker, the great South African historian, was asked to pass a vote of thanks. Instead he spent ten minutes dismantling Steward's cases with devastating facts and insights. He ended with the point that however noble the aims and objectives of apartheid, it was unworkable and economically impossible, but *above all* it was not implementable without untold suffering, misery and violation of people's rights, dignity and humanity. 'You see, Mr Steward,' concluded the historian, 'you have only missed out one thing – and that is Jesus – and he was interested in blokes.'

That was it. Apartheid not only did not have the dignity of the individual implicit in it, it was a direct denial of it – it was bad for blokes!

This, to my young undergraduate mind, was answer and insight enough. Moreover, I knew that whatever Huddleston was or wasn't, the encyclopaedic Eric Walker could hardly be labelled 'an unreliable observer'.

For my part, I was satisfied that Alexander Steward was indeed wrong. Huddleston, even a biased Huddleston, was more right than the professedly unbiased Steward.

And so said all of us.

The Margaret Thlotleng Society and intensifying confusion

Under the leadership of Michael Nuttall and Arthur Jenkins, another budding young South African historian, a bunch of us – all South Africans at Cambridge or Oxford – formed the Margaret Thlotleng Society. (Margaret Thlotleng was an old, poor, blind African lady in Sophiatown who used to go daily, come weather fair or foul, to Eucharist at Huddleston's Church of Christ the King. Old Sophiatown locals called her a saint.) Our aim was to do something reconciling for South Africa.

These were heady days. There were endless heated discussions, scores of strategy sessions, daily missionary prayer meetings, special Eucharists, two weekly CICCU Bible studies, plus non-stop evangelism. And in the vacs there was more of the same, plus crumpets and tea in stimulating house-parties at Cumberland Lodge in the great Park at Windsor, only a few hundred yards from the Royal Lodge.

Amidst the many frivolities and much fun and banter which we all enjoyed at Cumberland Lodge, South Africa and reflections upon it pressed upon us ever more incessantly. Nor did we want well-meaning British people to dull either our consciences or their own.

Michael Nuttall, Alasdair Macaulay and I duly burst into print in the London edition of *The Times*, our first effort being in May 1956.

Michael was our scribe, almost as articulate then as now:

> Nothing is more rooted, it seems to us, in the average White South African mind than the capacity for self-deception. It is sometimes deliberate enough to amount to sheer, blatant dishonesty. We deceive ourselves into believing that apartheid will work even though we know, deep down, that to work it will require large land grants to the African, and that the European farmer upon whose vote we depend will not give up his land . . . The great temptation to the White South African (ourselves included) is to exploit the complexity of his problems, and to hide behind facts which conveniently obscure the issues at stake. Mr Strydom is reported in one of the papers to have answered Father Huddleston with the significant refutation that the Nationalist Government has spent more per capita for the African population in South Africa than any other Government in Africa. This is wonderful news, and we are proud of it; but, ever so subtly, it evades the basic issue. A spiritual and a moral challenge is answered by a material rationalisation.

The letter covered many aspects of the South African problem and then concluded:

> We love our country. There is a great work to do there. We would urge, in humility, that well-meaning sympathy from British people not be confused with honest thinking about fundamentals. It is tragic that the conscience should be stilled when it ought to be stirred. Yours sincerely, etc.[14]

This letter seemingly won approval with the *Cape Times* of Cape Town, which editorialised positively on us a few days later (18 May 1956), and expanded:

No-one with an unblinkered mind, can really expect that the Black man, with the White man remaining standing on his shoulders, will also be keeping his eyes on the mirage of total apartheid, a mirage now made more distant than ever. No one can really expect the Black man to share and through generations to continue to share this national neurosis. If the majority of South Africans genuinely believe this will happen, they, or their children or their children's children, are going to be awakened from their fantasy-life by a shock of explosive force. And by then it may be too late to do anything about the realities. For, truly, deceiving others, bad as it is, is far less dangerous than self-deception.[15]

The words about being awakened from our fantasy-life 'by a shock of explosive force' were twenty years before Soweto 1976 and thirty years before Crossroads, New Brighton, Uitenhage and Alexandra 1986. It is the curious fate of those who read history right to be overwhelmed by those who read it wrong or not at all.

As time wore on, however, I became more and more sceptical about the effectiveness of political protest, and more and more politically and theologically schizophrenic. The conservative evangelical CICCU wasn't into this sort of thing. Its boundaries, then at least, were confined to personal faith and witnessing, and its patron saints limited to IVF (Inter-Varsity Fellowship) authors of the 1950s. Unforgivably, C S Lewis, by then a don in Cambridge, was out of bounds. That I heeded the strictures on Lewis and never sought him out constitutes one of my major regrets in life.

Even so, I owed CICCU much, and the vital personal and privatised faith which I saw among its members inspired me much more than the more socially aware and liberally minded members of the SCM (Student Christian Movement).

Compounding my crisis, Michael Nuttall, such an intimate friend, began to react against CICCU narrowness. Suddenly the beautiful Margaret Thlotleng Society was in tension. This tension became more severe at the time of the South African 1957 Treason Trials (156 people having been arrested for High Treason). It was proposed that we march from Cambridge to London, following another of our letters to *The Times*, and then picket South Africa House!

My doubts were now rampant. 'Not on your life,' I thought, 'no marching to London for me!' If I went at all I'd go by train! Which I did.

In the early hours of the morning, in a little bedsitter in London, I struggled desperately in prayer with whether or not to be part of the picket at South Africa House.

Then in reading in the letter of James that morning I came upon this verse: 'If you show partiality you commit sin' (Jas 2:9). 'Yes, that's it,' I realised, 'apartheid shows partiality. So it is indeed old-fashioned sin.' And what were most of those so-called Treason Trialists up for in the last analysis but for protesting about the partiality of the system? If some had been tempted or drawn into violence, the law would have to take its course. But where, ultimately, did the blame lie?

So, yes, I would picket. Yet deep inside, as I donned my black arm-band, I knew that for this form of protest I was a reluctant debutante.

All the same, my confusion hereafter intensified as my evangelicalism deepened, fanned week after week at Cambridge by undeniably marvellous evangelical speakers. Somehow they didn't seem to be much into concern for society. None ever mentioned South Africa. The talk was of justification, wonderful justification, but never of justice.

Finally, in anguish, I resigned with several others from the Margaret Thlotleng Society. Michael Nuttall was much grieved and our relationship was strained. (Its deep and beautiful repair came later when I was a wiser man.) But in the meantime I betook myself to the safety and security of personal, privatised religion.

By mid 1957, with all this still swishing in my mind and spirit, and with the long vac coming up, it seemed good to escape across the Atlantic by student charter and spend the summer in New York.

Unknown to me at that time, there awaited me in that Brave New World a mighty moment of calling, plus the dawning of new light for the way ahead.

5 Pilgrim's Progress

Progress is not an accident but a necessity.

Herbert Spencer (1820–1903)

Be diligent in these matters; give yourself wholly to them, so that everyone may see your progress.

1 Timothy 4:15

> He who would valiant be
> 'Gainst all disaster,
> Let him in constancy
>   Follow the Master.
> There's no discouragement
> Shall make him once relent
> His first avowed intent
>   To be a pilgrim.

John Bunyan (1628–1688)

Somewhat inauspiciously, our battered old propeller charter took three days of starts, false-starts plus repairs and more repairs before it finally got off the ground on a wing and a prayer. All envied the thrice-blessed student whose lucky stars had deposited him by the emergency exit!

Anyway, somehow we conquered the Atlantic, feeling a bit like Charles Lindberg as we landed in New York. But once safely in that mad and magical metropolis where my uncle and aunt were living, and where I would be staying for the next three months, all was novelty, excitement and exhilaration – the people, skyscrapers, freeways, Hudson River, Statue of Liberty, Empire State – *and* Billy Graham!

I should add here that a little while before this American trip, I had begun to think of theological training, with a view to doing a good job of scripture teaching, on top of my Latin and French, in some high school. This was how I understood my future career. However, when I made enquiries about English theological colleges, I was informed that scholarships were not available unless one gave the assurance and undertaking that one was going to enter the ordained ministry. I did not feel free in all honesty to make such a guarantee. In one fell swoop that ruled out all English theological colleges, because I felt unwilling to tax my parents' resources further.

A CALL IN MADISON SQUARE GARDEN

Not long after arriving in New York, I discovered from local newspapers that an enormous crusade conducted by Dr Billy Graham was on in New York City at that time (summer 1957). His meetings were taking place each night at Madison Square Garden. By this time my mind was moving along the lines of discovering a theological college in the United States where I could get suitable training. Not knowing any other Christian in the United States than Dr Graham, I decided to write to him personally and ask for his advice! Naiveté is sometimes an asset!

My letter arrived at the Crusade office, along with thousands of others, and eventually landed on the desk of a Japanese student from Fuller Theological Seminary. He read of the enquiry about theological colleges, immediately phoned me, and invited me down to Madison Square Garden. He told me he came from a theological seminary called Fuller, in Pasadena, California. He wanted to introduce me to some of his friends. By strange coincidence, almost every one was a student at Fuller Seminary. In fact, throughout the following three months, almost the only seminary I heard of was Fuller! It appeared to be a clear pointer. Before the summer was through, I wrote to Dr Edward John Carnell, President of the Seminary, applying for entry and a scholarship. One letter in one particular bag on one particular desk had shaped my whole future!

While my seminary enquiries proceeded, something else of profound importance was taking place in my life. As I attended the Madison Square Garden meetings night by night, something began to happen in my heart: I began to get a vision, I began to dream a dream, and I began to experience a call.

I remember one night pacing up and down the long corridors which flanked the Garden Arena itself. The meeting was over. Hundreds were being counselled in the Counselling Room. I had seen God at work in a wonderful way as the Spirit honoured the proclaimed word. I was seeing mass evangelism happening. Suddenly I found myself hearing within my spirit: 'Why not in Africa?' 'Yes, why not, Lord?' I replied. It was that simple. From that moment on my calling was clear and Dr Graham's part in it had been important and decisive.

Evangelism, the preaching of the gospel of Jesus Christ, now became clearly and irrevocably for me the basic building-block and the central commitment for anything and everything I ever proposed thereafter to do or be – whether in South Africa or beyond it. Indeed the Madison Square Garden experience took on more meaning to me with every passing day.

The eternal destiny of the human soul and the discovery during man's earthly odyssey of new birth and salvation became the matter of paramount importance. After all, as Jesus had put it, 'what will it profit a man, if he gains the whole world and loses his soul?' (Matt 16:26, RSV).

I knew now that I could never give myself unreservedly or totally to building only an earthly city or working only for a political kingdom. 'For the things that are seen are transient, but the things that are unseen are eternal' (2 Cor 4:18, RSV). The Prayer Book prayer had it right: 'We must live that we may so pass through things temporal that we finally lose not the things eternal.'

And night after night at Madison Square Garden I basked in hearing the cross proclaimed – 'the old rugged cross', as George Beverly Shea sang of it, 'the emblem of suffering and shame'. And without coming to that cross, I became assured, men and women were lost and under divine condemnation.

Clearing undergrowth on a wooded property in New Rochelle belonging to my uncle and aunt, I memorised scriptures relating to my new sense of calling. Into my heart went John 3:16–18 (RSV):

> For God so loved the world that he gave his only Son, that whoever believes in him should not perish but have eternal life. For God sent the Son into the world, not to condemn the world, but that the world might be saved through him. He who believes in him is not condemned; he who does not believe is condemned already, because he has not believed in the name of the only Son of God. And this is the judgment, that the light has come into the world, and men loved darkness rather than light, because their deeds were evil.

And I believed it.

I could never be a universalist.[1] Coming to Christ mattered, and mattered desperately and eternally. To preach his word would be my privilege and delight. After all, said another of my memory verses, 'God . . . desires all men to be saved and to come to the knowledge of the truth' (1 Tim 2:4, RSV). 'But how are men to call upon him in whom they have not believed? And how are they to believe in him of whom they have never heard? And how are they to hear without a preacher?' (Rom 10:14, RSV).

Yes, evangelism was the thing – and the greatest calling in the world.

I also basked in the new sense of my Lord's hand upon me and his promised guidance for all that lay ahead. Ethel Waters, great effervescent Southern mammy and minstrel that she was, sang it out almost nightly in the Garden: 'His eye is on the sparrow – and I know he watches me.'

I knew it too.

DRAMA IN LITTLE ROCK, ARKANSAS

Another drama, distant yet not totally unrelated in its Christian inspiration to that in Madison Square Garden, was being enacted in North America at that time. But the drum-beat was different. In Madison Square Garden it was Billy Graham, the evangelist. In Little Rock and the South it was

Martin Luther King. In Madison Square Garden the foe was the devil. In Little Rock they said it was Governor Faubus. For it was Faubus with his state troopers who was blocking the entry of young blacks to hitherto white schools.

On TV that summer of 1957 I watched the drama build up till finally President Eisenhower sent federal troops in to enforce the school integration process.

One of the most moving of all the media images of the civil rights movement of these years was the picture of little Elizabeth Eckford sitting alone on a bench in front of Little Rock Central High School, surrounded by an angry white segregationist mob. Her ordeal and solitary encounter with the hostile white mob was blazed across the wire services one evening, and the world's attention was riveted to Little Rock.[2]

Watching all this on TV up in New York, one asked oneself: 'From where does such courage and commitment come?' – a commitment of course which was sweepingly evident among blacks all across the South and had been so in a special way since 1 December 1955, when exhausted little Mrs Rosa Parks had refused on a Montgomery bus to give up her seat to a white man.

Had I been at Holt Street Baptist Church in Montgomery, Alabama, on 5 December 1955, I would have got the answer to my self-addressing question at the TV set in New York: 'Whence such courage and commitment?' The answer was heralding forth from a little-known black preacher called Martin Luther King. After describing the arrest of Rosa Parks, he added:

> you know, my friends, there comes a time when people get tired of being trampled over by the iron feet of oppression. There comes a time my friends, when people get tired of being flung across the abyss of humiliation where they experience the bleakness of nagging despair. There comes a time when people get tired of being pushed out of the glittering sunlight of life's July and left standing amidst the piercing chill of an Alpine November.[3]

Had I heard that word back in the late 1950s, I too would have already known, on the basis of what I'd seen and learnt in South Africa, that a time would come there too when blacks would say: 'We are tired of being trampled on – enough is enough.'

King went on:

> We, the disinherited of this land, we who have been oppressed so long are tired of going through the long night of captivity. And we are reaching out for the daybreak of freedom and justice and equality . . . In all of our doings, in all of our deliberations . . . whatever we do, we must keep God in the forefront. Let us be Christian in all of our action. And I want to tell you this evening that it is not enough for us to talk about love. Love is one of the pinnacle parts of the Christian faith. There is another side called justice. And justice is really love in application. Justice is love correcting that which would work against love.[4]

Of course I didn't hear King say all this – I only saw Little Rock erupting – but I knew it was part of a sweeping movement with a long history. And the issue was the same as South Africa's. And these were the sorts of things Trevor Huddleston and Alan Paton and Pat Duncan were on about. And here too in the South were white Christians, millions of them, all Bible believers of the Bible belt, yet supporting Faubus and all his works and propping up the segregationist way of life. Thankfully there were other Christian voices of protest from the black world, and some marvellous exceptions from the white.

Two other things gripped me in 1957 as I goggled at Little Rock, and even more so in 1987 as I re-goggled at the re-run in a six-hour video presentation of it all called *Eyes on the Prize*. The first is how really awful, evil, violent and self-deceived many Southern whites had become in the 1950s. The second thing was the different odds against South African blacks as compared to blacks in the deep South. The latter had the Constitution, the Supreme Court, the President, the Attorney General and the Federal Army all with them. South African blacks have nothing like that. They only have numbers. Plus of course history.

A VISION OF SOUTH AFRICA

As I returned to England at the end of the summer of 1957 for my last year at Cambridge, I did so as a called and commissioned man. I still could not see how my interest in teaching, my new call to evangelism and my concern for South Africa all fitted together, but I did not bother too self-consciously to try and resolve the matter. I knew the Lord was bringing it all together.

The academic year 1957–1958 finally ended. I received my degree in modern and medieval languages and left Cambridge more assured than ever of the faithfulness of God and more determined than ever to serve him on the continent of Africa.

After six months school-mastering in London, among some of Britain's 'wild-life', I took my modest earnings, plus a princely £60 from selling my old London taxi, bought a sea ticket and headed back to South Africa to await my entry, in October 1959, to Fuller Seminary in California.

During the magnificent sea-voyage home, God confirmed my call beautifully through a Pentecostal family, Jack and Ruth Holmes. The experience of seeing Table Mountain clothed with cloud early one morning while we were thirty or so miles out to sea, was one of those moments impressed indelibly upon my now burning soul. This was my place – South Africa, lovely land of promise and of pain.

In England I had seen Pat Duncan again and perplexed him with the story of my conversion and my altered perspective on South African issues. Now I saw him in Cape Town. Then I called on Joost de Blank, and in his great study at Bishop's Court in Cape Town I heard the controversial archbishop say: 'Although I am not worthy to lick Billy Graham's boots, yet it remains so that many evangelicals have neglected the incarnational concerns of the gospel.'

By this time I knew it was true.

'Maybe you are someone', he went on, 'who should try and bring these together.'

It was a relevant challenge to me, and a memorable one.

Nine months later I set off by plane for Fuller Seminary.

A TASTE OF EVANGELISM

Significant help soon came from Edward John Carnell, then President of Fuller Seminary. His classes in apologetics and in systematic theology, along with his book *The Case for Orthodoxy*, quickly became an intoxicant to me – and the single most liberating influence in all my four years of theological training.

My severe bigotry towards Christians with whom I disagreed also came under Carnell's gentle but persuasive assault. As to socio-political issues, Carnell made short shrift of dichotomies between the personal and the social.

The summer vac of 1960 saw four of us, as a student Gospel Team, travel the Eastern Seaboard of the USA with a high-powered California evangelist. We students tried our wings at evangelism, often with hilarious consequences, and spent the whole summer arguing over Calvinism versus Arminianism, and sovereignty versus free will, thereby creating alarm and despondency among the long-suffering pastors who hosted us.

In the first fascinating frolics in evangelism, the insistent word of the Spirit to my heart was that I should go back to Africa the following summer with my friend Ed to travel its length and breadth, meet leaders and spy out the land.

ABRAHAM VEREIDE

A key encounter in Washington that summer had been with Abraham Vereide, the old Norwegian saint, who had at Roosevelt's request launched a great spiritual movement among political leaders in Washington. Soon known as International Christian Leadership, a label it later shed to remain popularly known as the Prayer Breakfast Movement, this spiritual thrust presented another and intriguing angle on evangelism and social concern – namely the evangelistic reaching and spiritual discipling of leaders who in turn could shape society and the body politic more into the image and way of Christ.

What appalled Vereide, as he had written in 1934, was that

as he travelled around as an evangelist, he could see that
'politics seemed under the control of those who were not fit to
take the leadership'.[5]

Norman Grubb, Vereide's biographer, writes in *Modern
Viking*:

> Concern for the 'down and out' is fairly common. Their need is
> obvious. Concern for the 'up and out' is more rare. It takes a
> more discerning eye to see their need, and a rare combination of
> compassion, boldness and right approach to meet it. True leader-
> ship demands true men. True men are God's men. God's men
> have come to the cross of Christ, having discovered themselves to
> be untrue men, and have begun a new life of which the motivating
> center is God in them, and not themselves. This was Abram's
> apostleship. A leadership led by God. Men must first have God's
> salvation for their own needs, and then be God's representatives
> to walk in His ways and act by His spirit. The greater the sphere of
> influence in government or industry, the more responsible they
> are to make it plain by their personal living, by their conduct of
> affairs, and by their verbal witness, that Jesus Christ as Saviour
> and Lord is the only answer to the human problem.[6]

Vereide's main point was that 'the Church is the layman
and laymen must live and work out their faith in the real
world'.[7] He invited me to the 1961 Presidential Prayer Breakfast, the first one with John F Kennedy as President. A
thousand or more top brass were there. Billy Graham spoke
on 'The heart is deceitful above all things and desperately
wicked.' The gospel application of Jesus, his forgiveness and
his demands, was thorough and convincing. I observed that
Billy Graham was not given to compromise, not for President
Kennedy or anyone.

The experience made an enormous impression on me, all
the more so when Vereide called me to his room, and issued
me with a solemn and unforgettable charge to take on my
heart the leaders of Africa.

He stressed that to reach a leader genuinely and deeply for
Christ is potentially to touch thousands of followers and to
impact both society and the body politic. It was a glorious
vision, and one not to be laid aside.

AN AFRICAN TOUR

The chance to test this call came the following summer, in 1961. In faith I duly booked two tickets (for my friend Ed Gregory and myself) for a tour starting in Tripoli in Libya, moving across Tunisia and Algeria to Morocco, down through all the West African cities, into 'Congo' as it was, then South Africa, Rhodesia, Nyasaland, East Africa, Ethiopia and Egypt.

Money for the trip came in the day before we left!

After a meeting in Washington DC with African ambassadors, organised by Vereide, Ed and I set off on our three-month and thirty-thousand-mile journey. Key leaders from Sir Milton Margai, Prime Minister of Sierre Leone, and Tom Mboya of Kenya to the Crown Prince of Ethiopia were among the many we visited.

In Lagos, Nigeria, something particularly important happened which was to affect my whole life. Reading in Acts 18 about Paul's butterflies before going to evangelise the city of Corinth, I came on verse 9 (RSV): 'Do not be afraid, but speak and do not be silent; for I am with you, and no man shall attack you to harm you; for I have many people in this city.'

In an astonishing hour, the Spirit of God gave form to my incipient call to evangelism. My focus was to be the cities of Africa generally and the leaders within those cities specifically.

Waiting on God, I heard a further word: 'The first city will be Pietermaritzburg.' I accordingly wrote 'Pietermaritzburg (Lagos, Nigeria)' and the date in the margin of my Bible.

MISSION TO PIETERMARITZBURG

Amazingly, back at Fuller Seminary four months later a letter arrived from the Ministers' Fraternal of Pietermaritzburg, inviting us to come and take part in an interracial, interdenominational city-wide evangelistic campaign in that city in 1962.

The mission, which took place in August 1962 with the

fledgling African Enterprise Team, exceeded all expectations, and the city hall was packed to capacity for two weeks, with people of all races and church backgrounds getting involved. The dream and the sense of calling from Cambridge days, from the basement of Madison Square Garden and from the cabin in Lagos were taking on substance and coming to fruition. God was proving faithful beyond my wildest dreams.

And evangelism, as the basic building-block of all my future endeavours, was unequivocally in place.

ALBERT LUTHULI

In line with Vereide's emphasis on showing concern for leaders and learning from them, one day during the mission we met with Liberal Party leaders Peter Brown and Alan Paton, educationalist Susie Kochelhoffer and then (up the North Coast of Natal) with the banned Nobel Prize winner, Chief Albert Luthuli.

Albert Luthuli was undoubtedly one of the most impressive Christian gentlemen it has ever been my privilege to meet. Professor Edgar Brookes, parliamentarian, historian, scholar and Christian, who knew Luthuli intimately, wrote of him: 'He was an admirable chief, outgoing, patient, devoted to duty.'

First elected as President of the Natal branch of the ANC (African National Congress), Luthuli soon passed on to become President of the ANC as a whole. Said Edgar Brookes:

> He seemed to me to have no ambition, but as leader of the main political organ of the Africans felt it his duty to struggle with the government for his people's rights. The government deprived him of his chieftainship, tried unsuccessfully to have him found guilty of high treason, imprisoned him and for seven years banned him. ('Banning' means that the person concerned may not speak in public, may not publish anything, may not be quoted, may not take part in any social functions and may not leave the District.) Chief Luthuli, winner of the Nobel Peace Prize and Lord Rector of Glasgow University, was still subject to these disabilities when he died [in July 1967].[8]

The events leading up to Luthuli's banning were focused on nationwide protests from blacks against the hated pass-laws. On 21 March 1960 at Sharpeville, a black township forty miles south of Johannesburg, a throng of twenty thousand blacks without their passes had challenged the police to arrest them. When some stone-throwing started, the police panicked and opened fire, killing sixty-nine men, women and children and injuring 180.

Shock engulfed the country. Outrage erupted worldwide. Sickened with grief and anger, Luthuli and the ANC called for a day of mourning and stay-away on 28 March, the day earmarked for the funerals of the victims. He also publicly burnt his pass.

The Government then not only banned the ANC and the more militant PAC (Pan Africanist Congress), but also briefly imprisoned Chief Albert Luthuli. Shortly after his release he too was banned.

So here he was, confined as a sort of non-person in remote rural Natal – unable to write, speak, lead the ANC, or be quoted.

Two observations

Two remarks Luthuli made struck me forcibly. The first was about the ANC: 'The Government is very mistaken to think that by banning me the ANC will be destroyed. All that will happen is that the movement will go underground, move away from its commitment to non-violence, and fall into the hands of more extreme leaders.'

Founded in 1912 (two years before the National Party) in frustrated reaction to the exclusion of blacks from the franchise in the Union Constitution of 1910, the ANC had for no less than fifty years had a profound commitment to non-violence. And now Luthuli was prophesying that more extreme leadership would take over, and the commitment to non-violence be weakened. At the very moment of this utterance, a certain Nelson Mandela was emerging to take the lead.

South African-born journalist Michael Attwell writes of the post-Sharpeville, 'post-Luthuli-banning' period:

In the decimation of their [ANC] ranks after Sharpeville, Mandela looked the most promising of the surviving activists. They elected him leader of the National Action Council. Having failed to shake white domination by civil disobedience, black South Africa now entrusted Mandela with spearheading a new constitutional initiative. They called through Mandela for a new National Convention – this time between white and black, rather than white and white. They hoped thereby to negotiate peacefully a new and just dispensation for all South Africa's people.[9]

Apparently Verwoerd did not even reply.
Observes Attwell:

Had Verwoerd but known, had white South Africa but known, that this was the last brief time of asking, their response might have been different. A time would come when history would reveal this had been the last possible moment in which white South Africa could have dictated the terms for the future and ensured a peaceful resolution of the country's deep malaise. But lulled by Afrikaner triumphalism into a false sense of security, the precious instant slipped through their fingers without them even realizing it.[10]

Mandela went into hiding, and with many gave up the way of peaceful protest. A military wing of the ANC called *Umkhonto we Sizwe* (Spear of the Nation) was formed, and the first plans to sabotage installations were under way. After fifty years, the commitment to non-violence had ended.

If Luthuli's first striking observation in our meeting related to the radicalising consequences for the ANC of both his and its banning, then the second observation to impress us profoundly related to his Christian faith: 'The way forwards for South Africa', he solemnly affirmed, 'is the Way of the Master.'

To me, this was another crucial word, coming this time not from an evangelist or a theologian or a Southern civil-rights preacher, but from the leading black political figure of South Africa.

Not only was 'Jesus and justice' the goal for South Africa, but the Jesus way was *the* way for the country, said Luthuli.

The Christian end had to be pursued by Christian means, and for him this sprang from a deep personal faith which informed his political beliefs and methods, and held him deeply in every situation of life – even in prison.

In his banned book *Let My People Go* (which tells the story of the fifty non-violent years of the ANC as well as his own story), reflecting on the significance of his prison experience, Luthuli says: 'Frail man that I am, I pray humbly that I may never forget the opportunity God gave me to rededicate myself, to consider the problems of our resistance to bondage, and above all to be quiet in His Presence. My whitewashed cell became my chapel, my place of retreat.'[11]

Our time with Luthuli that September afternoon in 1962 had ended with prayer and poignancy. What, we wondered, was to become of this quiet man – manifestly a man of idealism, integrity, compassion and faith? Saluted by the world, here in his own country he was shut away and shunned. And from his isolation he knew and said that the summer of peaceful protest was passing. It struck me then as folly that white South Africans should not be allowed to hear what he had to say and to feel his heartbeat.

PROGRESS

As the spiritually adventurous summer of 1962 ended, and we headed back to the United States and a further two years of studies, I felt some advance had slowly but surely been made in the pilgrimage of marrying evangelism and social concern. The Pietermaritzburg mission and the Luthuli experience had captured the developing fusion. Here were the strands beginning to come together – the spiritual, the pastoral, the social, the political.

And so it was that by the end of 1964, when our little African Enterprise team finally set sail from New York for Durban, we were resolved as evangelists to preach the gospel with all our might to whoever would listen, whether high or low. Furthermore, we were settled in our minds and hearts that we would never make peace with apartheid. But instead

of mental anguish and theological schizophrenia over this
posture, there was now comfort and peace.

And this, I felt, was indeed progress!

Part Three

HOW TO BE AFRIKANER, SOUTH AFRICAN AND CHRISTIAN
(The Afrikaner dilemma)

6   Nationalism or Patriotism?

Protecting our culture and our nation – that is the whole
issue. The issue is not race. The issue is not that we are the
last bastion of civilization. The sooner we get over those
ideas, the better. The issue is whether the Afrikaner nation
will have a place under the sun.

Professor A D Pont

Standing as I do in view of God and eternity, I realize that
patriotism is not enough. I must have no hatred or bitterness for anyone.

Edith Cavell

Righteousness exalts a nation.

Proverbs 14:34

VARIETIES OF NATIONALISM

At heart, the story of South Africa is the story of a clash of
sectional and racially based nationalisms and of hitherto
abortive efforts to produce under God an all-encompassing
South African patriotism. By this I mean a racially inclusive
patriotism subservient to Christ, whose lordship we officially
embrace as a nation.

Afrikaner nationalism

Afrikaner nationalism has of course in recent history been
predominant. Its basic thesis was well articulated by former
Prime Minister, John Vorster. 'All other black nations govern
themselves,' he said. 'We have been in Africa three hundred

years and have the same right to govern ourselves as they. This right we cannot and will not forfeit.'[1]

Likewise Professor A D Pont, a founding member of the reactionary HNP (Herstigte Nasionale Party), affirms, 'The issue is whether the Afrikaner nation will have a place under the sun.'[2]

Nor can anyone deny that the Afrikaner has produced the most vigorous and developed nationalism on the African continent. More than that, it was the first, as Sir Harold Macmillan, the then British Prime Minister, recognised in his famous 'Winds of Change' speech in the South African Parliament in February 1960. 'Indeed, in the history of our time,' he said, very specifically to the Afrikaners, 'yours will be recorded as the first of the African nationalisms.'[3]

Black nationalism

Then of course, at the other end of the political spectrum, there is modern black nationalism, sometimes tribally inspired, which is summed up in the general African cry, 'Africa for the Africans' or in the specifically black South African slogan, 'The people shall reign' – meaning of course the black majority. When such black nationalism, even in more moderate forms, confronts Afrikaner nationalism, you have the classic collision of the irresistible force and the immovable object. Indeed that is the precarious stalemate of South Africa in the 1980s.

English-speaking South Africans

In between these two giant nationalisms stand the spectating English-speaking South Africans, pulled this way and that by the vestiges of Western liberal conscience on the one hand and the appeal of the Afrikaner gut cry for white solidarity on the other.

Some English-speaking South Africans are 'Gilbert and Sullivan' South Africans who remain English 'in spite of all temptations to belong to other nations'. Others are 'world citizen' South Africans who at one level belong to all nations in the Western tradition, yet at another level truly want, along with many Afrikaners and blacks, to belong deeply to this nation of South Africa but find the exclusive nationalism of both apartheid Afrikaners and black-power blacks hard to handle.

CHRISTIAN PATRIOTISM

Without a doubt, many from all backgrounds in South Africa are also Christians who know on the one hand that 'here they have no continuing city' and on the other that the healthiest patriotism is tempered, controlled and infused by the spirit of Jesus Christ. In fact they would go even further and affirm with Edith Cavell, the famous First World War nurse who said just before dying at the hands of a German firing squad, 'Standing as I do in view of God and eternity, I realize that *patriotism is not enough*. I must have no hatred or bitterness for anyone.'[4] Erich Fromm, the German psychologist, put it this way: 'Love for one's country which is not part of one's love for humanity is not love, but idolatrous worship.'[5]

It was with this posture of what I understood Christian patriotism to be that I for my part returned to my Beloved Country at the end of 1964 along with three other founding members of our African Enterprise team, Paul Birch, Dick Peace and Chris Smith.

First and foremost, our calling was evangelism and the proclamation of the gospel to lost souls. But how would this and our general stance on a Christian patriotism subordinated to the gospel work out, one wondered, especially in the face of both Afrikaner and black nationalisms? And how would the Jesus we had come to love and trust lead us in terms of an attitude to each of these giant forces? And how would or could a holistic gospel of personal faith and social concern, such as I had come to accept, relate to a context so national-istically charged?

Family influences

In the process of reflection on this issue of nationalism and patriotism, I felt much blessed in that a key and basic building-block had already been put in place by my maternal grandparents and by a sense of South Africa's history in the early part of this century. In Chapter 3 I mentioned their decisive friendship with the Boer Commander Deneys Reitz. I said I would elaborate. Let me now do so, since it was critical for me in shaping my own thinking, and, moreover, their experience together in Heilbron typifies and illuminates in flesh-and-blood terms the heart of the South African struggle to bring forth even the beginnings of a genuine national patriotism. In many ways understanding this struggle is both a prerequisite and a prelude to understanding the Afrikaner dilemma and the birth of apartheid, which we will look at in the next chapters.

After the Boer War had ended, grandfather was seconded to the Civil Service in the Orange River Colony (later Orange Free State) as a magistrate. He was posted first to Parys and then in 1908 to the Free State town of Heilbron, which, though small, was the centre of a large magisterial district. There he found that the local attorney was none other than the great Boer Commander, Colonel Deneys Reitz.

Both being men of generous disposition they began to forge a deep relationship out of their own post-war struggles. My mother, then just a little child, recollects that 'Deneys was a great wit and a real character, and they had great laughs together.'

Reitz at this point was however still struggling in his own heart with deep Afrikaner nationalist feelings. His father had been Secretary of State for the Transvaal Republic under President Kruger before the war began. 'At the conclusion of the peace treaty of Vereeniging,' wrote Reitz in 1933, 'my father refused to accept its terms and my brother Arend and I followed his example. Consequently Sir Alfred Milner, the British High Commissioner, ordered us to be deported.'[6] They were 'bitter-einders' like old Commandant Bester and Christiaan de Wet.

Father Reitz went to America, while Deneys and his brother headed for Madagascar, still giving vent to their Afrikaner nationalism and their anti-British feelings.

After a period of self-imposed exile in Madagascar, Reitz returned to South Africa:

After many wanderings I reached the little town of Heilbron on the northern Free State plains, and there cast anchor. The place had under fifteen hundred inhabitants, but it was the centre of a sturdy Boer peasantry who had fought bravely during the war, in the course of which they had suffered great losses. Their grim jest, 'my wife and children died in the concentration camps, my home is burnt down and my cattle gone, but otherwise there is nothing to complain of,' was a fair illustration of what many of them had suffered, and of their unbroken spirit. Now they were back on their ruined farms, patiently at work, and among them I lived for the next five years.[7]

And here, as I said, he also met my grandfather, Edward Reading. Though they had such different national histories, they became firm friends, both struggling with but committed to throwing off sectional nationalisms so they could become true patriots of a united South Africa, although the inclusive embrace of blacks, even for them, was not yet in view. The war had made the Boer–British issue their preoccupying fixation.

But the mood among Afrikaners around them was very different. While Deneys Reitz and Edward Reading sought to forget and forgive the past, others fuelled it with bitterness. Reflects Reitz: 'Vainly I advocated the ideal of a united nation, regardless of sectional distinctions, but my leaders would have none of it . . . At many an angry meeting I was howled down and sometimes roughly handled.'[8]

All the emotion in these rival views of Afrikaner nationalism and South African patriotism inevitably had to come to a head – and it did in the Boer Rebellion of 1914. This was the culmination of very understandable Boer negativism towards being dragged by their government into 'Britain's war' against Germany. Louis Botha and Smuts, with their wider sympathies, vigorously crushed this uprising.

My mother recalls this time vividly: 'I can picture coming into a bedroom in our home and finding Dad and Deneys pushing Deneys' revolver under some shirts in a drawer. You see, Deneys was going to come out against the rebels, and he was trying to make a getaway out of Heilbron before the rebels took over, which they obviously were going to do.'

Reitz had also received a private tip-off that a group of

rebels was expected in Heilbron that night, and that they were going to seize him and shoot him in his own backyard. He had to escape as lightly and unencumbered as possible, so he wanted to hide this extra weapon – a good rifle was enough.

My mother continued her recollection: 'When I surprised Dad and Deneys hiding the revolver, they looked put out, and casting glances at each other, said "Wait, come here." Then Dad knelt beside me, took my arm and whispered "You must be a good little girl, and we are going to trust you. You have got to help us. We are against the rebels, and you are in with us, and you don't tell anyone that Uncle Deneys has left his gun here." They made me promise and I felt terribly important and wonderfully burdened with this great secret!'[9]

Reitz adds the following interesting aside on the rebels: 'To them, as to all the rebels I ever met, the rising was but a more acute phase of our original political differences, and I never came across one man who thought that he had committed an offence in taking up arms against the Government of his country.'[10]

Basically it was a case of two clashing views of nationalism and patriotism.

Grandfather and his old friend were reunited to continue their friendship which was to affect both of them, not to mention me when I heard this tale, so profoundly.

Reitz and many other Afrikaners influenced my grandfather's South African patriotism to the extent that he could say in 1917 in a public meeting in Parys, where he had become a magistrate after leaving Heilbron, 'We are not British or Dutch. We are South Africans, and it is impossible for one section of the community to separate itself from another.'[11]

This line of thinking led to Grandfather's promotion in the Civil Service, till finally he had an office in Union Buildings as Secretary of the Public Service Commission. Reitz, who went on to become Minister of Lands in Smut's Cabinet, later wrote my grandfather a letter which I have framed in my office as a reminder of the spirit and posture which should, I believe, characterise our land if it is ever to be healed. Reitz's letter, dated 11 April 1934 and headed 'Union Parliament, House of Assembly, Cape Town', said:

You speak of our being able to 'talk old battles over without hate' and I would like to tell you that in my case the fact that I was able to speak of 'battles long ago' without bitterness as early as I did was largely thanks to you. When first I came to Heilbron I still nursed a good many narrow prejudices and I might easily have followed a far more rigid pathway than I did but for your having been my friend. You may not have realised it at the time how you were a potent cause towards starting me upon a broader outlook and a maturer view of past troubles. True, both General Botha and General Smuts had pointed out to me the road to follow, but in the narrow atmosphere of a country district I had begun to slip back into the old way of rancour and ill-will once more. Then in the course of our long friendship of those far off days, the liberal view you held, your friendly sentiments towards the older population, your lack of hatred and your love of the country of your adoption – all these insensibly led upwards towards a saner and wider horizon.

I am thankful to know that the road you and I have trod is now being justified by racial concord such as this country has never known and to you personally I owe an eternal debt of gratitude which this letter is a feeble attempt to express.

It was this wider and more inclusive spirit of patriotism and reconciliation, as typified by Reitz, which my grandfather held up to me as the way of healing for South Africa. It was the godly way, he believed.

ENCOUNTERING NATIONALISM'S DIFFICULTIES

It was as an overlay to this 'Grandfather-cum-Reitz' spirit and commitment that Christian conversion finally came in 1955, followed by my call to evangelism in 1957 and then four years of theological study (1959–1963) in the USA.

But I was soon to find as our African Enterprise ministry got under way in South Africa in early 1965 that all was not quite straightforward in this matter of the way faith informs and infuses one's nationalism and patriotism.

My first inklings of this came on 24 January 1965, the day Winston Churchill died. I was in Cape Town with the prominent Christian layman Sir Cyril Black, the Conservative MP for Wimbledon, who was visiting South Africa. I had met him in London to discuss the idea of getting a prayer-group going in the South African Parliament, similar to the one he and others had started in the House of Commons under Abraham Vereide's inspiration.

We agreed to meet in Cape Town and visit Mr Henning J Klopper, the Speaker of the House of Assembly and, as I had been led to believe, another notable Christian layman.

He had in fact been one of the founders of the South African Broederbond (a large Afrikaner Nationalist secret society) and its first chairman from its inception in 1918 till 1924. At that point Sir Cyril and I were blissfully unaware of this. Thus blindly did we rush in where better-informed English angels might well have feared to tread.

Had we known Klopper's history and that of the Broederbond we might have better understood his rejection of the idea of a prayer-meeting in Parliament to bring together Afrikaans and English-speaking MPs around the word of God.

'It is not necessary,' he said rather abruptly. 'All the Cabinet are Christians, and most have been in my Sunday-school classes!'

In many ways he was a dear old man, but spiritually there was something unresolved, I thought. Had I then known more of the Broederbond's history and of his prominent role in it, I might have better discerned the workings of his nationalistic but seemingly wounded spirit and maybe even shown some real understanding. (More on that later.)

In any event, Sir Cyril and I were unwittingly before the great founder of the Broederbond, naively and innocently suggesting that English and Afrikaner MPs meet together to pray, study the scriptures and seek the mind of God. Such a little group does in fact exist today (and I have met with it), but in 1965 the kindest thing you could say was that it was an idea whose time had not yet come!

In the next eighteen months, as our African Enterprise evangelistic campaigns got under way, we were to experience many different aspects of the problem of nationalism – and the complications arising from them.

In Ladysmith the town council banned blacks from our meetings, which forced us to put up a tent in the black township. In Vryheid some of the white locals said the communists had sent us. In pre-Independence Lesotho, all fired with nationalistic zeal, a communist-backed group said Verwoerd had sent us!

All this led me to say yes to an invitation that arrived during the 1966 Lesotho mission to speak on 'The Ethics of Political Nationalism as an Obstacle to Evangelism' at the Berlin World Congress on Evangelism later that year.

THE ADDRESS TO THE WORLD CONGRESS ON EVANGELISM

Berlin, with its hideous wall and its still-evident war scars, provided a salutary reminder of the awfulness of nationalism run riot.

As we walked beside sections of the Berlin wall, Francis Schaeffer told me, 'This wall is a warning to you people in South Africa, Mike.' In his view, pre-war Germany illustrates the devastating consequences of nationalism divorced from the lordship of Christ.

Sir Fred Catherwood, the European Parliamentarian, has correctly said, 'Christians cannot escape their obligations as citizens . . . the Churches were probably the only force which could have stopped Hitler . . . there are times when a movement of Christian opinion is all that stands between a country and moral disaster.'[12]

When I entered the famous Berlin Congress Hall on the morning I was to read my paper to a major seminar, two men fell in on either side of me, each taking a frozen elbow, and marched me to a corner.

They introduced themselves as Dutch Reformed delegates from South Africa. They had seen a précis of my paper and didn't like it. More than that, it was 'a pack of lies, distorted and unfair to South Africa'. I was therefore not to deliver it, and they would see that it was expunged from the Congress record. If I did deliver it, I would be in for the high jump, and they would tell 'four million Christians' in South Africa (the white ones of course!) that I was 'a traitor'. It was an ultimatum.

I was stunned, never before having faced such a threat. Stumbling away through the hall, I bumped into Rev. Robert Birch from Vancouver, father of Paul Birch, our AE director of music in the early years. I told him my dilemma. 'Would you like to pray about it?' he asked with concern. 'Oh yes, please, let's do so.'

He opened his prayer, 'No weapon that is formed against thee shall prosper; and every tongue that shall rise against thee in judgement thou shalt condemn. This is the heritage of the servants of the Lord, and their vindication is of me.'

Though he went on to pray, it was not necessary. The Lord had spoken to me. And my heart leapt, for it was Isaiah 54:17 (AV), one of several scriptures God had given me most profoundly at the inception of the African Enterprise idea, several years before. I would stand on the scripture and deliver my paper regardless.

Though Berlin dealt with a thousand other aspects of evangelism – from theology and preaching to relating the gospel to the cults or to communists *etc.* and *etc.*, nevertheless the seminar on nationalism and evangelism seemed to attract huge interest. The conference room was packed.

After a number of speakers, it was my turn. Thankfully I felt relaxed and at peace in spite of the explosion which I knew was to follow my paper.[13]

Absolute versus relative ethics

After discussing the origins and development of both white and black nationalisms in South Africa, I urged overseas people to avoid simplistic views of our problem, noting that if the emotions generated by nationalism within one ethnic group are complex, they are much more complex when two nationalistically motivated ethnic groups stand face to face within one country, as in South Africa. The agony of complexity and ambiguity must be appreciated by outside observers, and the temptation to reduce the problems to the over-simplified categories of literally black and white issues must be resisted. Over-simplification, I argued, has the appeal of neatness, but it lacks realism and objectivity, and often truth itself.

I went on to observe that what really creates the problem for Christian witness and evangelism is that powerful race feelings among both blacks and whites tend to foster what one might call the group ethic – an ethic developed by group-thinking along racial lines. The temptation on both sides of the racial fence is to subordinate Christian principle to political expediency.

This leads to what is perhaps the greatest problem which South African nationalisms raise for evangelism, namely the clash between the relative ethic of nationalism and the absolute ethic of Christianity. The call to Christian commitment is a call among other thihgs to an absolute ethic – an ethic which embraces means as well as ends. But some African national-isms, assuming a semi-religious dimension and defining their own ethical absolutes, begin to equate their own political progress with the divine will. Thus legitimacy is often defined in terms of the pragmatic. What the majority agree to be the most rapid and efficient way of achieving a desired end becomes *ipso facto* morally valid.

Ideals and ambiguities

In the face of this insidious and dangerous philosophy of *vox populi vox Dei* (*i.e.* 'the voice of the people is the voice of God') the church has a task to remind the body politic that the ideal is not simply self-government or majority rule, but good government and responsible rule. Power is to be used in the service of justice and truth, and no dichotomy should be permitted between what is legal in the technical sense and what is right in the ethical sense.

And, of course, if we start to say this, we find ourselves in collision with both the white philosophy of self-preservation without reference to blacks, and the black philosophy of self-realisation without reference to whites. True evangelism must confront *both* these philosophies, modifying both and being seduced by neither.

At the same time, the Christian seeks to understand what has produced these outlooks. He cannot condemn without entering into the agonising ambiguities on both sides of the fence. The Christian tries to understand what has produced each force. He recognises first that Africa's militant and sometimes excessive nationalisms have their roots in long bitternesses engendered by the indignities of the slave trade and some of the less happy aspects of white rule. The African's desire to fight back and assert his value and dignity is natural enough; but the church has to stand in firm condemnation of the nationalistic force when it serves causes beyond its original causes and when it reduces all life and value to a narrow equation with the so-called liberation struggle.

Condemnation and recognition

Equally difficult but equally necessary is a condemnation of that sort of nationalism that blinds its devotees to human sacrosanctity and value. This was seen in the Congo atrocities, I said, when the world waited, largely in vain, for any condemnation from African governments of the bestialities perpetrated by the rebels in the name of nationalism. 'My country right or wrong' is never a valid watchword, and when pressed into the service of any nationalistic group it must incur proper condemnation.

I then made a point which I always stress overseas when trying to help people understand South Africa: 'If the black philosophy of self-realisation is understandable, then equally so is the white philosophy of self-preservation. Of all instincts, that of self-preservation is the most powerful, and it is in fact just this force that lies at the heart of white, particularly Afrikaner, nationalism. Before condemning white nationalism, at least one must recognise the understandable emotion that inspires it. White fear of annihilation by an overwhelming black majority may be exaggerated at points, but extravagant statements by some leaders on the African continent have lent some substance to it.'

The Christian call

I wondered how my Afrikaner nationalist friends were taking all this. It was the moment as I ended my paper to make what seemed to me then, and still does, the most difficult of calls – a call that I as an English-speaking South African find as hard to work out as perhaps any Afrikaner would.

The call is to the white nationalist, whether English or Afrikaans, for charity in spite of dangers, unselfishness in spite of risks, faith in spite of fear. White nationalism has to be reminded that the Christian ethic is to 'lose one's life in order to save it', whereas it is the very reverse of this – save your life in order not to lose it – which stands at the ethical heart of most white South African thinking.

Here one sees a partial obstacle to the evangelisation of South Africa's whites. The fact is that the injunction to love, carrying with it, as it does, the injunction to unselfish promotion of black interests, appears to involve just that kind of political action which will lead to racial suicide for the whites. Evangelism's task is thus to help people, through Christian commitment, to work through the dilemma of whether they can in fact dare to love and leave the consequences with God, whether they can dare to lose their lives in order to save them. This is no easy task when politics seem to advise realism about human nature and a selfish protection of one's life, so as not to lose it.

The nature of Christian allegiance

My parting shot was that the challenge to faith has to be the starting-point for the solution. But to be meaningful it must also be accompanied by both the proclamation and the demonstration of the supranational nature of Christian allegiance. The body of Christ is not a pretty idea, but it is an authentic spiritual reality uniting all kinds and conditions of people. The Church in Southern Africa must therefore beware of National identifications. In crossing racial boundaries, it must also demonstrate within itself that sort of society which it desires to see in the body politic. Guarding not what is old but what is ageless must be our pressing concern. In this capacity we must speak bi-directionally to both white and black nationalisms, promoting what is good in both, refusing to tolerate what is evil in either. Patience, faith, love and the New Testament ethic must be preached as basic ingredients of all policies and the essential prerequisites of all national progress.

These were my thoughts then. Nothing I have seen or experienced in the twenty-two years since then has caused me to alter them.

RECONCILIATION AND FORGIVENESS

No sooner had I finished than the Rev. van Jaarsveld (not his real name) leapt to his feet and launched a diatribe of such vigour that it left the whole place thunderstruck. Fortunately I had no need to defend myself. One delegate after another got to their feet to do it for me.

Of course the anti-Cassidy stirring of these two Afrikaner brethren hurt my spirit, and I felt antagonistic. They were, I felt, doing just what I lamented, putting nationalism before Christ. But what about me? Was I innocent?

Next day Dr Dick Halverson of Washington DC was speaking in a plenary session about early church evangelism being the overflow of a reconciled fellowship. 'Reconciliation was the absolute prerequisite to fellowship and effective evangelism,' he said.

He went on: 'In the apostolic church, the relationship between believers and God and between fellow believers was paramount. The light and warmth and love, the forgiveness and acceptance that emanated from that unique community, penetrated a jaded, bored, loveless, weary culture and awakened the spiritual hunger of both Jew and pagan. "See how they love one another!" it was said of them.'

'But today', said the American preacher, 'one of the greatest stumbling-blocks to the world outside the church is the way Christians treat each other. It is not inconceivable that today's world might be inclined to say with some justification as it views the church, "See how they dislike one another!"'

The message was convicting me. Were not my hurt feelings, my antagonism to the two Afrikaner brethren and even my Englishness obstructing now my own capacity for faithfulness to the Lord in South Africa and my ability to love these brethren who were roughing me up?

Then Halverson gave the knock-out blow with two scriptures: 'By this shall all men know that ye are my disciples, if ye have love one to another' (John 13:35, AV) and 'Therefore if thou bring thy gift to the altar, and there rememberest that thy brother hath ought against thee; leave there thy gift before the altar, and go thy way; first be reconciled to thy brother, and then come and offer thy gift' (Matt 5:23–24, AV).

The Spirit spoke within: 'You need to go and apologise to those men. You have bitterness towards them.'

'But Lord . . .' I expostulated. 'Look what they've done to me all over this Congress. *They* should apologise to *me*.'

'No – if you know your brother has something against you, go first and be reconciled. *You* make the move!'

What a battle I had! Was I who had spoken on political nationalism as an obstacle to evangelism now going to let just such nationalism vanquish my own spirit? Yes, I was starting to allow this – and it scared me.

Suddenly I resolved the issue. I would seek their forgiveness.

At the tea break they were almost the first people I saw in the crowded refreshment lobby.

I went up to them. 'Brothers,' I said, holding out my hand, 'please forgive me for my hard feelings towards you since yesterday.'

Joubert (not his real name), stared straight through me, rejected my hand, and turned away. Nationalism, I thought, has won.

Van Jaarsveld looked me compassionately in the eyes and held out his hand. And I loved him. Nationalism, this time, had lost.

Years later, in 1970, I was privileged to work with him during an African Enterprise mission in Johannesburg. I found him a dear, sensitive man. But he had been much wounded by the past. 'You know,' he told me later with quivering lip and watering eyes, 'I can remember after the Boer War having to walk round Pretoria with a placard round my neck which read: "I am a Donkey. I cannot speak English."'

The wound had been with him for life. And what had inflicted it? The answer was devastating: English nationalism.

I started to see that my own history and my British forebears in South Africa were much to blame for where the Afrikaner had finally arrived.

In fact, not only did Britain and the English hound the Boers round South Africa in the nineteenth century, and then out of greed and imperialism decimate them in the Boer War, but they also connived in a racist constitution being given to South Africa in 1910. Beyond that, we English-speaking South Africans have continued in largely unadmitted guilt, with our absurd smugness, our rank hypocrisy (pointing at the Afrikaner and *saying* one thing while we *do* another), our aiding and abetting of the system, plus our current conservatism and racism. Furthermore, we have often refused to struggle with the same pain, integrity and cost as many Afrikaners who are trying in the 1980s to change. All this I have come to see, but this is to anticipate.

The Berlin 1966 Congress ended and I returned home to South Africa, thankfully rejoicing in the joy of my Lord, in the freedom of the Spirit, and in a relaxed patriotic love for my land. No, I was not a traitor; I was just a sinner saved by grace who was trying to prevent an all-inclusive patriotism becoming sectional nationalism.

Yet I also returned home soberly, for it was time to reflect with feeling on the Afrikaner nationalist's dilemma of how to retain his own national identity without betraying his Christian faith. His proposed resolution of this was of course what had produced apartheid.

On my return to South Africa, a leading Afrikaner intellectual and a prominent layman read my paper and phoned me. 'I am sorry about what happened to you at Berlin,' he said. 'It is a pity that we did not have a couple of men from the more moderate stream of Afrikaner church life representing us. I have read your paper, and I can't see what all the fuss was about!'

This conversation brought home to me that there were in fact members of a different, if not dissident, stream in Afrikanerdom who would have found Van Jaarsveld and Joubert as problematic as I did.

Even so, I knew I had to try and grasp with greater compassion what really lay at the heart of Afrikaner nationalism.

7   Understanding Afrikaner Nationalism

God created nations. They exist for Him. They are His own. And therefore all these nations, and in them human-ity, must exist for His glory and consequently after His ordinances, in order that in their well-being, when they walk after His ordinances, His divine wisdom may shine forth.

Abraham Kuyper

From one man he made every nation of men, that they should inhabit the whole earth; and he determined the times set for them and the exact places where they should live.

Acts 17:26

There is neither Jew nor Greek, slave nor free, male nor female, for you are all one in Christ Jesus.

Galatians 3:28

In 1965 I had met two Afrikaners who carried the past with them. One was Klopper in his Parliamentary Chambers. The other was Dominee van Jaarsveld at the Berlin Congress. Both were ardent apartheid exponents. They were fine men, yet, I felt, men wounded by history.

Their posture and responses evoked a basic question: What had produced these wounds, this mind-set and the philosophy of apartheid?

For those like myself who do not share the history of the Afrikaner, it is extremely difficult to penetrate, comprehend or do justice to the nuances and finer points of the Afrikaner saga at this point, or to capture them with fairness and accuracy.

For me, with my British history, colonial conditioning and then overseas influences in student days *etc.*, the struggle to break free from the imprisoning limitations of my *own* history has been very real.

Yet it has also been my desire, especially in the last decade, to try to get some 'feel' for this beleaguered people who have always been a minority struggling against the tremendous odds of both British and black antipathy.

In this most difficult of climates the Afrikaners have with courage tried to carve out for themselves a national identity, a secure place in the sun and an honourable life in the family of nations.

At the centre of this process has been the pulsating heart-beat of Afrikaner nationalism.

As I see it, there have been ten major steps, if one stays with the headlines of history, in the development of this nationalism.

An understanding of these ten steps is vital – for appreciating the Afrikaner dilemma; for understanding how South Africa got to this place; for deciding what Christians and the church should do about it.

We need to look in turn at each of these phases, and will consider five in this chapter and five in the next.

THE TRAUMA OF DEFEAT (1652–1910)

Perhaps Henning Klopper's Broederbond and its genesis is as good a place as any to seek some first clues to a deeper understanding of the rise of Afrikaner nationalism and the birth of apartheid.

We must remember how shattered Afrikaners were at the end of the Boer War. At the peace of Vereeniging in 1901, J D Kestell, a great field-preacher wrote: 'I saw lips tremble of men who had never flinched before the enemy. I saw tears welling up in eyes which had been dry when they had seen their loved ones laid away into the cold earth.'[1]

It should not surprise anyone that bitterness was a

spontaneous, deep and virtually irrepressible Afrikaner reaction after that war.

An Afrikaner prophet writes compassionately and truly:

> Among those who belong to a defeated and subjected people there can most obviously and most easily be the reaction of enduring and growing resistance. It becomes 'nation-consciousness'. In its most uncompromising form, it becomes militant nationalism, finding its sustenance in a burning resentment. It has no theories, only the belief that the group has suffered injury, that there must be redress: power must be wrested from the oppressive opponent. Only in this way can things be righted.[2]

This emotion had its roots in the whole unhappy struggle between Boer and Briton and Boer and black, going back to the earliest history of the country and working right up to the Boer War itself.

That Afrikaners, no less than any other vanquished group, should thus react, and often with bitterness, should mystify no one. While individuals can rise to sainthood, it's much harder for a nation to do so.

Be that as it may, it is clear that an understandable and deep national grief bound this people. And national grief always binds people more poignantly and powerfully than national triumph (just ask the Jews about the Holocaust or South African blacks about Soweto 1976). In effect the Boer War, and especially the loss of twenty-eight thousand women and children in the concentration camps, was to Afrikaners what the Holocaust is today to Jews. The war, the survivors of the camps, the angry defeated nation and its church all helped shape a national psyche and bred massive national resolution in the Afrikaner.

Not surprisingly, that bitter grief has pervaded the whole of subsequent Afrikaner history.

History's prisoners

An old Afrikaner, a right-wing voter to whom I spoke in the Northern Transvaal in Treurnicht[3] country, told me of the

Afrikaners' resolution to form a nation and then of their final imprisonment in their own history.

'History holds us,' he said as he poured a cup of steaming hot coffee as we sat together in his lounge.

'Let us start at the beginning.

'A group of people trekked out of the Cape Province, to the Free State, Natal and Transvaal. We are anchored to that history. We have a Day of the Covenant which is part of that history and which we celebrate because we see it as a day when the creator intervened in our affairs and rescued us as a nation. It was a victory for the Christian faith, and that made it possible for the whites to settle in this land. In the course of time, there was peace. Initially it seemed impossible. But then came the First Boer War in 1880, then the Second Boer War (1899–1901). The Afrikaners then lost their national freedom. It took three years, and a very powerful nation, to take it away from us. Then once again, after the war, the Afrikaner wanted his freedom as a nation. So he consolidated after the Boer War. Then came the struggle. Our children couldn't speak Afrikaans in schools. If they did, they had a card round their necks saying "You're a donkey, you spoke Dutch."'

'That blasted placard again,' I thought to myself as I sat in the old man's home and looked wistfully out across the vast expanse of empty Africa which was now his private and encapsulated world.

'You see, Mr Cassidy, notwithstanding this great attempt to destroy us, we remained a strong nation, free from all the nations on earth. Servants of the almighty. Free from the rest of the world. That freedom is very valuable to us. It is built into us. Every nation has its own place. And we want ours. *We* will not let it be endangered.'

Commenting on this history, Professor David Bosch has noted that the early Afrikaner settlers found themselves caught in a pincer movement between on the one hand an alien and unsympathetic administration bent on anglicising them, and on the other the advances of the vastly more numerous blacks.

Many Afrikaners tried to escape from the pincer by trekking

north, across the Orange River, to establish the three northern republics of Natal, the Orange Free State, and the Transvaal. Time and again, however, their efforts at political self-determination were thwarted, as the British annexed or conquered one newly acquired Afrikaner territory after the other. Natal (1842), Basutoland (1868), Griqualand West and the Kimberley diamond fields (1871), and the Transvaal (1877). In the First War of Independence (1880–1) the Transvaal was victorious. But twenty years later with the Orange Free State it succumbed during the Anglo-Boer War (1899–1902).[4]

Grief, pride, politics and religion

Reflecting on the Afrikaner national grief, David adds:

> For Britain the war was no more than a passing episode; for the Afrikaners, who lost eight times as many women and children in the concentration camps as soldiers on the battlefield, this was the most crucial event in their history, the matrix out of which a new people was born.
>
> Immediately after the war Lord Milner embarked on his vigorous policy of anglicisation and banned the use of the Dutch language from all schools. This was regarded as a total onslaught. Having lost their political freedom on the battlefield, Afrikaners were now to lose their identity through the schools. In the Afrikaner's darkest hour, it was above all the Afrikaans churches that rallied to the people's aid. Church and people became virtually indistinguishable.[5]

This astonishing ministry from the church to a shattered, demoralised people, struggling to keep their identity and find a place in the sun, was obviously a critical factor in bringing forth the almost invincible Afrikaner fusion of politics and religion. And if a man's politics and religion coalesce, whether consciously or otherwise, you have a virtually unbeatable combination.

The Afrikaner aim was not just to secure identity but to regain honour and national pride. And who can deny that to any man or nation? As Alan Paton said to me once, 'The Afrikaners were determined to undo all the evil that had been done to them by the British.'

Even so, the heterogeneous composition of South Africa kept the insistent question before the Afrikaner: To mix or not to mix? To many, with Hamlet, it was more a case of 'To be or not to be?'

A DIVISION OF ATTITUDE (1910–1918)

Not every Afrikaner answered the question with opposition to mixing English and Afrikaner. Thus Louis Botha, Smuts and the Reitzes of this world were for conciliation and forgiveness. But we should not wonder that there were great numbers within Afrikanerdom who could not with the huge personal losses they had sustained rise to the magnanimous and forgiving heights of Reitz, Botha or Smuts. These felt, on the contrary, that Afrikaners could advance only by doing their own thing and passionately embracing (both as a way of spiritual self-protection and as a means of political recovery) what they called their '*eie*' (*i.e.* their 'own' things).

W A de Klerk observes with insight: 'Between the militant nationalists, prepared for almost any means, including violence, in their struggle for power, and the patriots, reasonably rejecting political bondage because it is unworthy of the free intelligence which is the human being, a spectrum of related attitudes may emerge.'[6]

The spirit of Louis Botha

The most striking figure on the side of conciliation was Louis Botha.

His daughter, the late Mrs Helen de Waal, reminisced about him in 1972, saying: 'I never heard his voice raised in anger against any of us, not against anyone. He would always say "Remember that other people's feelings are deeper than you know."' He was, she said, passionately for 'a united South Africa'.[7]

Speaking at the graveside of Louis Botha on 27 August 1919, Smuts captured the spirit of his leader in moving terms:

His great work was the Union of South Africa; his untiring efforts through all difficulties were directed to the unity of the people of South Africa, to the promotion of a strong feeling of national brotherhood among all sections of our community, to the healing of old wounds and the laying to rest of old enmities.[8]

In any event, the South Africa Party, formed in 1904, continued its labours of reconciliation after Union (1910) with Botha and Smuts at the helm. Also including some Britishers, it did not focus exclusively on rebuilding and rehabilitating the Afrikaner: this to many Afrikaners was its fatal flaw.

Our 'own' things

That being so, it was understandable that another spirit would eventually predominate among Afrikaners. Thus the more nationalistic Afrikaners, under J B M Hertzog, had formed the National Party in 1914 (coincidentally only two years after African leaders, with some of the same emotions, had formed the African National Congress!).

Hertzog's line was that if conciliation meant the 'eie' or 'own' things were to suffer, then conciliation was out. South Africa should be ruled only by Afrikaners, he said.

These emotions inevitably produced the Boer Rebellion of 1914. And who could blame those far-off freedom fighters who fourteen years after final defeat in a dreadful conflict refused to go and fight on the side of their victor against some distant and foreign foe? Nor should we marvel that their sympathies were with the Germans in both the First World War and the Second, for is not my enemy's enemy my friend?

On the night of 17 April 1918, a Nationalist Party meeting addressed by the Party's Cape leader, Dr D F Malan, was broken up by a vandalising opposition mob. Malan, originally a Dutch Reformed pastor, was fired by the church's duty to help rebuild the shattered morale of his people. But by 1918 he had left the Christian ministry to enter politics full time.

The breaking up of his meeting, with members of the audience being assaulted, had a profound effect on him as well as on three other young Afrikaners, H W van der Merwe,

D H C Du Plessis and Henning Klopper (later to be Speaker of the House of Assembly).

THE EMERGENCE OF THE BROEDERBOND THINK-TANK (1918–1921)

Still in their late teens, these three young men met the next day on a hillock in Johannesburg. With Henning Klopper as founder and moving spirit, the three pledged themselves to form an organisation, 'the Broederbond' or 'Band of Brothers', to stand by the Afrikaner and help him be restored to his rightful place in his fatherland. They received helpful advice from another Dutch Reformed pastor, Rev. J F Naudé, father of the famous Beyers Naudé.

Said Klopper at the inaugural meeting on 5 June 1918: 'Our aim is a Brotherhood of Afrikaners.' On 2 July 1918 the following aims were formulated: 'A melting together of Afrikaners . . . to serve the interest of Afrikaners at all times . . . to bring Afrikaners to consciousness, to create self-respect and love for our own language, history, country and volk.'[9]

They had – unwittingly perhaps, but certainly in fact – brought to birth one of the most powerful think-tanks our world has ever seen.

The meaning of 'brotherhood'

Though initially non-secretive, semi-religious and cultural, the society in due time (1921) became secret, more political and more unashamedly committed to Afrikaner domination and the promotion of all things Afrikaans.

Smuts of course, Afrikaner though he was, was dead against this, and said many years later in a 1945 parliamentary debate: 'When we have an organisation that wants to promote the interests of one section or of one race by an attitude of secrecy and keeping everything shrouded in darkness, you have to be careful.'[10] He found this 'dangerous' and 'in conflict with the interests of the country, and that is un-Afrikaans'. He could not approve of 'exclusive race politics and the promotion of race interests'.[11]

One Afrikaner friend told me that his parents were among many rank-and-file Afrikaners who resented the Broederbond for its exclusivism and deplored its elitism.

But that wasn't how Klopper and his friends saw it. The Broederbond was a thing of beauty, a noble thing. It earnestly sought to uplift the Afrikaner and was based on that most beautiful of bonds called 'brotherhood'.

What this meant to those in the Broederbond was well described many years later at its fiftieth anniversary in 1968 (by which time it had eight thousand members), when its then chairman, Dr Piet Meyer (also at that time chairman of South Africa's National Broadcasting Corporation), reflected on the Broederbond's early and later inner dynamics and commitments: 'Brotherhood is selective, confidential leadership continuously extended as the inner-mechanism, the heartbeat of the Afrikaner-volk. Brotherhood means fully considering and digesting the problems facing our volk from time to time, and studying the facts to ensure clarity and effective solutions.'

Dr Meyer said the Broederbond was formed as a different kind of answer to long-standing problems facing the Afrikaner – subservience to the English and Britain, a feeling of national inferiority, impotence, bondage, exploitation and poverty. The Broederbond's response was: 'Your honour is in your name, your Afrikaner name; your Afrikaner ancestors, their faith, ideals and sacrifices, their language and history. Your honour is in your faith, your ideals, your mother-tongue and your fatherland's history. Betray that and there is nothing left.'[12]

Dr Meyer then went on to celebrate the special and divine mission of the Broederbond:

Broederbond membership, broerskap, is that and much more. This 'more' is not something from us and by us. It comes from outside us and above us. It is something which God established Himself: otherwise it remains inexplicable and inconceivable. It is something which we as Broeders have in common with all

Christians on earth. Broerskap – the Afrikaner Broederbond – is a gift from God to our volk to strive and realise its separate destiny to the greater glory of His name.[13]

Through this 'Brotherhood' there was, as many Afrikaner leaders now saw it, a vehicle to redeem and re-establish the Afrikaner's place in South Africa.

Not surprisingly, as the Broederbond think-tank developed its religio-political mysticism within the bonds of brotherhood, questions about the future shape of the nation and the destiny of the Afrikaner volk leapt up like challenging sentries to ask who was going where and how and why. The need for study and reflection of every sort pressed itself upon the membership, some of whom saw the intellectual need primarily in theological terms, others in more political terms.

While endless reflection went on at home, other groups went overseas to study, some going to Holland and others to Germany. These two countries became the sources from which two massively important streams of destiny would flow back into the far away Fatherland and mix with local and indigenous theological thinking.

TWO STREAMS – ONE THEOLOGICAL, ONE POLITICAL – FORM IN HOLLAND AND GERMANY (1920s and 1930s)

To try and get some grasp on this story, I once asked a leading Afrikaner this question: 'Politically and theologically, how did we get to the place where we now are in South Africa?'

He responded at once, saying: 'One must start with the *theological* side, because what has happened in our country is due more to a theological development than a political one.'

The theological stream

Kuyper

The young Afrikaner theologians who went to Holland to study, chief among them S J du Toit (considered by some

to be the major father of Afrikaner nationalism), now
came under the influence of a key Calvinist thinker, the great
Dutch theologian, Abraham Kuyper, the founder of the Free
University of Amsterdam.

Kuyper insisted that all spheres of life owe their existence
to God's decree in creation and to the common grace he
showers on all his created order. Thus decreed into the fabric
of life, *each sphere has lordship, rule, and sovereignty over
itself under God.* It can run its own show, as it were, without
reference to the other spheres. This would apply, for
example, to areas such as family life, economics, education,
art and so on. It would also apply to church and state, so that
one could validly insist that the church stick to spiritual things
while the government gets on with governing and politics.
The result is that *neither is answerable to the other, but to God
alone.*

Not only did this principle apply to church and state, but
also to nations! '*For God created nations.* They exist for Him.
They are His own. And therefore all these nations, and in
them humanity, must exist for His glory and consequently
after His ordinances, in order that in their well-being, when
they walk after His ordinances, His divine wisdom may shine
forth.'[14]

It is not hard to see how this stress on 'nations' as decreed
by God is but a step away from the elevation of nationhood
into an inviolable unit.

Kuyper's thought applied to South Africa

Back in South Africa, as David Bosch has noted, 'Kuyper's
ideals were adapted to local circumstances. As they blended
with the existing socio-political realities, they underwent
some significant changes.' The slogan 'isolation for survival'
emerged. Adds Bosch: 'For the first time in South African
history sustained theological (or ideological) arguments
suggested that Afrikaners should neither fraternize with
foreigners nor break down the walls of racial separation
instituted by God; like Israel, the Afrikaner's salvation lay in
racial purity and separate schools and churches.'[15]

In fact one Kuyperian pastor, as far back as 1907, proposed

a thorough-going political and social segregation. The Rev. W J Postma's suggestion was to 'give the black nations a piece of ground where they can establish their own schools, churches, prisons, parliaments and universities. If we go there we must not ask to own ground or vote. And if they come here to work they must not play tennis!'[16] Note that this was in 1907, not 1948!

Biblical support for separatism

In a genuine search for a political and theological way forward, three classic texts were used to support the separatist line.

The first was Genesis 11 – the Tower of Babel story. The understanding of the story was that man sinfully attempted (against God's plan) to preserve the unity of the human race and its homogeneous nature. But God in judgement upset this proud plan, scattered the human race, confused the languages, and ordained the division and wide distribution of races and nations.

The second text was Deuteronomy 32:8: 'When the Most High gave the nations their inheritance, when he divided the sons of men, he fixed their bounds according to the number of the sons of God' (JB).

The third was Acts 17:26: 'From one single stock he not only created the whole human race so that they could occupy the entire earth, but he decreed how long each nation should flourish and what the boundaries of its territory should be' (JB).

Again, the idea is that God has given various nations their separate existences. This implies that they should remain separate. If there is no racial separation, racial mixture will follow and God's will and plan will be denied. What is more, politically all will be lost. Israel was held to be the classic precedent for this principle. *National pluralism, based on 'pluriformity not uniformity' in creation, is the divine will.*

Covenant holiness

There was another key theological principle. Prof Adrio König of the University of South Africa explained it to me once when I sought his insights about the theological genealogy of apartheid.

'Well, Michael, there's one thing you mustn't miss,' he said, 'and that is the Afrikaner's understanding of the covenant and holiness. You see, Afrikaners interpreted Old Testament holiness, seen as covenant separation from the heathen, in terms of their own separation from the black heathen. The New Covenant was thus reinterpreted in terms of the Old. In other words, the Afrikaners attached religious significance to their separateness, at least initially, with whites being Christian and blacks being heathen. If the Old Testament people of God had to be separated from the heathen, then so did Afrikaners. God required it.'

Seeing pennies starting to drop, Adrio went on: 'I mean, if you look at the modern Mixed Marriages Act or the Immorality Act [forbidding marriage or sexual relationships across the colour line], you can see from this perspective how they happened, can't you?'

As Adrio further explained the idea of the maintenance of separate identity as an Afrikaner's holy obligation to his or her nation, I could quickly see how if they were to lay all this down – as the Afrikaners are now being asked to do – it would involve a denial of something hitherto totally integral to their religious pilgrimage. One can see how this has produced a trauma of gargantuan proportions.

In passing, it is perhaps instructive to reflect that if apartheid was in the first instance a theological construction, then its dismantling must in the first instance also be theological. In other words, the Afrikaner churches are vital to the process. Political figures or parties or overseas investors banging their heads against the granite of apartheid won't by themselves affect it. Perhaps right here lies a crucial historical clue for all solution-seekers: they mustn't miss the churches and theology.

The political stream

While the young theologians were in Amsterdam in the 1930s, something else was happening among several young Afrikaner political scientists.

Seven in number, they were labelled by Smuts 'the coffee party' because of their endless reflections over coffee on the future of South Africa! All of them later became eminent South African politicians and scholars.[17]

In the 1930s they were all at German universities, being inspired by the ideals of German nationalism.

Derek Morphew identifies six key ideas in the philosophical background to their political thought:

1. God is to be identified very closely with nature. (Jacob Boehme 1575–1624)
2. Not only is God identified with the world and with nature, which make up the 'whole', but this being so, *individuals* are only part of the whole and are therefore less important than the whole and unable to affect it (*i.e.* they are not fully 'free'). (Baruch Spinoza 1632–1677)
3. If the whole is more important than the parts, then the state is more important than its parts (*i.e.* than the individuals comprising it). (Frederick Schelling 1775–1854)
4. The individual who would be absorbed into the divine whole must now make it his goal to be absorbed into the state, which is the whole. This is both his religious and his political duty. (Johann Fichte 1762–1814)
5. If a nation would triumph in its upward struggle to civilisation, it must remain pure and unique, or it loses its fight. Morality is therefore defined in terms of what is good for the upward movement of this pure and civilised state. (Johann Herder 1744–1803)
6. A nation stays pure in this struggle by maintaining its own language and culture (Herder). In this, controlled education is a key (Fichte)[18]

One can well imagine the excitement and enthusiasm with which this thought of national progress via a divinely mandated preservation and propagation of national purity was received and imbibed by those young Afrikaner political scientists.

The developing orchestra of apartheid was now beginning to be heard via the soundings of these far-off notes from foreign instruments. For the 'coffee party', the music was already playing and the chords were coming together; these young men from a nation and culture under threat were beginning to discover the much-needed blueprint for survival!

THE MEETING OF THE TWO STREAMS AND THE BIRTH OF APARTHEID (1940s)

Many other influences were of course being processed by the Broederbond think-tank, but the convergence in South Africa of these two overseas streams was like the bringing together of fire and methane: there was spontaneous combustion.

Here at last there was what seemed to be a morally valid, theologically justified and politically legitimate way not only to secure survival for the Afrikaner volk, but to triumph and as a nation mount on eagles' wings at the Southern end of Africa.

A policy emerges

As part of the coming together of the two streams a remarkable book by Dr G Cronjé, one of the Amsterdam theologians fired up by Kuyper, now came forth and was of key significance. Published in 1945 and called *'n Tuiste vir die Nageslag* (*A Home for Posterity*), it was intensely and enthusiastically discussed in the Broederbond.

It set forth a full-blown apologetic for what would become apartheid. 'The racial policy which we as Afrikaners should promote', said Cronjé at the beginning of his book, 'must be directed to the preservation of racial and cultural variety. This is because it is according to the Will of God, and also because with the knowledge at our disposal it can be justified on practical grounds.'

'Indeed', he added,

the Boer people have themselves gone through the crucible of imperialist and capitalist domination and exploitation. They still show the wounds and bruises of it all. Their national life and culture have been disrupted. As a nation they almost perished because they served the interests of other people. They know what it means to see the *eie* [one's own] destroyed, but they also know what it means to promote through their own efforts a national revival and restoration.[19]

The book then works out the extensive details of his suggested grand scheme of 'Apartheid' or 'Separate Development'. Now these famous words appear clearly.[20] And to implement apartheid was the Afrikaner's Christian duty, and one to be done 'whatever the cost'.[21] What its cost would be was perhaps fortuitously hidden from the enthusiastic author.

Nor did the radical nature of this 'total and final solution'[22] daunt Cronjé. In fact, he said,

> we can be of one mind that the more radically racial segregation is applied, the better it will be. Indeed the more consistently the policy of apartheid could be applied, the greater would be the security for the purity of our blood and the surer our unadulterated European racial survival. Total racial separation . . . is the most consistent application of the Afrikaner idea of racial apartheid.[23]

Cronjé felt this would take about twenty-five years to work out – in other words only about one generation would have to suffer a bit, but then an assured future for the white race would have been won, along with justice for all, and we would all live happily ever after.

Dissident voices

By no means all Afrikaner theologians and thinkers saw it this way. A number of dissident voices had sounded across the theological landscape long before the political and social climate encouraged dissidence of any sort.

One such was Professor J du Plessis of Stellenbosch Theological Seminary, who was actually submitted to a heresy trial in 1929 because of his questioning of the South African version of the Kuyperian system of theology. This questioning was in effect seen as treasonable to the Afrikaner cause and made it difficult for others to come out in opposition.

Yet there were others who did so, coming, surprisingly enough, from the church's pietistic and missionary stream, whose lineage went back to Scottish evangelicalism and the ministries of men like Andrew Murray. In fact, as early as 1860 the Rev. D P M Huet, who described himself as a 'zealous adherent of the missionary cause and a defender of those who were hated because of their missionary work', denounced blatant discrimination against blacks in church and society.[24]

Particularly noteworthy during the 1940s and 1950s, when most Afrikaner theologians and intellectuals supported the apartheid ideology, was the witness and stand taken by Professors B B Keet and Ben Marais. These men conceded that there could be some practical grounds for racial segregation, but they rejected any theological basis for it. As early as 1939 Keet sounded a warning about the growing enmity between whites and blacks based on black resentment caused by the way white Dutch Reformed churches were agitating for racial segregation. Keet, who used the Dutch Reformed Church's magazine *Die Kerkbode* as a platform for his criticisms, went on to publish in 1955 a watershed volume called *Waarheen Suid Afrika?* (*Whither South Africa?*). Keet's hand was strengthened by Professor Ben Marais during the 1940s as both men ceaselessly challenged the Dutch Reformed churches' attempts to justify apartheid in the light of scripture.

Into the tradition of these two great opponents of the theological justification of apartheid came other stalwarts, most notably the famous Beyers Naudé who with a number of others from the missionary wing of the church challenged the idea that there could be social implications of the gospel as far as poor Afrikaners were concerned but not as far as blacks were concerned! They denounced this schizophrenic notion, insisting that the social and political implications of the gospel must in fact transcend the narrow confines of nationalistic self-interest and embrace *all* people made in the image of God.

The two streams become one flow

When all was said and done, however, these were by and large voices crying in the wilderness. In the 1940s they were very definitely running against the stream of things. The dominant mood of the day was being carried by one particularly powerful figure, Dr Daniel F Malan.

Malan's view, first articulated decades previously, remained simple and unambiguous:

> Our church has received from God a special calling in respect of the Afrikaner people with which it is so intimately related. It should therefore also be regarded as [the church's] duty to be national itself, to watch over our peculiar national interests and to teach our people to detect the hand of God in its history and genesis; it should also keep alive in the Afrikaner people the awareness of its national calling and destiny.[25]

In 1943 Dr D F Malan became the one major Afrikaner leader in whom these great streams of theological and political thought converged. In him they were channelled ever more fully into a single flow. And from this flow emerged the word 'apartheid' as integral to the political vocabulary of this powerful leader.

He was leading the *Herenigte Nasionale Party* (Reunited National Party). His view became enshrined in the policy conclusions of a great *Volkskongress* (People's Congress) which met in Bloemfontein in 1944. The Congress decided that in the interests of the white and non-white populations of South Africa a policy of apartheid should be followed, 'so that each of the non-white population groups will find the opportunity to develop according to its own characteristics [*aard*], in its own area, so as to acquire eventually full control over their own affairs'. It also said that 'it is the Christian duty of the whites to act as guardians over the non-white races until such time as they have reached that level where they can look after their own affairs'.[26]

In 1945 apartheid became the official policy of Malan's party. With the policy now in place, the time had arrived for a giant-killing battle with Smuts and the English in the United Party. A general election was only three years away: there was no time to lose.

8   The Dilemmas of Winning with Apartheid

I have earnestly asked myself whether the advocates of total unity of the different races can bring justice and fairness to everybody. I am absolutely convinced that integration in a country like South Africa cannot possibly succeed . . . I am seeking justice for all the groups and not justice for only one group at the cost of the other three . . .

If meddlesome people keep their hands off us, we shall in a just way, such as behoves a Christian nation, work out solutions in the finest detail and carry them out. We shall provide all our races with happiness and prosperity.

Hendrik Verwoerd

Unless the Lord builds the house,
its builders labour in vain.

Psalm 127:1

The last chapter charted the first five steps in the development of South African nationalism, outlining the convergence of the theological and political streams of Afrikaner nationalism in the Broederbond and noting the ascendancy of Malan's Reunited National Party, with its belief in apartheid.

A theologically legitimated notion of apartheid was now enshrined in the policy document of the People's Congress. But could it usher South Africa into a new day of happiness, peace and national prosperity for all groups, as its supporters claimed? We turn now to the remaining five steps that lead to the present.

A POLITICAL VICTORY IS WON (1947–1949)

Malan saw his task as twofold: first to build up and establish
the Afrikaner, and second to shake him free (in political
terms) of the English-speaking sector, but in the nicest way
possible.

Wanting to understand more of the English side of 1948, I
spoke to Harry Oppenheimer, a former director of Anglo-
American, and one of South Africa's great gentlemen. He
had been very much part of Smut's United Party (UP) in the
1940s.

Smuts

I first asked him if he knew Smuts.

'Well, yes,' replied South Africa's leading businessman. 'I
knew him insofar as it was possible for someone quite young
to know him. My father was a tremendous admirer of his, and
I was brought up to look on him as a sort of hero. He came to
Oxford for my twenty-first birthday party and made a speech
there.'

'And what of Smuts' political posture?' I asked.

'He was fairly conservative, you know,' said Oppenheimer.
'In many ways to the right of the present Government. But he
and we in the UP differed in one extremely important respect,
in that Smuts' so-called Native Policy was based on the Fagan
Commission's Report of 1946. This had said that blacks were
in the white cities to stay and there was no question of them
going back to the tribal lands. This meant the large and
permanently urban black population would have to be
accommodated socially and politically.'

'So what would he have done had he won in 1948?'

'His line,' replied Oppenheimer, 'was to let things evolve
and deal with problems and issues as they came up. He never
had a clear franchise policy for blacks. However, by 1948 he
had seen clearly that the first stage involved admitting that the
problem could not be solved simply on a tribal basis but *only
on a South African basis*. This meant recognising black people
as an integral part of the modern industrial South Africa. That

to our mind then involved moving inevitably towards the situation which the Government is reluctantly having to face up to now, forty years later.'

Malan

'And Dr Malan? What do you recollect of him?'

'Oh, he was a nice chap. Rather a solemn fellow, but with very good manners.'

The former Chairman of the Anglo-American giant then began to chuckle, as our conversation triggered a recollection.

'But he did make a few funny remarks in my presence. I remember going somewhere in the Western Province to talk at a place called Rondegat, meaning of course, "Round Hole" in Afrikaans. Malan was there too, and he said of me that he had never seen a better example of a square peg in a round hole! Then he came to the Free State to open or shut something on one of our mines. He was very nice, and in his speech said, "The Honourable member for Kimberley and I sit opposite one another in the House of Assembly and therefore there is no possibility of our stabbing one another in the back!"'

Becoming serious again, Oppenheimer added, regarding Malan's status as a Dutch Reformed minister, 'I must add, however, that as I heard him in those days, I thought, perhaps unfairly, that his position as a man of religion was rather subordinated to his political views. The fact is that he, and more especially the highly logical Verwoerd, saw rightly that you could not carry out the sort of policy they had in mind and try to meet the political aspirations of black people only in tribal areas. Unless you stopped the flow to the towns, and gradually reversed it, apartheid would not work. Unless one could reverse it there would be no stopping integration politically as well as economically. I think Malan and Verwoerd saw that very well. But the lesson they drew from it was not that you had to find a solution to integration, but that you must get rid of the blacks in the cities. You must unscramble the omelette.'

'And where did Malan's strength lie?'

'It lay, I think,' Oppenheimer went on, 'in his party's ability to forge a political party to represent the way of thought and ethos of Afrikaans-speaking South Africans in a particular way. And so long as you worked to keep the vote to white people only, and so long as two-thirds of white South Africans were Afrikaans-speaking, you had a recipe for staying in power for ever.'[1]

Mamelodi township

Leaving the rarefied atmosphere of 44 Main Street in Johannesburg, I drove over to the dusty hustle and bustle of the black township of Mamelodi near Pretoria to put a similar set of questions to Professor Nico Smith, the Dutch Reformed pastor there, and former Professor of Missions at Stellenbosch University.

At 44 Main Street one might have thought the answer to South Africa lay in the right use of financial muscle. In Mamelodi, where one could hardly manoeuvre one's car for people, one realised it would be settled by numbers. The town's unofficial population, probably twice the official figure, is estimated at 320,000, with sixty-five per cent of them under twenty!

'Malan saw this,' said Nico Smith. 'So did people like my father. Seeing all the black people coming into the cities, with no separation, I can remember my father telling us of the danger that the blacks were just overwhelming us. One gains certain impressions as a child, and so I also began wondering what would happen. But for my father all those things added to the concept that the only solution was separation. My father always said this was the reality of South Africa. We have different people and cultures. They are irreconcilable. The only solution is to separate and let each group have their own place. At that stage we still thought it would be possible to divide the whole country. But fear was a big thing.'

As Nico Smith spoke, it brought to mind Alan Paton's observation to me that Malan pushed the survival issue and exploited white fear of overwhelming black numerical superiority so as to breathe intense and gutsy new life into the National Party's appeal to the white rank and file.

'What of Smuts, Nico?' I asked this modern Afrikaner prophet who has broken with the system so courageously. 'How did he see this thing of black numbers?'

'As I understand it, Smuts was a very pragmatic man. His whole concept of "let things develop" also included that one must handle every situation as it comes. So I believe he was thinking that at the correct time, if it was necessary to give the vote to the blacks, it would have to be accepted. I remember that back in 1950 he stood up in Parliament in a very serious mood and warned the Nationalist Party (it was very clear at that time that they would do what they had promised in terms of separating the people), that if they continued in this way they would ruin this country. He said South Africa would become a world problem. I can remember how as students we laughed about that. And of course it happened like that exactly. I always think Smuts died from total despair. He just couldn't take it that the Nationalists were really doing what they had started to do in 1948.'

Nico went on: 'You see, Smuts' whole line on letting things develop and not manipulating society with social engineering to fit a political blueprint was based on his conviction that if one did that the whole society would be polarised and everyone would be turned against everyone.

'But people like my father', said Nico, 'much opposed that. Afterwards I discovered how much he had been influenced in his own thinking, although an intellectual man, by the DRC [Dutch Reformed Church]. You see, the moment you have a theological justification for believing in the absolute necessity of different cultures being kept separate, and for peoples keeping their own identity, then you cannot end up with anything other than apartheid. Smuts, however, resisted this whole theology.

'And make no mistake, it was a theology. Malan used theology to preach liberation, and it was not much different from the liberation theology used today by blacks!'[2]

Smuts the international Afrikaner

In reflecting on this period of South African history, it often occurs to me that Smuts (great man though he was) and the English-speaking South Africans were, in the words of Martin Luther King, 'sleeping through a revolution'. Like many whites today who are insufficiently aware of the black revolution which will sweep them into chaos unless they wake up before the summer is ended, Smuts and his United Party had their minds too much on other things and were inadequately attentive to the mighty Afrikaner revolutionary happening going on around them.

Primarily, Smuts' mind was on the wider world and the Charter of the League of Nations, which he had helped to draft, not on the Afrikaner farmlands and the frightened poor white workers who felt themselves to be under economic threat from a potential black African deluge. He was *par excellence* an internationalist and a friend to other giants on the world stage, Churchill, Woodrow Wilson, Roosevelt and others.

As an international Afrikaner, Smuts was virtually a contradiction in terms. But, as W A de Klerk comments, his perspective was seriously flawed:

> For Smuts, in the light of the tremendous things which had taken place on the world-stage, the bickerings and theorizings at home must have seemed much like . . . twittering birds: unreal little bodies chirping away into balmy nothingness. Had his ear been closer to the ground, perhaps, instead of tuned to the cosmic music from greater, more splendid fields, he might well have discerned deeper notes at home which would have given him cause for alarm . . . The twittering of the birds in fact foreshadowed the dawn. It was, however, a threatening dawn, rising broodingly, silently, in a murky sky – the upcoming Afrikaner Revolution.[3]

Smuts had his eye not just on the world generally but on England specifically. Hence his invitation in 1947, just a year before South Africa's next general election, to the British Royal Family to tour South Africa.

I remember it very well. I was eleven years old, and went home from boarding school in Johannesburg for an unforgettable week in Basutoland.

Of course Smuts was not with the Royals in Basutoland, but everywhere else he was their incomparable and confident guide. Politically there was nothing to worry about. And surely the response of warm-hearted South Africans, Afrikaners included, must have blinded him further to the real, underground political realities.

Peter Townsend, the King's equerry on that Royal Tour, describes the Royal reception in buoyant terms in his moving autobiography *Time and Chance*. Like Smuts, neither he nor the King were remotely aware of what lay beneath the happy welcomes. They, however, had better excuses for ignorance.

'It was an exhausting, but fabulous journey,' recalled Townsend.

From my own point of view, while I was lucky to average four or five hours sleep a night, I had the good fortune to get to know and to love that beautiful, romantic, colourful – in one word, beloved – country.

Everywhere, even in the toughest Nationalist republican strongholds, South Africans gave their King and Queen a warm and heartfelt welcome. It obviously sprang, not from any political feeling, but straight from the hearts of that multi-racial, multi-national people.

There was another reason. The simplicity and sincerity of the King and Queen appealed to the South African people. They immediately became a great hit.[4]

He went on:

As they trekked across South Africa, the Royal Family were welcomed by all races. People shouted from the crowd 'Stay with us!' or 'Leave the Princesses behind!' Black and white, they had trekked in from farms, miles away, by car, on horseback, or by foot, to places where the train halted.

The horsemen – boys and girls too – often galloped alongside the train. A gnarled old giant, mounted on a clean-legged Basuto pony, caught up with the train. Breathless, he told me, 'I'm a Dutchman and a nationalist, but the King's visit is doing us a lot of good,' and added, 'Yes, I'm a Boer. I fought the British in the Boer War and joined the rebellion in 1914. Now I've seen the King, I'm through with being a republican.' Then he whipped off the handsome belt from around his waist and handed it to me. 'I've had it thirty years,' he said, 'Here, give it to the King.'[5]

However, if many blacks were still loyalist and Royalist, fewer and fewer Afrikaners were. Thus did I wonder as a little boy, when going occasionally from Maseru to the cinema in Ladybrand, just over the border in the Free State, why it was that fewer and fewer people stood when 'God save the King' was played at the end of the show. No one explained. Maybe no one understood.

Smuts and the race issue

Townsend, as a relaxed traveller with Smuts, was well placed to pick up the old man's thinking on the racial issue at that historic moment just before the 1948 election.

Seemingly Smuts was not without his own fears of the 'Swart Gevaar', or black danger. Perhaps they were also at the back of Smuts' mind when he and Townsend had a long moonlight conversation in the shadow of the mighty Drakensberg. In Townsend's evocative words: 'It was when we came to the Natal National Park Hotel, high in the forbidding Drakensberg range, that, one night before dinner, I had a long talk with Smuts – alone, under the stars, while lightning cleft the darkness, momentarily revealing the massive peaks towering up behind us.'

After giving Townsend a thumbnail sketch of South African history, Smuts came to the present moment of 1947 in South Africa.

The 'native problem' . . . was of course South Africa's greatest problem, but he did not see in it all those many difficulties and dangers. It was, after all, the world's problem: there were more blacks than whites in the world and if only the whites – in South Africa and the world at large – would stop their futile fighting between themselves, they would come to an understanding with the blacks. That would not happen in his lifetime, but Smuts did not think in terms of the present moment or place: he was hundreds of years ahead, thousands of miles away.[6]

But Smuts' summer, unbeknown to him, had passed. A wintry earthquake of immense proportions was about to engulf him. He enjoyed the blissfulness of being unaware. The parallels with South Africa in the 1980s are obvious, to say the least. Says Townsend in even more blissful ignorance: 'And so the King of South Africa journeyed on among his people, Boer, Bantu and British.'[7]

Edgar Brookes, later the Chairman of African Enterprise, notes in his biographical reflections his disappointment that Smuts, whom he admired as a man 'brave and merciful and big in mind and heart', was 'weakest in the area where men such as I needed him most . . .'[8]

Brookes feels Smuts hesitated on colour questions mainly

because of his political position. He had lost a large proportion of the Afrikaner intelligentsia who had gone into the Nationalist ranks. He was determined not to become merely the Afrikaner leader of an all-British Party. His solid core of Afrikaans-speaking supporters, apart from a few intellectual leaders of outstanding merit, consisted of men who had been on commando with him or with General Botha during the Boer War, and were thus not the type of men to respond to liberal doctrines of race or colour. Whether General Smuts really believed in liberal policies or not I could never make out.

He adds:

Smuts once committed himself to the view that 'segregation has fallen on evil days'. But beyond this he did not go . . . No doubt he was right in feeling that the bulk of the white electorate was deeply conservative on the colour question, but he did not win it over by his refusal to support liberal ideas. He lost the sons of his own old burghers, and he also lost the black leaders and some of the best younger white men who expressed liberal views. With all these faults he remains the biggest figure in South African parliamentary history.[9]

A victory for apartheid

Smuts lost the 1948 election when it came. Malan and apartheid had carried the day of destiny.

Smuts had turned a blind eye and a deaf ear on both Afrikaners and blacks. Not so Malan; no two groups were more within his purview. Meanwhile, from the sidelines, the black majority of South Africa watched in anguish.

Smuts in fact lost his own parliamentary seat to a political unknown called Wentzel du Plessis. For Du Plessis, the world opened up on the wings of apartheid: 'For me,' he said, in a British television interview some years later, '"apartheid" is not the dirty word people claim, and which they throw about like bits of slush and mud. Apartheid is a fact of nature, there are not two people in the world who are the same.' He then spoke reflectively of the 1948 victory: 'The horizons were lifting, the skies were clearing. There was promise in the air. And we were going to avail ourselves of that opportunity. Which we did.'[10]

Indeed they did.

Thus it was that in 1948, as segregationist law and practice (which had for centuries been an accepted pattern of much imperial and West European social behaviour) receded across the world, South Africa's new Government stepped openly and proudly on to the stage to enforce and reinforce the past.

FURTHER THEOLOGICAL UNDERGIRDING OF APARTHEID (1950–1960)

Apartheid was now the official policy of the country. With the blacks politically enraged and the first distant sounds of world uproar in the air, the task was twofold – to begin to press apartheid into practice and to justify it still further theologically.

A huge amount of literature undergirding the apartheid system was published. Theology was at its heart, but it embraced philosophy, anthropology, sociology and political science. It flooded into quarterlies, journals, newspapers and books. Comments W A de Klerk: 'The collected material would constitute a fair-sized municipal library . . . What had started with Diederichs [one of the members of the 'coffee party'] had been a trickle. Now it became a flood.' It is an impossible task, says De Klerk, to absorb it all. And neither, he says mercifully, 'is it necessary'.[11]

In fact all we need register at this point is that from 1950 to 1960 the various Dutch Reformed churches poured themselves into the task of justifying apartheid and seeking to reconcile it with scripture. Backing their efforts were the Broederbond think-tank and other more modest off-shoots such as the South African Bureau for Racial Affairs (SABRA), which was founded expeditiously in 1950, just two years after Malan's victory.

Binding the nation

SABRA's line was consistent with the two streams emanating from Kuyper in Amsterdam, with his divinely decreed nations, and from Fichte, with his German exaltation of the volk. This theologico-political thinking now burst into floodtide to cascade across the nation and sweep all before it.

As SABRA saw the new binding together of Afrikaners and the necessity that this be to the exclusion of other groups, it said:

> One of the basic values which lends meaning to the concept of 'apartheid', is the value of national binding [*volksverband*]. National binding has for us a very deep and real meaning and value. Just like the individual, the nation has an intrinsic worth and dignity. The worth of the nation is even higher than the worth of the individual: therefore we may with justice and good conscience demand from the individual that he bring the greatest sacrifice to the nation, as in time of war.[12]

'Colour', SABRA added, 'is for us important because it is indicative of national and cultural binding . . .'[13] Hence integrationist ideas and especially practice were to be resisted in the names of both theology and political wisdom.

Not that it was unimportant to care for people of other
races. 'In the policy of separate development', said SABRA,

> it should be fundamental that we grant unto others what we claim
> for ourselves. This is playing practical politics, but the moral
> grounds and the deepest justification for it is that all other people,
> *in casu* the non-Whites, are our fellow human beings, that they
> bear in themselves the image of God; with an own intrinsic worth
> and dignity which is not to be assailed, and which we should
> always respect. Moreover, it is a fact that in our particular ethnic
> situation separate development offers the only true potential for
> the non-Whites to come to self-realization as human beings.[14]

Then came SABRA's professedly Christian punch-line:

> But above all we are Christians who stand under the command of
> the Master that we should love our neighbour as ourselves . . . It
> is therefore essential to the meaning of apartheid, that together
> with the separation between nations and cultures, the Whites also
> accept the responsibility for the well-being and development of
> the non-Whites.[15]

Theology and politics

In a nutshell, what we have in the above quotations is
politicised theology and theologised politics. One wonders
whether any theologians or any churches in history were ever
so profoundly caught up and involved in the political life and
development of their nation. Where any Afrikaners derived
the currently popular notion that the church should keep out
of politics is a mystery: to be sure they did not get it from their
own history.

All of which causes us to ask: If the apartheid system took
this much theological, philosophical and socio-political
thought to wind it up – with the National Party Constitution
even being drawn up by a theologian (J D du Toit) – is there
any chance whatsoever of it being unwound, except by similar
theological, philosophical and socio-political thought? A few
Western liberal and democratic ideas fired across the floor of
Parliament won't do it; nor will the odd ANC bomb beside a

Pretoria police station or in a Johannesburg cinema – that's for sure.

If theology provides the clue to the genesis of apartheid, so must theology provide the clue to the process of its dismantling. Thus Afrikaners and the Dutch Reformed Church, who put it together ideologically, must be the primary and humble agents under God in dismantling it. In this they need compassion, encouragement and prayers. Thankfully the Dutch Reformed (NGK) Synod of 1986, in a development of great consequence, has put that theological process of turning from apartheid under way.

Those on the receiving end of the system, even back in 1948, felt they had good reason to doubt there was any political altruism built into the apartheid edifice as it went up and as they experienced it. But to those Afrikaners who were the chief architects of it all, the grand design of apartheid policy was a beautiful building ushering in peace and prosperity for all – it was too bad about the ugly but necessary scaffolding which had to go up beside the building to get it into place. Which brings us to the eighth step in the process.

ERECTING SCAFFOLDING TO SUPPORT THE BUILDING OF GRAND APARTHEID
(1960–1966)

Back in 1948, although apartheid's proponents felt themselves to be well-intentioned and their policy humane, blacks and most South African English-speakers at that time saw it more in terms of a legislative *blitzkrieg*, demolishing the all-too-modest fabric of reasonable South African race relations.

Though Malan was the first South African Prime Minister (1948–1954) to represent the ascendant pro-apartheid party, followed by J G Strydom (1954–1958), H F Verwoerd was the most brilliant and dominating figure from 1958 through to his death by assassination in 1966. (It was Verwoerd who on 31 May 1961 took South Africa out of the British Commonwealth.)

Verwoerd

I saw Verwoerd in the flesh only once, and that was in 1965 in the Pietermaritzburg City Hall, at one of the only three political rallies I have ever attended in my life. It was just after Rhodesian UDI, and both nation and world were waiting for Verwoerd's policy statement and reaction. He spoke brilliantly, fluently, incisively and technically on his and South Africa's viewpoint for over an hour without notes of any sort. ('No notes' was normal for him.)

The man was intellectually brilliant. And it was this brilliance which he, together with Malan, harnessed to put into place one of the boldest and most massive legislative superstructures of social engineering ever to be devised by any government anywhere at any time. It governed every aspect of black life, from residence and work to family life, sex and education.

Observes W A de Klerk, with a Churchillian touch: 'Never in history have so few legislated so programmatically, thoroughly and religiously, in such a short time, for so many divergent groups, cultures and traditions, than the nationalist Afrikaners of the second half of the twentieth century.'[16]

In his book *The Puritans in Africa*, de Klerk, Afrikaner sage that he is, stresses something we have already spoken of, but which rings strange to English, African or overseas ears: the well-intentioned nature of this whole endeavour. Most apartheid critics cannot conceive of any sincerity, good intentions or honour in the aims behind apartheid's grand design. And in this apartheid's antagonists perhaps fail the Afrikaner and wound his integrity. De Klerk puts it this way, and then comments on what world criticism about apartheid missed. Never, he says, has such a small minority of all those affected legislated 'with such a high sense of purpose, vocation and idealism. Never have so few drawn such sharply critical attention from a wondering world. Never has such a volume of criticism been so wide of the mark.'

This criticism, which was directed against the 'harsh, oppressive policies' of the Nationalist Government and against the 'tyranny of apartheid', was in de Klerk's view ineffective because it did not understand that 'the manifest harshnesses, the patent injustices, were all the oblique but necessary results of a most rational, most passionate, most radical will to restructure the world according to a vision of justice; all with a view to lasting peace, progress and prosperity'.[17]

I know when I heard Verwoerd speak at that rally he was nothing if not sincere – misguided perhaps, but not insincere. Maybe therein lay his tragedy.

Just after becoming Prime Minister (3 September 1958) he addressed the nation saying: 'The policy of separate development, "is designed for happiness, security and the stability provided by their home language and administration for the Bantu as well as the Whites."'[18]

Later he said, in the quote which heads this chapter:

> I have earnestly asked myself whether the advocates of total unity of the different races can bring justice and fairness to everybody. I am absolutely convinced that integration in a country like South Africa cannot possibly succeed . . . I am seeking justice for all the groups and not justice for only one group at the cost of the other three . . .
>
> If meddlesome people keep their hands off us, we shall in a just way, such as behoves a Christian nation, work out solutions in the finest detail and carry them out. We shall provide all our races with happiness and prosperity.[19]

In the interest of God's kingdom

While the world thundered, the English fumed and the blacks cried out in anguish as they were bolted into pre-planned places in the apartheid scaffolding, most Afrikaners, and especially the Broederbond, saw something beautiful for God – and from him.

Hence the doxologies to the Most High in 1968 at the fiftieth anniversary of the founding of that greatest of victorious think-tanks, the Broederbond. Devout old Henning Klopper, whom I'd met in Parliament with Sir Cyril Black in 1965, waxed eloquent in paeans of praise to the Most High for his instrument on earth – Afrikaner earth at least. 'Yes,' he said, 'it is in the interest of the Kingdom of God that the Afrikaner Broederbond shall be there.'[20]

Then he recalled the symbolic Ox-wagon Trek which he himself had organised in 1938 to celebrate the centenary of the Great Trek, and which many felt paved the way for Malan's 1948 victory, so wildly and enthusiastically was it received:

> When the volk was depressed after the 1938 election, with only 27 out of 140 members of Parliament, God gave us the Ox Wagon Trek. Through the grace of God the Broeders executed it. It was not that the Broeders sought to become big and powerful in the nation. God used them in this instance too. They planned it, but God used them as instruments to make the trek what it was. Many people told us in places where the Trek arrived, 'It is wonderful, it is from God.' The Afrikaner Broederbond is just as wonderful, and it also is from God.

Then, in the reflected glory of the mighty apartheid edifice as it arose out of the labours of Malan, Strydom and Verwoerd, Klopper could ask:

> Do you realise what a powerful force is assembled here tonight between these four walls? Show me a greater force on the whole continent of Africa! Show me a greater force anywhere else in the world, even in your so-called civilised nations. We support the State, we support the Church, we support every big movement born from the nation. We make our contribution unobtrusively, we carry it through and so we have brought our nation to where it is today.

He went on:

> We have supplied the leaders to our nation. Pity the nation without a leader! Every time, a leader could be chosen for the nation from the ranks of the Afrikaner Broederbond. When we lost Dr Malan, we had Advocate Strijdom. When death claimed him we had Dr Verwoerd. When he died so tragically, God had another man ready for us [John Vorster].

Klopper then told about a foreign journalist who had visited this country:

All he could say about the Afrikaner nation was that it was a miracle. That is because we accepted God our Father as our Saviour in every crisis. In those dark days when it was difficult, we went on our knees with all our problems and God gave us a solution.[21]

This was clearly how Klopper and others sincerely felt about the building. It was beautiful. Nay, it was a temple: it was God's – and this regardless of the ugly, though temporary and necessary, scaffolding. It would be required only 'for a generation', said Verwoerd. Twenty-five years or so of pain, and then all would come right – like a child when the tiresome and painful plaster of paris is taken off, and its broken arm is mended and everything is all right again.

THE SCAFFOLDING BECOMES THE BUILDING (1966–1978)

There was now to come a fateful and searing time for the Afrikaner national psyche. A few people woke up one day to see and say that the ugly scaffolding had become the building: what was temporary had become permanent; what was to uphold the building was now inseparable from it – the fairy had turned into a frog.

More horrifying still, while a few saw this and said so, others didn't. They liked the framework a lot. For now it looked like a fortress, and it felt good inside. It was safer than a pretty building. It was handsome too in its own way, like a castle. Thus, quietly and insidiously, when no one was looking, the castle became a calf – a golden one – and idolatry entered the soul of a nation.

This period happened, as I see it, in the home straight of the Verwoerd era, and in the first half at least of the Vorster era (1966–1978). For blacks it was a desperate time, as one shattering law upon another devastated their lives. For them there was no beauty here.

The Cottesloe consultation

It was thus with both shock and dismay that Afrikaners and
their church leaders heard the historic theological negative
pronounced upon apartheid in December 1960 at the World
Council of Churches (WCC) consultation at Cottesloe near
Johannesburg. This was held in the shadow of the Sharpeville
tragedy nine months previously (21 March 1960).

Everything the Dutch Reformed churches had theologically sanctioned in their massive corpus of apologetic literature on apartheid was now not only called in question but
denounced by a group of world theologians and Christian
leaders.

Prior to this, Afrikaner leaders had felt able to ignore as
eccentric and misguided the local thunderings of whites such
as Trevor Huddleston, Ambrose Reeves, Geoffrey Clayton,
Archbishop Joost de Blank, Alan Paton and a few others,
plus of course those vociferous black rebels like Luthuli, Z K
Matthews, Walter Sisulu, Robert Sobukwe and Nelson
Mandela.

But Cottesloe was different. This was the world church
speaking along with other South African Christian leaders.
And it was devastating. The views of the Church of the
Province in South Africa (Anglican) had already been conveyed, before Cottesloe, by Archbishop de Blank to Dr
Visser t'Hooft, the then General Secretary of the WCC. 'The
future of Christianity in this country demands our complete
dissociation from the Dutch Reformed attitude. Either they
must be expelled [from the WCC], or we shall be compelled to
withdraw.'[22]

Other Anglican leaders in the wider world opposed this
proposal. Instead, the WCC agreed to convene 'a consultation on Christian race relations and social problems in South
Africa'. In spite of de Blank's hostile line, of which he later
repented, the Dutch Reformed Church attended the
consultation, no doubt with anxiety and some trembling.

Part one of the final Cottesloe statement said that all unjust
discrimination was to be rejected. Part two said that all racial
groups of South Africa were part of the country and should
'have an equal right to make their contribution toward the

enrichment of the life of their country and to share in the ensuing responsibilities, rewards and privileges'.

The statement went on to resist emphatically Dr Verwoerd's plans to legislate that blacks and whites could not worship together. Said Cottesloe:

> No one who believes in Jesus Christ may be excluded from any church on the grounds of his colour or race. The spiritual unity among all men who are in Christ must find visible expression in acts of common worship and witness, and in fellowship and consultation on matters of common concern.[23]

Cottesloe's resolutions went on to other specifics. They called for more consultation between race groups and for recognition of the validity of racially mixed marriages. Migratory labour, low black wages and job reservation were all denounced. Delegates also called for the direct representation of coloureds in the central Parliament, for justice in trials, and for freedom of worship on a multiracial basis.[24]

In an addendum the consultation also said blacks could not, without violating Christian conscience, be excluded from full political rights.

Reactions and retractions

A truly significant thing here is that most of the Dutch Reformed (Nederduitse Gerevormeerde Kerk – NGK) leaders present accepted the consultation's findings, though one group (the Nederduitse Hervormde Kerk – NHK) rejected them out of hand. But from Verwoerd and Dr Koot Vorster (brother of John Vorster, the future Prime Minister) the reaction was electric and immediate. Such theological and political capitulation was to them unthinkable.

Verwoerd rightly discerned something that is still true today, that 'should the moral rightness and metaphysical soundness of the idea [of apartheid] be seriously questioned, and should it lose the full support of the Church, it could not possibly hope to retain the enthusiasm and loyalty of

Afrikanerdom'.[25] As far as he was concerned the theologians must retract.

And retract they did. The Dutch Reformed Church thus took the momentous step of withdrawing from the World Council of Churches.

A few stalwarts like Dr Albert Geyser and Dr Beyers Naudé, then acting moderator of the Dutch Reformed Church in the Transvaal, refused to be party to any recanting. Naudé's question was simple: 'Are we in these times of crisis prepared to listen again whether God perhaps has something to say to us? Or do we run the risk of our informing God that the route we are following is in every detail beyond question and also his way for us?'

Naudé's concern was that Afrikaner aspirations for their nation should also 'assure justice to all parties' so as to enable them to 'qualify for the blessings of heaven'.[26] So, to labour for this end, he, Geyser and others formed the inter-denominational and non-racial Christian Institute to encourage Christian dialogue in South Africa and to work for reconciliation.

The Dutch Reformed Church could never be quite the same again. Consciences became worried and questions of doubt persisted. This was especially true of some of the NGK leaders in the Mission Church, where they saw the horrific, painful, traumatic and sometimes tragic consequences among the blacks they served in their work. For example, the Group Areas Act, said the Dutch Reformed Mission Church in one report, 'caused suffering too deep to understand'.[27]

Freedom to preach the gospel?

Others, like Nico Smith, not only saw in their mission work the traumas inflicted on blacks by apartheid, but they found there were emerging profound questions and doubts related to the Broederbond and their participation in it.

Out in Mamelodi that dusty afternoon I visited him in April 1987, Nico Smith explained the crisis and how he resolved it. He had in 1963 been made Missions Secretary of his church in the Northern Transvaal, and as such he had the opportunity to travel abroad. In Switzerland he met the famous theologian Karl Barth, whose work he had studied at seminary. As the Mamelodi buses, cars, bicycles and people barrelled past in the street outside, Nico elaborated the telling tale.

Barth had just read a speech by Dr Verwoerd. 'What amazes me,' Barth had commented, 'is that what he said on race relations in your country is almost exactly the same as what President Davis said about race relations in the USA, exactly a hundred years ago. Must I now take it that you in South Africa are a hundred years behind the times?'

'I didn't want to argue with him about South Africa,' said Nico, 'so I didn't comment. But the observation and question made me think.'

'Then,' added Nico, 'Barth put another question to me, just as I was leaving his office. "Are you really free to preach the gospel in South Africa?" I replied we were. He then said, "Yes, but maybe some day you will discover an understanding of the gospel that is not in accord with your family and friends' understanding. Will you be free enough to preach then?"'

Nico went on: 'I couldn't answer Barth, as my family and friends all accepted the way I preached the gospel. He said "But it may become even more difficult! Maybe you will understand the gospel in a way in which your Government will not want it preached! Are you free enough to say you will be faithful to preach the gospel as you understand it and as the Holy Spirit may reveal it to you?"'

Nico said he was really embarrassed by these questions, but Barth's concept of freedom to preach haunted him as he returned to South Africa.

Freedom and tragedy

The question haunted him even more after he had under some pressure joined the Broederbond. The pressures within it to toe the Nationalist line put him, he found, in ever-deepening bondage. He felt increasingly unfree to follow his conscience.

'One night in 1973', Nico recollected, 'there was a real crisis in Parliament and in the Cabinet. The Broederbond and all its cells nation-wide were called together within hours. What I heard and what we were being asked to resolve brought things to a head. So I stood up and said, "Brothers, I want to tell you that this is the end of my time with the Broederbond."

'They had promised us that we would meet for only half an hour to approve a decision. But that night we sat in our cell until 11 p.m. Interestingly, the people who opposed me the strongest were the Dutch Reformed Church dominees. They were arguing why the Afrikaner Broederbond, the Nationalist Party and the Dutch Reformed Church were the only channels for change in the country.

'But I could no longer accept that. So I resigned. And at last I felt free. Free to preach the gospel according to what my conscience was beginning to say.

'That', concluded this theological pioneer, 'was twelve years ago. And the people who opposed me then are now walking out of the Broederbond for the very same reasons. Anyway, in spite of suffering and ongoing pressure, we have found our spiritual freedom, and that is what matters!'[28]

And so it was that a number of Afrikaner theologians, like Nico Smith, plus missionaries, laypeople and others began to tell their church and nation that the unacceptable scaffolding of apartheid had become not only the building but a dangerous idol. This being so, the system must be removed or else.

Words such as these from David Bosch (an Afrikaner himself) began to ring ever more frequently, uncomfortably and hauntingly in Afrikaner ears:

What we see unfolding now truly has the makings of a classical Greek tragedy. The stage for this tragedy is as large as Western Europe. Most of the millions of actors seem unable to comprehend where they are heading. They stride to their fierce disasters in the grip of truths more intense than knowledge, captives of their respective histories.[29]

Such words finally registered even in the heart of the then Minister of Defence, Mr P W Botha. In 1978 he would succeed Vorster as Prime Minister and initiate the tenth and final step in the story to date.

DISMANTLING THE SCAFFOLDING, BUT SAVING THE BUILDING (1978–1989)

Attempting to dismantle the scaffolding of apartheid has been the peculiar pain, peril and destiny of President Pieter W Botha. I will have cause to speak more of him and the actors of this era later, but I also want to make several brief observations about him here too.

Whatever people think of P W Botha, the history of the ten steps in the birth and growth of apartheid as catalogued in these last two chapters must surely establish him as a significant deviationist from historic Afrikaner orthodoxy. As such he must be credited with considerable political courage and with his own special niche in history.

When at Upington in 1979 he said South Africans must 'adapt or die', he was a brave political realist, bending his commitment and energies to at least the first steps in dismantling if not the apartheid building then at least the offending scaffolding. History must surely salute him for this, in spite of what many see as current back-pedalling or stalling.

I once chatted about President Botha to John Scott, the satirical columnist of the *Cape Times*. He said he once travelled abroad with the President as part of the Press Corps. One day, the President said to him *a propos* solving the apartheid problems: 'When I finally stand before my Lord, I don't want him to say to me, "You never even tried."'

I found this instructive, and it has generated sympathy in me as I've watched him seeking – albeit haltingly and to some extent vainly – to break free of the imprisonment of Afrikaner history. But the task is no simple matter, for the voluntary and successful undoing of conquest, other than by conventional colonial powers (which South Africa is not), has no historical precedent I know of.

Let it be registered, however, that although adept at dancing the Nationalist jig (one step forward and two steps backwards), President Botha's reforms have been considerable. But they are not enough, for alas as far as blacks can perceive, they affect only the scaffolding and the blacks are the ones on the receiving end. Hence their thundering with

Desmond Tutu: 'One does not reform a Frankenstein. One only destroys it.'

Be that as it may, we must nevertheless spare a thought of mercy and of prayer for the heroic Afrikaner people who, just when they have clawed their way out of a myriad perils and oppressions to win their place in the African sun, are now being asked to hand it all over.

More than that, the request of history is that the hard and perilously won 'national identity', the cardinal tenet and treasure of the nation's faith and soul, must now be laid on the altar and the roots of centuries be abandoned. It is a tremendous amount to ask.

And beyond that, Afrikaner theologians and church leaders are now being asked to renounce the epic theological apologias for separatism, wrought, as they have been, over the span of at least a century.

Amazingly, some are trying. Moderator Johan Heyns, reflecting on the 1986 DRC Synod, points out: 'What is very important is that we did in the past give to apartheid a theological and ethical justification. We have now completely abolished that. I believe this is a tremendous step forward.'[30] It is. Perhaps like Neil Armstrong's step on the moon, which was a small step for a man but a giant leap for mankind, so the steps of President Botha in the political realm and Professor Johan Heyns in the ecclesiastical, may appear small for mankind, but they are giant for that proud though poignant man of Africa called the Afrikaner.

To be sure, there are many miles to go amidst blood, sweat and repenting tears, as dreadful political and theological errors are faced. But let us not obstruct their way by denying that the first courageous and humble steps have been haltingly and painfully taken. Tragically, they have come when the summer is just about over. But perhaps, in wrath, God will yet remember mercy.

Part Four

THE TREE, THE ROOT AND THE FRUIT
(The links between structural injustice, theological error and black anguish)

9 No Grapes from the Bramble Bush
(A white education in the black experience)

Have you thought that we blacks are not quite human as whites are human: and therefore we don't quite experience ordinary human emotions?

Desmond Tutu

Only those who face their wounded condition can be available for healing and so enter into a new way of living.

Charles Villa-Vicencio

No good tree bears bad fruit . . .

Luke 6:43

BLACK ANGUISH AND PROTEST

We have reviewed the growth of Afrikaner nationalism and the strain, pain and struggle of this poignant people in the face of the harassments of history. But that, as we all know, is only one side of the story. The other is the profound experience of black anguish and protest, which though not originating in 1948, certainly intensified then. The grand system of apartheid is in place and operative. But what are its effects on blacks at an ordinary human level?

This is a key question raised by a central principle which Jesus often stresses – namely that a tree is known by its fruit: 'No good tree bears bad fruit, nor does a bad tree bear good fruit. Each tree is recognised by its own fruit. People do not pick figs from thornbushes, or grapes from briers' (Luke 6:43–44).

If the South African system and social structure, as developed in this century, and specially since 1948, is thought of as the *tree*, and if white privilege plus Afrikaner nationalism, all rationalised with some theology and political theory, is the *root*, then what is the *fruit*? What has the thing produced? And what will we do, if instead of figs we find thorns, and if instead of grapes we find brambles? Will we not have to re-examine the tree and deeply question its roots? Will we not perhaps have to hack down the tree, uproot it and start again with a new and rightly rooted tree which will produce good fruit?

As any hospital patient knows, understanding the problem, diagnosing the disease, and seeing where, how and why the illness developed, is a necessary prerequisite to successful surgery, appropriate remedy and restored health.

Knowing this, St Paul in his epistle to the Romans takes two and a half chapters ruthlessly to expose man's sin, the seriousness of his problem and its tragic consequences, not to leave his readers in condemnation, but so that he may bring them to 'the power of God for . . . salvation' (Rom 1:16) and thence to 'the obedience that comes from faith' (Rom 1:5).

The pattern is bad news before good news; we can't escape it.

In the early years of our African Enterprise ministry, we saw endless evidences of the fruit of the so-called South African way of life and its apartheid system. And of course subsequently these evidences have stared us in the face wherever we looked.

Curiously, the awfulness of the effects, the depth of black pain, and the intensity of black protest are not really understood by most South African whites because the system protects us from entering emotionally into what discrimination in general and apartheid in particular do to those on the receiving end. As beneficiaries of the system, South African whites cannot know what it is like to be the victims.

Tiny glimpses, however, of its dehumanising awfulness are caught if one either mixes socially with blacks or travels with them as we often do, being an interracial team involved in itinerant evangelism.

Actually there is a sort of ascending scale of offence, from the irritating, nuisance-value pinpricks of petty apartheid, to the devastating trauma of bearing the effects of grand apartheid every day of your life.

I'll start with the pinpricks.

PETTY APARTHEID

I think of a little thing like travelling by train to Johannesburg in 1970 with my colleague Abiel Thipanyane. Arguably, we should never have travelled by South African Railways, knowing what it might involve. But on that occasion we had no option.

First of all, we found ourselves in different coaches at different ends of the train. It would have been illegal to be together in the same coach. Then when we got to Johannesburg station we had to leave by separate exits (not required now) and ended up losing each other and failing to rendez-vous successfully. Once finally reunited, we hailed a taxi to go to our appointment.

'No blacks,' said the taxi driver. 'I'm not allowed to do it.'

Declining to accept this, I argued the toss with the driver.

'Alright, climb in. But it will be fifty cents extra for the boy!'

'Do you realise, sir,' I protested, 'that this man was offered the job of official interpreter to the Lesotho Houses of Parliament, and you call him "the boy"?'

'Calm down, Mike,' said Abiel laughing. 'This is nothing new. Let's go.' And we did – he patiently bearing it, and I fuming, angry and guilty, accepting it.

I think too of going fishing at an inland resort with my colleague Andrew Mohibidu and our respective children – only to find that the main fishing area was closed to blacks. By some strange and unusual quirk of Christian amnesia, it had not entered our minds to anticipate this. As a white I could have decided to defy this. But how much more vulnerable Andrew was! So by driving five or six kilometres we came to the black fishing area, where Andrew gave me my first lessons in fishing, while the fish remained curiously indifferent to whether we were black or white – simply by-passing us both!

Once again, like many blacks, Andrew graciously laughed all this off to save me embarrassment. But inside I was crying. And deep down we were both outraged. It wasn't really a pinprick. It was a stab at the heart of a man's humanity and dignity.

Beyond petty matters, the principle of discrimination on the basis of skin colour still prevails in the major areas of education, residence, political rights, the vote, race classification and often in the way blacks experience our police and legal system.

BANTU EDUCATION

I always knew there was much black pain and protest over Bantu Education. But 1980 was when this came home to me personally.

In 1980 our team was invited to conduct a city-wide Christian mission to the diamond city of Kimberley. I learnt early on that the place was in tumult, trauma and uproar because thirteen thousand young blacks were rioting and boycotting schools, protesting against the nature of so-called Bantu Education. Ten schools had closed.

On a reconnaissance visit to the city, I spoke to the black mayor of Kimberley's Galeshewe Township.

'I want to meet the young people', I told him, 'and find out their grievances. After all, we can't come and do a mission in this city and turn a blind eye to the fundamental problem which is turning the place upside-down. Our gospel preaching to both black and white will make no progress if we do.'

'You'll find it too hot, Mr Cassidy,' he replied. 'Besides, those kids won't speak to any white. They won't even speak to the Parents-Teachers Association, or to the black clergy. What chance do you stand?'

In spite of this, I resolved to persevere. Several weeks before the mission, I sent half a dozen of African Enterprise's young black and white interns into Galeshewe to try and make creative and positive contact with the leaders of the boycott. They ended up being locked in the township for three weeks when it was cordoned off by the police.

Miraculously, however, the upshot of all this was that when the mission opened I was told a handful of young black township leaders would meet me secretly at the Anglican deanery where I was staying. They all converged on the deanery by different routes and told me their story.

All subsequent meetings were also secret affairs – but in Galeshewe township itself, not in the city centre.

Slowly the picture of grievances emerged.

'The big problem', they said, 'is Bantu Education. And you know what Dr Verwoerd said, don't you?'

There were knowing looks all round.

'We are to be educated only up to levels suitable for certain forms of labour. We are not putting up with that. We want to see a unified system of education; we want qualified, not unqualified teachers; we want more high schools; we want freedom to choose our subjects; we want better recreational facilities; we want a better balance in the pupil-teacher ratio. And we're not going to go back to school till our demands are met.'

Though not all their demands were capable of an overnight solution, I knew they had a point. A big one.

The facts spoke for themselves. Verwoerd's notorious dictum about educating blacks only to the levels appropriate for certain forms of labour was part of black South African folklore and fuelled the suspicions of every black child in the nation regarding even the best efforts and intentions of the Department of Education and Training. It is strange how words from the past rise up to haunt the present and imperil the future.

I also sensed with these young people, as I have with many other blacks since that time, that another of their major problems with Bantu Education is the feeling that it lacks legitimacy because blacks themselves have never been consulted adequately as to what they themselves really want in their own educational programme. Unconsulted, they feel that whatever is given to them is foisted upon them and thereby rendered illegitimate.

Anyway, as we listened to the case presented by these

Kimberley young people, they began to give us their hearts and confidence. More than that, they started pouring into our evangelistic services and wanting to hand out our song books *etc.*

Amidst all this I sat down and drafted letters to Dr Piet Koornhof (then Minister of Co-operation and Development), Dr Ferdie Hartzenberg (then Minister of Black Education) and Dr Pieter de Lange, chairman of the De Lange Commission on Black Education. I also later visited Pretoria to meet with Dr Koornhof, Mr Hartzenberg and Mr Rousseau, the Deputy Director of Education – all of whom graciously received me. They hoped something could be done. I did too. But were they not captives of a flawed ideology which could never win favour with young blacks?

I shared the Government's reasonably open response with the kids, some of whom I almost got to Pretoria to meet personally with the authorities. This exacting enterprise in face-to-face encounter between the top authorities and the kids finally foundered on a tiresome technicality. But when this failed I restated my pleas, both spoken and written, to the authorities, including a statement of what the Kimberley kids themselves wanted to say to the Cabinet generally and to the Minister specifically.

In our letter to the Minister my African Enterprise colleagues and I put in a final plea in these terms:

> We think the student leaders are, for the most part, too intelligent to be taken lightly. We feel there would be a real danger in making promises that are not seen to be fulfilled practically and visibly within the relative short-term. Our fear is that if promises are made, and not fulfilled tangibly, then in the very near future, the Educational and Government authorities are going to have something worse than a boycott on their hands and the consequences and outcome of a 'second phase boycott' could be much more serious and much more difficult to resolve because the confidence and hopes of the youth would have been totally destroyed. It is shaky at the moment, but we believe that if we don't act to build effective trust very soon, we are going to lose this group of youngsters to many more forces of evil in our society.[1]

Sadly, eight years later (in 1987–88) very few young blacks feel much has changed substantially. Educational improvements, well-intentioned by the authorities and undoubtedly sincere, are all seen as still within the discriminatory framework, still within an unacceptable white ideology, and still – Government protestations not withstanding – within the supposedly well-disguised goals of Dr Verwoerd's tragic dictum about the aims of Bantu Education. Unsatisfied and unconvinced, black suspicion still rules the roost.

So black protest, both youth and adult, about black education rises to ever-intensifying crescendoes, never to be dulled or silenced till the last vestiges of apartheid are gone and all education is freed from ideological captivity.

By the mid 1980s the cry of black youth would be: 'Liberation now, education later.' This of course means that many of today's young people will grow up uneducated, which won't be terribly helpful to a future South Africa. But it is hard to argue with passions that are so rooted in the hurts of history.

Sipho's story begins

Of course there's nothing like a close encounter to bring things home. This was the case for me with the Kimberley mission. We had made such spiritual progress with these youngsters as the mission ended that many were ready and willing to respond positively to an invitation from us to come down to Pietermaritzburg to the African Enterprise Centre for a week of Christian discipling and spiritual nurture.

Accordingly, a group of thirty or so arrived by bus in early December, fully convinced as they entered lush Natal after the dry, dusty Free State that they had entered the promised land!

Sipho Mazwana (not his real name) was one of the prominent members of the group. Being a key boycott leader, he had been sent along by some powerful militants as a sort of political watchdog to the group.

During the week, the gospel of Jesus Christ, which he had not previously embraced, captured his hitherto embittered heart. The night before the group left to return to Kimberley, I met them to report on my interview that same afternoon with Minister Hartzenburg and Deputy Education Director Rousseau in Pretoria. I told them of my hope that there would be progress from the Government side, and encouraged them to go back to school.

Later in the evening, while I was saying a moving farewell to the group, Sipho came up to me, held out his hand, then without warning threw his arms round me and began to sob. I clutched him tight and he calmed. Then came a prayer I will never forget: 'Lord Jesus, make me an instrument of your peace in South Africa today.'

It was a poignant moment for me too. Here was a boy ready to be a reconciling instrument of peace and a positive, sensible and responsible force for Christ and for healing in our land. Also, no doubt, he would be seeking to get his thousands of mates back to school when the new term opened in January 1981.

In fact, he and others succeeded in this. And Kimberley's young people did indeed return in their thousands to school in January 1981 – believing their plea had been heard.

But going back to school was not to be Sipho's lot. For he was shortly to be put in prison, and not so long after that he almost died. The system was once again winning and destroying. Sanity and the future were losing.

I for my part was now to get some new insights into another area of profound black pain and protest – namely the experience many blacks have of our police, prison and legal systems. Not that these systems are by any means always brutal, unfair or unjust. I have met many policemen of honour and compassion, and have recently in a Natal court seen the South African legal system operating with great enlightenment and compassion towards black people. However, in the present section of my tale I unfold certain facts and experiences as they came to me.

THE BLACK EXPERIENCE OF THE SOUTH AFRICAN POLICE, PRISON AND COURT SYSTEM

The drive from Kenton-on-Sea to Pietermaritzburg is a long one – all of six hundred miles. As I opened the door of our home in mid January at the end of this journey, and at the end of a Christmas holiday, the phone rang. The New Year of 1981 was opening with a vengeance.

It was a white minister from Kimberley. Could I do anything? Sipho and twenty-two others had been detained and were in prison.

Sipho's story unfolds

In the weeks and months following, I did everything I could. I wrote endless letters back and forth to the Ministers of Police and Justice, to get these youngsters released. But all was in vain. The Minister said that Sipho and seventeen others had not been charged with any crime but were being detained 'as witnesses' so as to prevent them being 'intimidated'! Five of the twenty-three had charges brought against them.

Nineteen months later, when Sipho was finally released after a dreadful and desperate ordeal, I brought him to Pietermaritzburg to my home. He told me his story over successive days in eighteen sides of taped testimony, later reduced and edited into a twenty-one page legal affidavit. Periodically he would break down in the telling and reliving of it all, and we would end the session for that day.

However, I was staggered to find that, against all odds, the love of Christ was still reigning in his heart, and the spirit of forgiveness was miraculously alive in his spirit. And as I heard more of the story, my mind boggled at how much there was to forgive.

The picture which emerged made my hair stand on end, my heart break, and my spirit so angry I could hardly contain myself.

The whole protest and boycott, Sipho said, had started with

'one overriding desire – to have Bantu Education eradicated completely from our schools'.

His part in this led to three experiences of detention which were later recorded in affidavit form.

The first was an ordeal of beatings, interrogation, solitary confinement and being deprived of food. It lasted for three days.

During the second period of detention his interrogators used a device called the 'helicopter'. He was strapped by his waist at an oblique angle over a framework consisting of a horizontal pole and a vertical pole. Hands and feet were spreadeagled and tied to the upright pole. Then clips were attached to his elbows and knees. While dangling precariously at an awkward angle, all the blood circulation to his hands and feet stopped and filled his body with unbearable discomfort and pain.

'A whistle was left dangling from the pole near my face. When I had had enough I was to thrust my head towards it, secure it in my mouth and blow. It meant I was ready to talk.' Then the interrogation would begin.

'When I was put up on the helicopter for the first time, I lasted barely fifteen minutes. I was also terrified.'

The third time of detention was to bring new experiences of horror.

15 January 1981 was the day before school was to open again. Sipho was all set to return.

'In my mind the boycott was now a thing of the past. I was a different person and I wanted to catch up on the months of schooling I had lost and get my matriculation.'

At 3.30 a.m. six men in the dark of the morning positioned themselves before the front and back doors. Sipho was wakened and told he was needed for questioning, but he would be home again that same day.

'Knowing this, I willingly got dressed and went with them.'

That 'day' lasted nineteen months.

Sipho began to descend into a brutal, meaningless hell.

He described an early episode in these terms: 'Two of them grabbed my feet and another two my arms. They lifted me up, swung me high into the air and dashed me against the wall and on to the floor. I thought my back had been broken.'

Then the two black policemen took him into an office where they closed the door.

'They punched me, they punched me, they punched me, for a very long time – in my face and all over my body. One of them grabbed my genitals and began to squeeze them, but the other man stopped him before the pain was too great.'

They then stood Sipho against the wall.

'They began to smash my head against the concrete. Many, many times they rammed my skull against the wall until I became dizzy and lost consciousness.'

There was blood everywhere. Sipho's head was broken open at the back. Blood was coming from his mouth.

'I was unconscious, I think, for several minutes – how long I cannot say. When I regained consciousness, I was forced to fetch a bucket of water and a rag and wash my blood off the floor and wall of the office.'

After a first short spell in solitary confinement, Sipho was moved to a long narrow cell containing a hundred 'awaiting trial' prisoners.

A boy of seventeen among ruthless criminals: in itself it was illegal for a juvenile to be held thus. But Sipho's conversion experience came to him afresh as he faced this congregation of needy men.

'During the day many searching discussions took place in the cell. I had found a Bible and was able to read to the prisoners and pray with them. In the evening they asked me to pray, so I would pray out loud for the whole cell. Before we prayed, we sang hymns.

'Every day many of these prisoners would be taken up to the courts to be tried for serious crimes. Several of them developed a real faith in God and went up to face their accusers, confident that God would help them. Many were acquitted or came away with greatly reduced sentences. These stories of acquittals filtered back down into the cells and had a real impact on the others who then believed in God.'

But there was harsh objection to the vibrant singing and praying, and Sipho was accordingly frequently put into 'Koeloekuhts' – the solitary cell – and denied two meals for a day.

But the hell was to deepen.

Seven months of solitary in a remote town in the Cape called Plooysberg were to follow for Sipho when he was moved from the 'awaiting trial' cell.

In his dark, lonely solitary confinement cell a bucket of water was given him which was meant to last for a week. When the water became putrid after a few days Sipho got his drinking water out of the toilet cistern.

He began to have frequent bouts of illness. Complaining to the station commander produced a response of Epsom salts regardless of the sickness. A stock of unused Epsom salts began to grow in his cell.

'To deal with my headaches,' said Sipho, 'I would fashion a bandage out of a torn T-shirt and fasten it around my head to quell the throbbing pain. While I was doing this I would pray for healing. I believe God did touch and heal me.'

Month after month the lad sat in his darkened cell.

'I remember how happy I was when I found two ants. I spent the whole day with those ants, playing with them on my fingers and even talking to them. There was nothing else to do. I began to rip up the blankets, pulling out the threads and making ropes. I spent days making them and undoing them. I even undid the hem of my trousers just to have something to do. At night it was impossible to sleep. They kept the light on, but also I had been suffering from acute insomnia for years.'

Eventually Sipho began to rampage round his cell until he would collapse exhausted on a mat on the floor, then pray and fall asleep. Finally came acute depression.

'I thought over my past, present and future, and decided that I was a nobody and therefore had no real reason to live. I took a white T-shirt, fashioned a rope out of it, tied it to my neck and climbed a wall dividing the cell from the toilet area. Then I jumped off the dividing wall.'

But the suicide attempt failed. The T-shirt rope was too elastic, and it broke as he leapt to the floor.

'As I lay there I seemed to come to my senses. I believe God spoke to me and showed me that it was cowardice to do this thing. I decided I would not be a coward, that I would face my problems and the effects of solitary confinement head-on, no matter how hard they were. God made it clear to me that he had not allowed me to succeed, because he had a genuine reason for my life – an assignment which he wanted me to accomplish for him. He spared my life to give me another chance.'

So the young prisoner began to sing again, loudly, so that any passing human being could hear. And there were the ants, of course: Sipho watched them for hours as they carried crumbs of food he gave them, up and down the cell.

'This was an enjoyable exercise. They told me that there was still life around me operating in the way God intended life to be lived.'

Finally the hideous, lonely months ended. Sipho was moved to another prison with one other companion from the school boycott who had also been in solitary. Though they had known each other well, they could not communicate.

The food was better there, and on occasion they were allowed out to exercise by washing the station commander's car.

Eventually the two boys began to relate. They started to read the Bible together – whole books in one sitting. Acts was particularly stirring, and especially the accounts of the apostle Paul.

'St Paul's courage in the face of persecution and imprisonment' said Sipho, 'was a real source of encouragement to us. In reading of the power he had through the Holy Spirit, we were able to understand and claim this power for ourselves. Paul had endurance because he had hope and faith. So we knew, no matter what our situation, we could endure.'

This endurance was to be tested one more time.

Sipho gets to tell his story

The two black policemen who had first beaten up Sipho took him from his cell and drove him several miles along a desolate road to a concrete wall duct which runs under a bridge. They showed him the statement he had made to them when first detained. It had been falsified in three places.

They began to apply their pressure. He should 'become a witness for the State' and withhold information relating to the circumstances of his detention and his treatment during the experience.

'I told them I would not even discuss such a possibility until my statement had been corrected to its original form.'

They were not pleased. They made it clear that they wanted Sipho to say he had not been cruelly treated at their hands. There were four others who had been detained at the same time and they had all told the courts they had not been badly treated, the men said. This was because they wanted to lead better, safer lives.

'I was told that these boys would now be going on to higher education, while I would be going to further prison if I told the truth.'

The men began to talk of Robben Island (the boy was naturally scared stiff) and also of what could happen to Sipho's uncle. So he agreed not to tell the full truth in court. The men then backed off. Much pleased with his agreement, they assured him of job opportunities and security from the state once the trial was over. As a parting shot, they said that if he were to tell the truth in court no one would believe him and he would be prosecuted for perjury.

Back in the cell Sipho learnt that his friend had been through a similar ordeal. The two then made a pact together to tell all in court.

On their way to Kimberley to give evidence the two boys were told by the police of two detainees who had given evidence for the defence and who were now to be tried for perjury. The boys were thoroughly unnerved.

'I had to pray that God would give me the strength to tell the whole truth once in court. I prayed he would keep me resolute.'

From 12 to 20 August 1982 Sipho appeared for the defence. The beatings, the helicopter, the isolation, the attempted suicide – all came out. The state prosecutor challenged him about the assaults and torture. The onus lay on Sipho to prove he had actually been tortured.

'While I was describing solitary confinement to the court, the Holy Spirit gave me the ability to describe the ordeal vividly. Many of the people in the court were weeping openly.'

The magistrate apparently concluded that this testimony was the first convincing evidence that had been given in this whole case by defence witnesses. Because of the honest questioning he faced, Sipho felt free to tell everything, even the names of those who had assaulted him.

'At one stage I was asked if the men who had tortured me were in the court, and if so, could I point them out? They were both there, so I pointed them out to the court.'

Was he not frightened to give evidence while they sat there watching? asked the advocate.

'The truth will remain the truth even if they are in the courtroom. And the truth is that they beat me up and assaulted me, and nothing can change the truth of this.'

Witness Sipho Mazwana was now released and free to go. It was nineteen months since I had received the phone call from Kimberley saying he had been detained as a witness, which, according to correspondence I had received from the Minister of Police, was 'to protect him from intimidation'!

What does God require?

As Sipho's horrific story laid hold upon my being, I had to ask myself what the love of God and the gospel of Jesus Christ required of me. To be sure, I couldn't just walk away from his pitiful plight. I had to do something. And Jesus' principle gave added impetus: 'whatever you did for one of the least of these brothers of mine, you did for me' (Matt 25:40). And if I did nothing, the converse would most surely on 'that day' apply to me: 'whatever you did not do for one of the least of these, you did not do for me' (Matt 25:45).

Here unquestionably was 'one of the least' – broken, devastated, lost and rudderless. Above all, here was a victim of the system I had allowed to take root in my land. I could not abdicate responsibility. Besides, the Bible had an endless stress on caring for 'the *fatherless*' (Deut 10:18; 14:29; Job 29:12; Ps 10:14; Hos 14:3, *etc.*). The apostle James even defines 'pure religion' not in terms of pure theology or beautiful church services, but in terms of what we do about 'orphans and widows in their distress' (Jas 1:27). And was not

Sipho fatherless, both literally (his dad had died years before) and metaphorically?

The Lord's word seemed to come to me saying: 'You cannot be responsible for all the detainees in the country. But you can become responsible for this one I have put in your path.' Was I meddling in politics? Or was I simply carrying out the dictates of Jesus' love for the little ones of this life? The answer was to me self-evident.

Step one was to help him get his education going again. Kimberley's black schools were not keen on 'ex-detainees' and Natal black schools said they could only take Zulu students not Xhosas. Finally I felt constrained to approach Richard Todd, the Headmaster at that time of Hilton College. Marvellously Richard opened the way for Sipho to get a full scholarship to this great private school for two years.

With his parents deceased, Carol and I are now *in loco parentis* and have seen him thus far half-way through his university studies.

One thought gripped me after coping with the horrors of Sipho's story. If his experience was the fruit of the apartheid tree, then we were dealing not with a good tree but with a bramble bush, for there were no grapes anywhere. Not anywhere.

10 A Victim a Day on the Jericho Road (The regular violation of black dignity)

Apartheid is the finest blend of idealism and cruelty ever devised by man.

Alan Paton

Your brother's blood cries out to me from the ground.
Genesis 4:10

Sadly, Sipho's story is not the end of the tale. Far from it. To comprehend the depths and extent of the South African problem, we have to look further at the fruit of apartheid. This will involve moving from symptoms to diagnosis, and then into God's Calvary answers, God's challenges, God's Holy Spirit hope and God's saving way forwards.

My first-hand exposure and encounter with Sipho's experience really shook me up. It seemed incredible. I wanted to reject it. (Unpleasant truths are always hard to swallow.) But coming within my circle of acquaintances as it did, there was no way I could side-step it.

Then, of course, I found myself trying to rationalise it further. After all, if it was true, as I had satisfied myself it was, then was it not just an isolated case? After all, every country of the world, the UK and the USA not excluded, could probably produce its odd horror story of police brutality or abuse. Was Sipho's case not just some nightmarish exception?

The facts unfortunately supplied another answer.

DAILY VICTIMS

Everyone knows and loves the story of the Good Samaritan
(Luke 10:29–37). When others failed to be neighbour to the
wounded victim, he did not. He turned aside, bound his
wounds, put him on his donkey and took him to a place of
shelter, food, warmth and recovery. He also covered the
costs.

As the Samaritan journeyed on to his home, he no doubt
lamented the bad luck of the man who had fallen victim to this
rare and isolated robbery. But what if he found a wounded
and robbed victim every day as he travelled to work on the
Jericho road? Presumably he would have bound them all up,
exhausted his poor donkey with the additional daily load, and
boosted substantially the inn-keeper's profits from all this
new business! But would not his love and service have been
incomplete unless he had finally done something about the
structures and law enforcement procedures that allowed such
bandits to rob, wound or kill with impunity along the Jericho
road?

Would he not sooner or later have had to move his attention from the individual victims to the groups of people, the
political mind-sets and the social structures which played so
constantly, regularly and perilously upon the lives of those
individual and daily victims?

And what about the situation in South Africa? Regrettably,
the hard facts of our national life provide a clear and overwhelming answer whose implications and message must be
faced and understood before any of the Lord's answers will
ever be found. These facts come not just in physical brutalisation, but in political, mental, psychological and social
brutalisation as well.

For example, if one were to think only in terms of something as extreme as black deaths since the State of Emergency
in 1985, there is not just a victim a day on the Jericho road.
(The 8 September 1988 edition of the *Johannesburg Star*
quoted the South African Institute of Race Relations' calcula-
tion that 695 people died during the 1986–1987 State of
Emergency and 864 died between June 1987 and June 1988.)
In fact, even in early 1988 in our home area of Pietermaritz-

burg there were three to four deaths a day as a result of conflict between different black groupings, a conflict which many feel to be rooted in divergent black responses to the system. And though unrest-related deaths are currently not a daily phenomenon, they are still occurring every few days.

This poses the question: What is wrong, structurally speaking, with a society where this sort of lethal violence has become endemic?

DETENTION AND IMPRISONMENT IN SOUTH AFRICA – FACTS AND FIGURES

Let it be noted again here that nothing in this section invalidates the good work done with integrity by many in the South African police force. For numerous police brigadiers, officers and constables, both white and black, perform their incredibly difficult task with honour and impartiality in circumstances of extreme complexity and provocation. And many in all sections of the population, as in other countries, are thankful for this and salute it. As Gilbert and Sullivan observed, 'a policeman's lot' is often 'not a happy one' – or an enviable one. This I recognise, and I also acknowledge that the police need much prayer. But that said, it would seem inescapable that in this area of our national life (as in so many others) there are people and places where things have gone terribly wrong and where brutality, partiality and abuse have become deep and extensive. That this is so would seem to be demonstrated by the picture which often emerges of detention and imprisonment – often without trial – as they have functioned in this nation in the last forty years.

It is becoming clear that Sipho's experience was not an isolated thing. In a research study by Don Foster, Dennis Davis and Diane Sadler at the University of Cape Town, they affirm that since 1948 the 'use and abuse of these laws has become more extensive and the legislation itself more draconian with the passage of time. At a conservative estimate, about 70 000 people had suffered by the end of 1986 at the hands of the shadowy figures empowered by this legislation'.[1]

They open their book with this paragraph: 'It is approxi-

172   THE PASSING SUMMER

mately 25 years since detention without trial outside of war-
time was introduced in South Africa . . . Since then, despite
persistent and widespread protests against detention and a
considerable degree of critical attention directed at this system, very little change in a positive direction has been
forthcoming.'[2]

The Detainee Parents Support Committee (DPSC) in its
report for 1987 said a total of 9 194 people were detained in
1987. Fifty per cent of these by February 1988 had been
released without charge, while fifteen per cent of known
security detainees had been brought to trial. 3.46 per cent of
the total number had been convicted.

The Report further estimated that twenty-five thousand
people had been detained between the introduction of the
State of Emergency in June 1986 and the end of 1987, and that
forty per cent of detainees were aged eighteen or younger.

Official figures released in April 1987 by the former head of
police, General Johan Coetzee, said that 19 209 people had
been detained by 15 April 1987 and 14 965 released.[3]

Though the Government's and the DPSC's figures may
show discrepancies, even the Government's figures reveal
that detention with or without trial in South Africa is no isolated experience reserved only for the occasional Kimberley
schoolboy, but is an integral part of the governmental
apparatus in this land.

Says Professor Foster:

It has become apparent that detention without trial has increasingly assumed a central place within a vastly expanded
system of state security . . . In the space of a period of about 13
years between the early 1960s and the mid-1970s, the principle of
peace-time detention without trial had become an accepted part
of the apartheid regime.[4]

And what is it all for? The Cape Town researchers concluded that 'the central purpose is the gathering of information, especially to monitor all opposition, but also to
remove key people from political organizations'.[5]

It must be an effective means of intimidation. 'As a mode of
psychological violence,' says Foster,

the substantial number of deaths in detention and the widespread rumours of vicious treatment and torture at the hands of the security police both work to generate a climate of fear that operates in favour of the state, at least over the short term.

The same processes in the longer run are likely of course to undermine the legitimacy of the state in serious ways.[6]

The realities of detention

Unhappily, the stories of 'vicious treatment and torture' are not just rumours. The documented cases are now so extensive and numerous that we can with confidence say that Sipho's experience was not unique.[7]

Here I will briefly deal with another real-life case.

Vusi Khanyile

Not all detainees are school children, rioters or boycotters. Some are among the sanest and most needed leaders in the black community. A case in point is my long-standing friend Vusi Khanyile, Chairman of the National Education Crisis Committee, and Special Assistant to Dr Stuart Saunders, Vice Chancellor of Cape Town University.

A devout evangelical Christian, a man of peace, a responsible and balanced leader who tried to keep young people in school rather than out, Vusi is at the moment of writing incarcerated.

In December 1986 he had been due to give a paper on black education at Natal University, Pietermaritzburg.

His phone call came mid afternoon to my office at the African Enterprise Centre.

'Mike, can I come out to see you? I have some problems.'

I felt privileged that he would call, and fifteen minutes later he was with me. The police had told the Professor of Education, Dr Schreiner, that they would be there to hear Vusi's talk. Now Vusi felt he couldn't give it. It would be read *in absentia* to the conference. He said he felt imperilled.

We had a rich time of fellowship and prayer in my office, and I urged him to stay with me a few days if possible rather than drive to Soweto that night as he was insisting. He was most anxious to see his wife and children, all of them being on the verge of moving to Cape Town.

But I could not prevail. He drove to Soweto that night, packed up his belongings with his family, but just before leaving in the small hours of the morning for Cape Town, the police arrived.

As of now, nearly two years later, he remains in police custody. As Professor Saunders records in the *UCT Alumni Magazine*: 'It is trite to record that no charges were laid.'[8]

All attempts by the University authorities and various friends to secure his release have failed, though from all accounts he has not been physically harmed. Thus has the very best sort of black leader been put out of action.

Psychological effects of detention

Of course all this causes the head to spin, especially when one realises that from September 1963 to November 1985, sixty-four people, including Steve Biko and the Trade Union leader Neil Aggett, have died in detention, and that from July 1984 to November 1985 a further seventeen died 'in police custody'.[9]

By early 1988 the figure stood at eighty-seven.[10]

We cannot leave this sorry subject without saying something about the psychological consequences to the victims themselves.

A *Sunday Tribune* report of 2 November 1986 quotes psychiatric research done on released detainees. As many as seventy per cent develop post-traumatic stress disorders. The conclusion is that 'children are particularly susceptible to anxiety disorders, depression, adjustment and behaviour disorders and psychotic episodes. Children frequently exhibit acute feelings of guilt, fear, isolation and depression on their release.'[11]

For example, fifteen year old detainee Johnny Mashiane of Alexandra was found displaying 'acute psychotic behaviour' on his release from detention, and had to be hospitalised for a month in a psychiatric ward. Confusion and disorientation persist, and he has been unable to return to school.

Other problems plaguing the released detainees include nightmares, headaches, insomnia, passivity, poor concentration, and impaired abilities to relate to people.

More serious yet are the long-term consequences to the country of a rampaging generation of radicalised and brutalised black young adults whose reason has fled and whose driving psychotic passion is the impulse of vendetta. The prominent South African journalist Allister Sparks puts it this way:

> The young blacks of today are the third generation to grow up under apartheid. They refuse to accept it . . . Not all the threats and detentions and teargas canisters and shotgun blasts in the world are going to make those kids accept the system. All that massive overuse of force can do is to brutalise them and turn them into a Khmer-Rouge.[12]

A biblical challenge

When one thinks of Jesus' profound, manifest and tender concern for those in prison, one's heart is deeply challenged. Beyond that, when he makes visiting and caring for those in prison one of the criteria by which on that final day we are judged worthy or otherwise of inheriting the kingdom (Matt 25:34), then one is almost overwhelmed at the delinquence in this area. Will Christians generally, and South African Christians specifically, hear him say: 'I was in prison and you came to visit me' (Matt 25:36), or will he say 'whatever you did not do for one of the least of these, you did not do for me' (Matt 25:45)? Rather crudely, he says it makes the difference between 'eternal punishment' and 'eternal life' (Matt 25:46).

THE COLOURED EXPERIENCE OF RACE CLASSIFICATION

A couple of years ago I was preaching near Durban to a so-called coloured congregation. After the service I went to tea with the pastor and his wife in their modern little home in their modern little township. The minister and his wife were beautiful, godly and articulate people.

As we chatted, some of their pain began to come through. The human tangle which emerged brought home to me the madness and cruelty of building a nation on race. One hardly had to look beyond the bounds of this one family to find all the grounds anyone, most of all any Christian, needs to cast the system to outer darkness.

A family's experience

The experience of coloured people somehow highlights the wickedness of racialism. Their 'inbetweenness' creates such human absurdities that the folly of operating a society on racial lines is made to stand out starkly in all its moral nakedness.

The Rev. Albert van Rensburg and his wife Jeanie said their whole family history and experience, plus that of their friends and even congregational members, had been bedevilled by South Africa's racial laws – especially the Population Registration Act (1950), which required a central population register in which all people were classified as whites, coloureds, asiatics or blacks.

Two other Acts which had hurt them, both of which are now mercifully repealed, were the Prohibition of Mixed Marriages Act (1949) and the Immorality Amendment Act (1950), which forbade marriage and sexual intercourse between whites and so-called 'non-whites'. Inevitably they had also been much affected by the Group Areas Act (1950). This augmented the various laws providing for racially segregated residential areas. Areas were thereby set aside for each group, and no other racial group could live or own land there. Any members of other racial groups already living there had to be removed.

'Like most coloured families,' said Albert, 'we have links into the white world which have made things very difficult for us. For example, my wife's two aunts both married whites. And her grandfather is classified white, but lives in the coloured area. They would come and visit once a month, but when they did so their European husbands would sit in the car down the road for fear of being found out that they in fact had wives who were not officially white. In fact, they wouldn't even walk into the house. All the nephews and nieces are exposed to this also and are traumatised by it. So you have the situation where the children are asked not to recognise their aunts if they see them in town, for fear that the aunts will be found out!'

As I sat dumbfounded, Albert said, 'Many coloured families have the same thing. They can't recognise so called white members of their family in public. If they meet, it has to be in secret.

'Then there's my sister who looks white. She went to a coloured school, but when she grew up and saw the life she'd have to live on the wrong side of the race line, she cut herself off from her family and jumped the tracks into the white world. She felt she'd have much better chances and job opportunities that way.

'You know,' said Jeanie butting in, 'I think those people who move over to the white side are actually more the losers than we are on this side of the line, because at least we have our family around us, but they have no one. Of course they do live with their new families, but always with the constant fear of losing everything if they are found out.

'And then, my goodness,' chortled Jeanie with a cynical little smile, 'when they have a child they just have to pray like mad that it comes out fair and without crinkly hair! Otherwise it would give the whole game away. And the child also could be shunned and probably have to be put out for adoption.'

She sat silently for a moment, letting the impact of it all sink in on me.

'Albert,' I said, 'to come back to your two aunts and their white husbands who stay two blocks away in their cars when their wives visit you: would those husbands not recognise you at all as family?'

Albert shook his head.

'No Michael. They can't. Not openly anyway. Actually, I can't tell you the trauma of that family. They really live at home behind closed doors and in constant fear. And this is most acute during any pregnancy. Then the fear of exposure is most intense of all.'

A sense of worth

As Jeanie poured me some more tea and lavished typical coloured hospitality upon me, Albert told me that a major part of his ministry involved trying to instill in his people a sense of value and dignity.

'You see, Michael, this race thing has given blacks and coloureds such an inferiority complex. They come to think that being white is somehow better, and they will therefore sometimes even break precious family ties and disown relatives to get on the right side of the line. So a big part of my ministry lies in convincing my congregation they are OK people and that they are somebodies.'

'Where does Christ come into this Albert?' I asked. 'How does he help with their hurts?'

'Well, they must know who they are in Christ. If they know who they are in Christ, it lifts them above all racial categories. The problem in our nation is that the church has failed to let the different people know their value and identity in Christ.

'But if you want a real story of the Lord's workings, you must hear Andrew's tale.'

Andrew also is a coloured. However, while he looks very coloured, his sister looks white. They were once together in Pietersburg, where, as Andrew put it, 'baaskap' ('boss-ship') is very strong.

'We were going to the station where she was to get on the train to go to Johannesburg. I was carrying her bags but walked behind her to try and look like her servant.'

As Andrew and his sister got into the train to head for her compartment, the white conductor informed Andrew that coloureds were not allowed in this section of the train.

'But he's my servant,' protested his sister. 'He's taking my bags to my compartment.'

'You see,' explained Andrew, 'we wanted to get to the compartment so we could say goodbye properly. But the conductor wouldn't have it.

'There was a tense silence,' reflected Andrew looking back over many years. 'She was so scared I would get angry and blow everything up for her. But I didn't expose her. It was awful. I just looked at my sister. We couldn't say anything. We couldn't say goodbye. We just had to look.

'Then as she turned away from me, I left the train without a word, and we have never seen each other since. Nor ever corresponded. I don't know where she is.'

Apparently this whole episode finished off Andrew's sister. She left South Africa, got married somewhere in Spain, and is now a wealthy 'Spanish' lady who doesn't know whether her lost and secret South African family are dead or alive.

'For years I felt so scarred by all of this and embittered towards the system,' confessed Andrew. 'One day a white child called me a bushman and I retaliated: "If it wasn't for your fathers and the black women I wouldn't be here."

'The child's mother was so embarrassed. But my feelings had to come out. But in the end I realised that carrying all this bitterness around wasn't going to benefit me at all. So I tried to control it myself.

'I also knew there was something lacking in my life. So I began to seek for the Lord. When I came to know him, I knew this was what I needed. I lost the chip on my shoulder and found I was able to love whites, blacks and everybody with the love of God.'

Annas' story

But what if you're a coloured who doesn't look white or coloured or Indian? What if you look African?

Our family was on our regular annual holiday in the Eastern Cape. (We are among the lucky ones for whom such things are possible.) One day an African lad turned up and asked if he could wash my car. His name was Annas. His face was unusually striking – full of character, with sensitive features and sparkling eyes that exploded into vibrant twinkles when he laughed. I hadn't seen such a lively fourteen year old in a long while.

So he washed my car and earned a little money. He was

saving, he said, for school books. He was hoping to get into the local township school now that he could no longer keep going to the farm school where his mother had worked.

But he had a problem. In excellent English he told me that while he looked African in every way and his mother was Xhosa, he was actually coloured and his surname was Pelzer. His coloured father was who knows where, and his Xhosa mother lived nearby on a farm. Any birth documentation or whatever on Annas was long since lost.

When he went to the local Coloured Affairs Department, gave his name and asked for fresh documents so he could get on with his schooling in a coloured school, they said they couldn't help him because he looked African. He must go to Bantu Affairs. Bantu Affairs said he was not part of their Department if his name was Pelzer. He must go back to Coloured Affairs.

Each year over the next few years, as I came to Kenton-on-Sea for my holiday, young Annas would turn up with his ongoing tale of woe about being shunted about in the desperate no-man's land between these two Government departments. And still he was not given permission to enter any school. Though helped by a wonderful godly volunteer social-worker from Kenton's Anglican Church, Mrs Jo Gardiner, Annas could not break out of this downward spiral. Each year he look more dejected and dissolute, and I started to hear how he was a 'ne'er do well' and a trouble-maker round the area, and that the police had their eyes on him.

Finally, at long last, in March 1978 Annas was classified as a black. Pathetically this involved abandoning his real surname (after all no African could have the Afrikaans surname Pelzer) and taking his mother's Xhosa surname. Delighted to have his status finally resolved, and hungry to get on with his education, Annas galloped excitely to the school in the local Kenton township – in fact called Kenton Emergency Camp (which incredibly it's been since before 1965!).

His excitement was short lived. The school authorities told him that now, in March 1978, he was too old to enter the Kenton 'Emergency Camp' school. Annas had been seeking entry since early 1975. The three years drifting in no-man's land had cost him dearly.

When I last saw Annas he told me he had finally given up the school idea and, though without a pass, was going to end his odd-jobbing for holiday-makers and go to Port Elizabeth or somewhere to seek work in the grey and gruesome shadows of cheap migrant labour.

In fact, as I later found out, Annas succeeded in the end in finding his so-called 'coloured' father, who was a worker on the railways. Father Pelzer succeeded in helping Annas get a job on the railways, but could not let on that this was his son.

Then something went wrong. Annas packed up the railways and headed back to Port Elizabeth and more job-hunting amidst a crisis of unemployment.

I don't know what's become of him, but it wouldn't surprise me if sooner or later he had fallen foul of the law. For at the end of his wait for the Kenton 'Emergency Camp' school, he was beginning to get into mischief.

There is another possibility though. Perhaps all that obvious but frustrated, angry and now almost delinquent intelligence would find an outlet somewhere quite different, like Lusaka, or one of the other places where many angry and militant young South African blacks go for guerrilla training.

So here we are, with all the Siphos in detention, all the van Rensburgs in tragic family mix-ups and all the Annas Pelzers in a no-man's land, swirling downwards from human potential to political peril. To be sure, in South Africa there *are* daily victims on the Jericho Road.

11   Black Rights and White Wrongs (The black struggle for human rights)

Our responsibility is also to help white people realize their privilege is at the expense of blacks.

Frank Chikane

And pity never ceases to be shown
To him who makes the people's wrongs his own.

John Dryden

You shall not wrong one another, but you shall fear your God; for I am the Lord your God.

Leviticus 25:17, RSV

Of course my friend Annas in his no-man's land was not just a victim of Race Classification and the Population Registration Act (1950), but of the whole battery of racist legislation going back over at the least the previous eighty years prior to that wretched law.

While modern Afrikaner Nationalists may have a lot to answer for since 1948, they are most certainly not wholly responsible for the racist framework they inherited and then developed.

BLACK LAND RIGHTS

Take for example the land issue, and its relationship to farming, residential, work and even voting rights.

In every society land is of vital importance, and throughout history, land ownership and acquisition have led to struggle, contention and even war. This has often set up a tragic cycle of attack and reprisal, invasion and occupation, exploitation and resistance, oppression and rebellion.

Europe was no exception, though with its long-standing knowledge of the gospel of love it should have known better. Thus when Western Europe rose in the eighteenth and nineteenth centuries to world supremacy, it capitulated to its acquisitive land appetites and colonised large areas of the world. And of course modern South Africa as we know it has its origins in this epic though questionable adventure.

Inevitably, therefore, as white (Afrikaner and British) expansion took place in the 1800s, the African population was compressed more and more into so-called 'reserves' or else into renting farming land from whites – and generally farming it remarkably well – and this often in spite of so-called 'anti-squatter' legislation (*e.g.* the Location Acts of 1869, 1876, 1884, all British in genesis) which sought to restrict this practice.

Leon Louw and Frances Kendall rightly make much of how successfully blacks farmed their 'reserve' and 'rented' land in the second half of the nineteenth century.

Thus for example in the Eastern Cape in 1865, following an agricultural exhibition, a Wesleyan missionary told the Commission for Native Affairs: 'Even this year (after the drought) I think their [the blacks'] exhibition far surpassed that of the Europeans. It was a universal remark in the district that the Fingo exhibition far excelled that of the Europeans both as to number and quality of the articles exhibited.'[1]

Likewise a Cape statistician at the time could note: 'Taking everything into consideration, the native district of Peddie surpasses the European district of Albany in its productive powers.'[2]

In fact in the 1870s the purchasing power of blacks in the Eastern Cape exceeded £400 000 (R 8 million) a year, and their exports 'were many and varied'.[3] 'They lived in brick houses (built by Europeans) and stocked them with furniture, crockery, cutlery, stationery and so on. They sent their children to multiracial boarding schools and employed labourers and leased portions of their land.'[4]

In 1893 a white Eastern Cape farmer from Alice told the Cape Labour Commission that 'blacks seem to be able to raise sheep here, the Europeans not', while in Port Alfred (the town from which my old friend Annas got shunted about), another white farmer complained: 'Europeans cannot compete with natives.'[5] By 1890, according to Kendall and Louw, 'there were between one and two thousand of these affluent black commercial farmers. Now, one hundred years later, you will have difficulty finding even one.'[6]

It is extraordinary that in a farming area where blacks once competed favourably with immigrant farmers from Europe and Britain, and once dazzled whites with their agricultural skills, we now have a situation of black poverty, malnutrition and economic stagnation, where black peasants are viewed by whites as bad farmers and poor entrepreneurs.

Louw and Kendall ask the obvious question and then provide the shameful answer: What went wrong? Why did blacks do so well in the Eastern Cape and indeed throughout South Africa, in the nineteenth century and fail so badly in the twentieth century?

Have blacks regressed over the past hundred years? Have agricultural and climatic conditions deteriorated?

No – the answer lies in changes which occurred in the blacks' economic and political conditions. Until the last two decades of the nineteenth century, blacks enjoyed a considerable degree of economic freedom; in this century they have been allowed almost none. How did this come about?

The truth was that white farmers felt threatened by blacks. Not only were the blacks better farmers but they were also competing with white farmers for land. Moreover, they were self-sufficient and hence not available to work on white farms or in industry – particularly in the Transvaal gold mines where their labour was badly needed. As a result a series of laws was passed which robbed blacks of almost all economic freedom. The specific and stated purpose of these laws was to prevent blacks from competing with whites and to force them into the workforce.[7]

The important thing to grasp from such a statement is that there was a heyday for black South Africans in the second half of the last century, when 'for a few short decades they were allowed to experience a relatively free market, unfettered land ownership, modern technology, equality at law, reasonable freedom of movement and unrestricted upward mobility for the enterprising. They responded magnificently.'[8]

However, such a heyday was not to last; several major Land Acts of the twentieth century added to black pain and protest.

The Native Land Acts (1913 and 1936)

The first of these was the notorious Native Land Act of 1913 which, though not applying to the Cape, meant that Africans could own only seven per cent of the land, thus preventing them owning land in ninety-three per cent of the country. This formal dispossession was something many leading blacks, such as Sol Plaatje, who was in the Mafeking siege at the same time as my grandmother, had anticipated and warned about.

In the Foreword to the new edition of *The Diary of Sol T Plaatje*, the Editor writes:

> The Natives' Land Act, no 27, of 1913 was the first enactment after the establishment of the union that posed a threat to African rights. A long and complicated piece of legislation, it provided, in essence, for the creation of 'scheduled native areas' in which Africans could own land. Outside these areas Africans were specifically barred from the future purchase or hire of land from anyone other than an African; within them Africans could not sell to non-Africans.[9]

Plaatje's perceptive analysis of events leading up to the passing of the Act does not obscure his central, cogently stated point: 'Awakening on Friday morning, June 20, 1913, the South African Native found himself, not actually a slave, but a pariah in the land of his birth.'[10]

The SANNC (South African National Native Congress – later to be called the ANC – African National Congress), which had just been formed the previous year (1912), sent two protesting deputations to the young South African Government and one to the British Government. The South African

Government declined to budge; the British said they could not intervene.

Finally, much later, came the famous Native Trust and Land Act of 1936, which this time *did* apply to the Cape. It provided for the increase of the area of so-called 'Native reserves' to *thirteen per cent* of the country!

On top of this there were two other major handicapping laws for blacks to cope with. The first was the Native (Urban Areas) Act of 1923, which by influx control restricted African ownership and residence in the cities. It has been amended seven times and consolidated once, and has been described as 'one of the most complex pieces of legislation ever devised anywhere'.[11]

The Apprenticeship Act (1944)

The second handicapping law was the Apprenticeship Act of 1944, which ensured that the standards required for acceptance into an apprenticeship were such that no black would qualify. This Act prevented blacks from entering over a hundred trades, and was so effective that by 1974, according to the Minister of Statistics, J J Loots, there were, for example, '19 259 white, 331 coloured and 426 Indian motor mechanics – but not one black'.[12]

The Group Areas Act (1950)

In the light of all this, it should not surprise anyone that blacks exploded in infuriated anguish and protest when, after the Group Areas Act of 1950, which tightened all this up even more, the unbelievable process of forced removals got under way.

Now, even from those places where black people had found solace and settled, sometimes for over a hundred years, they were to be forcibly removed to conform to Dr Verwoerd's visionary scheme of grand apartheid.

Voting rights

And what could they do about it? After all, they were voteless, and had been so from the Peace of Vereeniging (1901) onwards, with Britain's Alfred Lord Milner and his Government conniving not only in a segregationist form of life for South Africa but also in blacks remaining voteless after Union in 1910.

Not surprisingly, with each province being allowed by Britain to bring its own franchise arrangements into the Union, political power was entrenched in white hands.

In the more liberal Cape, 'Africans continued to enjoy the parliamentary vote but not the right to stand for parliament; elsewhere they were voteless.'[13]

All that blacks could do was protest, try to organise in political groupings, strike from time to time, riot occasionally, and keep appealing to the white man's conscience – and especially to his Christian conscience. But it was all to little avail.

THE BLACK TRAUMA OF FORCED REMOVALS

When removals really got under way, the pain reached breaking point. Explosions, both metaphorical and then literal, were around the corner.

Finally, when the black masses were faced not only with deaf ears but with the guns of Sharpeville, things took a new turn. And the ANC, after a *fifty-year* commitment to negotiation and nonviolence, finally turned to armed struggle.

One does not condone such measures – far from it – but one can scarcely fail to understand. Again, as I've noted before when discussing other aspects of the South African scene, personal encounters with those involved brought home to me the full enormity of the situation.

I always knew that forced removals were a dreadful thing, and I've been in my fair share of homelands and black townships, but somehow it all really got to me when my friend Peter Kerchoff took me to Compensation Farm in July 1981.

Peter picked me up from home after breakfast, and we set off out towards the majestic Drakensburg mountains ('mountains of the Dragon'). The scenery of Natal was a delight to the senses – gentle undulating hills, lush greenery, beautiful fields, streams everywhere, and finally all mounting in climax towards the craggy grandeur of the Drakensburg.

It was good, too, to be challenged by the social passion and compassion of Peter and his organisation, the Pietermaritzburg Agency for Christian Social Awareness, or PACSA. PACSA faithfully, bravely and relentlessly uncovers the facts on South African life, publishes them in regular fact sheets, and presents them challengingly to white Christians. And Compensation was one of those areas to be uncovered. I felt privileged to be getting some new insights.

'Black spots'

Compensation Farm was born from two sets of removals. The first was in December 1978 from a place inauspiciously labelled 'The Swamp', in the Peversey area of the Natal Midlands; the second was in July 1981 from a place called Kwa-Pitela, in the Sani Pass area of the Drakensburg.

Both of these had been labelled 'black spots' – a grim image, except that they were actually beautiful spots, but had blacks living on them. In that sense, yes, and in that sense only, were they black.

Though some places may indeed fairly be labelled black in the pejorative sense, most in fact are simply places where black South Africans live, often with freehold rights, in areas now designated 'white' by the South African authorities.

In Natal, beautiful Natal, there were back in 1963, by government conclusion, some 250 'black spots'. Estimates made in 1958 indicated that the clearance of these 'black spots' would involve the uprooting of 375 000 landowners and tenants, the destruction of 85 000 homes, 680 churches, 350 shops and 350 schools. By the end of 1967, about 77 000 people from a hundred black spots in Natal had been removed.[14]

Most South African 'black spots' were in fact in existence

even prior to Union in 1910. 'Some are farms owned by individuals; some are "mixed" suburbs of rural towns; some are country areas bought initially by a tribe or a group of individuals, where families live on small freehold plots.'[15] This is the distinctive thing about them. They are places of freehold ownership, generally where blacks own their land legally, in the belief that they should have indefinite security of tenure.

'The Swamp'

This was the case with The Swamp, which certainly did not look like any swamp to me as Peter and I drove past it.

In any event, swamp or no swamp, it was purchased in good faith by the late Charles Mndaweni, and completely paid off by 17 June 1898. It was seemingly happily lived on by his descendants and others till December 1978, a period of exactly eighty years. Then the hundred families were moved.

Old Mndaweni's title deed said: 'To hold the same unto the said Charles Mndaweni, his heirs, executors, administrators, or assigns with full power, to possess the same in perpetuity . . .'

However, on 3 April 1970 The Swamp was expropriated in terms of Section 13 of the Development Trust and Land Act (1936) and the Expropriation Act (1965), because it was a 'black spot'.

'Compensation Farm'

When we arrived at Compensation Farm – having passed en route the devastated village of Kwapitela – we were confronted by the pitiful spectacle of a mass of ordered little plots (each with a metal toilet and a tent on it) set into an uninviting and exposed hillside. (In fairness, a quite sturdy Community Hall and some classrooms had also been built.)

The Government called Compensation Farm 'Goed Verwagtig' ('Good Expectations'), but the blacks saw it differently, calling it 'kwa-Vula Mehlo' ('the place which opens the eyes', *i.e.* 'the Eye-opener').

During our visit I certainly had my eyes opened. We spent the afternoon there, talking to young people, women and old men. We also met several very sick people, and at least one dying person with whom we shared Christ and prayed. Adult men were conspicuous by their absence as they were now either working in neighbouring towns or seeking work. Previously, at Kwapitela, they had had employment on neighbouring white farms.

The people of Kwapitela had been happy to move here, so the official line ran, but I for one, unless all my powers of discernment have been overtaken by self-deception or chronic gullibility, was fully satisfied by what I saw and heard that day that the people had *not* wanted to move. Official assurances to the contrary left me cold.

I returned home truly sick at heart and heavy in spirit. Once again the system's fruit I saw was not figs or grapes. Again it was brambles all the way. More dangerous still, the brambles were hidden to most whites. Apartheid tends to put many of its victims out of sight. This helps the official media to tell us convincingly that there really are figs and grapes over there behind the hill.

Removals – for and against

By 1987 a staggering three and a half to four million South African blacks had suffered the resettlement experience of the people of The Swamp and Kwapitela, according to the National Committee Against Removals. They estimate that a further 2.2 million blacks are under threat.[16]

For

The Government case for removals is simply put. First of all, it fits the macro-scheme of grand apartheid and is therefore ideologically in line with the country's political philosophy.

Second, it is supposed to remove people from slums and

poverty – the so-called 'black spots', and resettle them in places of greater physical comfort and opportunity. No doubt on occasion this has been the case.

Third, as one Government Minister put it, 'The Bantu people like being moved . . . [They] like the places where they are being resettled.'[17] And of course there has been for a long time the strange idealism to which Alan Paton once referred. Said one official: 'Equity and reasonableness are the very touchstones of the white operation of the removal of black spots. No-one is forcibly removed.'[18]

Against

However, whatever the occasional pluses of these removals, the case against them is overwhelming.

Who wants to move?

The overwhelming evidence is that the people affected have *not* wanted to be moved. If there are any who have, I have not met them in twenty-five years, nor do I know anyone else who has. In fact the contrary is the case, and more often than not heavy coercion, if not force, has been required.

More honest was one Deputy Minister who, when asked in Parliament by a Conservative Party MP why physical resettlement of blacks was not keeping pace with land purchases, answered that the 'political climate' was 'opposed to resettlements', and moreover 'the Government was having tremendous problems in persuading people to move'.[19]

A violation of dignity

The manner in which removals have been carried out has more often than not been totally unacceptable, sometimes happening in mid-winter with trucks and bulldozers moving in during the small hours of the morning. This was the case, for example, with the removals from Nyanga in the Cape in 1981 when a thousand squatters were bundled so unceremoniously into buses back to the Transkei that mothers and children even became separated in the process.

The *Rand Daily Mail* went on to note that:

Johannesburg's Chief Rabbi, Mr B M Casper, making a rare entry into a national issue during his Sabbath sermon last night at the Great Synagogue in Wolmarans Street, Joubert Park, attacked the deportations and called on the Government to let justice and compassion prevail. 'The forcible removal of home-less squatters from their pitiful, miserable shacks, in the midst of winter, must surely touch even the most heartless of men. Every humanitarian instinct cries out against it,' he said.[20]

Quite so, these removals violate elementary human com-passion. It is not even every Christian instinct which cries out, but every human instinct. The thing defies the humanitarian principle of ordinary compassion.

Surely not even the most hardened Government ideologue can deny the personal suffering involved in being summarily and forcibly removed or ejected from one's place, even one's poor place, of domicile.

The radical outcome

As might be imagined, the radicalising effects of this sort of thing are considerable. I met one black intellectual who was becoming committed to armed struggle and revolutionary violence. As he told me his story it became painfully clear to me that his entire life over at least two and a half decades had been massively radicalised by the experience as a youth of being forcibly moved from his home in the Cape Flats. He said it was done in winter, in the small hours of the morning. 'What's more,' he said, 'I literally watched scores of babies getting pneumonia and then dying in subsequent days. Officials saw it as unfortunate. I saw it as murder.'

From that day to this he has been a passionate and relent-less opponent of the system. But it was the system which took the innocent youth of yesterday and made him the uncom-promising foe of today. So if he ends up taking part in violent acts of sabotage, where should the blame rightly be located?

An acceptable cost?
Then of course there is the prohibitive cost of it all, not just
in human terms but also in lost opportunities to develop
economically.

Forced removals are not only economic madness for whites
in terms of the tax costs involved, but they are productive of
yet more poverty for blacks. By January 1984 the cost to the
Government of land purchase for homeland consolidation
was R804 million.

Beyond that, the cost to blacks themselves in terms of
maintaining such businesses as they have had has been
adversely affected – even for good business entrepreneurs
such as the Indians. Thus, for example, an Indian member of
the President's Council, Mr M Rajab, said that

> the Group Areas Act had directly affected roughly 65% of the
> country's Indian traders and had indirectly touched every Indian
> business in South Africa. By 1978 25% of these businessmen had
> been moved from white CBDs (Central Business Districts) to
> Indian townships, while 40% had been told that they would have
> to move. As a result of a 'cascade' of discriminatory laws affecting
> Indians in business, the number of Indian traders had declined by
> 4% between 1960 and 1980 while the number of white-owned
> retail and wholesale outlets had increased by 50%.[21]

More serious than all of this, and far more damning too, is
the escalating spiral of dire poverty and deprivation into
which all this has placed black people, Africans particularly.

THE POVERTY/IGNORANCE SPIRAL

The thing that is hard for whites to understand, whether in
South Africa, the UK, Australia or the USA, is that the black
person is often trapped in a poverty spiral. In South Africa
this poverty cycle is particularly desperate, with one calamitous consequence following almost inevitably upon another.

Pictorially presented, it looks like this:[22]

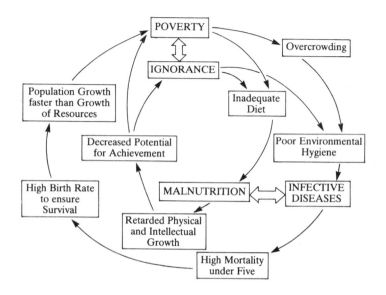

Cycle one

First of all, economic and political exploitation beget poverty. This undeniable but tragic fact of South African life goes on to spawn over-crowding, which leads to poor hygienic habits, which in turn generate disease and high infant mortality. All this breeds low morale and inadequate social care, which in their turn spawn a higher, not a lower, birth-rate.

All the economically advanced countries of the world have a low or even static rate of population increase. The poor countries, by contrast, are exploding. So poverty breeds, and it breeds prolifically. Conversely, as is often said, if you look after the quality of people's lives, the quantity will look after itself.

For South Africa this means a population of forty-five million by the end of the century, of which blacks will contribute eighty per cent of the increase and whites thirteen per cent. Eight out of ten children born in the next sixteen years will be black!

The first cycle of the spiral completes itself as population growth exceeds the growth or affordability of healthy food resources, leading to even more poverty.

Cycle two

As population growth exceeds food resources, leading to more poverty, more and more black people in general, and children in particular, suffer from an inadequate diet. This in turn degenerates into malnutrition, with some three to four black children in South Africa dying every hour, according to Professor Athe Moosa, head of the Department of Paediatrics at the University of Natal. This results in retarded physical and intellectual growth, then in a decreased potential for academic and other achievement, and finally in yet more ignorance, which feeds both things such as poor hygiene (in the outer-spiral) as well as poor work performance or even unemployment (in the inner-spiral).

So the cycles go on, until the final denouement of a socio-political explosion, when the victims say enough is enough. When that moment comes, every human instinct pushes people, rightly or wrongly, naively or realistically, to perceive the root of the problem in unjust political structures.

And of such stuff are revolutions made. Nor is it any use protesting that it's more complicated than that and pointing out that many other African countries suffer poverty and disease and population explosion. Black South Africans resist invidious comparisons with Sierra Leone or Upper Volta, which do not happen to be their countries of domicile. South Africa happens to be their country and their place of dwelling, heritage and preoccupation. Their cries are about life *here* rather than about less avoidable and worse misfortunes elsewhere. So while anxious 'comfortable' whites point out other Third World disaster areas, black South African ears, almost deafened by their own ineffectual cries of political protest over the last ninety years, are turned away and retune to the sounds of another, more distant – and for whites more dangerous – drum, whose name is revolution.

The hard fact is that blacks know (as all whites should also realise) that, unlike other Third World nations, South Africa has alongside its own Third World components a First World economic and political infrastructure which could substantially eliminate the discrepancies, severely retard the downward black spiral and, with political justice, mutual trust and the combined efforts of all in a non-racial democracy, build a stunning nation to bless and inspire the world.

The first step in this process requires us to understand where we have gone wrong, and how we can get it right. This is the first responsibility of all South Africans, but most especially the nation's Christians.

There is a definite link, which must now be explored, between structural injustice, theological error and black anguish. As Desmond Tutu has said: 'When Moralists are uncertain about the moral quality of an act or policy, they will often seek to find out what the consequences of such an act or policy are. If these are evil, then the probability is that the original act or policy itself is evil.'[23]

The development by the church of an understanding of the theological link between South African structural injustice and black pain is now, in the light of all that we have discussed so far, a pressing responsibility which we must shoulder.

To that we now turn.

Part Five

IF MY PEOPLE . . .
(The church's responsibility)

12 Understanding
(The church's responsibility for spiritual comprehension)

Let him who glories glory in this, that he understands and
knows me, that I am the Lord who practises steadfast love,
justice, and righteousness in the earth; for in these things I
delight, says the Lord.

Jeremiah 9:24, RSV

Do not be like the horse or the mule,
Which have no understanding . . .

Psalm 32:9

God be in my head and in my understanding.

Sarum Missal

After leaving school, and then shortly after leaving university, I had a couple of very happy spells as a prep-school
master.

One of my most common questions in class was, 'Now,
boys, do you understand that?' This alternated with regular
juvenile laments over French irregular verbs or Latin past
participles: 'Please, Sir, I don't understand' they would wail.

But never was my delight greater than when a stare as
vacant and expressionless as the inside of a hub-cap gave way
to an illumined sparkle of smiling comprehension once I'd
tried to explain: 'Oh, thanks, Sir, *now* I understand.' That
always made my day!

200 THE PASSING SUMMER

UNDERSTANDING IS CRUCIAL

Understanding why things are or how things work, or why we've made mistakes or where we must change course, is a crucial part of both personal and corporate life.

If understanding fails, then meaningful and right action is torpedoed, effective turning jeopardised, and corrective measures (if we've been wrong) sabotaged.

It's not surprising, therefore, that the wisdom of the ages can affirm in the Arab proverb, 'Understanding is the wealth of wealth.' More significantly, the Bible everywhere underlines the importance of understanding.

Thus God's word to Israel through Moses carried this lament: 'they are a nation void of counsel, and there is no understanding in them' (Deut 32:28, RSV). The writer of Proverbs can exhort: 'get wisdom: and with all thy getting get understanding' (Prov 4:7, AV). His harsh judgement on the 'fool' is that he 'takes no pleasure in understanding' (Prov 18:2, RSV). The Old Testament prophet Hosea applies the principle nationally: 'a people without understanding shall come to ruin' (Hos 4:14, RSV). Faulty presuppositions in the life of a nation will bring it to the dust.

Our Lord, too, was endlessly concerned as to whether people understood what he was saying. 'Have you understood all this?' he asked the disciples (Matt 13:51, RSV). A little later he said to Peter, 'Are you also still without understanding?' (Matt 15:16, RSV).

He told the scribes that the first commandment involved loving the Lord their God not only with all their hearts and souls but with all their minds (Mark 12:30). One scribe responded, saying he grasped by this that Jesus meant God was to be loved 'with all the understanding' (Mark 12:33, RSV). Jesus said he was right.

All this brings me to the basic conclusion that the church's first responsibility anywhere and at any time is *understanding*. Without this we remain defective in worship, in word, in work, in deed, in evangelism, in renewal, in prophetic witness, in societal concern, and in everything else. Not understanding God, not understanding his Christ, not understanding his word and not understanding our calling, character or context, we flounder around destructively, like blind men in a dark room.

Something like this has happened in South Africa.

In Part 3 we discussed how the grand scheme of apartheid, not without some sincere and good intentions on the part of its original exponents, was put in place. However, the account in Part 4 of its consequences and fruit in terms of massive black pain and protest must alert us to the self-evident fact that something terrible has gone wrong.

What has gone wrong, and how to begin getting it right, can become evident only as we reach certain key and basic understandings. But our understanding must be true to the Bible as our final authority in the things of God. So it was that a major agenda of Jesus with his disciples after his resurrection was to 'open their minds to understand the scriptures' (Luke 24:45, RSV).

We must further understand that the scriptures apply to all of life, not just to certain safe and select little compartments.

All this being so, each believer can well afford to pray with a saint of yesteryear: 'God be in my head and in my understanding.'

UNDERSTANDING THE CREATOR'S CHARACTER

As a fellow struggler myself in all of this, one major step forward in my own understanding came in 1969, when our African Enterprise Team was invited by the combined churches of Nairobi, Kenya, to conduct a city-wide evangelistic campaign there.

That was the first time I began to grasp that our creator God wanted to be understood in his character. It came about through the teaching of the great missionary statesman E Stanley Jones, who had spent most of his life in India, and who joined our team for that outreach.

The big thing he had to say was that the universe and all creation and everything in it is God's. More than that, it is Christ's. It came forth from his character, was stamped with his mind, impregnated with his laws, and can be managed only in his way. Failure to understand this, said Stanley Jones, would mean getting everything wrong all down the line, whether for individuals, for the church or for society as a whole.

All this was in the Bible, I knew, but somehow it had remained till then an academic truth for me. In Nairobi in 1969 I came to understand it, at least in measure. And since then it has not been a truth which *I* have held, but one which has held *me*. There are many facets to it, with huge implications for both our personal and our societal life and witness.

What sort of God?

The sixty-four thousand dollar question, determining all else, is this: What sort of God is God? What is he like, this God who has put us and everything together? And how does his character affect our witness?

One of the clearest and most dramatic pointers to an answer comes in the book of Jeremiah.

Speaking through the prophet, God urges his people to get their priorities, values and understandings right:

> Thus says the Lord: 'Let not the wise man glory in his wisdom, let not the mighty man glory in his might, let not the rich man glory in his riches; but let him who glories glory in this, that he understands and knows me, that I am the Lord who practises steadfast love, justice, and righteousness *in the earth*; for in these things I delight, says the Lord.' (Jer 9:23–24, RSV)

This is a breathtaking affirmation. First of all it tells us what God is like. He is a God of unswerving love, justice and righteousness. That is his fundamental character.

Second, this passage says that knowing this sort of God personally is the *summum bonum* of life, the highest good, the pearl of great price, the thing of ultimate, final and eternal importance. A person can have everything else life has to offer – intellect, wisdom, political power, influence, riches and everything money can buy, but if he or she misses this, they have missed everything. For this is really what life is all about. St Paul's perspective was right when he said that he counted everything 'as refuse' in order that he might 'gain Christ and . . . *know* him and the power of his resurrection' (Phil 3:8–10, RSV).

When I came to know Christ as a young undergraduate, I was fully persuaded that this was the ultimate blessing of life, and that telling others of him in witness and evangelism was the highest of all privileges and the greatest of all responsibilities.

Robert Benson, a theologian, got the gist of Jeremiah when he said: 'There is but one thing in the world really worth pursuing, and that is the knowledge of God.'

Third, says the Lord through the prophet, part of that ultimate knowledge of God is *understanding* him and his true character. Of course, lots of people know him, but they seemingly fail to understand certain basics about him, even as someone may know a friend but not understand him too well. Of course we can never understand God exhaustively, but we must understand certain fundamental truths about him.

Central to these is the truth that he is not just the possessor of these attributes of love, justice and righteousness, but that he *practises* them. He works them out in deeds. That's the kind of God he is. That's his character. He is an active, working, functioning God, caught up in certain divine deeds and praxis.

Fourth, our God astonishingly lets us in on the arena where he does all this: *on earth*. His activities of love, justice and righteousness are not just in heaven, but on earth. This ties in with Jesus' instruction to pray for the kingdom to come and his will to be done on earth (Matt 6:10), and fits in with the psalmist and St Paul's reminder that '*The earth* is the Lord's' (Ps 24:1; 1 Cor 10:26).

So God practises works of love, justice and righteousness on earth. That's the special arena of his activity, says Jeremiah.

Finally, says the Lord in our passage, these are the things in which he delights (Jer 9:24), and he therefore wants to see them displayed in his people too. The prophet Micah makes it unmistakably plain. 'He has showed you, O man, what is good; and what does the Lord require of you but to do justice, and to love kindness, and to walk humbly with your God?'

(Mic 6:8, RSV). Obedience to this creates stability, balance and harmony in all human relationships. The converse is also true, that when among his people 'justice is turned back, and righteousness stands afar off [and] truth has fallen in the public squares' (Isa 59:14, RSV), then it displeases him (Isa 59:15) and he cannot delight in his people. Moreover, while they are 'heaping oppression upon oppression, and deceit upon deceit' (Jer 9:6, RSV) – all convincing evidence that they do not understand the character of God – then they show themselves to be religious only outwardly, but not inwardly.

So then, the people of God do not show a concern for justice and execute it merely because the Bible says they must, but because the very character of the active God they worship requires it. So when the Lord says 'seek justice' and 'correct oppression' (Isa 1:17, RSV), it is because 'just and right is he' (Deut 32:4, RSV) in his character.

Likewise, when we understand that love and mercy and a special care for the weak, powerless, needy or oppressed are integral to his character (*e.g.* Matt 25:39, 45; Isa 1:17; Lev 19:13; Ps 72:1–4; 1 John 3:17; Jas 1:27), then we will take these concerns upon our own hearts and show special concern for those least able to fend for themselves and protect their own interests.

And all this must be worked out *on earth* – because that is where God, our model, is working it out. Likewise, if he shows no discrimination but is impartial in his love for every human, then we cannot be party to anything discriminatory, and will resist it with all our hearts.

If, then, we want to know the first place where apartheid and all racial discrimination has gone wrong, it lies in a violation of the character of God which we have failed to understand. Therefore, when South African Christians, or any others for that matter, distance themselves from a deep concern for justice and acts of mercy they reveal a serious failure to understand the character of our creator God. Jesus punches this point home to back the Old Testament with the New: 'Woe to you, scribes and Pharisees, hypocrites! for you tithe . . . [but] have neglected the weightier matters of the law, justice and mercy and faith' (Matt 23:23, RSV). Who can fail to feel the sting? We *all* stand guilty. Lord, have mercy.

UNDERSTANDING OUR DIVINE CREATION

Once again we must go back to the creation story for the vital understanding that we humans are not an accident in a lonely solar system, resulting from the random workings in a godless universe of impersonal energy plus time plus chance. No, we must understand that we are divinely and purposefully created – made man and woman by God and in his image. This makes us hugely valuable and endowed, as the US Constitution rightly affirms, with certain 'inalienable rights'.

These we grasp in new measure when we are brave enough to look all the way back to creation. Especially is this true for South Africans. This is the new spiritual Great Trek on which we must embark: not forwards to some New Republic, but backwards to the Garden of Eden.

Comments John Stott:

> The origin of human rights is creation. Man has never 'acquired' them. Nor has any government or other authority conferred them. Man has had them from the beginning. He received them with his life from the hand of his Maker. They are inherent in his creation. They have been bestowed on him by his Creator.
>
> Put in another way, human rights are the rights of human beings, and the nature of human rights depends on the nature of the human beings, whose rights they are . . . Fundamental, therefore, to human rights is the question what it means to be human.[1]

There are at least two major things the scriptures say about how God has created us and what it means to be human.

Dignity and worth

First of all, God's creation of man gives him dignity and worth.

A classroom of children was asked to 'Name one of the most important things to happen in the last hundred years.' One little enthusiast with a tousled mop of red hair answered sincerely: 'Me!' He was right. Being created by God in his image, he is immensely important and valuable, and is endowed with a dignity and value which are not to be violated, refused or withdrawn, for they are God-given. R C Sproul, an American theologian, captures this beautifully:

> It is because God has assigned worth to man and woman that human dignity is established. It is because mankind bears the image of God that he enjoys such an exalted rank in the nature of things. From his creation to his redemption, man's dignity is preserved. His origin is significant – his destiny is significant – he is significant.[2]

Though small in size, human beings have immense significance and value given them by God. And the resulting rights, paradoxically, come by God's grace alone, as does his salvation. All is a gracious gift from God. So in one sense one has no right to human rights apart from God. It is crucial that we grasp this, because if people's rights were of their own making or of the making of other humans, they could just as easily remove them. But coming as they do as a divine gift within the creation package, their inalienability is totally secure (see Appendix 4).

Not that the Bible uses the term 'human rights' to describe what is due to our little tousled friend in the classroom, but the motivation for the development of the term was certainly deeply Judaeo-Christian.[3] Thus René Cassin, the major author of the Universal Declaration of Human Rights, could affirm that the major root of the Declaration was the ten commandments.[4] The ethicist Stephen Mott can insist for his part that human rights are a 'crystallization' of the claim every person has, like that little boy, that he be valued 'as an end' in himself.[5] He is not therefore, for example, to be abused or brutally used as a means for the state to achieve the end of gaining some needed information, as happened to Sipho. This is a violation of value because it is 'using' another man.

The great Jan Hofmeyr was right on target when on 9 September 1938 he cried out in the South African Parliament: 'The issue is simply this. Are we going to allow non-Europeans to be made pawns in the White man's political game? One safeguard goes today, the next will go tomorrow.'[6] At which he resigned from the cabinet. He saw that when you forsake the Bible's view of human value you put yourself on the slippery slope to human rights violations: people become pawns.

Jesus' example

We must also give due note to the fact that although the concept of dignity and value stems first of all from Genesis and creation, it is further backed up by Jesus and the New Testament.

Says Reg Codrington, a South African Baptist leader, 'Jesus valued the individual, especially those society cast out, such as the woman at the well, Zacchaeus and so on.'[7] Yes, indeed, Jesus always saw past shabby external appearances, past the shame of sinful living, past social class, and past economic levels, to the priceless value of one human life. An angry South African politician once said to me, 'I despise you!' And such attitudes to political critics or opponents are not uncommon in South Africa, but Jesus never said to anyone, 'I despise you!'

Least of all could he ever have done it on the basis of skin colour. For that would leave a man more helpless and devastated than anything.

President Julius Nyerere of Tanzania put it this way:

If a man discriminates against you because you have appalling table manners, it is bad – but not that bad, because you may improve your table etiquette, and his discrimination against you will end.

If a man discriminates against you because you are a sloppy dresser, it is bad – but not nearly that bad, because maybe one day you may acquire fancy apparel and his discrimination will certainly come to a welcome end.

But, if a man discriminates against you because you are Black, then you have had it! This kind of discrimination leaves you with no way out. It leaves you with your back pressed hard against the wall, because it is this type of ruthless discrimination that is aimed at the very foundations of your being.[8]

Herein lies the true awfulness of South African racism, that it has caused millions of black people made in the image of God to despise themselves and question their worth and value in the sight of God. Persistence in this will produce, if we are not careful, the first generation of black atheists who have thrown the Book away, tossed God out, and taken to the gun.

Equal before God

The Bible's creation story also confirms that, having worth and value in God's sight, we are all, 'in all that matters most', equal. This is the second major meaning of being human.

Being equal before God, we all have the human right not only to be equally treated by one another, but especially by the state. The state that understands all humans to have been divinely created by God will not discriminate against one to the benefit of another or show partiality to one at the expense of another – as when in South Africa we give the vote which affects the Nation's Central Parliament to a semi-literate white youth of eighteen who can't pass his Junior Certificate exam while denying that same vote to, for example, my black friend Dr Khosa Mgojo, who has a PhD in Greek and Hebrew from Harvard!

When the early Transvaal Republican Constitution and its modern counterparts insisted on 'No equality in Church or State' it was guilty of failing to understand both the biblical doctrine of creation and the totally non-partial posture of Jesus towards all human beings. This posture prompted the Pharisees once to say: 'Teacher, we know you are a man of integrity. You aren't swayed by men, because you pay no attention to who they are' (Mark 12:14). 'That is,' observes John Stott, 'he neither deferred to the rich and powerful, nor despised the poor and weak, but gave equal respect to all, whatever their social status. We must do the same.'[9]

When people fail at this point, says the writer of Proverbs, and indulge, for example by political partiality, in oppressing the poor, they do not just violate the value of the poor person, they 'show contempt for their Maker' (Prov 14:31).

So, to detain thousands of people who disagree with

apartheid, because they feel it violates their humanity, is not just to deny the detainee's human value but also shows contempt for the maker and creator of both detainee and detainer. This is what the Bible in general, and Proverbs in particular is saying.

The consequences of a recovery of a biblical view of humanity

What then are the consequences if we do finally recover, recognise and understand the human dignity, value and equality due to all on the basis of their divine creation?

First of all, we will responsibly contend for the cause of those to whom basic human rights have been denied. This is love's demand – of which we will say more later. That means I must stand up for Sipho or Albert van Rensburg or for poor Annas in his 'no-man's land' between Bantu and Coloured Affairs.

Second, we will work for the development of massive movements of social reform which the rediscovery of human value will spawn. This is not wishful thinking. It is a historical possibility rooted in solid historical precedent.

E M Howse, a recent chronicler of the distinguished 'Clapham Sect' which supported William Wilberforce (1759– 1833) in his labours for the abolition of slavery, observes that from this group's endeavours and from the evangelical revival of which they were a part, 'there appeared in England a series of religious and humanitarian movements which altered the whole course of English history, influenced most of Europe, and affected the life of three other continents'.

Howse then makes the fascinating observation that 'these movements sprang out of a new doctrine of responsibility toward the underprivileged, a doctrine which received its chief impulse from the evangelical emphasis on the *value of the human soul and hence of the individual*'.[10]

In other words, understanding our divine creation and all its implications is not just an airy-fairy Bible idea dangling irrelevantly over South Africa like a frazzled piece of string over a drowning man. Rather it is a critically important truth, which if understood by black and white alike could lead South Africa into similarly significant 'movements' of humanitarian concern which could steer it out of its calamitous cul-de-sac on to the Lord's highway of national salvation.

UNDERSTANDING OUR FALLEN CONDITION

A theological wag, making a play on the American practice of calling Autumn 'the Fall', penned this limerick:

> There once was a young man named Hall,
> Who fell in a spring in the Fall.
> T'would have been a sad thing
> Had he died in the Spring,
> But he didn't, he died in the Fall.

While the fellow won't be made Poet Laureate, his theology wasn't too bad! Because the Bible does say, and says unequivocally, that in man's rebellion against God, as recorded in Genesis 3, he fell from his original place of perfection to a new condition not of complete badness but of seriously spoilt goodness.

So, although there are huge implications, as we've seen, from our glorious dignity and our amazing value as creatures made in the image of God, there are equally consequential implications which flow from an understanding of our fallen condition.

The extent of fallenness

The first thing to say about our sin and human fallenness is that it is universal. 'All have sinned', says St Paul (Rom 3:23) sweepingly, and 'all . . . are under the power of sin' (Rom 3:9, RSV). No one, white or black, rich or poor, high or low, escapes its ravages. There is therefore not much room for optimism in the Bible as to what man, unaided, can achieve.

Derek Crumpton, a prominent South African renewal leader, has said:

Apartheid is in the heart of natural man. It is basic tribal suspicion, enmity, jealousy and greed, plus the desire to dominate and control, for fear of being subject to the control of others. No constitution, no laws, will change that in this country any more than it has in Washington DC. The heart has to be changed. That is an evangelical action, a spiritual process of change and growth, a liberation from natural self-centredness into the new man for Christ and for others. And that, as we know, is a long process.[11]

This brings us to the seriousness of sin.

Sin's seriousness

Sin has, says the Bible, totally corrupted us – body, mind, spirit and will. When John Calvin spoke of 'total depravity' he did not mean that we are at every point as bad as we could be, but that at no point are we as good as we should be. In other words, the effects of sin have affected man totally, throughout his whole disposition.

The heart, seen as the seat of man's inner nature, is thus singled out by Jesus as the place from which flow 'evil thoughts, murder, adultery, sexual immorality, theft, false testimony, slander' (Matt 15:19).

The heart of the problem is indeed the problem of the heart.

The consequences of fallenness

This being so, it is not surprising that the personal, social and political consequences are many and varied.

Simon Maimela, a black theologian at the University of South Africa, puts it eloquently:

The Bible teaches us that humans, though originally good creatures of God, have through the fall become corrupt, twisted, misdirected and are deeply immersed in sin that pervades their lives and work (Gen. 8:21; Ps. 51:5; 58:3; Jn. 3:6; Rom. 5:12–21; 7:7–20). Because of sin humans do not love and serve each other as they should; they love and relate to each other wrongly; and they organise their communities in irrational paths (Gen. 4:8–14; 1 Jn. 4:7–12, 19–21).[12]

This irrational organising of our communities, plus failing to love as we should, plus relating wrongly, has of course another whole set of consequences in the socio-political arena which is the focus of this volume.

Blacks and whites are *both* fallen

The obvious example is the way white South Africans have so irrationally and wrongly organised their society. However, the biblical doctrine of sin and of the universal fallenness of man alerts us to another critically important reality – namely that blacks, too, not only have been and are but will be just as prone to a wrong and sinful ordering of South African society when they move from being under-dogs to top dogs.

Having underlined something of white fallenness, fairness requires that we look at the black side too.

I said earlier that when this whole set of social implications from creation began to come home to me we were in Kenya for a city-wide mission to Nairobi. I was therefore in the land not long since delivered from the ghastly awfulness of Mau Mau atrocities.

When the mission ended, I went up to Uganda, where violent nightly happenings in the street near my lodging place might have alerted me, had I had the foresight, to the imminent advent on the scene of a certain Idi Amin. Milton Obote then 'liberated' Uganda from the brutal Amin. Then, while he was President, at least 200 000 of his tribal enemies were murdered in the Loweru Triangle alone. The bestial aftermath of this I saw later with my own eyes as I travelled through that area – dubbed by one journalist as 'the killing fields of Africa'.

Thus easily, as the Bible would warn us, can today's liberator become tomorrow's oppressor, and today's violent and self-righteous revolutionary become tomorrow's brutal or even more self-righteous defender of the status quo.

It has been my enormous privilege and delight to travel through, and often minister the Christian gospel in, most of Africa's countries. I can truthfully say that I love Africa and Africans, but I have few illusions about black rule or the angelic nature of black hearts, or about the immunity of the black disposition from oppressiveness, selfishness, greed or corruption. How could I, when I have been in and seen some African countries sliding into Marxist takeover, seen others wracked in tribal civil war, seen others tottering in organisational chaos or reeling in economic shambles, and seen still others floundering in massive political confusion or even moral declension?

In the same vein, Professor Ayittey (a Ghanaian Professor of Economics) writes with unusual humility and political honesty in the *Wall Street Journal* and *The Times* (London 1985) in these terms:

> Apartheid is an abomination . . . but if one looks beyond skin colour, similar characteristics also can be found in many black African regimes.
>
> In black Africa, the two classes are not whites and blacks but the elites (the educated class and the military) and the people (the peasants). The elite minority, which controls the government, does not share power with the people. But as in South Africa they disenfranchise the peasant majority.
>
> Some African leaders who advocate majority rule and one-man-one-vote for South Africa do not give their own black people the right to vote. Many have declared themselves president for life. Other black regimes are military dictatorships or farcical 'democracies' . . .
>
> Despite the parallels, world-opinion tends to apply radically different standards of morality to South Africa and black Africa. There are indeed 16 million oppressed blacks in South Africa. But some 400 million people live elsewhere in black Africa, a majority under despotic rule. Why is so little attention given to their plight?[13]

Just as Professor Ayittey spares nothing in his castigation of his own continent, South African whites in general and Afrikaners in particular find naught for their political comfort in black Africa, whose political story thus far offers little reassurance. In fact the reverse. Black Africa and its fallen-ness have made the white task of doing the right and courageous thing harder rather than easier.

Ayittey puts it this way: 'Some of the remaining support for apartheid may be caused by conditions in black Africa itself. When South Africans look across their border they see the same atrocities the black African governments accuse them of committing. Furthermore, these governments have, through misguided policies, reduced their economies to tatters.'[14]

This is tough stuff, hard for blacks or starry-eyed overseas idealists to face. But it is no harder than that which Afrikaners or English-speaking South Africans have to face about them-selves as well. Unless black fallenness is faced with as much realism as white fallenness, and unless blacks and whites each take their own and each other's fallenness seriously, we will all drift off into even more sentimental self-deception and obtuse political pipe-dreaming than already afflicts us.

In other words, we have to free ourselves from either white or black utopianism and face the seriousness not just of personal but also of social sin.

Speaking of our social and political institutions, Professor Stephen Mott writes:

> Our institutions are not just a constraint on sin (a conservative attitude toward institutions); they themselves are full of sin. The structures of social life contain both good and bad. Because of the hold of self-interest we will tend to see only the good in those social forms which favour our interests unless we have a strong theology of sin. Our social life is fallen with us, and no social system is beyond the need of reform or perhaps even of reconstitution.[15]

Grasping this kind of reality should therefore prompt those whites who make ANC renunciation of violence the condition of negotiation to ask themselves how nonviolent their re-sponse would be, were a black government to mete out apartheid treatment and oppression on them as whites. The Boer Rebellion of 1914 provided an instructive clue: Afrikaners took to violent rebellion when they felt unfairly handled.

Likewise, facing personal fallenness might prompt ANC or Pan African Congress front-runners to ask themselves whether on accession to power they would carry Freedom Charter principles into their dealings with Inkatha (Chief Buthelezi's political movement) or Andries Treurnicht. Or would the Freedom Charter also fall prey to the corrupting ravages of political power, in this case in the hands of blacks?

I once asked a high-powered South African black politico whether he had any basis for assuming that black rule in South Africa would be better than in the rest of Africa.

'We are the exception,' he said. 'We are mature.'

'Possibly,' I thought. 'But don't be too sure.'

But it would not be impossible if he and his colleagues could protect themselves, by the power of Jesus, by the wisdom of his word and even by constitutional safeguards, from the corrupting personal and political consequences of human fallenness.

Nothing that has been said in this section absolves South African whites, and especially South African Christians, from working with all vigour for black rights and freedom, and for a new order in the land.

We are in fact obliged to obey God in this, even if we perceive the potential consequences as risky, and even if a worse order under blacks were to replace apartheid. The possibility of others also getting into political sin in no way allows us to bask in ours! However, there is no need to capitulate to the disaster scenario for South Africa if both blacks and whites also understand and co-operate with the moral laws of the universe as stamped into its fabric by Jesus, the cosmic Christ.

UNDERSTANDING THE COSMIC CHRIST

This insight was perhaps the most significant aspect of what came home to me through E Stanley Jones in that Nairobi mission back in 1969.

What he underlined was this. Jesus is not just a great religious prophet and the finest man who ever lived. He is either much more or much less. In fact, the New Testament says he is much more. It says he is the cosmic Christ. He is the one behind the universe.

Thus, while God the Father was the author of the creation idea, Jesus the Son was the agent in the creating process.

So St John, for example, can say in the prologue to his gospel that 'all things were made through him, and without him was not anything made that was made' (John 1:3, RSV).

Likewise, St Paul could write: 'all things were created through him and for him . . . and in him all things hold together' (Col. 1:16–17, RSV).

The writer to the Hebrews is equally succinct and definite about this cosmic Christ: 'He . . . bears the very stamp of [God's] nature, upholding the universe by his word of power' (Hebrews 1:3, RSV). Jesus was not just a rather unusual Middle Eastern prophet, trotting out a few bits of pretty religious advice, rather, he is the creator, Lord, upholder and sustainer of the entire universe. This also is what he himself claimed: 'All authority in heaven and on earth has been given to me' (Matt 28:18, RSV).

That being so, the Jesus stamp, says the Bible, is on and written into the very fabric of the universe. And if this is so, we must tell society, both governments and governed, that for life to work, whether private, marital, social or political life, the game must be played Jesus' way.

The pattern built into the universe

What this means is that in all phases of life in the universe there is 'the way' and 'not-the-way'. In chemistry H_2O produces water. We may fight the formula or twist it into something else, but in the end we have to surrender to it and accept it or we won't get water. Two parts of hydrogen and one of oxygen is the way, and everything else is not-the-way.

Likewise, when I fly from Durban to Johannesburg, there is a way to fly and there is not-the-way. Check with the pilot and he will tell you that every moment he must obey those laws upon which flying depends – or else! There can be no moral holidays in the air. He obeys or breaks. And he gains mastery only by obedience. Aviation did not invent those laws or impose them; it discovered them.

Now if obedience to laws holds good in the physical realm, what about when we come to the business of human living and when we move over into more subtle relationships like the social, the moral, the spiritual or the political? Does chance reign there? Can we do as we please and get away with it? Or do we find there something which demands obedience if we are to live happily and in peace? And is that something which demands our co-operation not merely a set of conventions and customs built up by society but something written into the nature of reality? The philosopher Immanuel Kant (1724–1804) once said, 'Two things strike me with awe: the starry heavens above and the moral law within.' What he meant was that the laws of those two worlds are equally dependable, equally authoritative, and equally inescapable. And there is a way and 'not-the-way' written into both. If we obey the way, we get results. If we don't, we get consequences, dreadful consequences.

In other words, we accommodate our lives, bodies and functions to the laws of the universe as we know them. It also follows that if God is behind everything, then human beings should fit into the environment which is there. And this is indeed the case, for example, in the physical realm.

So for the Christian it is not surprising that my lung system is in correlation to the world's atmosphere, for the same reasonable God made both my lung system and the atmosphere, and he put me in this world. He gave me an eye which registers colour and a world which is colourful. He gave me an ear to hear sounds and a world full of sound.

In short, the Christian believes that in every area and realm of life there are God-given laws built into the fabric of reality. God has spoken both in nature and in the Bible, and the whole created order belongs to him.

Jesus as the Logos

This pattern that God has built into the universe connects with the Bible's picture of Jesus himself – especially where

John in the prologue to his gospel speaks of him as the *Logos* –
the Word – the self-expression of God.

The ancient Greek philosophers had seen that there was a
divine reason or mind in the cosmos. This mind gives it
coherence, unity and order. This is also the basis of the
inherent morality which they sensed as something real. So
they gave it a name. It was called the Logos (*i.e.* the word or
self-expression of God).

Even before the appearance of Jesus Christ, the human
race had become persuaded of a moral order behind the
universe. This they saw not only in the physical and moral
nature of man, as they experienced it, but in the nature of the
universe as they perceived it. All this testified to them to the
reality of a 'Logos' behind everything.

The world was thus poised morally, spiritually and intellectually for the arrival of Jesus Christ. For as St John says: 'In
the beginning was the Word [*logos*], and the Word was with
God, and the Word was God . . . And the Word became flesh
and dwelt among us, full of grace and truth; we have beheld
his glory, glory as of the only Son from the Father' (John 1:1,
14, RSV). Here, said John, is the lawmaker behind our planet
and the universe: he has stepped on to planet Earth and we
have beheld his glory.

Jesus' disclosure of morality

Christians believe that what Jesus was, as seen in his earthly
life and ministry, God is always. Jesus' nature is God's nature.
Not only that, but in his humanity he was the natural, normal
man *par excellence*, whose life was in absolute accord with the
natural order and the cosmos.

Because he is the agent in creation, and seeing that 'without
him was not anything made that was made' (John 1:3, RSV), all
reality, and all the cosmos, has his stamp upon it.

What Christians believe, therefore, is not that Jesus imposed a morality on man, but rather that he exposed more
fully and completely an intrinsic morality in the universe
itself. A good and moral action will therefore have not only
Jesus and scripture behind it but the universe and the cosmos

as well. Conversely, a bad or evil action will therefore stand not only under the judgement of God and scripture, but also under the judgement of life and the cosmos.

Consequently, in each action we commit cosmos or commit chaos, according to whether the action is good or bad. A good action is integrative and constructive; a bad action is disintegrative and destructive.

Christian ethics are therefore always on the side of fullness, happiness, true fun, completeness, peace, health, political stability, justice, social harmony, and so on.

Laws cannot, therefore, be 'broken', but one can be broken by them. No one breaks a law; he can only illustrate it in operation. To jump off the Empire State Building is not to break the law of gravity – only to illustrate it!

Morality and reality

To be moral, therefore, for the Christian, whether in personal, family or political ethics, is not to be narrow, prudish or politically obtuse, but simply to co-operate with the moral and spiritual structure of reality. Moral obedience is not obedience to an arbitrary decree, but to the way things are.

The moral law, then, is seen to be part of the way the world is made. That which is 'good' is that which enhances life by obedience to its inherent constitution; that which is 'bad' is what is out of relation to the structure of the world and life as it has been designed by God.

The moral law is the law of nature, and the law of nature is the law of life. In other words the laws of God's world all interlock – and when man is called to be sexually or financially or politically moral, he is simply being called to play the game of life according to the rules of the game established by the author of the game for our happiness and well-being.

Morality and salvation

Likewise, when Christians call on people to find salvation in Christ, they are calling them to an all-embracing harmony in which their divided souls can be unified in right relationships with the world, with other people and with the infinite moral and spiritual fabric of God's universe.

This is why Christians believe that in Jesus the end and meaning of human life and the universe is revealed. In him is the basic structure of morality. For a person to come to Christ is the way to become genuinely human. It is the way of fulfilment.

The commandments of Christ are not therefore capricious and arbitrary. Nor is something good because God commands it, but rather he commands it because it is good. Moral laws are therefore the expression of his own being, and the laws of God are the laws of life. This means that to love God with the whole mind, soul and strength is to be rightly adjusted to life and the total reality around us, whether in private life, home life, business life or political life.

Morality and contemporary politics

So then, when governments segregate or discriminate or pervert justice, they violate the moral law of the universe, and the hugely negative and reactionary consequences of this serve only to demonstrate this violation. The law in effect has not been 'broken' – it has only been illustrated!

So the Lord can speak to ancient Judah, just before he judges them with Babylonian conquest, and explain that in their many sins of injustice, greed and violence they are 'sinning against themselves'. The moral law of the universe is catching them out.

God's word is simple and clear: 'Woe to him who increases what is not his . . . You have devised a shameful thing for your house by cutting off many peoples: *so you are sinning against yourself*' (Hab 2:6, 10, NASB).

Likewise, St Paul can say of the immoral person that he 'sins against his own body' (1 Cor 6:18, RSV): he hurts himself. He does not break the law; the law breaks him.

In other words, whether in political, personal or social morality, to go against the Lord's ways, which are the rules of the universe, is to hurt oneself.

Apartheid and all its works therefore constitute one gigantic national project of self-inflicted wounds. The discriminating way is the way of shooting ourselves in the foot. Persisted in long enough, it must become the way of national suicide.

We are free to choose in politics as in life, but we are not free to choose the consequences. A law, which operates regardless, will always have the last word.

So the Jesus way is not just for those who accept or buy into the Christian scriptures: it is for all.

The Jesus way and the South African way

The implications of this seized my imagination back then in 1969 as I began to see why and how Jesus could say 'I am the *way*' (John 14:6), and the reason why Christianity was described in the first century as 'the Way' (Acts 24:14; 9:2; 19:9; 24:22).

The disciples had found the way not only for salvation (Acts 4:12) but for living life and making it work – in any and every sphere, whether personal, marital, social or political.

So 'the way' is the way to do everything – the way to think, to feel, to act, and to be in every conceivable circumstance and in every relationship. It is the way that is written into the nature of everybody and everything. This makes the moral universe all of a piece, with its laws inherent in reality itself.

This means that the way we are made to work is also the way God wants us to work. Creation thus works his way or else works its own ruin. And the history of humanity is nothing but a long confirmation of this truth.

All this raises acutely the issue of how we do things not only in our personal lives but also in our nations. The relevance for South Africa and its so-called 'way of life' is devastating.

It means there is a 'Way' and a 'Not-the-way' for South Africa to order its society. And the choices will confront us at every turn in our national life. Will it be the Jesus way of justice, love, care for the poor and powerless, compassion, respect for families, equality of opportunity, *etc.*, or will it be the non-Jesus way, with all its dire consequences?

As these truths slowly became part of my life from 1969 onwards, I began, not surprisingly, to see that the way we have organised our social and political life in South Africa, and the way our Government has conducted affairs these last forty years, is simply not the Jesus way. It has been out of accord not just with God, the Bible and world opinion. It has been out of accord with the universe and its moral fabric. In other words, the South African way, the racist way, is a deadly experiment in how not to do it. The catalogue of black pain and protest (Part 4), not to mention world outrage and our slowly disintegrating nation, should alert us to the fact that whatever our grand racial and constitutional theories about how to organise and run our society, we are not doing it the right way.

As South Africa erupted in 1976, and became ever more traumatised in the following years, I sought in 1980 to explain this principle to a leading South African politician and Cabinet Member, emphasising that the fundamental issue facing us in South Africa is whether we live in a moral universe or not. If we do not, then we can discriminate and get away with it. But if we do live in a moral universe, we can't and won't get away with it. And the judgements of life, of history and of the universe will become the judgements of God, because he has made one sort of universe and not another – a universe in which we reap what we sow (Prov 22:8).

I concluded in these terms:

Exactly how all this is to be worked out within the realities of the South African situation is for those of you who are Christian politicians and statesmen to decide. But of this I am sure – anything that breaks with Christian principle will not work. It will only produce the kind of mounting fury which is now threatening to engulf our whole society – if not right now, then within a few years. It is self-deceiving to see all this as the work of a few agitators. It is not. It is a reflex in the machine, as it were, to what happens when the rules are broken. It is the cogs in a watch grinding to a halt because of sand which should not be there.

Put differently, it is life and the universe in *reaction*. This is not to discount agitating, exploitive or even Marxist elements. But Marxists are never foolish enough to exploit anything except *just*

causes. The devil always has a sound eye for the genuine griev-
ance! We can only head him off by cleaving to what is right – no
matter how much the darkness may call us to the dictates of
expediency.

So my challenge is to encourage subordination of policy to
principle, bearing in mind that it is better in the eyes of both time
and eternity to lose in the short term with what must ultimately
win, rather than to win in the short term with that which will
ultimately lose.[16]

And this I firmly believe. It is also why at times we have to
say no to some of the things Caesar may require of us. We will
come to this in chapter 18, but for the moment we note Martin
Luther King's affirmation that there are times when 'a moral
man can't obey a law which his conscience tells him is unjust'.
This is not to be politically perverse, but because 'there are
times when a manmade law is out of harmony with the moral
law of the universe'.[17]

RIGHT UNDERSTANDING AND RIGHT
THINKING
ARE IMPERATIVE

The key thing to grasp is that right actions, right policies and
right attitudes are seriously imperilled, if not rendered impossible, unless rooted in right thinking. All Christians,
especially those in South Africa, must think these things
through, and grasp that so much of South Africa's life and
action has been rooted in the soil of wrong understanding. So
the tree has come up wrong, and the fruit is therefore
inevitably wrong.

The soil of right understanding and right thinking, however, will receive and nourish the seed of the right trees which
will in turn bring forth the right fruit. Grapes and figs will
emerge instead of thorns and brambles.

The key lies, as we said, in ever and always praying – with
courage too – 'God be in my head, and in my understanding.'

13   Getting the Act Together (The church's responsibility to connect the vertical and the horizontal)

If you preach the Gospel in all aspects with the exception of
the issues which deal specifically with your time, you are
not preaching the Gospel at all.

Martin Luther

Jesus went throughout Galilee, teaching in their syna-
gogues, preaching the good news of the kingdom, and
healing every disease and sickness among the people.

Matthew 4:23

If understanding is the church's first responsibility, whether
in South Africa or elsewhere, its second lies in the challenge of getting the act together whereby vertical and horizontal components of the gospel are brought into balance.
This we in African Enterprise saw most clearly in 1970,
the year after the Nairobi mission, when we went to Johannesburg and Soweto for a year-long city-wide evangelistic
mission to that great metropolis. What made the whole
exercise so difficult was that again and again we found the
churches and pastors polarised and alienated as to whether
evangelism and social concern could combine. One man's
piety was another man's poison. One conservative denomination even pulled out of the mission because I preached in
the Anglican Cathedral! Such absurdities brought home to
me how far we all were from facing the true and urgent
demands of witness to our country. It all reminded me of the

Russian Orthodox Church just before the 1917 Revolution. While the whole Tsarist social order was on the verge of being overturned, the main issue in the church was whether priests should wear vestments or not! The contemporary church's ability to major in minors still seems to know no bounds.

THE RESPONSE FROM SOWETO

The main indicator as to the urgency of the hour and the perilous detachment of the church was Soweto. Apart from the endless evidences of apartheid's pain and trauma as we met with people there, we also met hundreds of black teenagers who said they were through with the evangelical gospel because they said no evangelical Christian seemed to worry about their plight or about the issues of justice.

'Not only that,' said some of the teenagers, 'but we see the Bible as the instrument of the status quo and the system, because the Government makes us pay for our school books but gives us the Bible free! Why is that? It must be to make us passive and accept our lot.'

But to try to alert rank and file Christians (the problem was rarely with Christian leadership) to the structural problems and injustices of the system, as the Soweto young people articulated them, was to get oneself labelled 'political and unspiritual', a 'communist' or worse!

In fact we felt so strongly that Soweto was going to 'blow' unless these issues were faced, that in desperation I went to the Mayor of Johannesburg to speak to him about the youth of Soweto. He said he would tell the Prime Minister, John Vorster.

The hard reality was that by the end of 1970, though three hundred churches had participated in the mission to the city and many people had been won to Christ, some of us were nevertheless profoundly disturbed by the seemingly congenital inability of the churches to get their act together and bring mission, evangelism and social concern into a healthy and balanced union of holistic ministry to a country headed, as we could so clearly see, for massive tragedy.

Our team members, along with the Mission '70 Chairman

John Rees, by then newly elected as General Secretary of the South African Council of Churches, began to dream of bringing together the various wings of the South African Church for a massive combined conference on mission and evangelism.

John would invite his friends from the more ecumenical and socially concerned wing of the churches, and we in African Enterprise would go for the more overtly evangelical.

We felt it could be quite an instructive party, and it was. It was called the South African Congress on Mission and Evangelism, and it took place in March 1973 in Durban.

DURBAN 1973

Eight hundred top church leaders from all across the South African church spectrum, with the exception of the Dutch Reformed Church, finally came together. 'The fundamental, the sacramental and the sentimental – all are here,' said one astonished and bemused overseas participant!

This is not the time or place to relate everything the Congress said and did as that tale is chronicled elsewhere.[1] But for the purpose of this book, the exciting phenomenon to note, as far as South Africa was concerned, was that for the first time on a wide scale in the South African church Christian leaders from different sides of the spectrum began to learn from each other and to see that a major responsibility of the church is to bring together the vertical and horizontal – the personal and the social, the evangelistic and the activistic and the pietistic!

One of the most helpful contributions leading all of us better to grasp how these two dimensions of the church's responsibility fit together came from the British theologian Canon Douglas Webster, of St Paul's Cathedral in London.

He noted that mission and evangelism are related words but they do not mean the same thing. Mission is a comprehensive word with a large meaning. Evangelism is a more restricted word with a sharply defined meaning. To evangelise is to tell or bring good news. Mission however has about it a sense of action, posture and process. It speaks of all the church is sent to do. 'Evangelism is centred in news, which must be reported in words, about a person, an event, a series of events. It's concentrated. Its concern is with the gospel itself . . .'[2] Webster pointed out, however, on the basis of Luke 4:18–19, that the mission of Jesus included a great deal more than evangelism.

Many speakers, both black and white, also stressed that mission and evangelism could not proceed effectively unless the South African set-up and system was faced and challenged.

The gospel under threat

Dr Manas Buthelezi, now a senior Lutheran bishop, put it this way in a prophetic utterance of perception and warning:

> The future of the Christian faith in this country will largely depend on how the gospel proves itself relevant to the existential problems of the Black man. This is so, not only because the Blacks form the majority in the South African population, but also because Christendom in this country is predominantly Black.
>
> But the major threat to the Gospel, and indeed to the society as a whole, is that the Whites have incarnated their spiritual genius in the South African economic and political institutions and have thereby sabotaged and eroded the power of Christian love. They have virtually rejected the Black man as a brother.[3]

In Dr Buthelezi's eyes, the crime of a white Christianity divorced from structural concerns was a crime against what Christian love was meant to be all about. White Christian credibility would be destroyed unless white Christians saw this.

Beyers Naudé, also a great prophet, pressed the point home further. His concern was to see 'a renewal of man's individual life and the renewal of society to reflect more truly the lordship of Christ over all spheres of the life of man through the establishment of the Kingdom of God on earth'.[4]

After Durban

The Durban Congress of 1973 was in the view of many a
watershed experience for the South African church. What it
said was that while evangelism must remain integral to the
very lifestyle of the church if it would stay true to its Lord's
great missionary commission, the Christian message as a
whole could not and should not be divorced from its context.

This meant that personal witness and social action, pietism
and activism, prayer and praxis should all come together. Our
resolution after Durban '73 was to do better.

However, as the Durban participants returned to their
congregations and organisations, some went back changed
people and others went back just the same. Beyond that,
some of the changed ones found great success in moving their
congregations towards greater balance of the vertical and
horizontal while others met with nothing but frustration and
rigid adherence to one emphasis or the other.

A vital question

All of this raises an important question: Why is it that some
individuals, groups or congregations are able to get their act
together and grow and progress, as the Durban Congress was
urging, while others can't, and won't and don't?

Every Christian basically, I believe, wants to blossom into
new biblical balance. And I think there is a way to move
towards this. And it holds good regardless of where you live –
whether in South Africa, Europe, the USA, Latin America or
Australasia.

UNDERSTANDING OURSELVES BETTER

It all starts with realising that none of us has 'arrived'. In every
person there is room for growth. Nor are we all at the same
place. So we need compassion for each other as we seek to
grow and move on to the new place God has for us. It is of
course important to understand that faith is not something

which never changes, though from time to time we do get stuck. In all of us faith changes and develops as we gain new insights. The exact nature of that change and how we can progress to the best place the Lord has for us is what we need to consider now.

In biology a study of the variety of life forms is clarified by their classification, even knowing there are exceptions. While no person made uniquely in God's image can be neatly categorised, the study of our personal and spiritual development can be separated into several phases. This allows us to assess how we grow. It also enables us to understand ourselves and others better.

In my own struggles some real light on the complicated nature of this growth and change process in myself and in others has come from two Roman Catholic scholars, John Walsh and Jim Fowler. In their studies they show that our psychological and emotional development is markedly similar to our spiritual growth, and they describe six phases to demonstrate this parallelism.[5]

These phases can also, according to their thesis, be seen in groups, congregations, denominations, *etc.*

THE WALSH/FOWLER THESIS

In a tabulated form, the Walsh/Fowler thesis could be summarised something like this:

Phases of Psychological and Emotional Growth	Means of Spiritual Growth	Code Words
Phase 1: Pre-school child (0–6 yrs)	Child's image of God and church being formed more by feelings and emotions than didactic content.	'Feelings' 'Vibrations'
Phase 2: Junior school child (6–12 yrs)	Child's faith grows through hearing and reading stories with help from parents, teachers, Sunday school teachers.	'Stories' 'Parents' 'Teachers'

Phase 3: Early teenager (13–16 yrs)	Faith grows or fails to grow as young person follows peers and significant others in non-judgemental way. Many can get stuck here.	'Conformity' 'Peer-group' 'Parade'
Phase 4: Late teenager to young adults (16–30 yrs)	Faith personally appropriated and internalised. Often involves agonising reappraisal. Instinct to opt for one model, style or package. Us/them mindset very common.	'Personal appropriation' 'One model'
Phase 5: Older adults (30 yrs and over)	By resolution or mere good fortune the person may be exposed to several models or emphases. Validity is seen in the other models, which begin to be embraced, integrated and incorporated.	'Many models' 'Both/and' 'Developing integration'
Phase 6: Any age (but more often over 45)	The believer harmoniously resolves the polarities and the different emphases, often by ongoing positive experience of others reflecting such holism.	'Harmony' 'Holism'

Now we look at the phases in more detail.

Phase One: The pre-school child, 0–6 years old

In this phase the child does not absorb information about faith as much as feelings and emotions, even vibrations, about God, Jesus, the church, and life in general. The child starts getting feelings as to whether God is a great big angry ogre up there, or a loving, caring, heavenly Father. Feelings will also develop as to whether the church is a happy, caring place or a tedious and boring one. The child's subconscious is being shaped at this time. The code words here might be '*feelings*' or '*vibrations*'.

Phase Two: Junior school child, Ages 6–12

Faith grows in children of this age through hearing or reading Bible stories of Moses, Goliath, Jesus and Saul, the bad guy who turned out good! The key word here is '*stories*'.

Phase Three: The early teenager, Ages 13–16

The key words here are '*conformity*' and '*parade*' – as when one keeps in step in a parade. The individual wants to be doing what the group does. It is normal at this phase to take on the attitudes, standards, or values of that group, because security is found there.

Another characteristic evident in all of us at this phase of life is that of following 'significant others' in a non-questioning and undiscerning way. In the primary school stage, 'the significant others' were our parents, teacher, pastor, or perhaps an older brother or sister. In the adolescent years the significant others are found in the peer group.

As far as the development of our faith is concerned through this phase, if a young person is a Christian, he will basically go along with the way the group prays, or sings, or thinks about Christ.

Interestingly enough Walsh and Fowler feel that ninety-five per cent of Christians tend to stick at this phase where they find their union and their security through *conformity to the group* or to the particular religious parade in which they happen to be marching, whether a conservative Baptist parade, or a hand-waving Pentecostal parade, or an activist Catholic parade, or a free-for-all Anglican parade like mine! Basically people feel emotionally, culturally, or aesthetically, comfortable in the parade in which they have been raised.

Phase Four: The late teenager and young adult, Ages 16–approx 30

This is a time when faith moves for many people from being something nominal to being much more personal. Something handed on by others is now personally appropriated and internalised.

Fowler and Walsh liken this phase to the opening up of a sort of spiritual knapsack in which various things have been placed by parents and teachers and significant others throughout phases 1, 2 and 3. Now we empty the knapsack, examine the contents, toss out a few things here and there and personalise that which seems really meaningful to us.

Sometimes this can involve an agonising reappraisal of what has been handed to us by others, or else it may be quite straightforward. But the point is that a moment comes when we realise we have to face Jesus personally and give an account of our own lives in a responsible way. We realise that we can't just hide in our group and say to the Lord at the end of the day: 'Well, our group didn't think this or that was too important.'

The interesting thing about this phase is that we tend to opt for *one model* or *style* of Christian expression. We adopt an either/or mentality and with those who differ from us we become confrontational, taking an 'us/them' attitude.

In my own experience, after conversion at Cambridge, I embraced all things overtly evangelical and rejected all things seemingly non-evangelical. I accordingly adored my conservative evangelical friends and distanced myself, often with appalling rudeness and bad manners, from the college chaplain and chapel whose theological orientation was different from that of the Cambridge Inter Collegiate Christian Union. CICCU was evangelical, so I embraced that, whereas the Student Christian Movement, whose emphasis was more social, was, to my mind, totally beyond the pail in every possible way. I was the classic one-model man and my model was the only way. In fact, in my mind, between the Intervarsity Fellowship of Britain, whose books and teachings I embraced, and the early church, there was, nothing but nineteen centuries of irrelevant heresies, with the exception of one or two good blokes such as Martin Luther and John Wesley!

People in phase four cling to one model and throw the rest away. They can't cope with two sets of theological criteria which appear to be pulling in different directions. So, a person who opts for evangelism in a big way won't opt for justice or social protest because these reflect models too different from the one he or she has embraced.

Phase Five: Adults from 30 onwards

The code words here are '*many models*' and the key dynamic is *both/and*. In other words, people who reach this growth point, says Walsh, are Christians who start to incorporate many different models into their Christian life, walk, work and witness. These can see good in different models and indeed in different polarities. So the intellectual who is interested in theology and apologetics may find great fulfilment in a Pentecostal prayer group where he can sing, dance, clap and have a charismatic burst-out! Or else the person who is concerned with justice and socio-political matters may also be an ardent evangelist, personal soul-winner or even a vigorous intercessor who participates in half-nights of prayer. Or you have the New Testament evangelist who will bring to his ministry a strong component of the Old Testament prophet.

People in phase five will be mature, integrated and liberated Christians who can hold different challenges and emphases in creative tension and bring together the various strands of scripture. But there is still a touch of tension and struggle to hold it all together, so there is still more growing needed.

Phase Six: Any age, but most likely 45 or 50 plus!

In this phase, the person has basically resolved polarities and holds the different emphases and balances of scripture in harmony. This person, who is obviously a rare bird, will be, according to Walsh and Fowler, a 'God-lover, a people-lover, an explorer, a pioneer and a taboo breaker. He will also be in tune with the heartbeat of the universe and his ministry will be prophetic.' Key words are '*harmony*' and '*holism*'.

Where do we fit?

While all of us would probably want to peg ourselves pretty low down in these phases, say as conformist phase threes or one model phase fours, I think it is true and fair to say that it is possible for people to be at one or two different phases at the same time, according to different aspects of their character and experience. At times I feel I am just beginning to get the act together (phase five) and then suddenly I feel very threatened by someone else's model, style or emphasis. At other times I feel very exhilarated, challenged and stimulated by being around people with different emphases from my own, but I sometimes find this makes me insecure, and I tend to shrink back into the little womb or bunker of my own group or congregation. So I find staying open to other Christians with different emphases and postures difficult, but worth the effort.

The implications of the Walsh/Fowler thesis

There is obviously going to be tension within groups and between groups. This can in fact operate in three ways.

How phase fours see phase threes

It is likely that the 'one-model' phase fours do not like the conformist and perhaps nominally Christian phase threes because phase fours see themselves as more spiritually serious and also think their model is the only viable and right one. So they look down on phase threes with pride and superiority, and have the view that everything new is good and everything old is bad. If they have left the Anglican Church for a Pentecostal church, they will tend to think that everything in Pentecostalism is good and everything in Anglicanism is bad.

If they were once into pietism and prayer meetings, but now are into social activism and protest, they will tend to reject the former and see relevance only in socio-political witness. If a person was once big on social concern and then became disillusioned with it, they will fixate on prayer, spirituality and perhaps evangelism. As far as justice is concerned, they will not only throw out the baby with the bath-water but throw the bath out as well! So these groups will have problems with each other.

How phase threes see phase fours

Phase threes (the 'conformist' people who don't question) will not like phase fours (the people who have bought passionately into one model or another) because they will see one-model phase fours as conformist phase threes who have either gone wrong or gone fanatical. It is also true that the uncritical phase threes who follow their significant leaders without evaluating or questioning, will feel a threat from phase fours who have very vigorously embraced one option and are now very self-consciously and vigorously propagating it.

I remember when I committed my life to Christ at Cambridge, not only did I reject the Anglican womb which had nurtured me but also a number of people within that womb became very unhappy about my embracing the evangelical model so wholeheartedly. They wanted me back in the safe, comfortable and sometimes more sociable and respectable forms of the faith. In other words, their attitude was 'This religion business is fine, so long as you don't go overboard.' South African student friends coming over to Cambridge were told by their parents not to get all fanatical like Michael! It was a case of 'sensible phase threes' warning possibly gullible threes not to become 'fanatical phase fours'!

It should also be noted that if a lot of hitherto conformist phase threes begin moving to phase four, or if a whole society which has been conformist and uniform suddenly moves into a phase four mindset, those still in phase three will develop a siege mentality and feel very threatened and insecure.

People with such a conformist mindset will begin dashing

for cover to find security in familiar political groupings or in a new denominational framework where all the old familiar landmarks, attitudes, teachings *etc.* are still secure.

This, say Walsh and Fowler, is why religious sects and sometimes new, conservative Christian denominations will flourish in insecure or unstable societies. As insecurity and instability build up the religious instinct begins to clutch at the familiar and resist anything which questions or challenges it. In South Africa people like Desmond Tutu become terrifying to people who are stuck in phase three conformism.

How phase fours see other phase fours

A third area of tension, in terms of the groups we have outlined, is that one-model phase fours, all people of great conviction, will probably not like each other because they have different and seemingly opposing models according to which they operate. So the social justice people might resent the prayer people; and the evangelists, who stick to preaching the old-time gospel, will resent and hold suspect the social analysts and all those who want to 'contextualise' the message.

The role of phase fives in church and nation

One of the things which emerges from all this, note Walsh and Fowler, is that those in phase five (who hold many models in tension) will be the ones most likely to offer the most effective ministry in a world or society that is full of one-model phase fours. Phase fives, who have integrated the various models, are more likely to be skilful, loving, sensitive, caring and patient as they approach the earnest 'one-model phase fours' or the conformist, more nominal phase threes. To phase fours, for example, they will say: 'I affirm what you have done and the model you have embraced, but I challenge you to recognise that there is more than one model. Please think about this.' To the conformist phase threes, who are perhaps more nominal in their faith, they will, as my friend Robert Footner did for me at Cambridge, present the challenge of a fuller surrender and commitment to Christ.

It is obviously also true that if the leadership of nations, churches or denominations is at phase four, with a tremendous loyalty to one model, then those leaders will gather other phase four people into a grouping around their model. So the us/them mentality will continue strongly. But if the leaders themselves are at phase five, they will be able to see the importance of all sorts of different models and be able to encourage and develop 'a communion of communities rather than a collection of cliques'.

In South Africa this is vitally important for the church in terms of allowing and indeed encouraging multiple responses to the situation without letting any one group anathematise the other. Not everyone is going to be called to respond in exactly the same way. But everyone must embrace and affirm the particular witness, emphasis and calling expressed through another group. The Lord is the great orchestrator of the whole church and he doesn't call the violins to play the same orchestral tune as the flutes, nor does he ask the clarinettist to try and bang the big drum!

It is really a matter of getting back to the body of Christ principle of St Paul in 1 Corinthians 12 and 14. The body has many parts, and not all the parts have the same function, but all need to be in sympathy, in harmony and in working co-operation with each other. It is all so obvious really. But if we stick in phase three conformity or phase four exclusivism, we will not see the importance or relevance of the whole body of Christ. We will merely encourage the activities of our own exclusivist sector and exclude the arm, leg, eye or ear of the other individuals or groups whose emphases and contributions are different from our own.

THE SOUTH AFRICAN SITUATION IN THE LIGHT OF THE WALSH/FOWLER THESIS

The phase three response

All of this sheds light on the South African situation, where people are resistant to talk about social change or justice because it constitutes a psychological and material threat. And if social or political prophets thunder in frustration and anger about our lack of commitment to justice, we just get more and more insecure and curl up in our little group or gravitate to our phase three womb to keep us safe.

We may even be inundated by horror stories of injustice and the awful consequences of apartheid *etc.*, but we will resist the implications of these because change frightens us. It threatens to disrupt our familiar world. Every white in South Africa knows this, myself included.

Indeed, if I am honest with my own heart, I have to admit real fear and insecurity about what massive social change in South Africa would mean. I see it as a threat to my lifestyle, my comfort, my privilege, and indeed my psychological peace and equilibrium. Yet I know that my Lord, my gospel, my Bible, the march of events, the course of history and the sheer injustices of the current system oblige me to gear up not just spiritually and psychologically but also politically to move from a politically conformist phase three or one-model phase four to a political phase five, where altogether new options have to be faced.

Of course another fatal flaw in the phase three mindset is the inability to admit that there actually are any more phases beyond phase three. Similarly, phase fours, may be so bound up in their model that they actually become completely unaware that there are any others of consequence.

The need for a wider experience of others

Another problem if we get politically or spiritually stuck in phases three or four is that our limited exposure to other groups, other peoples, other denominations, other models or other emphases will so restrict our awareness of the true state of things in our church, country or society that we will actually wonder what on earth all the fuss is about!

However, the more a person sees what goes on, the more socially and spiritually aware he or she becomes, not only of the need, but of the biblical and theological bases for grappling with that need.

I remember my friend George Irvine in Port Elizabeth saying that it was only through constant *exposure* to black pain in the townships that he actually and finally allowed the political penny to drop and became aware of the compelling imperative as a Christian to do something about the causes – whether economic, political or social – of that pain.

Part of the problem is that there is often a huge distance, which we won't spot if we remain blinkered or restricted, between the violence which can be in a system or structure and the final and awful effects of that systemic violence. So we just look at a result – for example, young blacks burning down a school – and remain utterly perplexed and baffled as to why they should do so. And unless our political, social or religious experience takes us from our one-model living into the 'black' context of those young blacks, we will remain permanently bewildered and perplexed by such behaviour.

But if we come out of a phase three womb or a one-model phase four, and if we meet those young blacks where they are, then we may start to understand the long linkage which ends with their violent act of destruction, typifying their deeply rooted resentment of particular aspects of the overall system, and especially of Bantu Education.

The Christian leader

Walsh and Fowler feel that their thesis has special relevance for Christian leaders, particularly those who seek to be more prophetic.

They say prophetic leaders or pastors often make the mistake of being judgemental or angry or menacing. Such attitudes can only lock people in either phases three or four and can never liberate them. There is a need to remember that no one has 20:20 vision on either the problems or the solutions.

So the leader, pastor or prophet who wants to move people on to a different phase will, as a self-confessed Christian struggler, have to turn from the often-employed tactics of impatient tough talk to issuing a challenge in love to people to look inside themselves so as to recognise the longings and desires which are there ready to expand, develop and grow in the faith.

The need for more . . .

In all of us there is a primal cry for more. We want more of the Lord. We want more of reality, more understanding, more insight, more ministry effectiveness, more relevance, and more truth.

It would also be true in the South African context that deep down we all want more harmony, more peace, more justice, more safety, more prosperity and more hope for the future. We want to blossom individually and as a nation. We want more recognition and acceptance in the world. We want more guarantees that all our children, whether white or black, will live together peacefully in the future.

If we can face one another under God with these deep inner desires, we will actually start to dislodge ourselves from being stuck at one phase or another, and begin to move forwards towards that 'more of the Lord', 'more of one another' and 'more of God's peace in our country' which we all long for. In other words, we have to ask the Lord and seek the help of each other to break out of our ghettos and adolescent phases so that we can move towards a new place of spiritual, social and political maturity so that a land such as South Africa may be healed and saved.

14 Practical Steps Towards Biblical Balance
(The church's responsibility to seek ministry holism)

When I was a child, I talked like a child, I thought like a child, I reasoned like a child. When I became a man, I put childish ways behind me.

1 Corinthians 13:11

The taking of the cross means the death of self, of personal ambition and self-centred purpose. In the place of selfish attainment, however altruistic and noble, one is to desire alone the rule of God.

George Eldon Ladd

One must reach the point of 'not caring two straws about his own status' before he can wish wholly for God's kingdom, not his own, to be established.

C S Lewis

There is no use talking about love if it does not relate to the stuff of life in the area of material possessions and needs. If it does not mean a sharing of our material things for our brothers in Christ close at home and abroad, it means little or nothing.

Francis Schaeffer

Once we realise that mission and evangelism belong together, and once we accept that we need to move from a phase three conformism or a 'one-model' phase four mindset, we will be asking ourselves how practically we can step out of the valley of dangerous lopsidedness to the new place of spiritual maturity and more effective witness which the Lord has for us.

To do this there are – according to my own struggles, which are still continuing of course – a number of truths which when held together in tension bring us to that new and better balance which God has for us as we relate to our societies.

We can present this as a wheel with a hub and a number of spokes which all flow out into an all-encircling rim:

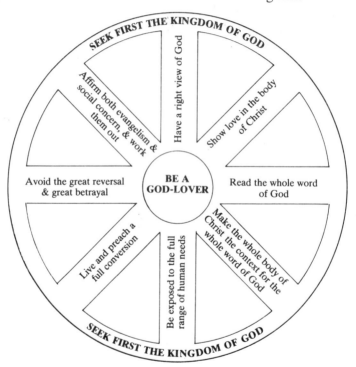

THE HUB: BE A GOD-LOVER

The scriptures first call on us to love this God, whose nature is revealed in creation, in Jesus, and in the biblical text, with all our heart, soul, mind and strength (Matt 22:37; Mark 12:30).

There is no way that we will move to a place of greater growth and to a higher stage of spiritual maturity unless we are motivated towards this by a fundamental and deep love for the Lord our God.

Clearly this love will make us want to obey him and follow his will and purposes as we understand these more fully through his word and his people. The lover of God will be the 'obeyer' of God, and the obeyer of God will not shrink from where that obedience will take him, even if it means forsaking the safety of a phase three womb or a phase four model for the dangers of a phase five adventure in witness.

One of the richest expressions of this love of God comes in the form of praise and worship. The prophet Habakkuk, who prophesied to Judah towards the end of the seventh century BC, got it wonderfully right when he burst out:

> Though the fig-tree does not bud and there are no grapes on the vines, though the olive crop fails and the fields produce no food, though there are no sheep in the pen and no cattle in the stalls, *yet I will rejoice in the Lord, I will be joyful in God my Saviour*. The Sovereign Lord is my strength. (Hab 3:17–19)

This scripture was first brought meaningfully to my attention by a former colleague, Quentin Smith, who had been a pastor and chaplain during the anguished years of civil war in what was then Rhodesia. Everything around them was in turmoil, 'But,' said Quentin, 'Habakkuk's word and the Spirit of God are teaching us to praise and worship our God regardless.'

Ultimate security

There is something else significant here. As we think about the different societies, systems, and pressuring ideologies around us, we find in worship and praise of God that we are making a statement to the Lord, to society, to our authorities, and to the principalities and powers of darkness (*cf.* Eph 6:12), as to where our ultimate security really lies. In worship we are able to stand before the world free of its menacing pressures. Being free of the rewards, punishments and controls of the systems around us, we are able as Christian people to be delivered from the threats of those systems.

Of course the systems themselves will find this threatening

and menacing. My late colleague Festo Kivengere of Uganda told me that at the height of the Amin years and troubles they would quite often have incidents when Amin's soldiers would come into a church, take the pastor out of the pulpit, stand him outside the church and shoot him dead. The Christians would then come out of the church, forgive the soldiers, bury the pastor, continue praising and loving God, and then put up yet another preacher for the following Sunday! Nothing Amin or his henchmen could do could stop the church worshipping and praising its Lord.

Ultimate loyalties

In a sense what worship does is to make a statement not only about where our ultimate security lies but where our ultimate loyalties lie. That is why both worship and politics can raise the same questions. For example, whom do I love most? Jesus and his word, or the political party, ideology or nation? And to whom am I most loyal? Is it to Jesus or is it to Caesar? And, a particularly South African question, Where do I find my real identity? Is it in the supra-racial community of the Lord's people, or is it in my tribe or party or volk?

If we are real God-lovers and worshippers, the answers to all those questions and their implications become self-evident in each of our lives.

SPOKE ONE: DEVELOP A RIGHT VIEW OF GOD

The opening section of our chapter on understanding (chapter 12) spoke of the character of God. If we don't understand God and his nature aright, our action and behaviour in the world will be all wrong. For example, if we think of him only in spiritual terms and if we forget that he became incarnate and lived concretely on our planet Earth, then we will think that only spiritual things are important and we will ignore the physical, concrete and earthy. But as C S Lewis used to stress, Christianity is the most physical of the world's religions because it exalts matter and the body and doesn't drive a

wedge between body and soul. Jesus' incarnation therefore
stands against that sort of dichotomy.

As we think of our God not only as spirit but also as the
incarnate Christ, we will also remember the message of our
Jeremiah text (Jer 9:23–24), where the Lord revealed himself
as the one who '*exercises* kindness, justice and righteousness
on earth'. Being concerned about those things here on Earth
is therefore a logical outflow of our understanding of the
nature and person of God.

SPOKE TWO: MAKE THE SHOWING OF LOVE IN THE BODY OF CHRIST A PRIORITY

There is no use hating or despising the person who needs
healing or growth. In fact only those who really have a
genuine love for the church of Jesus Christ and its people will
be able to confront them with their failings, faithlessness and
imbalance and then call them back to their true vocation and
to a more rounded witness. As Dr Edgar Brookes once said to
me: 'Many overseas people are quite unable to help us here
because they love neither South Africa nor South Africans.'
No one can move if he is just placed under endless judgement.

It is also important for the prophetic messenger to recognise that the need which we all have in phase three for love,
security and union *is actually a valid and legitimate need*.
Every one of us needs the assurance that we are loved, and we
need people around us to confirm to us that we are acceptable
and OK. The prophetic American writer Jim Wallis puts it
this way:

> Our identity and security depend upon that love and confirma-
> tion. Only then do we feel safe and secure, fully capable of loving
> and being loved. Christian community is the environment that
> provides confirmation, comfort and challenge. We no longer
> need the authority of a system to affirm and authenticate us,
> because we now recognise and worship a higher authority. When
> our source of security becomes God alone, we can safely act
> independently of the systems around us. The love made possible
> through Christian community can provide the necessary inner
> authority we need to act more faithfully in the world.[1]

SPOKE THREE: READ THE WHOLE WORD
OF GOD

In the early years of my ministry I found two remarkable
things happening to me.

The first was that I started (through a system John Stott put
me on to) to read the whole Bible cover to cover on a regular
basis. The system, requiring reading four chapters daily,
began with Genesis 1 (the beginning of everything), Ezra 1
(the beginning of the restoration – after the exile), Matthew 1
(the beginning of the gospel) and Acts 1 (the beginning of the
church). So at any one time one was required to be reading in
four different periods of biblical history. This was a great
blessing. The second was that our interdenominational interracial evangelistic ministry in African Enterprise was exposing our whole team and myself to the whole body of Christ on
a regular and sustained basis. This not only became rich and
rewarding and sometimes terrifying, but was also highly
edifying. More than that, these two experiences gave me an
insight into how Christians can remain imbalanced, locked in
ghettos and even deaf to the wider meanings of the word of
God.

Prior to these two things, I had found that I endlessly
gravitated towards those passages which reinforced my current convictions. That pattern began to be disturbed only
when I studied or faced the scriptures together with others or
in fellowship with people of other persuasions and backgrounds within the body of Christ. And even then I sometimes found that other people had fallen into the same trap as
myself. Thus, for example, I met one man who literally saw
nothing in the Bible except a message relating to the poor, the
fatherless and the oppressed. His main thing was visiting
prisoners. So a mass evangelist like Billy Graham, a Christian
politician like Mark Hatfield or a gospel singer like Cliff
Richard would be anathema to him. All this underlines that
reading *all* scripture is a key part of the process of growth.

SPOKE FOUR: MAKE THE WHOLE BODY OF CHRIST THE CONTEXT FOR THE STUDY OF THE WHOLE WORD OF GOD

South Africa is a classic example of the way an isolationist and ghetto-style study of the scriptures can block our understanding of the word of God and prevent us reaching the new places of biblical balance where all Christians should stand.

After I gave a lecture at Sydney University in Australia a student asked me: 'How is it, if South Africa is a country which is over seventy-five per cent nominally Christian, that the church could seemingly have failed so often to hear and understand what the Bible says?' It was a penetrating question. And the answer to it constitutes not only a causal explanation for the phenomenon but one of the major rungs in the ladder out of the valley of Christian lopsidedness.

For me in my own struggles at this point the answer has come from embracing the whole body of Christ in fellowship, so that not only is every Christian my brother and sister, but he or she is also my teacher. Not that I am a quick learner in this way, because I sometimes find such learning threatening. However, given that all of us are a bit heretical at one point or another, there is glorious blessing in allowing my heresies to be corrected by my brother's insights and his heresies to be corrected by mine.

To me the kind of thing which imperils our true understanding of the word of God and its balances was the line taken by one major South African denomination when faced with the challenge of participating along with five thousand other South African Christians of all races in SACLA (South African Christian Leadership Assembly). The major aim of that historic Congress was to 'examine together what it means to be faithful and effective witnesses to Jesus Christ as Lord in South Africa today'.

The directive from the denomination's senior executive to all local church councils was aimed at dissuading them from participation, and it said: '*We* as a church need not discover what it means to be faithful and effective witnesses of Christ in South Africa. We daily study God's Word and know what it is.' What a disastrous study in isolation!

In Bible study, as in everything else in the church's life, we cannot say, to use Paul's analogy of the eye trying absurdly to be independent of the hand: 'I don't need you!' (1 Cor 12:21).

This becomes obvious when we admit, as we must, that we all read the Bible as coloured by our own personal and historical presuppositions.

For example, I can read the text only through the interpretive grid of my own history as a white, middle-class South African, with a colonial history in former Basutoland (now Lesotho), a distinctive social circle, and a particular set of educational influences. I can't read it as a teenager in Soweto, who has been detained and perhaps shot at, and who has maybe seen his friends mown down in police gun-fire. That has not been my story or background. Nor can I read the Bible as an Afrikaner farmer whose parents fed him from birth on stories of British Boer War atrocities or the 'swart-gevaar' (black danger) or the primacy of the Afrikaner Volk. Those influences make each of us come to the biblical text with our own, sometimes massive, distortions.

Clearly the only way to prevent such a thing is to study our Bibles in the context of the fellowship of the whole body of Christ. Maintaining the unity of the body, with its miscellaneous sets of correctives, checks and balances, is therefore vital to our appropriation of the whole message of scripture and to our embracing of a rounded understanding and practice of biblical ministry. With the help of our denominational, racial or even theological 'Samaritan' (the person with whom we have no dealings), we can progress out of our historical prisons into the glorious, mature liberty of the children of God.

SPOKE FIVE: BE EXPOSED TO THE FULL RANGE OF HUMAN NEEDS

I referred earlier in this book to my friend Peter Kerchoff taking me to the squatter camp at Compensation Farm. One couldn't be exposed to that need and suffering and then walk away saying, 'My job is only to preach the gospel from an air-conditioned pulpit or to hand a gospel tract to some desperate, suffering squatter.'

Perhaps in South Africa one of the things white ministers could do is to bus their comfortable congregations into the nearest squatter or removals camp for a Sunday excursion. So shattered would people be that no one would have the heart or head to say evangelism and prayer meetings constitute the total responsibility of the church.

It's not such a weird idea, for in March 1988 two movements, Koinonia (started some years ago by Nico Smith) and the NIR (National Initiative for Reconciliation, launched in 1985), co-sponsored a black/white encounter conference in the black township of Mamelodi, which brought white conferees to live in the township for four days to experience the black world and its political pains and needs. Black conferees, for their part, stayed in white, mostly Afrikaner, homes in Pretoria. The mind-boggling and eye-opening experience of human encounter and discovery of one another's needs, problems, hopes and fears, affected each of us hugely, and challenged each participant both to new balance and to new identifying care in Christ's name. Each group was changed by exposure to the different needs of the other.

In tiny measure, each of us was trying to work out the principle by which Jesus came and entered our life situation, with all its suffering, and by that became one who 'was able to be touched with a feeling of our infirmities' (Heb 4:15). He felt what it was like to be human and he felt human pain and trauma. Becoming the wounded God, he could and can minister to a wounded humanity.

Likewise the prophet Ezekiel, speaking of the Jewish people in Babylonian captivity, could say, 'I sat there among them seven days – overwhelmed' (Ezek 3:15). Just being with those exiles in their pitiful place of judgement and lostness overwhelmed him.

On the other side of the coin, if the Christian social activist never looks to the spiritual needs of the human soul, which lie beyond justice, the vote, food, clothes and education, and so on, then he will miss a major component required of a rounded Christian ministry.

Edgar Brookes, as socially and politically concerned a

person as South Africa has produced in this century, was right on target when he said in the Durban Congress in 1973:

> Pay every Black person a fair wage, see that good food is obtainable at a reasonable price, build a model community with opportunities for freehold purchase and abolish the pass laws, and still you will not necessarily have heaven on earth; you may only have built a superior and better ventilated hell. We cannot make the gospel a mere means to a political or social end. This is a lesson grievously needed to be learned by many social reformers who reproach the Church because it has not created ideal living conditions.[2]

The fact is man does not live by bread, church or the vote alone, but by 'every word [including the evangelistic gospel word] that comes from the mouth of the Lord' (Deut 8:3).

In other words, if we balance out our gospel witness by exposing ourselves to all areas of human need, then we cannot forget the 'soul needs' for Christian salvation: divine forgiveness, a sense of meaning and purpose, and the assurance of eternal life.

To stand as I did this week (while working on this chapter) by the bed of a dying child and her grieving parents and to face the eternal issues and mystery of life and death, is to know that the vote, the good school-room and a higher salary are totally inadequate unless the eternal need for Christian salvation is also addressed and discovered. After all, 'What good will it be for a man if he gains the whole world, yet forfeits his soul' (Matt 16:26)?

SPOKE SIX: LIVE AND PREACH A FULL CONVERSION

Being an evangelist, conversion is one of my favourite words. And it is the ultimately matchless experience any human being can know.

Thus C S Lewis, describing his conversion, could write: 'I was brought kicking and struggling into the kingdom of God by the sheer evidence on behalf of Jesus' claim.' Dr

Alexander Wood, a Cambridge physicist, declared, 'I believe Jesus Christ has verified himself in my experience and he can do so in yours.'

My favouritely worded testimony, perhaps because it accords so fully with my own experience, comes from Temple Gairdner, the famous Anglican missionary to Cairo: 'That sense of newness is simply delicious, it makes new the Bible and friends and all mankind and love and spiritual things, and Sunday and church and God himself. So I've found.'

This whole experience of conversion was well described theologically by Leighton Ford in the Durban Congress of 1973:

> Conversion, biblically speaking, is a metaphor of motion. A man is going one way. He stops, turns around and walks back in the opposite direction. This act of conversion includes what he turns from, what he turns to and the act of turning itself. To a Christian, conversion is unique in that the turning pivots on the person of Jesus Christ . . . Conversion therefore is far more than an isolated religious or emotional experience. It is a complete re-orientation of the personality towards a new centre as a result of a real personal encounter with Jesus Christ. It is nothing less than becoming a part of God's new creation in Christ.'[3]

And St Paul summarises the result as 'a new creature' who has forsaken the old for the new: 'if anyone is in Christ, he is a new creation: the old has gone, the new has come!' (2 Cor 5:17).

But what is included in the 'old' we leave behind and the 'new' we embrace?

In 1975 our team was invited to do a major city-wide evangelistic campaign in Pietermaritzburg. Night after night literally thousands of people came to the Royal show grounds as we shared the gospel of Christ.

By Thursday night I was quite the local hero. Then on Friday I preached on 'Jesus Christ and the Future of South Africa' and stressed, which I should probably have done more clearly earlier in the week, that repentance means, among other things, forsaking old racist attitudes and abandoning our old acceptance of political injustice and discrimination. It is not just turning from private sin but from collective sin too.

Conversion means reorienting around the new way of Jesus, embracing his new kingdom values, and accepting new moral standards for private and societal life.

At this, hundreds of whites freaked out: 'Why did Michael spoil it by getting political? After all, to be converted to Jesus is enough. Let the politicians worry about apartheid and all that.' While being verbally assaulted by whites after the meeting, some militant blacks came up to tell me I was 'totally irrelevant'. Militant blacks and conservative whites were equally hot and bothered – which made me conclude I just might have scored a bull's-eye.

In my view, conversion is of little ultimate consequence if all it means is that we start having some warm feelings of peace and begin having a Quiet Time for devotions each day but remain basically unchanged in the totality of our being. Surely when Jesus called those early disciples it was not just to a changed intellectual position or some happy emotions but to a total transformation of life, behaviour and world-view. As Jim Wallis notes: 'There are no neutral zones or areas of life left untouched by biblical conversion.'[4]

So conversion, which brings us to Jesus and into his church, will also take us out into the world. In other words:

> Our conversion cannot be an end in itself; it is the first step of entry into the Kingdom. Conversion marks the birth of the movement out of a merely private existence into a public consciousness. Conversion is the beginning of active solidarity with the purposes of the Kingdom of God in the world. No longer preoccupied with our private lives, we are engaged in a vocation for the world. Our prayer becomes, 'Thy Kingdom come, thy will be done, on earth as it is in heaven.' If we restrict our salvation to only inner concerns, we have yet to enter into its fullness.[5]

This means that our conversion will often put us at odds with the conventional mindset or practice of our society. In South Africa it must make us clash with apartheid. To say our conversion does not relate to apartheid is to deny that we are fully converted.

SPOKE SEVEN: AVOID 'THE GREAT REVERSAL' AND 'THE GREAT BETRAYAL'

In his fine book *The Great Reversal*, the American author David Moberg says that evangelical Christians were once very much part of a forward movement of unity, evangelism and social concern. Then they went into a great and tragic reversal.

It was not always the case that so-called evangelical Christians read only half the Bible and ignored the major socio-political issues of their time. Indeed social history in both England and the United States, as Moberg demonstrates, reveals that Christians who were theologically conservative played a major role in social reconstruction and social welfare. In fact they had 'a profound impact . . . upon the abolition of slavery, prison reform, humane treatment of the mentally ill and improved working conditions for industrial labourers'.[6]

There was however, Moberg admits, one lack: these nineteenth- and early twentieth-century evangelicals tended not to see all the 'structural' issues behind poverty, racism and so on. So they did *welfare* work to alleviate problems rather than undertaking *social action* to get at their causal roots so as to prevent them claiming more victims.

Even so, despite that caveat, concerned evangelical believers spoke up for the under-dog and championed the poor.

Then came the 'Great Reversal'. From 1910 until the 1930s, a major shift took place in evangelical circles on social issues. The trouble was that many of those who weakened in their adherence to the Bible's authority, the deity of Jesus and the supernatural dimensions of scripture and Christian witness were the ones who became more and more enamoured of the 'social gospel', which began to replace evangelism and missionary work. This was 'the Great Betrayal'.

The more theologically conservative evangelicals, fighting for biblical authority, the deity of Jesus and for biblical supernaturalism, overreacted and tossed out the baby of social concern with the bath water of liberal theology.

The American theologian Carl Henry sees the poor 'social-concern' track-record of modern evangelicals as coming from at least two causes: 'The first was the neglect of the Good News of salvation for sinners by social gospelers, because that imposed upon conservatives the staggering burden of biblical evangelism and missions throughout the world.' A second cause of imbalance was rooted in a reaction against the attempts of liberal Protestantism in betrayal of biblical faith to achieve the kingdom of God on earth 'through political and economic changes, excluding the supernatural redemptive facets of Christian faith'.[7]

In other words, at least part of the reason for the Great Reversal was the concentration by evangelical Christians on other *legitimate* issues involved in responding to the Great Betrayal. But in the process they developed serious 'blind spots to current social evils'.[8]

None of this excuses any of us caught up in the Great Reversal; we all need to move forward with the *whole* message and ministry of scripture.

SPOKE EIGHT: AFFIRM THE LINK BETWEEN EVANGELISM AND SOCIAL CONCERN, AND SEEK TO WORK THEM OUT

In 1974 a major Congress on World Evangelisation was held in Lausanne, Switzerland. The matter of getting the gospel out in new ways around the planet was its major item of concern. But its other major concern was to work out and express how evangelism and societal concern and the demands of justice all interlink and come together.

In the *Lausanne Covenant* these various dimensions were wonderfully drawn together, particularly in Clauses 4 and 5 on the Nature of Evangelism and Christian Social Responsibility respectively. (See Appendix 4).

Though these two great arms in Christian endeavour of evangelism and social concern on occasion function separately, they should in fact normally operate together, with acts of social concern being either a *consequence* of evangelism or a *bridge* to evangelism or a *partner* in evangelism. The ideal is probably that of partnership, where evangelism and social concern operate as the two blades of a pair of scissors, cutting through human need and bondage of every sort.

One American writer and evangelist, Robert Speer, wrote at the beginning of this century: 'Wherever the Gospel goes, it plants in the hearts of men forces that produce new lives and it places in the communities of men forces that create new social combinations.'[9] Evangelism is thus critically important because you can't have socially responsible Christians without having produced Christians in the first place!

I see such positive forces in the life and ministry of Caesar Molebatsi in Soweto. He lives and works in that demanding place as a true evangelist and a true social reformer. Caesar and many of his evangelical friends put out a document not too long ago called *Evangelical Witness in South Africa*. Their group, calling themselves 'The Concerned Evangelicals', say this in their courageous document: 'We believe that one cannot meet the spiritual needs of people effectively if this does not touch on or have any bearing on their social needs. Evangelism therefore cannot be separated from social action and social justice.'[10]

Yet there can occasionally be a practical outworking of someone's specific calling which effectively results in some separation of evangelism and social action. Sometimes the demands of a specific situation or audience may justify some separating of evangelism and social action, but more commonly it is the distribution of spiritual gifts within the body of Christ which may have this effect. Not everybody is gifted in the same way. Some are gifted as evangelists (Eph. 4:11), while others are called very specifically to 'service' (Rom 12:7; 1 Pet 4:11) or to 'acts of mercy' (Rom 12:8). The point is that we are not all called to do exactly the same thing. We have different specialised callings, but we are to use them for the common good, and are neither to over-inflate the importance of our own contribution nor to deflate the value of someone else's (see 1 Cor 12:14–26). But this can't be an excuse for remaining lopsided and saying, 'You do your thing and I'll do mine.'

If we belong together in the body of Christ, we all have to support each other, whatever our given place and calling in the body. Mercifully I am not called to be Archbishop of Cape

Town or to do what Desmond Tutu does or to have exactly his emphasis. But I do need to encourage him in his ministry, and I do. Equally mercifully, from the point of view of students, I am not called to be an academic like David Bosch, while he is probably equally thankful that he does not have to come with me into tropical West Africa to conduct an evangelistic campaign to the Liberians in Monrovia while struggling with tropical heat, a touch of malaria and the proverbial tummy-runs! But I must support David, and he must support me; and we do. This is what the body of Christ is all about: mutual support and interdependence.

In South Africa there is a rampant movement across the nation of neo-Pentecostal congregations calling themselves the Rhema Church. They have wonderful worship, music and a great evangelistic ministry. Many people anathematise them for not showing much socio-political concern. I don't, because I too believe in worship, music and evangelism. But I would want to urge them to add to those concerns more fully the necessary and urgent concern for the injustices of the society in which they minister. And I would not want them to reject Desmond Tutu or Frank Chikane for agitating about justice.

The point is that we have to relate to one another in the body-life of the church of Jesus Christ, and only by this can our various specialisations work together for the glory of God, the extension of his kingdom and the saving of society. We need each other.

THE RIM: SEEK FIRST THE KINGDOM OF GOD

We come now to what holds these 'spokes' together: seeking first the kingdom of God. This is the rim of the wheel. In terms of our diagram (p. 242), our growth in balance flows out from our love of God, which is at the centre. Then it goes along the eight spokes into the rim of the wheel, which is our seeking first the kingdom of God. From the rim of the wheel it flows back along the spokes into our love of God.

In other words, Jesus' teaching on the kingdom of God, and

our seeking of it, is the all-embracing outer truth which holds everything together once we are in a love relationship with the living God. Our mentioning of this last is not because it is last in importance but because it belongs with that which is first in importance – namely our loving the Lord our God with all of our heart, soul, mind and strength. Neither the hub nor the rim of a wheel stand as more important than the other. Both are of paramount importance because the spokes radiate from the hub into the rim and from the rim into the hub in total interdependence. So both love of God and seeking the kingdom are of *first* importance. In one sense they are the same thing put differently!

One of the loveliest choruses to come out of the Charismatic Renewal of the last decade is 'Seek ye first the kingdom of God'. The beautiful melody adds weight and emotion to this matchless and celebrated injunction from Jesus. In fact, once we do start to seek first the kingdom, we will find all other things, including a whole and balanced ministry and witness, will be added to us. This needs just a little more spelling out so that we see its full implications.

Jesus as the king of the kingdom

The main thing about kings is that one submits to them, especially if one is in their kingdom. And surely this is what Jesus meant when he opened his public ministry with his very first recorded words: 'The kingdom of God is near. Repent and believe the good news!' (Mark 1:15).

What he was really saying was something like this: 'I, as the king of heaven and the universe, have now come down to earth. So my kingdom is in some special and new way being inaugurated here on this planet. Therefore things can never be quite the same now that you know about the kingdom which I have come to inaugurate. This you must see as Good News to be believed and you must accordingly lay down your weapons of rebellion and bring yourself in full submission to me and I will bestow on you the many blessings of my kingdom. I will also reign in your life for your good, and for the good of your societies.'

Now the fact that Jesus had to talk about us repenting and surrendering suggests that in our hearts there is an inclination away from submitting to his kingship and his reign because our fallen human natures tell us we should stay in charge and do things our own way. We basically want to be king and do not want to submit ourselves to the reign and rule of Jesus Christ in our lives, relationships, and over our societies.

But Jesus wants us to do it his way. And getting everything back under his control is what he has intended since the original fall of man.

The kingdom is at hand

When Jesus says the kingdom of heaven is at hand, or has come near, he is really saying that heaven and the way it is ruled has now come within our reach and experience. Human beings can enter the kingdom of God *now*. And we do it by repentance and faith. This means turning from our sins, in other words from doing things our own way and not his, and then surrendering or believing in him as one believes in a doctor who is going to take out one's appendix. After such a surrender the agenda of Jesus becomes ours in the world around us.

As we do this and give ourselves to him an amazing thing happens. Jesus described this to Nicodemus, the Pharisee who came to see him by night, as a 'new birth'. And the incredible thing about this new birth is that without it a human being will not even 'See the kingdom of God' (John 3:3), let alone 'enter' it (John 3:5).

'Thy kingdom come'

If we are in any doubt that the kingdom of God speaks about God's rule not only in heaven but also on earth, we have only to think of how Jesus taught us to pray: 'your kingdom come, your will be done on earth as it is in heaven' (Matt 6:10). Surely Jesus is saying that 'The Kingdom of God is a society upon earth where God's will is as perfectly done as it is in heaven.'[11]

When we look at this definition we will also find in it an answer to the rather puzzling fact that the kingdom or reign of God is often spoken about in the scriptures in three different tenses – it is past, present and future, all at the same time. One could look at it like this:

THE KINGDOM OF GOD

HAS COME	COMES	WILL COME FULLY
(when Jesus came and announced it)	(and is present in the lives of those who believe in him and obey him)	(when Jesus comes again and everything alien to the kingdom is put under his feet)

One scholar has summarised it this way:

> An analysis of 119 passages in the New Testament where the expression 'Kingdom' occurs, shows that it means the rule of God; which *was* manifested in and through Christ; *is* apparent in the Church; gradually develops amidst hindrances; is triumphant at the second coming of Christ (the end); and *finally* perfected in the world to come.[12]

People and relationships in the kingdom

The most exciting implication of what Jesus says about his kingdom is that it is really all about *people*. It is not about a physical realm. This rule is over people and over the hearts of people.

The kingdom of God is basically the kingdom of right relationships. It is about Jesus so reigning and ruling in the hearts of his people that they not only relate rightly to him, but to the other people in the church of Christ; and to still other people who are spiritually lost or in distress or in need in the society around them; and finally to those people (not to be abstracted as the state) who govern the society in which they live.

So the kingdom or reign or rule of God is being expressed or effected as his *people* do four things:

1. *Preach the gospel of the kingdom to other people* not yet submitted to Jesus, the king. (Here God's rule is working personally and evangelistically.)
2. *Work out loving and right relationships with other people* – especially in the church. (Here God's rule is working communally and relationally.)
3. *Care for any people in any kind of need.* (Here God's rule is working practically and physically.)
4. *Work for justice and rightness in the way one group of people, the strong, treats another group of people, the weak.* (Here God's rule is working socially, economically and politically.)

CONCLUSION

If I think back over the years to the people, churches or ministries which have struck me as most truly Christian and most vitally attractive, the quality which always surfaces for me as an explanation is that of balance. They bring into harmonious unity and equilibrium the many-faceted concerns of our Lord, and like a prism or rainbow of many colours they radiate beauty and wholeness. They shine forth as the real thing. And one looks at such people and says: 'I like what I see!' Or one tastes such a church and says: 'To worship and serve here is beautiful.'

In fact one is tasting salt which has not lost its savour. And salt makes one thirsty – thirsty for the Water of Life and for the kind of life and witness and heart from which flow rivers of living water to a parched world.

15 Reaching for Reconciliation (The church's responsibility to be united and uniting)

A love of reconciliation is not weakness or cowardice. It demands courage, nobility, generosity, sometimes heroism, an overcoming of oneself rather than of one's adversary.

Pope Paul VI

To reconcile man with man and not with God is to reconcile no one at all.

Thomas Merton

We implore you on Christ's behalf: Be reconciled to God.
2 Corinthians 5:20

Therefore, if you are offering your gift at the altar and there remember that your brother has something against you, leave your gift there in front of the altar. First go and be reconciled to your brother, then come and offer your gift.
Matthew 5:23–24

It is a grim and glorious thing to be gripped by reconciliation in South Africa today.

It is grim because so many white Christians see reconciliation as political and therefore to be shunned, and most black Christians see reconciliation as cheap and therefore to be ignored.

But it is glorious too because it is central to the heart of Jesus, pivotal to the New Testament, and inescapable for South Africa. This is because, whatever anyone says now, reconciliation is destined sooner or later to be an idea whose time has come. And if we contemplate what John Vorster said was too ghastly to contemplate, we should let the time for the coming of the reconciliation idea be now.

Not that it will be, can be or dare be easy and cheap. For it is a desperate, difficult and dangerous business, as we shall see. But it must be the business of the day – now, not when both land and people lie in ashes.

RECONCILIATION STARTS WITH MAKING THE VERTICAL PRIMARY

There's no way round the primacy of the vertical (our relationship with God) over the horizontal (our relationship with others). We must start here, with each of us being personally reconciled to God, born again of his Spirit and filled with his Life and Calvary-love, and then preach it. Otherwise others, caught up in the preoccupations of the horizontal, will forget it too.

This came home very clearly to me in 1968–1969, when Festo Kivengere and I first teamed up to minister and travel together, first in Nairobi (1968–1969), then across the USA in 1970, and thereafter all over the world from Nicaragua and Costa Rica to Cairo and Sydney.

In Festo's own experience he had to be converted to Jesus Christ before he could, for example, forgive and be reconciled with a white missionary whom he hated. That power of Christ in his heart triggered both a new motivation to be in fellowship with his enemy and a new power to do something about it. A fifty-mile cycle ride through the mountains to sort this out was both evidence and proof that he meant business.

In my own experience, too, I know that nothing short of conversion to Jesus Christ could have motivated me to want to preach round Africa with black Ugandans or find my fumbling way over miscellaneous British barriers to Afrikaner friends.

So the vertical is where it all starts; it cannot and must never be forgotten. This in turn makes evangelism always crucial.

In 1980, at a Renewal Conference, Pastor Justus du Plessis, a South African Pentecostal leader, rightly warned against thinking of reconciliation in exclusively horizontal categories: 'We cannot even begin to deal with reconciliation before we have dealt with the awfulness of sin and God's sole remedy for it in . . . the blood of Jesus Christ.'[1]

Thank goodness there are Pentecostals, Baptists and Rhema people around to remind us of this biblical emphasis. As St Paul says, the thing '*of first importance*' is to know 'that Christ died for our sins according to the Scriptures . . . [and] that he was raised on the third day' (1 Cor 15:3–4). And Jesus for his part told us to 'Make every effort [the Greek is *agonizomai* = agonise] to enter through the narrow door' (Luke 13:24) to Christian salvation. In other words, do anything to get in there . . . but get there. If your hand or foot or eye looks like blocking you from entry to eternal life, remove it or pluck it out, but get there. The gaining of eternal life is the pearl of great price; it is to be valued beyond all else.

So reconciliation between God and man is fundamental – for both the next life and for this. Indeed without it there would be no church here at all.

RECONCILIATION MEANS TESTING WHERE I AM WITH GOD BY WHERE I AM WITH MY BROTHERS AND SISTERS

Roy Hession, that perceptive exponent of the 'Calvary Road', has written:

The work of the Lord Jesus Christ on the Cross was not only to bring men back into fellowship with God but also into fellowship with their fellow men. Indeed it cannot do one without the other. As the spokes get nearer the centre of the wheel, they get nearer to one another. But if we have not been brought into vital fellowship with our brother, it is a proof that to that extent we have not been brought into vital fellowship with God. The first epistle of John insists on testing the depth and reality of a man's fellowship with God by the depth and reality of his fellowship with his brethren (1 John 2:9; 3:14–15; 4:20).[2]

He also makes an observation of profound importance for
all of us who live in alienated and polarised societies such as
South Africa, Northern Ireland or the Middle East:

> Some of us have come to see how utterly connected a man's
> relationship to his fellows is with his relationship to God. Every-
> thing that comes as a barrier between us and another, be it ever so
> small, comes as a barrier between us and God. We have found
> that where these barriers are not put right immediately, they get
> thicker and thicker until we find ourselves shut off from God and
> our brother by what seem to be veritable brick walls. Quite
> obviously, if we allow New Life to come to us, it will have to
> manifest itself by a walk of oneness with God and our brother,
> with nothing between.[3]

Now when one realises how profoundly and seemingly
irrevocably apartheid has disrupted relationships between
blacks and whites, and put massive barriers between believers, one can see how perilous are these human barriers to
our relationship with God. The fact is that our spirituality and
gospel faithfulness can so easily become casualties of our
horizontal alienations. Beyond that, and equally alarming,
our horizontal reconciliations become almost impossible because we have suffered such spiritual leakage that we actually
do not have the spiritual resources for the totally demanding,
costly and humbling business of reconciliation. And that is
when we toss it out.

The common white South African rejection of reconciliation is often a totally self-deceiving fig-leaf to hide the nakedness of spiritual, moral and political bankruptcy. The black
word that reconciliation is irrelevant is a confession that an
unacceptable biblical shallowness and an understandable
political despair have made them forsake the lamb role which
Jesus mandated (Luke 10:3) for the wolf role which he
forbade. All of which makes for a demoralising scenario. Nor
is it one which will resolve itself till we go back and put the
building-blocks in place all over again, to see what reconciliation is really all about.

That requires, among other things, a new humility with
each other.

RECONCILIATION INVOLVES A PILGRIMAGE TO CALVARY

Let me go back to an earlier part of my pilgrimage, not only in the ministry of reconciliation but also in my struggles with my own pride in all this.

It has been a long road, and there is still a long way to go – as the road winds uphill all the way from the interpersonal and vertical to the interpersonal and horizontal, and then on to the inter-group and finally to the structural. As we reach each horizon, thinking we've got to the top of the hill, another one opens up and the Spirit of God calls, 'Come on. There's more. You can't stop there!' And the Lord might even whisper: 'Why all the whimpering? Did you believe that reconciliation was the easy option?'

I suppose that the first time the challenge of horizontal reconciliation became deeply real for me was, as I narrated earlier, when the Holy Spirit pressured me at the World Congress on Evangelism (in Berlin 1966) to go and get right with the two Afrikaners who had so hammered me after my paper on 'Nationalism as an Obstacle to Evangelism'. It involved not just eating a slice of humble pie, but almost meant consuming the whole thing!

What I saw then in embryo, and which I see more clearly now, is that reconciliation is not the easy way out. Anger, bitterness, verbal vendetta and personal distance are much easier. They are also much more delicious because they feed the old nature and its self-importance so exquisitely.

But to see that God's way up is down, and to climb down from self-righteousness to assume blame and responsibility is to struggle desperately with the inner constraints of one's own sinful and proud heart. This is what makes the first steps into the reconciliation arena so hard – it involves dealing with one's own heart before that of one's adversary.

In a way, it really is a question of getting oneself to Calvary – that toughest of tough turf on which to stand. The proud, stiff-necked 'I' has to bow its head and die, for as long as we lay all blame at the other person's door we are done for – whether individually or nationally.

Roy Hession has written:

> The story of man's first quarrel with God in the third chapter of
> Genesis is closely followed in the fourth chapter by the story of
> man's first quarrel with his fellow, – ie Cain's murder of Abel.
> The Fall is simply, 'we have turned every one to his own way' (Is.
> 53:6). If I want my own way rather than God's, it is quite obvious
> that I shall want my own way rather than the other man's. A man
> does not assert his independence of God to surrender it to a
> fellow man, if he can help it. But a world in which each man wants
> his own way cannot but be a world full of tensions, barriers,
> suspicions, misunderstandings, clashes and conflicts.[4]

To have mastered the art of getting one's own way is to have
lost the art of reconciling love, because it means one has made
putting self first one's way of life.

Yet when we look at Jesus the whole picture is so different,
with its humbling images of the dove and the lamb. For here is
the true humility of deity. Here is the model for proud
humans. Here is the God who in Paul's words 'took the form
of a servant' – a scandalous idea for us South African whites,
who know what servants are all about. Paul's description does
not stop there, however. He goes on to say how this God of
ours 'humbled himself and became obedient' – and not just
obedient, but 'obedient to death', and not just any death, but
the ultimate death, the most awful ever devised by man:
'death on a cross' (Phil 2:7–8).

Paul in using this language shakes us out of all possible
complacency and self-comfort with the simple exhortation
(which is one of the first building-blocks in the ministry of
reconciliation): 'Your attitude should be the same as that of
Christ Jesus . . .' (Phil 2:5). More than that, we are 'in
humility' to 'consider others better than [ourselves]' and 'look
not only to [our] interests, but also to the interests of others'
(Phil 2:3–4).

When I read those requirements they seem impossible, to
the extent that I wish I could ignore them or I wonder if the
philosophy of revolution might be more sensible: reconciliation is so hard and the alternatives are so much easier.

All of which agonising serves to underline that the ministry of reconciliation involves the self-crucifying art of getting ourselves to Calvary.

RECONCILIATION INVOLVES THE PREREQUISITE OF CONTACT

The late Seth Mokitini, a wonderful old South African Christian leader, was once walking with a friend in the street. As a man passed them on the other side of the road, Mokitini's friend said: 'I don't like that man.'

'But I didn't know you knew him,' responded Mokitini.

'I don't really. Not well anyway,' said the friend.

'Well', concluded the old African sage, 'that explains why you don't like him!'

First-hand contact and personal exposure to the different and distant brother or sister is crucial to the relational and reconciling process.

We saw this beautifully illustrated at PACLA (The Pan African Christian Leadership Assembly) held in Nairobi in 1976. This was an outflow of our Durban Congress of 1973, where we saw many marvellous happenings of deep reconciliation. Believing that the whole of polarised Africa needed this type of experience, some of us then initiated PACLA, drawing together leaders from forty-eight out of Africa's fifty-one countries.

One of the things we quickly learnt was that new levels of reconciliation come about when there is contact between people who have hitherto seen themselves as enemies or as at best very distant brothers.

One Kenyan girl, finding out just before PACLA opened that she had unbeknown to her been doing conference preparation work in PACLA's administrative offices with some of my white African Enterprise South African colleagues, suddenly blurted out: 'I can't believe it. I suddenly find these whites are South Africans. Oh, goodness! What shall I do? I already love them too much to hate them!'

Contact had opened her heart. Imagine what might happen if all the barriers in South Africa went down: real meaningful contact between equals would suddenly begin, and who knows what would follow?

Evanson Kangongoi of Nairobi, one of the stewards, decided he could develop new friendships most deeply and quickly by inviting people to his home. In the first group to visit his home was a black American and a white South African. Said Sydney Luckett, the South African, later: 'This was for me one of the deepest experiences I had at PACLA.'

You see, all Syd's stereotypes of blacks and black homes were suddenly blown apart.

Mrs Salome Mbevi of Kenya rejoiced to meet the first Sudanese person she had ever known. 'You know, brother,' she confessed, 'when I thought of the Sudan, I have always previously thought of oases and camels. Now I will think of you!' Whether the Sudanese brother found that a source of satisfaction, history does not relate![5]

When stereotypes go, and there is personal contact and mutual exposure in fellowship, then new avenues of reconciliation open up. If South Africa has a problem, it is in the stereotypes 'apartheid' has allowed to develop. We all relate to ghosts. Reconciliation, on the other hand, insists that we work at breaking stereotypes.

RECONCILIATION MEANS EMBRACING THE WHOLE BODY OF CHRIST AND THE UNITY ALREADY THERE

Again our experience at PACLA was instructive in this, because time and again we saw reconciliation frustrated and alienation escalated by the difficulty Christians have in accepting one another as fellow members of the body of Christ.

But if we do accept one another on that basis the consequences are extraordinary: especially if we see that through Christ we are *already* united!

The evening before PACLA opened, Majongwe Daidansou, a very fine Christian leader from Tchad, came up to me and said: 'You know, brother, there is some shaking in our delegation about the presence of the South Africans. What should our attitude be?'

'Daidansou,' I replied, 'the brothers have got to come to terms with the fact that in Jesus Christ we belong together. We are together part of the church, however objectionable we South Africans may seem to you. We are related, even as Peter, with all his prejudice towards Cornelius, became related to him in Christ. This is what the church and the gospel are all about. Brother, you must get this through to your friends.'

'I'll try,' said the West African leader, 'I'll try. But it may not be so easy. The feelings are very strong.'[6]

Before my own address to the PACLA conference on the theme of 'Fellowship and Unity within the Body of Christ', I was introduced by Festo Kivengere, who until his recent death led our own African Enterprise East African teams.

Festo shared how we had ministered as miracle brothers – a black Ugandan and a white South African – and how this had come about through the reconciling love of Christ. Then he launched me with a great public embrace of love.

Sitting in the Assembly, Simone Ibrahim of Nigeria was touched in his heart by this demonstration of Christian brotherhood. 'In fact in that moment', he testified later, 'the Holy Spirit worked in my heart and I began to feel that perhaps after all violence was not the way in Southern Africa. Maybe God really could bring an answer by the power of Calvary love.'[7]

Thus can even a seemingly small demonstration of the supra-racial nature of the body of Christ work its miracle-working power.

In my ensuing comments, I zeroed in on Ephesians 2:11–22, where Paul makes his theological reply to the huge strain on fellowship created by that epic ancient-world divide between Jew and Gentile.

In this passage St Paul reminds the Ephesians that

'at one time you *were* strangers. Now you *are* fellow citizens. At one time you *were* without God. But now you *are* members of the household of God. At one time you *were* afar off from God and each other. But now you *are* near. At one time you *were* alienated. But now He *has* made you one with us. At one time there *was* a dividing wall of hostility between you. But now He *has* broken down that dividing wall.'

Paul thus contrasts the past or previous situation of division which did exist, not with the new situation of unity in Christ which might or could or should exist, but with the new situation of unity in Christ which *does* exist. 'He *has* made us one' (verse 14). It is true now in the present. In Christ it has happened. It is not just a unity for which we must work as Christians, but one which already exists for us as Christians because of Jesus and His cross. Paul is speaking not just of a future possibility, but of a present reality. The major basis of our fellowship, therefore, is what God has already done in bringing us into Christ as we respond in repentance and faith to Jesus' death, resurrection and offer of forgiveness.

It is not that the whole structure of Christians may one day be joined together by some future ecumenical breakthrough; but rather, as we see in Ephesians 2:21, that the whole structure is already joined together. We *are* one. Our job is to show it.[8]

RECONCILIATION REQUIRES HEARING EACH OTHER

Even to begin the process of reconciliation, another basic prerequisite is that we hear each other. Again South Africa makes things very difficult for itself by, so to speak, putting its people into almost hermetically sealed compartments, so that we can't hear what the other person is saying, nor can we feel his heartbeat.

The struggle for this hearing process to happen was also dramatically evident in PACLA. Especially was this so when the time came for an Afrikaner, of all people, to address the Assembly.

As the programme chairman of PACLA, I had been approached with numerous protests about putting David Bosch on the programme for a plenary address. But I adamantly refused to remove him, knowing that much good would come from blacks throughout Africa, hearing from one whose nationality they automatically despised and abhorred.

By one of those special Holy Spirit ironies it was Bosch's

moving paper on 'The Church as the New Community' which brought the PACLA conference to Calvary and to spiritual breakthrough.

Speaking to the deep and desperate alienations in the church throughout Africa, the Dutch Reformed Professor noted that

> reconciliation is no cheap matter. It does not come about by simply papering over deep-seated differences. Reconciliation presupposes confrontation. Without that we do not get reconciliation, but merely a temporary glossing over of differences. The running sores of society cannot be healed with the use of sticking-plaster. Reconciliation presupposes an operation, a cutting to the very bone, without anaesthetic. The infection is not just on the surface. The abscess of hate and mistrust and fear, between black and white, between nation and nation, between rich and poor, has to be slashed open.[9]

David then shared a deep and moving experience which he and his wife had had:

> One evening, about a year ago, my wife and I had a visit from some black ministers of our church. Our discussion inevitably was on what it means to be Christians in South Africa today. The attitude of the blacks was: 'In spite of everything you two whites say tonight, you still belong to the group of the oppressors. You benefit from the system, we don't. You are privileged, we are not. You remain white and we black, your feet remain on our necks.' We talked until the early morning hours and it seemed as though we would never be able really to find one another. We were not people, but blacks and whites. We were not people, but categories. Eventually, when the blacks were preparing to leave, my wife broke down and wept, pleading for understanding and acceptance.

At this point David's own deep emotions were evident to all as he struggled to hold back his tears. The sense of melting spirits, brokenness and repentance began to sweep the auditorium, because for the first time the vast majority of those African leaders were actually hearing and feeling the heartbeat of a real live, flesh-and-blood Afrikaner. And imagine if every Afrikaner, or South African English-speaker, for that matter, likewise really heard and felt the heartbeat of the African cry.

David concluded:

So those blacks left our home. But the next day one of them returned, on behalf of the others. He said: 'Your wife's tears made all the difference.' If it can still happen in South Africa that a white woman weeps because of a desire for real, human fellowship with blacks, then this is something that cannot be explained logically. It must be of God.[10]

Bishop Michael Nuttall, who was also present, reflecting on that meeting, said: 'That night Anamie Bosch's spiritual gift of tears watered the church in Africa.'

At that moment in PACLA we saw the reconciling power of the cross, because we had seen and *heard* a man at the cross.

Graham Cyster, a South African black from the Cape, and now an active Christian worker for reconciliation and for justice in Cape Town, said to an overseas friend: 'You know, Chuck, the other day I told you I was thinking of emigrating from South Africa and giving up. I've changed my mind. While there is one white man in South Africa who feels like that I am ready to go back and live for the Lord in that situation.'

A delegate from an independent African country confessed: 'Oh, I can't believe what is happening to me. I am under conviction. God is rearranging my whole thinking.' Said another: 'Suddenly I see I am part of the problem we face. My own lack of forgiveness and understanding has been part of the problem. I thought I was so free of complicity. I thought it was *their* problem.'[11]

That night, as I saw the miracle of the whole eighty-plus South African contingent being taken into the warm, forgiving and compassionate heart of black Africa, it was brought home to my heart not only that reconciliation is costly, but even more basically that it is actually possible. The impossibles can indeed find each other when they take time really to 'hear' each other in depth.

This applies to groups as much as to individuals. Similar

miracles of listening and healing took place between groups of French-speaking blacks and groups of English-speaking blacks, between groups of Arabs and groups of Africans, and especially between Angolan 'internals' and Angolan exiles – the latter seeing the former as sell-outs, and the former seeing the latter as deserters.

And was it not all happening in the land where Jomo Kenyatta, on behalf of the black group, had said at Independence to the English settlers, as the white group: 'We must forgive one another; we cannot build a new nation together unless we do so on the basis of forgiveness'? So one caught glimpses of reconciliation working at the group level too, where the Spirit of Jesus was allowed free sway.

RECONCILIATION INVOLVES FORGIVENESS

In early 1977, a couple of months after PACLA, those of us who had been at that historic gathering launched a new expression of reconciling faith and hope in the shape of SACLA – the South African Christian Leadership Assembly.

Mounting it was an adventure full of unbelievable difficulty, complexity, opposition and often trauma. But SACLA finally came to pass, attended by six thousand leaders of all races in Pretoria in July 1976.

Many incredible things happened, especially in the development of a network of new relationships across South Africa. Hundreds of these still hold and operate today to bless this land and to hold back the forces of even more serious alienation.

One of the most significant experiences for many of us was the challenge to forgiveness which all the mutual misunderstanding and wounding, either from the system or from other individuals, had brought into our lives.

One black said: 'I must now write a letter to an "unforgiveable white".'

A girl from the Soweto Committee of Ten said: 'I need to seek forgiveness for my antagonism to Gatsha Buthelezi.'

A black couple who were staying in an Afrikaans home and were made to use the 'outside' toilet rather than the indoor one had to muster the courage to confront their host and hostess, reveal their sense of affront, and then forgive the perpetrators. The gracious Dutch Reformed couple saw the painful offence to the human dignity of their guests, asked forgiveness from their side, and terminated the offensive and humiliating arrangement.

This was an interesting little episode, bringing home the truth that reconciliation will often mean honest confrontation, pain, struggle, tears and anger before there is healing.

I remain convinced that healing begins with unilateral forgiveness and ends with unconditional acceptance.

In my own case, in SACLA I found myself much wounded by a critic out in South-West Africa whom I believed to have damaged both SACLA and me. But while smouldering over this, I found the Holy Spirit saying, 'Before you give your talk at SACLA on the Holy Spirit, go, and first be reconciled to your brother who has something against you. Forgive him and go.'

Though it cost me an air ticket paid from my savings, I knew I had to forgive and go to my brother.

In another instance, a Dutch Reformed leader went to a Cabinet Minister to malign my motives in initiating SACLA and effectively to slander my name. Again I had huge struggles with forgiveness, my flesh rather calling me to pronounce multiplied anathemas on the offending brother.

As it happened, David Bosch went to the Cabinet Minister in question late one night.

'Have you come to talk about SACLA?'

'No,' replied David, 'I've come to talk about Michael! You've listened to a slanderous story without knowing the facts.'

That was brotherhood at work. But what of this requirement of forgiveness? To be sure, all sorts of blacks at SACLA, especially many who now experienced forced removals, had a huge struggle facing the forgiveness mandate when Dr Piet Koornhof (Minister in Charge of Black Affairs at the time, and therefore responsible for many removals) got up to address the Assembly.

One moving post-SACLA episode of forgiveness came my way many years later when I was in Zimbabwe to address a meeting of church leaders. A white pastor came up to me looking very distressed and a bit awkward.

'Brother,' he said, 'I want to ask your forgiveness. You will never, ever know the extent to which I shamefully tore you personally to the ground and opposed SACLA. But it has taken a ten-year civil war here and the loss of forty thousand lives to teach me you were right in your concerns for justice and reconciliation in South Africa. If there's anything I can ever do to make amends I would like to.' I just loved him and thanked God for him, and of course forgave him with all my heart.

The demands of forgiveness

However, when any of us rises to the demanding heights of a major act of forgiveness, even if it is only once, we then encounter the even more shattering demand of the gospel. Peter found out about it when he asked Jesus: 'Lord, how many times shall I forgive my brother when he sins against me? Up to seven times?' (Matt 18:21). In theory we know the Lord's reply only too well. The only problem is we don't do it too well!

'"Seventy-seven times"? Lord, you must be joking,' we protest. 'And from the heart too,' Jesus adds, just to keep us totally at his feet and dependent too.

Forgiveness is unilateral, he reminds us. It doesn't depend on the other person getting it all right and being nice to us.

It is imperative that we emulate Jesus' command and his example and learn to forgive others. Martin Luther King puts it this way: 'We must develop and maintain the capacity to forgive. He who is devoid of the power to forgive is devoid of the power to love . . . And forgiveness is not an occasional act: it is a permanent attitude.'[12]

Jesus' example

What a mandate! And what a challenge! Yet how we protest! But our Lord's example stands inescapably like an immoveable rock on the landscape of our souls, and we're meant to follow him.

The supreme example in Jesus' ministry is at the crucifixion, when he prayed, 'Father, forgive them . . .' As Sister Margaret Magdalen in her remarkable book *Jesus Man of Prayer* has put it, 'over-familiarity with the facts has made us casual',[13] so it is worth reminding ourselves that crucifixion 'was a hideous, obscene form of execution. In the world of that day none was more agonising and long drawn out.'[14]

Yet it was amid all this excruciating darkness and horror, and as those hardened soldiers began their cruel work of nailing Jesus to the cross and plunging it with a hideous jolt into its socket, that the world heard the immortal words: 'Father, forgive them, for they do not know what they are doing' (Luke 23:34).

As Sister Margaret asks: 'What *must* the soldiers have thought? Curses and oaths they expected and probably got frequently; but a prayer for forgiveness must have been totally outside their experience . . .'[15]

Here then was love miraculously and marvellously going out regardless and undiminished towards the perpetrators of evil, and at its heart was forgiveness.

Why was this? Because forgiveness is God's unique way for his children to deal with and positively redeem pain that is inflicted on them:

> Forgiveness describes the positive, redemptive response to pain, in which, for love's sake, the hurt is contained by refusal to return it with anger and in which love and goodwill are maintained unbroken towards the offender . . . The original hurt is isolated and so, being contained within the hurt person, is not instrumental in bringing about an increase in the total amount of pain and a consequent proliferation of evil . . . A pain has been transformed by grace into a source of love for both people.[16]

My colleague Festo Kivengere illustrated this admirably when Idi Amin had him as Number One on his hit list. With Archbishop Janani Luwum murdered, Festo, now the target, was forced to flee as an exile. His spirit became very bitter towards Amin. Then, at a Good Friday service in London, the

Lord spoke to him: 'If Amin had been among those soldiers hammering the nails into my hands, would I have said "Father forgive them – all except that big, heavy one from Uganda"? Or would my forgiveness not have gone to Amin too?'

In this letting go and setting free are to be found the inner secrets of forgiveness, for we set free both the offender and ourselves.

RECONCILIATION IMPERATIVES MUST DRIVE US TO OUR KNEES

The gospel demand for forgiveness drives those concerned for reconciliation to their knees. Only here will we ever win through. To hear Jesus say, 'Love your enemies and pray for those who persecute you' (Matt 5:44) is to hear one of the toughest demands our lives can face, but also to be let in on the deepest clue to interpersonal or inter-group reconciliation and healing.

Imagine if Mr Mandela and President Botha were praying for each other daily. Imagine if Mr Tambo and Andries Treurnicht truly lifted each other to the Lord each night. Imagine if Inkatha and UDF leaders found it in their hearts to intercede faithfully for one another. Imagine if you and I hourly upheld our main known enemy in prayer.

We shrink perhaps. Yet why? We shrink from such thoughts – or even actions – because it is too hard on our sinful natures, for we know God would get busy on us and on our hearts and attitudes if we let our enemy in so close that he intruded, *as Jesus said he must*, on our prayer lives.

For myself, though not approving many things done by either the National Party or the ANC, I have found it fruitful, to my own spirit at least, to pray for P W Botha and Piet Koornhof (and even Treurnicht) as well as for Mandela and Tambo – plus Slabbert, Buthelezi, Tutu and others. My prayer is that their minds will 'converge on the mind of Christ' and that my mind and heart, as God's servant, will be right towards them.

Perhaps here there has to be from all concerned with

reconciliation the prayer-posture of standing in the gap as
intercessors both for the major polarised parties in a situation
and for our own attitudes to those polarised from us:

> 'Standing in the gap' is a mediatorial work. The mediator is one
> who stands between two parties, representing the one to the
> other. Moses stood as one of and with his people, identifying with
> their sin, offering his life as atonement for it. But he also stood as
> God's man to his people, declaring God's law, mercy, love and
> forgiveness.[17]

This is why I value South Africa's intercessors and treasure
those who pray for me, who encourage me to pray for myself,
and who pray and intercede for South Africa. They are not
drop-outs, they are the front-line shock troops who enable the
Lord to let us busy little activists help with the odd rear-guard
action here and there.

So let us not bluff ourselves into thinking that we can get by
without prayer: it would be like asking the eagle to soar
without wings (*cf.* Isa 40:30–31).

RECONCILIATION IS GENERALLY IMPOSSIBLE WITHOUT COST AND CONFRONTATION

In SACLA 1979 the places of greatest growth and healing and
reconciliation were the small groups where people levelled
with each other in costly confrontation. Often there is no way
through without this. As in marriage it can often be the most
loving thing possible to confront, difficult though that is.

Confrontations with the forces of law and order

In 1983 our African Enterprise Team was invited to minister
in Israel among Palestinian and Israeli believers. Again and
again we saw costly tears of collision, confrontation and then
healing.

At our African Enterprise Centre a young African woman

who had been wounded in police cross-fire and then imprisoned during the Soweto riots of 1976 met a former South
African policeman who had come on a course there. They
entered a deep, costly and painful time of confrontation. But
from it came healing, growth and a new yearning to be part of
the solution in South Africa and not part of the problem.

A friend of ours, Lawrie Wilmot, in the Eastern Cape, told
us of seven young black detainees who had been badly beaten
up by some police who said they had been endangering the
public peace. On release the black lads went to the police
station with Wilmot with the intention of laying charges. But
once there they found that the offending constables had
already been severely disciplined by senior police authorities,
and in one case legally charged and punished. In the confrontation between the youths and the Special Constables, all
the latter expressed deep sorrow and repentance.

Lawrie reported that 'Six of the seven detainees said that as
they had recently become Christians they would not now lay
charges but would forgive the assaults done to them seeing
that the constables had shown costly repentance.'

Then one of the ex-detainees asked if he could lead in
prayer. 'I wept silently', says Lawrie, 'as this man began to
pray. He and the six detainees with him stood up. I will never
forget that scene. In front was this white policeman, a senior
policeman, in whose office we were, with its plush carpeting
and all that. Then there were these three Constables rigidly at
attention. But the man in charge of the situation was now this
young black ex-detainee, who incidentally at that stage was
still on a charge of public violence of which he has now been
acquitted.'

'Here', Wilmot later said, 'we were seeing costly reconciliation and kingdom progress at work.'

The 'National Initiative for Reconciliation'

In mid 1985 a number of us felt, as we cast our eyes and hearts
across South Africa, that we were watching our nation and its
polarised groups moving like two alienated people in a
crumbling marriage towards 'irretrievable breakdown'.

Only a costly reconciling initiative from Christian people seemed capable of doing anything to repair or heal the breach. One of the things which struck us then, and which grips me still, is that South African Christians are to be found in every grouping, from the super-conservative Conservative Party on the right to the ANC on the left. Imagine if all those believers, who profess a superior loyalty beyond nation and group, would mix as a mighty army of reconcilers to bring together the two ends of the spectrum plus everything in between! Could not the nation be healed?

Some seventy of us from across the land took the initiative to call together four hundred church leaders from forty-eight denominations at a short three-weeks' notice for what we called the 'National Initiative for Reconciliation'. We convened in Pietermaritzburg in September 1985 with a full house of invitees – bishops, archbishops, moderators, black and white, young and old, left and right, radical and conservative. From angry AZAPO youth to an anxious but precious fifty-six man contingent from the Dutch Reformed Church.

As we attracted huge interest and press attention from across the country, we sensed several things.

Bondage, Exodus and Jordan

First of all, while many whites felt themselves to be a people in Exodus to some degree or other, most blacks still felt they were held in the grip of Egyptian bondage.

Yet we also realised, as I noted in my own opening address, that to the extent that any of us are in Exodus, we in the church certainly cannot expect the secular leaders to cross the Jordan to some new Promised Land of political solution until the religious leaders have crossed it first.

In Joshua's case the people had to be led across the Jordan by the priests: 'as soon as the priests who carry the ark of the Lord . . . set foot in the Jordan, its waters flowing downstream will be cut off and stand up in a heap' (Josh 3:13). More than that, 'The priests who carried the ark of the covenant of the Lord stood firm on dry ground in the middle of the Jordan, while all Israel passed by until the whole nation had completed the crossing on dry ground' (Josh 3:17).

In South Africa, Christians have made the fatal error of expecting politicians to cross the Jordan ahead of the priests – *i.e.* ahead of the church. There is no hope for national reconciliation without the body of Christ first showing the way and paying the price. Some Christian leaders constitute notable exceptions, but the rank and file of the church of Jesus Christ has not really forded that Jordan by which the wilderness of racism, discrimination and prejudice is left behind. And until we have done so, and until we have come to costly reconciliation within the church, it is hard to expect politicians and political parties to negotiate such a crossing successfully. Besides, it is only by the collective faith and costly obedience of the people of God that the waters of Jordan can be made to part.

Yet black Christians feel white ones are not interested in either costly obedience or costly reconciliation, because we refuse to repent of our participation in injustice. It is a hard accusation to evade. Frank Chikane can thus give us the staggering information that the white man who supervised his torture in detention was a deacon in his own denomination who knew Frank was a pastor in that same denomination!

Called to be reconcilers

Comparing the black struggle with forgiveness to that faced by the Afrikaner, Archbishop Desmond Tutu said at the Conference: 'I believe the Afrikaner has found it difficult to forgive. He certainly has found it very difficult to forget the experiences of his people in the concentration camps at the beginning of this century. How do white people believe that we can forgive or forget the pass raids, the single-sex hostels, the brutal re-settlement camps, the exclusion from decision-making processes, the raping of our South African citizenship?

'But having said all that,' observed Tutu, 'we are nevertheless called to the business of forgiveness and reconciliation. God is not saying, "Do you like it or don't you like it?" We are called to it.

'But how do you forgive someone who has not yet asked to be forgiven? Forgiveness is something that you offer. It is available, but it has to be appropriated. I have sometimes had quite insensitive letters from white people urging our people to be longsuffering. I feel such words are a discredit to the Gospel of Jesus Christ. How can you ask forgiveness of someone when you still have your foot firmly planted on his neck? You have got him down there and you say, "Forgive me for putting my foot on your neck." '

The absurdity of this registered profoundly, I believe, at that moment in every white soul in the NIR Conference, and we were ready to receive the unpleasant truth that Desmond punched home: 'My brothers and sisters, reconciliation is not cheap, nor is it an easy option. You hear people in this country say, "Why don't you get involved in reconciliation rather than confrontation?" Who said reconciliation excludes confrontation? Who says reconciliation is easy? We must know what we are asking for when we say we must be ministers of reconciliation, because reconciliation cost God the death of his son. True reconciliation, my brothers and sisters, is costly. It involves confrontation because the cross was a confrontation with evil. The cross showed the evil of evil. Are we ready even to die? Are we ready to die physically, to die to our popularity, to die to our security? Are we ready to be made fools for the sake of Christ?'

Cheap or costly reconciliation

Interestingly, and perhaps paradoxically, this line on costly reconciliation was backed by an Afrikaner, David Bosch: 'Cheap reconciliation means meeting in the hope that we shall not clash too much, that we'll be "soft" on each other, that at the end we'll go home unscathed, breathe a sigh of relief and return to "normal". Cheap reconciliation suggests that meeting like this is a softer option than confronting each other in the "real" world outside.'

Cheap reconciliation, Bosch stressed, manifests itself in other forms as well. It is practised where one party wholeheartedly admits that they are wrong and the other party right, but nothing changes. It is also in evidence where one party attempts to ingratiate itself with the other party by constantly fawning on it. This happens at both ends of the spectrum: blacks buttering up whites, whites seeking favour with blacks. In both instances we have servility at the expense of honesty and of real change.

Cheap reconciliation also means tearing faith and justice asunder, driving a wedge between the vertical and the horizontal dimensions: it suggests that we can have peace with God without having justice in our mutual relationships.

In summary, then, cheap reconciliation means in Bosch's view, applying a little bit of goodwill and decency to South African society, but that, he said, is like trying to heal a festering sore with sticking plaster or treating cancer with aspirins.[18]

Awareness of others' sin

David also pointed out something I've seen again and again in South African Christian gatherings, and it was present even in the NIR – namely that

in ordinary inter-human communication people are usually more aware of the sins of others than of their own sins. To use a biblical metaphor: I am more aware of the mote in my brother's eye than of the beam in my own . . . 'Reconciliation' in such a context would mean, then, that the other party has to agree to *my* point of view, has to be won over to *my* position. But, of course, he usually adopts the same position. And so we both remain unyielding. The fronts harden. We adopt the language of 'winners' and 'losers' and seem to suggest that the winner should take all.[19]

Blindness towards our own sin

All this highlighted one of the most lethal aspects of the problem of reconciliation: each person or group's blindness to their own sin. Thus, for example,

the people in Jesus' last parable in Matthew (25:31–46) who did not minister to the hungry and the naked for the simple reason that they never consciously 'saw' those unfortunate victims of society, are not acquitted by Jesus for not being aware of the others' needs; on the contrary, they are pronounced guilty and sent into eternal punishment.

All these are cases not of innocence but of pseudo-innocence. If a pastor today attacks a colleague for referring to injustices in our society and then claims that he is totally unaware of any injustice in South Africa, he is not just ignorant, he is misguided and blind. Not being aware of our guilt may be our most terrible guilt.[20]

However true that may be – and true it certainly is – I was particularly struck at the NIR by the Afrikaner group's willingness, when confronted, to face its culpability, and even the English-speakers faced a little of theirs. Blacks by and large seemed too preoccupied with understandable accusations to face much culpability in themselves. Nor did guilt-ridden whites feel able to help them face any of their own faults or sins, not even in the matters of retaliatory violence *etc*. But it remains the case that final reconciliation will elude us in South Africa until *both* white and black have equal courage and honesty to confront each other in love, face their own and each other's faults, and then give and receive forgiveness as appropriate.

IN ALIENATED SOCIETIES RECONCILIATION HAS TO FIND ITS WAY INTO STRUCTURES

In one of the opening papers at the NIR Conference this point was made in hard-hitting terms by Dr Bonganjalo Goba, then a lecturer at the University of South Africa. 'South Africa', he said, 'is a society whose very socio-political structures are an insult to the integrity of [black] people; a society whose very foundations spell doom and despair.'[21]

In fact Goba saw these structures as under the judgement of the word of God and envisaged no reconciliation between black and white till this structural issue was faced. Nor, he stressed, could the current reform process help, because, as he saw it, 'it promotes and accentuates conflict by excluding the key partners in the conflict'. If the constitution and structures of a future South Africa are decided by one group who impose their solution on the other groups, there will never be national healing.

Amidst the crisis and chaos in many of our black communities, said Goba, church leaders have been calling for superficial peace and reconciliation, without calling upon the rank and file of Christians to deal with the system and its accompanying structures.

It was very difficult, emotionally speaking, for most whites at the NIR Conference to come to terms with this because it meant facing the issue of ultimate black majority rule in South Africa, which would mean a real sacrifice of white privilege and power. But this didn't bother the former opposition MP Graham McIntosh, who impishly told the NIR delegates: 'You don't have to be a politician to know majority rule must finally come, you just have to be a mathematician!' It is doubtful whether all whites at NIR agreed with this, but certainly all realised that structural issues had to be faced.

As we take up this issue of structural reconciliation in chapter 21, we can leave it for the moment. But there is still one key point to make here in this connection. It relates to our relationships even *after* structural change has come.

The point is that we mustn't imagine that just removing injustice is the whole story. All that social justice does is to make social peace possible. But it is not inevitable, says Klaus Nurnberger, because 'Structural change does not necessarily change the spirit of obstinacy in the stronger and the spirit of revenge in the weaker section. Therefore reconciliation is necessary through the Spirit of Christ.'[22] By this both parties to the conflict will come to the place of bearing with each other and with the painful consequences of the conflict once the causes of conflict are removed.

This will be necessary in South Africa, as it has been in Zimbabwe, because, after all, a just constitution only creates a theoretical framework within which the real work of fashioning good relationships still has to happen.

This being so, as Klaus has noted,

the suffering involved in reconciliation can be substantial because the stronger section has to forgo the advantages it derived from the structural imbalances and maladjustments of the past while the weaker section has to forgo its claim to the advantages it could gain from revenge or restitution in the future.

White South African Christians in particular will have to keep to the forefront of their minds and at the centre of their souls that 'all chances for genuine reconciliation will be destroyed if such fellowship appears to be designed to appease the wronged party or to cover up the cause of the conflict'.

In other words, any serious labourers for reconciliation in a society of conflict must be 'unambiguously and explicitly committed' to dismantling unjust structures. Otherwise, observes Nurnberger, 'it will make no contribution to a solution of the problem but only undermine the credibility and influence of the church of Christ further'.[23]

Now that some of these structural concerns were more deeply interlinked in our hearts with the spiritual mechanisms of national reconciliation, it was not surprising that the NIR Conference should have called for, among other things, not only new initiatives of nationwide evangelism and a National Day of Prayer and Repentance, but also a delegation to visit President P W Botha to share concerns related to the structural side of things (see Appendix 5 for NIR Statement of Affirmation).

I was not sure whether President Botha would see all this in the same way. I had my doubts. Anyway, I was to find out soon enough.

16   Humbling Ourselves
(The church's responsibility to labour for spirituality and revival)

It is the duty of nations as well as men to owe their dependence upon the over-ruling power of God; to confess their sins and transgressions in humble sorrow, yet with assured hope that genuine repentance will lead to mercy and pardon.

Abraham Lincoln

A spiritual awakening is a movement of the Holy Spirit bringing about a revival of New Testament Christianity in the Church of Christ and its related community. It may significantly change an individual, a group of believers, a congregation, a city, a country or even eventually the world.

J Edwin Orr

If my people, who are called by my name, will humble themselves and pray and seek my face and turn from their wicked ways, *then* will I hear from heaven and will forgive their sin and will heal their land.

2 Chronicles 7:14

'RESURRECTION DAY'

The day after the NIR Conference ended, one of the stranger and more memorable Christian meetings in my experience took place at the African Enterprise Centre in Pietermaritzburg. Several of us had been secretly planning it for weeks, and the majority of my own staff did not know anything unusual was on the go until all sorts of VIP cars and people began sweeping up the drive-way into our off-the-beaten-track property.

It was in fact a top-level nationwide leadership group, with every sort of unlikely combination present – left and right, black and white, Government and opposition, friend and foe, predictable and unpredictable.

Certainly I had never before seen such a set of incompatible people present in one room in South Africa. Nor had anyone else. In fact had the press known they would have 'gone bananas'. But we kept it secret, quiet and hidden, to allow maximum freedom of encounter, confidentiality and bold-ness in discussion.

Nellis du Preez (my administrative assistant) and I code-named it 'Resurrection Day' in our planning processes be-cause we wanted it to symbolise a sort of resurrection of hope!

Though not quite raising the church from the dead, the day nevertheless stands in my memory as a vivid and symbolic reminder that in Jesus Christ the otherwise impossible bar-riers can be crossed – that in Jesus Christ incompatibles can meet, communicate and find each other. Beyond that, the day reminded me that the church of Jesus Christ does indeed have the potential to be a mighty force for healing, change and solution, if only it would humble itself, pray, seek God's face, repent of its sin, rise from slumber, shake off its paralysis and 'get going' for God.

One national leader said to me over lunch, 'How on earth did you guys get this group together?' 'On the Jesus ticket,' I replied. 'We didn't do it. He did. Each person has come because of their loyalty to Jesus Christ, and for no other reason. It is *he* who has thrust us out of our corners into encounter.' The figure, a household name in South Africa, shook his head in disbelief: 'I just can't believe what I'm seeing with my eyes.'

With tears running down his cheeks, another participant, an Afrikaans MP, said a little optimistically: 'If only my children could have been here today to witness such a group. They would see a new South Africa being born.' An optimist, as I say, but hope was being reborn in him, as in many of us.

A self-humbling charter

We made the charter of the day Paul's astonishing doxology in Philippians 2:1–11, where he celebrates the self-emptying, self-humbling servant spirit of Jesus Christ, and urges his readers to be 'like-minded'. Not only that, but to 'do nothing out of selfish ambition or vain conceit, but in *humility* [to] consider others better than yourselves' (vs 3). Such humility, the apostle says, will lead each to 'look not only to [his] own interests, but also to the interests of others' (vs 4).

The key, as we noted, is for each of us to covet and embrace that 'same mind' (vs 2, RSV), which actually is ours and our right in Christ, 'who made himself nothing', took 'the very nature of a servant . . . [and] humbled himself and became obedient to death – even death on a cross' (vs 7–8).

The incredible thing is that as all these mighty ones (with a few of us little ones as catalysts) practised a little of that self-emptying and self-humbling spirit, communication began to flow and all of us knew with certainty that Christ *could* indeed heal the land if only each one of us could struggle more to emulate the self-humbling principle we saw ever so tantalisingly at work that day.

Somehow, for one brief moment, like shipwrecked men cast adrift on a stormy sea, that group met, touched hands and hearts, looked into each other's eyes with human recognition, and then were swept apart by the swirling currents and hurricane blasts of South Africa's turbulent life. But in those precious, poignant hours, in my own heart at least, a vision was born (or rather reborn): what if we really let God in, really humbled ourselves, really prayed, really sought his face, really repented of our national sins? What then?

Jericho and Ai strategies

A clue to the answer comes in the Old Testament story of Joshua. Particularly in the experiences at Jericho (Josh 6) and at Ai (Josh 7–8).

Have you ever thought how utterly crazy and how humbling to Joshua's self-respect as a military commander must have been God's word to him on the subject of Jericho? It was surely too much to be told to march round the city six times with your soldiers and then on the seventh have your priests blow their trumpets and let out a great 'haroosh!' (Josh 6:1–5). Not exactly a standard battle plan in the Israeli compendium volume on 'Tested Tactics for Taking Canaanite Capitals'! Yet that is what God asked: and it worked.

This was what I call a 'Jericho strategy': a divine battle plan which makes no sense to the ordinary human intelligence, yet which is the Lord's way through in a given situation. It is the divine strategy marked by 'the foolishness of God' which 'is wiser than man's wisdom' and by 'the weakness of God' which 'is stronger than man's strength' (1 Cor 1:25). It happens when God chooses 'the foolish things of the world to shame the wise; the weak things of the world to shame the strong . . . [and] the lowly things of this world and the despised things . . . to nullify the things that are' (1 Cor 1:27–28).

Then, by contrast, there is the strategy God called on Joshua to follow in the next battle for the land of Canaan as the Israelites came to the city of Ai. Here there was a conventional battle plan with standard military tactics, an ambush, a shoot-out and all that (Josh 8:1–23): the Ai strategy. Exactly the sort of thing any other military commander using his head and experience would have been able to conceive.

Two strategies: the one humanly foolish, the other totally sensible to human wisdom and common sense. The only factor in the Ai strategy that is different from a secular army's workings is that even the Ai strategy, with its conventional military tactics, couldn't and didn't work (Josh 7:1–5) while there was serious sin among God's people (Josh 7:16–21). (And that's true of the church too.) But once dealt with, and removed (Josh 7:22–26), the Israelite army could move on to victory (Josh 8). (This, too, is true of the church.)

For South Africa or for any other troubled nation to be healed and saved by God, both strategies have to operate through the church of Jesus Christ.

In this chapter we will mainly consider Jericho strategies as we think of what is required from the church of Christ in order for a nation to be forgiven and healed. Secular politicians or politically orientated Christian activists will not see much here to give grounds for hope. But in what follows is the key to all else.

A WORD IN THE NIGHT

The key is found in that well-known, and well-worn but eternally true and valid verse, 2 Chronicles 7:14. Here is the word to King Solomon, the son of David, received during a night-time visitation from his Lord: 'If my people, who are called by my name, will humble themselves and pray and seek my face and turn from their wicked ways, then will I hear from heaven and will forgive their sin and will heal their land.'

It is a familiar verse that we have all read or heard before. But our very familiarity can blind us to its implications. We must look at it once again, though now as if for the first time, taking into account its original historical context, in order to see its relevance to the South African situation of the late twentieth century.

'If my people . . .'

This is a word addressed to those in any nation who profess to belong to the living God by repentance and faith. If they, not the total population, do their bit, God will do his – and supernaturally too – to heal the nation.

Lifting this into a professedly Christian context such as South Africa's, it means that the healing of the nation lies in godly obedience from the Christian church. That means church leaders, rank-and-file laity, plus those professional and political leaders and all others who profess to be Christian. If *they* act according to the Lord's declared purposes and requirements, a supernatural thing will happen: God will hear from heaven, forgive the sin and heal the land.

Is the church ready?

Yet the church seems a rather unlikely candidate for national heroics, and that for a number of reasons.

Trapped in the past
First of all, it seems endlessly chained to the past. Says a
poetic spoof on 'Onward, Christian soldiers':

> Like a mighty tortoise
> Moves the Church of God;
> Brothers, we are treading
> Where we've always trod.

The trouble is, we love the safety of sameness, and deplore
the danger of difference, so we keep things as they are.

'Sleeping through a revolution'
Second, there's the problem of slumber. Like Israel, we keep
saying, 'Lord, wake up!' – 'Awake, awake! Clothe yourself
with strength, O arm of the Lord' (Isa 51:9) – as if it's God
who's asleep. In fact scripture is rather specific on this, and
describes the Lord as one who 'neither slumbers nor sleeps'
(*cf*. Ps 121:4).
    No, it's we who are asleep. Small wonder that Martin
Luther King could once preach a sermon to American whites
entitled 'Sleeping Through a Revolution'. Small wonder also
that the Lord replies to Israel saying, 'Don't tell me to wake
up. You wake up' – 'Awake, awake, O Zion . . . Shake off
your dust; rise up' (Isa 52:1–2). What wakes a national
church? Does it always have to be disaster, by which time
stirring from slumber can be too late? Or do prophetic
warnings sometimes work?

'Turning a deaf ear'
Third, there is the problem of deafness – especially deafness
to the prophets. For example, most whites cannot abide the
prophetic warnings coming from men like Desmond Tutu,
Frank Chikane and Alan Boesak. To see them on TV or in the
press is a signal for a freak-out because we whites don't want
to hear what they are saying.
    Inevitably I am often asked by South African whites and
others overseas what I think of Archbishop Tutu. My reply is
this: 'Tutu knows his Lord, and is an incredibly important
man because he is saying many prophetic things our nation

needs to hear. Beyond that, he is articulating a deeply valid
black cry. This does not mean he is infallible, or that he gets it
right 100% of the time. Who does? But if we remain deaf to
what he is saying about justice our nation will live to regret it.
Beyond that, in a decade or so, when real extremism may hold
sway, we will be longing to have one or two "moderates" like
Tutu around. So we must listen now, while there is time.'

This deafness to prophetic utterances is one which also
characterised the nation of Judah in Jeremiah's time (the
seventh century BC), during the closing days of the southern
kingdom. This must have continually frustrated Jeremiah and
created huge agony of spirit, as it has always done in the souls
of those prophetic men and women whose words have fallen
on deaf ears. In fact there can be no pain greater than to warn
those one loves of imminent danger and catastrophe, and see
it go unheeded.

With the aching heart of the godly patriot, Jeremiah
warned the people of God (see Jer 7:1–11) of the awesome
divine judgement coming upon them through the Babylonian
armies of Nebuchadnezzar, accompanied by famine and
plague, unless they repented of six national sins: false
religion, injustice, oppression, violence and murder, idolatry, immorality.

All these things in varying degrees characterise South
African life, and there is no reason to imagine that we, the
world's most markedly Christian nation by official profession
(certainly a people called by his name) will escape the Lord's
judgement if we persist with injustice. If God finally removed
his protective covering from Judah – his very special people –
why should we be different?

But Judah was deaf. Jeremiah lamented in agonising loneli-
ness: 'To whom can I speak and give warning? Who will listen
to me? Their ears are closed so that they cannot hear. The
word of the Lord is offensive to them; they find no pleasure in
it' (Jer 6:10).

'Everything's going to be fine'
More than that, Jeremiah had to contend with a religious
establishment that told the people all was fine: 'They dress the
wound of my people as though it were not serious. "Peace,

peace," they say, when there is no peace' (Jer 6:14). Yet Jeremiah knew that superficial religion was self-deceiving.

The peril of this sort of thing is everywhere present, but especially I believe in South Africa, because here there are still certain religious leaders and followers busy telling people all is going to be fine if only we can stop the total onslaught from all the communists out there.

That there are some enemies out there I don't doubt, but they or others just might end up being God's Babylonian agents of judgement on us unless we deal with our national sin of racism, which has scandalised and shamed the Christian gospel worldwide. Nor do we or any other nation involved in serious sin have endless time to sort ourselves out.

Time is running out
In Jeremiah's period Judah finally overran the time-clock of history, and judgemental disaster became inevitable and divinely decreed. The prophet was even told three times to stop praying for the nation: 'So do not pray for this people nor offer any plea or petition for them; do not plead with me, for I will not listen to you' (Jer 7:16; 11:14; 14:11).

With the divine silencing of the prophet's intercession, the nation lost its only remaining form of supernatural, protective covering. Nothing could now save Judah, for their security could not be divorced from their faith in God.

In extensive prayer for South Africa, and for the right line to take in this book, I have not felt the Holy Spirit saying our time has gone – though many others think it has, and they feel that God has declared it so. They may be right. However, my own attempts to discern the Spirit's word lead me to believe not that our time has gone, but that it is going. Not yet must we say with Judah: 'The harvest is past, the summer has ended, and we are not saved' (Jer 8:20).

But the summer is *passing*, and passing quickly. Not indefinitely will South Africa have it within its power to repent and change so that cataclysm may be averted. A moment will come – unless Christian people and our professedly Christian Government repent of all institutionalised racism – when the unthinkable will happen and God will say: 'Do not pray for the well-being of this people. Although they fast, I will not listen to their cry . . . Instead, I will destroy them' (Jer 14:11).

This is why so much in South Africa depends on its church. It really is a case in South Africa of 'If my people . . . If only my people will humble themselves . . .'

The need for national humility

In 1985, in the months before the NIR Conference, I felt while travelling around South Africa that I was seeing a new thing – the birth of an embryonic national humility. Everywhere I went across the nation I found people, high and low (but especially high), saying, '*We* have gone wrong.'

To me it was like the 'cloud as small as a man's hand' (1 Kings 18:44) which Elijah's servant saw rising from the sea as a token that God was going to break the three-year drought of judgement which had come on the people of Israel.

Now here in South Africa was a little cloud of national hope rising from our sea of self-sufficiency. Here was some embryonic national humility appearing on a hitherto hopeless national horizon. It made me excited.

The 'National Day of Prayer'

My feeling seemed confirmed by the willingness of multitudes in the church after the NIR conference to prepare for, in spite of extensive controversy, a National Day of Prayer and humiliation set for Wednesday 9 October 1985.

Real prayer is indeed an expression of humility. And humility is needed at all levels – from the grass-roots up to leadership. Imagine what might happen if our national leaders were to come clean and in humility say, especially to blacks: 'We are dreadfully sorry about apartheid. It has been wrong, sinful and misguided. Please forgive us and help us to set it right and build a new nation on justice.'

Indeed it has occurred to me that if President P W Botha, or whoever succeeds him, would take just fifteen seconds on national television to utter those words of humble confession,

the whole political climate in the nation would change overnight. All would rally to try and help fix things.

'Is the President ready for anything like this?' I wondered
back in September and October 1985, as I prepared to see him
privately in preparation for a delegation to him from the NIR
Conference. Of course it was also vital to have my own heart
right and in humility before the Lord and before this man of
power.

The weekend before my Tuesday meeting with President
Botha, and before the Wednesday (9 October) Day of Prayer,
I escaped with my family to friends in Southbroom, on the
Natal South Coast. My big fear was that 9 October would end
up a day of battle and not of prayer, because we heard that
two factions were emerging in the nation's townships – those
who would stay home to pray and those who would go to work
– and we feared that certain elements might set off nationwide
clashes between the two. I said to one black in Durban:
'What's going to happen on Wednesday?' 'The people are
going to fight,' he said, sending chills down my spine.

So at Southbroom I prayed and wrote in my journal: 'No
violence at all of any sort on Wednesday – but rather a miracle
of God's peace and calm, with your Shalom, Lord, made an
actuality in SA – for once – on that Day.'

Back home on Monday, Nellis du Preez told me: 'I've got
good news and bad for you. The Prayer Day is to be debated
on national TV tomorrow night – after you've seen the
President.' Then, knowing I dislike being on TV, Nellis
added: 'And the bad news is, you're on!'

Nellis then told me that Elton Trueblood's *Abraham
Lincoln, Theologian of American Anguish*, a copy of which I
wanted to give to President and Mrs Botha (as I had done
years before to John Vorster and Ian Smith), could not be
acquired anywhere. I was sorry about this because what had
struck me so much about Lincoln was his grasp of the place of
national humiliation before God, with special days of fasting
and prayer.

Lincoln and national humiliation
Apart from a tremendous personal life of prayer ('I have
sought His aid', he once said simply), Lincoln issued nine

separate calls during his forty-nine month presidency for public penitence, fasting, prayer and thanksgiving.

The first of the nine calls (12 August 1861) characteristically brought 'humbling ourselves' to the fore in recommending 'a day of public humiliation, prayer and fasting to be observed by the people of the United States'.

Lincoln's own part in this memorable pronouncement began with the recognition that

> it is fit and becoming in all people, at all times to acknowledge and revere the Supreme Government of God; to bow in humble submission to his chastisements; to confess and deplore their sins and transgressions in the full conviction that the fear of the Lord is the beginning of wisdom; and to pray, with all fervency and contrition, for the pardon of their past offenses, and for a blessing upon their present and prospective action.[1]

There is no suggestion here of vindictiveness towards the people of the Confederacy and not one judgemental line. In this first 'National Fast Day', the emphasis was upon personal contrition rather than upon blame of others.

It is worth registering here also that Lincoln saw the American Civil War not as an accident of history but as 'a terrible visitation from the hand of God'.

What were the national sins of which to be so painfully conscious? The answer fits white South Africa like a glove – pride arising from self-sufficiency:

> 'Intoxicated with unbroken success, we have become too self-sufficient to feel the necessity of redeeming and preserving grace, too proud to pray to the God that made us!' The prayer requested was the double one, the pardon of our national sins, and the restoration of our now divided and suffering Country.[2]

Tragic and desperate as it was, the ordeal might, Lincoln believed, become a blessing if it could bring forth true humility.

Another remarkable feature of Lincoln's prayer concern, and one which likewise cuts painfully close to the South African bone, was his prayer call to the nation for what he called 'insurgents'. He asked not for judgement on them but for a change in their hearts. So he asked the nation to pray for God 'to subdue the anger, which has produced and so long sustained a needless and cruel rebellion, to change the hearts of the insurgents, to guide the counsels of the Government with wisdom adequate to so great a national emergency'.[3]

This surely is also 'the largeness of mind' (1 Kings 4:29) King Solomon was given. Beyond that, here is insight into a President in whose thinking prayer and self-humbling came to dominate.

Preparing to meet the President

In my airport hotel room in Johannesburg early on Tuesday 8 October 1985, I woke to reflect on the day: a meeting with President P W Botha, plus a debate on national television. It felt daunting, and it was.

Carol rang early with a word of encouragement from James 1:5–6 (AV): 'If any of you lack wisdom, let him ask of God . . . But let him ask in faith, nothing wavering.'

'Ask the Lord for wisdom, sweetheart,' she said. 'And don't waver. As for the President, love him and speak for those with no voice.'

Though not having the Lincoln book, I resolved to affirm that if President Botha would be a Lincoln he needed to say before God and the nation that he was sorry about apartheid and would dismantle it.

Then I wanted to add that our problem is a breakdown of relationships so there is no trust and no understanding between black and white. Moving to the political agenda before there is trust is therefore hugely problematic. I wondered if a really top group of across-the-board black leaders could not meet informally and privately with the President and four or five of his colleagues.

I also wanted to plead for some concessions to be made as the NIR group came to meet him with the requests emanating from the conference in general and the black group in particular. There was a great need for something from him to assure the rank and file of black Christians especially that dialogue and negotiation paid off.

After prayer I felt constrained to take a substitute gift – an Afrikaans version of Oswald Chambers' devotional classic

My Utmost for His Highest. In part of the inscription I wrote: 'As I see it, two things are needed now – and constantly in the Christian walk. One is repentance. The other is faith. Jesus spoke of these two in the first recorded words of His public ministry (Mark 1:14–15). They are not just the way to Christ. But they show the way to walk *in Christ.* All of us in South Africa (Church, State, Nation, English, Afrikaners, Blacks, high and low, powerful and powerless) must *repent* of what we have done wrong over multiplied decades. We are all in it together. If we do, Jeremiah 18:7–8 will operate and our land will be spared by God's intervention and power.'

A difficult encounter

It was strange to sit in the waiting lounge outside the office of President P W Botha in Union Buildings, Pretoria, and see the gallery of past South African Prime Ministers all staring, larger than life, from their frames along the wall. There were Malan, Strydom, Verwoerd and Vorster – all heroes here in these sacred precincts, but villains in many ways in the world from which I came. 'The gaps of South Africa,' I thought to myself. Throughout these reveries my dominant prayer was still love for the President.

Minutes later I was in his office – but contrary to what I had expected we were not alone, for, disconcertingly, he had two others with him. This I knew would prejudice any real meeting of minds or hearts, and it did. I quickly concluded that this was not the President's day. Nor was it to be mine. I was immediately aware on entry to the room that this was not to be the sort of encounter for which I had prayed.

The President began by standing to read me part of Romans 13! He had his view on this, and I of course had mine (see chapter 18), but I felt constrained at that moment to hold my peace.

What followed in the next bruising hour is perhaps best left unrecorded in these pages, as it was a sad saga of the victory of those South African chasms which have landed us where we are.

At the end of the time, I said to him: 'Mr President you have completely missed my heart.'

'And you have completely missed mine,' he responded.

I could not deny it. The South African tragedy had won again.

Dejected, I drove back to Johannesburg with Nellis du Preez, scoring myself zero on the interview and feeling a total failure with God, man, the church, the NIR and myself.

Of special concern was the realisation there would be no NIR delegation to the President. I wondered if a major interdenominational and racially representative church delegation would ever be ready to go again. Had the summer for such things now passed?

And where did 2 Chronicles 7:14 and old Abraham Lincoln's line on national humiliation fit in all of this?

That worried me most of all.

The place and priority of prayer

Ah yes, 'If my people, who are called by my name, will humble themselves *and pray* and seek my face . . .' With the NIR National Day of Prayer due to take place the next day, and with a nationally televised interview on the subject only hours away, and with the unhappy encounter with the President now personal history, it was good to turn one's heart again to the only place possible – the place of prayer and seeking the Lord's face – which I did with vigour that afternoon in my hotel room with Nellis.

Then came the evening interview on TV. I felt as exposed and vulnerable as I have ever felt when I went on prime-time TV that night to debate the Day of Prayer with a senior Afrikaans theologian and the head of the South African Association of Chambers of Commerce (ASSOCOM). What understandably concerned many industrialists was the 'absence from work' factor required by the day. In fact many blacks wanted the day to be more of a strike day – a stay away – than a Day of Prayer. For others it was a 'pray away' – a combination action of prayer and protest.

Though understanding this profoundly, the day for me, and for most white Christians who struggled hugely with any strike component, was just what we called it – a national and deeply necessary Day of Prayer and fasting and humiliation. On the other hand, having the exercise on a working day, and not on a Saturday or Sunday, was good for whites because for once we were doing something the way blacks wanted it and we were being forced into an exercise that was a little less easy and cheap than what we were accustomed to. To pay the price of standing with black Christians in this way was therefore salutary for many whites. That extra touch of cost, even in terms of misunderstanding or criticism from employers or whoever, paid reconciling dividends of its own.

As I arrived at the television studios a top Afrikaner in SATV, a Dutch Reformed man, pulled me aside to say he was praying for me.

'I don't need selling on the NIR,' he said. 'My pastor went to that conference and he went one kind of man and returned another. It's been unbelievable.'

Down in the studios the lead interviewer told me: 'I'm sorry, it's going to be very confrontational!' That was all I needed to boost my morale! But I held on in faith to the Lord – 'not wavering', as Carol had said.

I knew many were praying for me. An African leader told me later he fell on his knees by his TV set the moment he saw me come on. And, praise God, I survived the ordeal and felt wonderfully strengthened by the Lord throughout.

Afterwards a young Afrikaans girl came up to me and said, 'Praise Jesus. Come with me.' Then, taking me up a precipitous staircase, she ushered me into the monitoring room – which looked like a sort of space-age, James Bond-type wonderbox of electronics. A whole bunch of technicians were up there: 'We were all praying for you, Mike,' they said. 'Well done. The Lord helped you.' Precious people, one and all, and they made me feel heartwarmed and encouraged.

At 10.30 p.m. that same night I was taken down to the radio interview rooms in the bowels of the earth of SABC, a few hundred yards from SATV. A young man of radiant disposition met me and sat me down opposite him, with a microphone between us, to interview me on the Day of Prayer for *Radio Today*, a prime-time early morning programme next day.

How would this go?

I needn't have worried.

'Mike, I've followed your ministry for years. I'm a Christian. And I'm on your side. Now listen, I'm meant to ask you some very tough questions, but let's just pause to pray the Lord will help you answer them!'

He beamed, as did I, and we prayed. He was tough, and I was clear – and the Lord was there!

The day arrives

The next day dawned bright and clear, with all the news media full of the Day of Prayer.

Nellis and I flew home to join in services in Pietermaritzburg, while reports poured in that night and in the next days from all across the nation, saying how thousands of people had come together for prayer in and from every corner of the land.

Most moving to me was the front-page headline and full-length picture in Soweto's *City Press* of what they called 'the busiest road in South Africa', from Soweto to the city. It was totally deserted, save for one lone cyclist. The huge headline, surely the strangest in South Africa's history, came from the heart of Soweto and simply said, 'HEAR US, O LORD.' The report opened by saying: 'Tens of thousands of people answered the call for a prayaway in cities and towns throughout the country yesterday . . .'

I phoned a friend in Soweto that evening and he said: 'Mike, it's incredible. The place is like a ghost town. We have never seen it like this. Trains, buses, and taxis are mostly empty and nearly a hundred per cent of our shops are closed and about sixty per cent of the people have participated. What's more, people are genuinely praying – many in large services and others in homes.'

In Johannesburg city centre both Standard and Barclays Banks gave all their staff extended lunch hours so they could attend prayer meetings, as did Anglo-American and the Chamber of Mines.

A Cape Town friend phoned us to say the day was 'fantastic and marked by incredible quiet'. Over thirteen hundred people had participated in the St George's Cathedral lunch-hour service. There were also reports of Christians of all denominations meeting in each other's churches to pray together – 'In Cape Town we broke out of our islands as never before,' said another participant.

In King William's Town black domestic workers and white housewives came together to pray through the evening.

The Rev. George Irvine, chairman of the Grahamstown district of the Methodist Church, reports that an ABC TV crew were detained by police for the afternoon of 9 October, but turned up regardless at the Port Elizabeth Cathedral to film the praying there!

The Rev. Mvume Dandala, then of Wellington Methodist Church in New Brighton, reported a steady stream of worshippers – 'We never had less than a hundred throughout the day,' he said.

The *Sunday Times* in an editorial stated:

> When the moderator of the Northern Transvaal Synod of the Nederduitse Gereforemeerde Kerk conducts a service in an Anglican cathedral, harmony within the divided arm of the Church seems to move a giant step nearer. When the service conducted by Dr Johan Heyns is for the National Day of Reconciliation then national harmony *must* be inching closer.

From all Reef Townships, said Methodist leader Ron Brauteseth, came police reports of the quietest and most peaceful day in years. John Allwood, Director of World Vision, wrote: 'We will never fully know the extraordinary dimensions of what God did that Day.'

Company Director Richard Scallan phoned me the next day: 'At our company we put out chairs for sixty to come and pray in the lunch hour. Over two hundred turned up. I'm amazed.'

Phillip Heber Percy, director of the Spar Supermarket chain, called in to report: 'Over two thousand people in our chain of stores participated in the Day of Prayer yesterday.'

One white woman in Pietermaritzburg said: 'I went into our church and saw one lone black woman on her knees before God. It moved me more than anything that's happened to me in years.'

Amazingly, concerned Christians all over the world joined us in prayer that day. And so it was, for example, that the Pope, speaking to seven thousand Catholics in St Peter's Square, could call Catholics everywhere to pray that 'South

Africa should soon find peace founded on justice and recip-rocal love through a sincere search for just solutions to the problems that torment that dear country.'

The Anglican Primate of Australia, Sir John Grindrod, said: 'We are standing with you,' as Anglican bishops appealed in the dioceses for prayer for South Africa on 9 October.

Then our friends Sam Hines and Ross Main phoned through from Washington DC, and said: 'We were praying with you in groups in our church on 9 October.'

The Latin American evangelist Luis Palau, for his part, put out the prayer call all across Latin America on hundreds of stations.

And so the stories came in from far and near. To be sure, more Christians in South Africa and worldwide prayed for this stricken nation that day than at any time in our history.

Did it pay off?

Certainly, because God hears prayer, and he knows in his strange purposes and economy what was wrought in the heavenlies that day for this land. Maybe at the least it bought us a little more time.

Prayer must come first. Not that one can use prayer as an excuse for inaction or indifference to things we can and must practically do, for there is much that can effectively be done once we have prayed, but there is nothing that can be effectively done until we have prayed.

This is why intercessory prayer has to go on, and why in the NIR we have continued to call Christians to a monthly day of fasting and prayer on the first Wednesday, Thursday or Friday of each month. Thankfully hundreds across the nation observe this, though many more could and should be involved.

Why bother praying?

First, *because prayer keeps spirituality and dependence on God to the fore* in what could otherwise become a morally and spiritually bankrupt struggle for political change wrought in the corrupting dynamics of human strength and energy alone, and producing a latter state worse than the first.

This problem applies as much to blacks as to whites, because of their deeper pain and more passionate involvement in the perilous interaction of mechanisms of political struggle and power. And matters of power always corrupt and are therefore in need of the controls which spirituality brings.

Carl F Ellis, a black American writer on the Civil Rights years, has noted that if the black quest for freedom 'has become a quest for independence from God, then we will end up on the junk heap of the nations – a junk heap of slavery far worse than what we ever experienced [previously]'.[4]

He then adds the following important observation, with its implicit warnings:

> We saw that the closer a people get to liberation, the more their own ungodliness and God's judgment will show. Liberation is insufficient if it is not accompanied by a quest for godliness in every area of life. Liberation alone will lead to self-oppression because a liberated ungodliness will always do its thing, and that thing is sure to bring death (Rom 6:23).

And is not prayer the primary posture where seeking first the kingdom most truly takes place? It is also the place and posture where we engage in the quest for righteousness.

This too is crucial, says Ellis. In fact,

> the quest for righteousness in every area of life must be on the top of the Black agenda if we are to become the people God created us to be (Mt 6:33). The more an oppressed people seek to construct their resistance to oppression around the Word of God, the greater will be the likelihood that the oppression will be broken, the smaller will be the likelihood that the resistance movement will be destroyed by the ungodliness of those involved in it, and the smaller will be the likelihood that they will lose compassion for their fellow human beings.[5]

That is why prayer must stay central: because it keeps spirituality centre-stage in the struggle. Otherwise the latter state, as we said, can be worse than the first. Battling a beast is futile if it makes one bestial oneself, yet that is just what political struggles can do.

Second, *prayer is simply commanded in scripture* from

Genesis to Revelation. In St Paul we find special pride of place given to prayer for rulers and political leaders: '*First of all*, then, I urge that supplications, prayers, intercessions, and thanksgivings be made for all men, *for kings* and *all who are in high positions*, that we may lead a quiet and peaceable life, godly and respectful in every way' (1 Tim 2:1–2, RSV).

The South African Renewal leader Derek Crumpton has said:

> I believe most strongly that the major failure of the Church in South Africa has not been its failure to speak out against and to oppose apartheid and the Nationalist Party's political philosophy (or religion). This it has done consistently and *ad nauseam*. Its real failure has been its failure to give itself to real, authentic, meaningful and prolonged prayer and intercession and probably fasting for God to intervene in His own sovereign way for the establishing of his Kingdom and the relief of suffering through good, honest, wise and just government.

Crumpton and his colleagues accordingly have a weekly night of prayer for the nation and related needs. Not, he says, that this absolves the church of the responsibility to speak prophetically to the nation 'concerning righteousness and justice in our national and local affairs. But it needs to be done in ways which can be heard by those to whom it is addressed.'[6]

Third, *prayer is vital for 'pulling down strongholds'*. Of this more in chapter 17, on liberation. Suffice it for the moment to note the relevant Pauline passage:

> For though we live in the world we are not carrying on a worldly war, for the weapons of our warfare are not worldly but have divine power to destroy strongholds. We destroy arguments and every proud obstacle to the knowledge of God, and take every thought captive to obey Christ. (2 Cor 10:3–5, RSV)

Prayer is crucial because it comes against external forces of spiritual darkness, identified mysteriously by St Paul as 'principalities and powers'. In Ephesians 6:11–12 (RSV) the apostle puts it this way: 'We are not contending against flesh and blood, but against the principalities, against the powers,

against the world rulers of this present darkness, against the
spiritual hosts of wickedness in the heavenly places.'

The overall picture is of a variety of evil forces unified
under the ultimately evil force, 'the devil' (Eph 6:11).

Michael Green notes that

> there has been a tendency to demythologise the concept, and
> regard them not as fallen spiritual beings but rather as the
> structures of earthly existence – the state, class struggle, propa-
> ganda, international corporations and the like, when they be-
> come either tyrannical or objects of man's total allegiance. This
> has the double attraction of divesting ourselves of belief in so
> unfashionable a concept as a hierarchy of angels, good and evil,
> stretching between man and God; it also enables us to find a good
> deal more in the New Testament about our very modern preoc-
> cupation with social structures. The truth of the matter is that
> words like principalities, powers and thrones are used both of
> human rulers and of the spiritual forces which lie behind them.[7]

So what we are saying here, stresses Green, is not that the
principalities and powers may not infest government, public
opinion and the like. It simply avoids the confusion of
identifying them.

That said, we must not miss the point that the New Testament is here speaking of *real* cosmic spiritual powers which
may indeed gain access to and manifest themselves at some of
the world's power points, and in many of its structures.

In fact, says the American devotional writer Richard
Foster, these 'powers' do in fact often, explain 'the destructive bent of power that we see all around us'. So

> we must not dismiss this teaching as the relic of a prescientific
> era . . . The powers are created realities . . . (Col 1:16). [They]
> were once related to the creative will of God; however, we no
> longer see them in this role. They are in revolt and rebellion
> against God their Creator.[8]

Of course, not to believe in these things if they really don't
exist is wise. But how dangerous might it be to refuse to
believe in them if they actually do exist, simply because they
are currently outside normal twentieth-century categories of

thinking or experience. A child might just as well not believe
in space travel because it is outside his personal experience,
seeing he never flew in Friendship 7. But John Glenn did.
Space travel is not outside reality. Nor are these spirit forces,
just because we may think them outside our experience. In
any event, the New Testament is quite clear. These 'powers'
exist, and it is against them that our warfare really lies. That's
why looking at the intractable South African problem
through man's purely natural and political eyes will never be
adequate, and why the natural human political weapons will
never suffice.

Prayer and intercession immediately now take on new
significance and relevance once we accept the possibility of
spirit forces energising human beings, albeit generally unbeknown to them, in their social, political or even religious
structures. And obviously this applies equally to blacks as to
whites.

As Richard Foster observes:

> The powers . . . do not 'possess' just individuals but organiz-
> ations and whole structures of society. Institutions can and do
> often become nothing more than organized sin. There are fun-
> damental spiritual realities that underlie all political, social, and
> economic systems. In back of brutal dictators and unjust policies
> and corrupt institutions are spiritual principalities and powers.[9]

Whether or not we invariably see institutional power operating this way, nevertheless, at the least we may affirm that
there are often spiritual powers at work behind human and
institutional powers. These need to be 'identified', especially
when one looks at organisations or even whole nations which
are seemingly held in a grip of steel by particular concepts or
ideologies. Apartheid is of course the classic example. That is
why we must grasp that when we speak of 'the spirit of a
group' or 'the spirit of apartheid', we are not just using a vivid
phrase but are accurately describing the reality with which we
are dealing.

In other words, we need to grasp that unless we face the
'spirituality' of institutions or ideologies we are only tinkering
with externals and failing to get to the heart of the matter.

Martin Niemöller, Dietrich Bonhoeffer and a few others in the Confessing Church of Germany saw and discerned these hellish powers at work in the Third Reich and its demonic perversions of the German Nationalistic spirit. But most German Christians in the 1930s did not. The tragedy is that spiritual hindsight of such things cannot save a nation. The thing is to see them while summer is here, not when it is past.

Finally, let it be registered that to go against such demonic powers in anything other than the power of prayer and with the whole armour of God, is to court disaster and be guilty of strategic folly. And to fail to discern where such powers are at work and take appropriate spiritual and prayerful measures is the spiritual equivalent of wandering into Rommel's Panzer divisions with a bow and arrow. Not that we can allow ourselves to go overboard and blame such forces for everything bad that happens in ourselves or in the political arena. That would be to absolve ourselves of responsibility. To give too much emphasis to these 'powers' outside us is to rob humans of responsibility and to make them, as Michael Green says, 'pawns in a celestial tug of war between God and the devil'. But if we give too little weight to these things we fail to account for persistent and massive individual and collective human wickedness.

It is small wonder, therefore, that in the divine scheme of things God can say that 'If my people . . . will humble themselves and *pray and seek my face* . . .' then all sorts of amazing things can happen, like the healing of the land.

But this cannot happen before one other spiritual prerequisite is met – the turning from our 'wicked ways'.

The need for national repentance

When we start thinking either individually or nationally of humbling ourselves and praying, it is never long before we realise we've botched things up pretty badly and need to stop doing so.

This means rather more than an apology to God and men, saying, 'I'm sorry,' and then carrying on as before. It actually means stopping the offensive behaviour, whether personal, social or political. 2 Chronicles 7:14 calls it 'turning from our wicked ways'. The New Testament calls it 'repentance' (Gk., *metanoia*), which means a change of mind *leading to a change of direction and action*. It is what the prodigal son did: he saw that his behaviour in the 'far country' was wrong, and he stopped it and went home.

Repentance will of course in the South African context mean different things to different people. For example, it used to amuse me in the 1970s, when I frequently visited old 'Rhodesia', to find 2 Chronicles 7:14 doing the rounds there with quite different interpretations put on 'wicked ways' depending whether one was white or black. For whites the 'wicked ways' from which the nation had to turn were the wicked ways of Muzorewa, Nkomo and Mugabe; for blacks the wicked ways were those of Ian Smith. Neither group seemed overly enamoured with facing just what its *own* 'wicked ways' were!

Recognising our own culpability and sin is always difficult. Some years ago, when my daughter Debbie had her friend Sarah over for the night at our house, some chocolates went missing and we suspected these two as the likely culprits. The truth came out, however, in prayers that night, when young Sarah announced to God that 'Debbie, Lord, has something to say sorry about!' (The Lord's view on the subject of course remained hidden to us!)

We must understand that we can't do one another's confessing or repenting, only our own! South African blacks and whites both have to see this.

Repentance from rigidity

In this book we have already looked at some of the things which might be required from each group, so now I will major on something required from both.

The Old Testament prophet Hosea (eighth century BC) had a very suggestive and powerful exhortation for the kingdom of Judah during a time of major religious apostasy when the people had become rigidly set in evil thinking and practice. He told them: 'Sow for yourselves righteousness, reap the fruit of steadfast love; break up your fallow ground, for it is the time to seek the Lord, that he may come and rain salvation upon you' (Hos 10:12, RSV).

The image of rain and salvation gives, I believe, a picture of renewal which is not only personal but social and political, because the sins from which this 'rain of salvation' could free them are almost all socio-political. Thus the list in verse 13 includes iniquity, injustice, dishonesty and false confidence in military power (*i.e.* chariots, warriors, fortresses, *etc.*). This 'salvation' which could 'rain' upon them, and which is akin to the healing of the land idea in 2 Chronicles 7:14, can come about if they do four things: 'sow . . . righteousness', 'reap the fruit of steadfast love', 'break up [the] fallow ground' and 'seek the Lord'.

The first two things – righteousness and love – we have already talked about, but what is this breaking of fallow ground which seems a prerequisite to a successful seeking of the Lord?

The answer holds a key for South Africa: fallow ground is ground which has been tilled but which now lies waste and needs to be broken up and mellowed before it is suited to receive grain. Hosea is saying that something tough, rigid and hard must be broken up.

If we look across from Hosea to Isaiah and consider a similar passage about 'seeking the Lord' and receiving his 'rain', Isaiah 55:6–10, we find that the prophet there stresses that the precondition for this 'salvation rain' is that the 'unrighteous man' forsakes 'his *thoughts*' (vs 7).

Why should he do this? Because God is not to be found in man's 'thoughts' and the 'ways' they produce, seeing that 'as the heavens are higher than the earth', so are his thoughts higher than ours (vs 9).

If we link the two passages, we see that the fallow ground which has to be broken up is man's rigidity of thought, his fixed mind-sets, his hard and weather-beaten attitudes of yesterday, his inflexible views and policies on this, that and the next thing, plus his infallible unyielding rightness on everything under the sun. In those rigid thoughts, inflexible views and the 'ways' they produce in man, God is not to be found.

If, therefore, we want to seek the Lord successfully and find his rain, his personal renewal, his societal salvation and healing in the land, we must break up the fallow ground of mental rigidity and turn from our rigid 'ways' (activities, practices, policies, *etc.*).

If any reader thinks of his own society, and if I think of mine, one realises what a killer rigidity of thought and intellectual inflexibility is.

In our case in South Africa everyone's views are set in concrete. No one will budge. Each of us knows the problem. So the Lord can't get a look in. Thus whites have inflexible, unbending views of Tutu or Boesak or the ANC or Mandela. Blacks have equally rigid, unyielding mind-sets of P W Botha or the Parliament or capitalism or the best constitutional framework, and especially on any opposing black political grouping.

But maybe the Lord has a different view of Mandela and his potential than the white electorate or Government. Maybe the Lord sees Tutu differently than does Treurnicht. Conceivably God thinks of President Botha's efforts differently than the UDF Central Committee does. Maybe God has a special role for Buthelezi. Who knows? Certainly we never will while we remain hidebound by rigidity of thought.

For the moment, though, *we're* not interested in flexibility. *We* know what's what. And *we're* not going to change our minds. Not for God or anyone. So he looks on – while we remain unhealed. That is unless or until we hear Hosea saying: 'Break up the fallow ground' of all that rigid, infallible, inflexible and arrogant thought and the false ways, personally, socially and politically, into which it has led you. Why? Because it is the time (Gk., *kairos*) to seek the Lord whose thoughts on all that are so totally different and as high above yours as the heavens are above the earth.

What is to be forsaken

As to the ways to be forsaken, they must for South African whites include oppression, injustice, discrimination, materialism, greed, acquisitiveness, selfishness, fearfulness, faithlessness and unbelief.

For blacks 'the wicked ways', whether in black individuals

or groups, could include bitterness, hatred, the spirit of vengeance and violence, internecine strife, self-pity, power-hunger and, sometimes, the spirit of blame to cover for laziness, lack of industry and initiative or plain inefficiency.

God's promise

But the Lord's promise stands: if his people (*i.e.* especially the church) will humble themselves and pray and seek his face, he will 'hear from heaven and will forgive their sin and will heal their land'. What a glorious promise! Not that I think scripture leads us to any utopian expectations for our nations in what may be the home-straight of history (just look at Matthew 24 or 2 Timothy 3). However, we do know from scripture, and from Paul's exhortation to pray for leaders (1 Tim 2:1–2), that God does desire us to lead lives which are 'quiet and peaceful'. And this is not least, I believe, because he 'wants all men to be saved and to come to a knowledge of the truth' (1 Tim 2:4) – a desire which is much imperilled if people are living in social contexts of revolutionary upheaval and political convulsion.

Peace/Shalom

This means at the least that the Lord wants societies living in stability, peace, order, political justice and equity of economic life and opportunity. This is really the Old Testament picture of *shalom*, which speaks of peace, wholeness, completeness, full health and comprehensive well-being in society, and which was central to God's intentions for his people. This 'shalom' was not to exist simply as an individual's state of inner calm and soundness of being in every way, but as an expression of his right relationships with other individuals around him, and between his group and other groups. At its heart are right relationships. So the famous St Augustine could see his 'city of God' as the city of right relationships where God's order for society was followed and worked out according to his word.

All of which brings us to the place of religious revival, and its effects upon societies in terms of aiding their 'healing'.

Revival

The late J Edwin Orr, one of the greatest authorities on the subject of revival, defines a spiritual awakening as 'a movement of the Holy Spirit bringing about a revival of New Testament Christianity in the Church of Christ and its related community'.[10] It may significantly change an individual, a group of believers, a congregation, a city or a country, but it accomplishes 'the reviving of the Church, the awakening of the masses and the movement of uninstructed people toward the Christian faith; the revived Church by many or few is moved to engage in evangelism, teaching and social action'.[11]

Interestingly enough, these great spiritual movements have been found historically to have certain inner laws or features which regularly characterise them.

As far as South Africa goes, one of the more interesting laws was articulated by James Burns, a great Scottish divine who published a book in 1909 called *Revivals, Their Laws and Leaders*.

Burns notes that the first law of great religious movements is that they 'usually synchronise with some crisis of national development, or with some profound change coming over the social or political life of a people'[12] (and if that doesn't describe South Africa, I don't know what does). To back this up, he shows how the mighty twelfth-century reawakening under St Francis of Assisi came when Europe was

> passing out of the darkness of the Middle Ages; the feudal system was breaking up; men were gathering in cities; a new sense of corporate life was beginning to emerge . . . At this time universities began to spring up; there was a widening of sympathies which the Crusades did something to foster; and over the whole of Europe there was passing the ferment of new ideas. The period thus marked the close of one stage of human development, and the beginning of another.[13]

Then there were the great reforming movements of the sixteenth century under Luther in Germany and under Calvin and Zwingli in Switzerland, and generally throughout Europe. This period, says Burns, was again a crisis time in human affairs:

Europe . . . was now, in the sixteenth century, passing from youth to the first dawn of conscious manhood. Men were forming themselves under larger combinations; loyalty to the city was giving way to loyalty to the state. It was the time when peoples were arising conscious of a vigorous, national life; when kings were creating courts, and forcing the nobility to acknowledge their supremacy; when Europe was rearranging itself under modern geographical and national divisions.[14]

When we think of Wesley's eighteenth-century England and consider the condition of England at the time of the revival, we see that she was passing through just such a period of change. The old order was changing, giving way to something new: the birth of the great manufacturing class and of industrialism, which was to revolutionise society and produce the most momentous changes in its political and commercial conditions. In such times, says Burns, 'all things seem to unite and cry out for a revival'.[15]

Emotions such as these are, I believe, being stirred in South Africa in these years. And hearts which are caught up in the agonising upheavals of these times are indeed starting to cry out to God for his mercy and help. In such a context a mighty spiritual revival could come upon this land, but it will remain elusive, I believe, until blacks let go of bitterness and whites let go of apartheid. That, as I see it, is the condition for revival in South Africa.

In this there can be no patching as far as apartheid goes if it is the *new* wine of spiritual renewal which interests us. Jesus put the principle clearly:

No one puts a patch of unshrunken cloth on an old garment; for if he does, the patch which he uses to fill in the hole tears the garment apart, and the rent is worse than ever. No one puts new wine into old wine-skins. If he does, the wine-skins burst, and the wine is spilled and the skins perish; but they put new wine into new skins, and both are preserved. (Mt 9:16–17, NAS)

Jesus knew that there comes a time when patching is folly and when the only thing to do is to scrap something entirely and start again. When the garment is wet the new patch will shrink and tear the garment open; likewise, unless new wine (which is still fermenting) is put in a new and elastic wineskin, the gases it gives off will burst the old skin.

Patching up apartheid or putting the new wine of mini-reform into the old apartheid wineskin can only be catastrophic – and certainly counterproductive of any healing of the land through spiritual renewal.

The time is upon South Africa for the new idea: no patching, no old wineskins, but the new idea. And may it come hand in glove with God's reviving and healing work across the land.

The consequences of revival

A final point: genuine spiritual renewal will always have social consequences.

The late Francis Schaeffer said in a lecture shortly before he died:

> A lot of the evangelical camp like to tell us we have to have another revival. But they have forgotten something. Namely that every revival, whether it was the Great Awakening before the great Revolution, or whether it was in Scandinavia or with Wesley or Whitefield, has always had three parts. First it has called for the individual to accept Christ as Saviour. Then it has called Christians to bow their hearts to God and let the Holy Spirit have his place in fullness in their lives. But there has always been a third part. It has always brought social change.[16]

Writing of Charles Finney, probably the greatest American revivalist ever, John Stott has likewise noted:

> He was convinced . . . both that the gospel 'releases a mighty impulse toward social reform' and that the church's neglect of social reform grieved the Holy Spirit and hindered revival. It is astonishing to read Finney's statement in his 23rd Lecture on Revival that 'the great business of the church is to reform the world . . . The Church of Christ was originally organized to be a body of reformers. The very profession of Christianity implies the profession and virtually an oath to do all that can be done for the universal reformation of the world.'

It is hardly surprising to learn, therefore, that through Finney's evangelism God raised up 'an army of young converts who became the troops of the reform movement of his age'. In particular, 'the anti-slavery forces . . . were drawn largely from the converts of Finney's revivals'.[17]

An awakened church should always return to shoulder its responsibilities for a hurting world. And never was this more true than in the eighteenth-century Wesleyan revival. Eighty-four thousand children were down England's mines when the eighteenth century opened; prison conditions were horrendous; slavery was an accepted part of the nation's economic life. There were also 160 different crimes punishable by death. England was drinking half a million gallons of gin per annum and it was said that every sixth house in London was selling spirits. Walpole, the Prime Minister at the time, wrote: 'There is scarcely a member [of Parliament] whose purse I do not know to a sixpence and whose very soul I could not purchase at the offer.'

Then along came the Wesleys with their passionate evangelistic preaching, their mighty movements of prayer and their compassionate concern for the poor and oppressed – not only at home but also abroad in the slave ships and even in the American colonies. Said John Wesley in a letter of 1775 about the Colonies to the then Prime Minister Lord North:

> In spite of all my long rooted prejudices I cannot avoid thinking, if I think at all, that these, an oppressed people, asked for nothing more than their legal rights and that in the most modest and inoffensive manner that the nature of the thing would allow. These men will not be frightened – they will probably dispute every inch of ground, and if they die, die sword in hand.[18]

As these comprehensive commitments and concerns were worked out, the Spirit of God began to sweep across the nation in reviving healing power.

The social consequences were massive. Says one modern chronicle, part of which we quoted earlier:

> The evangelical revival grew in power, at a period critically opportune, and created a moral sentiment that permanently changed England's attitude to distant and defenceless peoples,

and to her own brutal and degraded masses at home. Within a lifetime, like a group of mountain springs, there appeared in England a series of religious and humanitarian movements which altered the whole course of English history, influenced most of Europe, and affected the life of three other continents.

These movements sprang out of a new doctrine of responsibility toward the unprivileged, a doctrine which received its chief impulse from the Evangelical emphasis on the value of the human soul, and hence the individual. The first expression was in the abolition of the slave trade. Then the implications of the doctrine of responsibility widened.[19]

Imagine such a movement in South Africa, and its effects upon the nation, the region, the continent and the world.

Human unbelief says it could not be; natural sin says it could not be; a paralysed church says it could not be; the wider world says it could not be. But God says it could be – if his people there, who are called by his name, will humble themselves and pray and seek his face and turn from their wicked ways, *then* it could be.

17   Liberating the Captives (The church's responsibility to promote freedom in Christ)

The African wants to be liberated at all levels – spiritual, theological, political, economic and cultural.

Mavumilusa Makanzu of Zaire

The Liberty Jesus brings is all-embracing, not merely socio-political.

Derek Morphew

The Spirit of the Lord is on me,
  because he has anointed me
  to preach good news to the poor.
He has sent me to proclaim freedom for the prisoners
  and recovery of sight for the blind,
to release the oppressed,
  to proclaim the year of the Lord's favour.

Luke 4:18–19

THE KAIROS DOCUMENT

Not long after I sat down in President P W Botha's office for that somewhat fateful interview on 8 October 1985, he threw a question at me: 'And what of the *Kairos Document*?' – as if perhaps I had been personally responsible for it (I had in fact not even been a signatory).

The President was referring to a powerful theological document, drawn up by 150 or so South African church leaders and theologians, predominantly but not exclusively black, and calling itself 'a Christian, biblical and theological comment on the political crisis in South Africa today'.

In fact it was a shattering theological critique of the South African situation and the responses to the crisis from both church and state.

It said that 'the *Kairos*, the moment of grace and opportunity' had come and that this now was 'the favourable time' in which God was issuing 'a challenge to decisive action'. And this was seen as urgent because this 'is a dangerous time' and 'if this opportunity is missed, and allowed to pass by, the loss for the Church, for the Gospel and for all the people of South Africa will be immeasurable'.[1]

The *Kairos Document* goes on to classify existing church responses to the political crisis in our country according to three kinds of theology: a *state theology*, which uncritically supports and legitimises the policies of the Government; a *church theology*, which supposedly appeals to abstract Christian ideals without ever really taking a stand or applying those ideals in a rigorous and costly manner; and a *prophetic theology*, which sees the conflict primarily in terms of oppressor and oppressed, and which calls Christians actively to take sides with the oppressed in their struggle for freedom.

The document ends with a call to action which urges all Christians and churches to 'side with the oppressed' in faith and action. This is to be done by joining and supporting existing movements in their fight for justice, openly confronting the apartheid regime and even advocating civil disobedience, organising its own programmes in consultation with mass-based political groups, offering moral guidance (*e.g.* helping people to understand their rights and duties to resist tyranny), and by transforming church liturgies and activities to reflect and promote the liberating mission of God in our crisis.

As the President fixed me with his stare, my mind raced over the just released document, hastily and superficially read a few days previously, late at night and amidst a mild dose of flu.

Though not a theologian able to make quick and accurate theological judgements, I felt that the document had a mix of vital insights along with some unfair caricatures, some extravagant over-statements, plus some very tough theological language with which I could not easily come to terms.

I knew I could not express unqualified support. Nor would I express unqualified condemnation.

'It's like the parson's egg, Mr President,' I replied, ' "good in parts".'

The President did not quite see it this way. How could anything be good in parts? It was either good or bad. As far as he was concerned it was 'communistic' and in every way deplorable. He was also angry at the document's references to his Government as a tyrannical and racist regime.

I could see clearly that this not only outraged him but genuinely mystified him. How could anyone see his Government that way? Was he not trying his best to reform the country and was he not 'God's servant' in the situation?

President Botha then asked a hard thing. He wanted me on TV that night ('How', I thought, 'does he know I'm going on TV?') to denounce the *Kairos* people and disassociate myself from them, and also to put out a press statement to that effect within twenty-four hours. Certain consequences would follow if I failed. And he would be watching.

I thought of many I knew, in the black world especially, who had signed the document and I knew that this for them was not just an academic affirmation but a massive cry of pastoral anguish, theological frustration, political pain and utter emotional trauma. Though their document, by my limited insight, seriously lacked theological and political precision, I knew I could not dissociate from them in that way, whatever the cost to me. To say they'd got their theology wrong, at least at that early moment, and remain comfortably looking on at their plight from the grandstands of privilege while my black friends cried for release seemed to me the ultimate and glib expression of the cheap cop-out.

'No, Mr President,' I said, 'I can't do that.'

The President, understandably from his point of view, was incensed. I felt sympathy for him, and hoped he felt some for me!

In fact my heart went out to him, and I saw the chasms again: the mighty South African chasms, the seemingly unbridgable chasms of mutual 'uncomprehension'. I also saw *Kairos* blacks in the prison of their pain and anguish and frustration and anger, and the President in the prison of his isolated, distant and seemingly uncomprehending world of massive power, huge privilege and paralysing pendulums. These pendulums were oscillating between the 'left swing' call for reform and the 'right swing' threats of his own party, his own tribe – and his own heart! I sensed a man who wanted to move but couldn't.

Hadn't Jesus said something about coming to release captives, whether powerless or powerful, white or black, and regardless of the nature of their prisons?

It made me want to think again about what it really meant for people, and for nations too, to be free.

THE NATURE OF FREEDOM

What did it mean for me to be free? And for blacks to be free? And for President Botha and Afrikaners to be free? And *what* of Black Theology, which gave birth to *Kairos*?

Anyway, it seemed good to go back to scripture and start again from there. If freedom and liberation constitute a major biblical theme, how can or should the church in general and the South African church in particular work this out as part of the ministry of our Lord Jesus Christ on earth?

And what is the relationship, if any, between spiritual and political freedom? After all, the New Testament tells us 'if the Son sets you free, you will be free indeed' (John 8:36). President Botha is a believer: is he free? I am a believer: am I free? Desmond Tutu is a believer: is he free? Gatsha Buthelezi is a believer: is he free?

Has not Jesus anything to say? My pilgrim ponderings tell me he has. But the building-blocks of his way mean going back to basics for all of us, and the so-called Nazareth manifesto (Luke 4:18–19) is as good a place as any to start.

THE NAZARETH MANIFESTO

In South Africa the endless South African political factions, all professing to be Christian, plus the multiplicity of Christian groups, many of them alienated, all combine to underline the peril of any spiritual or so-called liberation enterprises which do not start where Jesus started at Nazareth that day, with 'the Spirit of the Lord . . .'

The role of the Holy Spirit

Deep Christian spirituality, where the Holy Spirit is empowering and in charge, has got to be the matrix from which all human endeavours flow, especially those which relate to the four categories of this scripture – the poor, the captives, the blind and the oppressed. And if Jesus had to move 'in the power of the Spirit' (Luke 4:14) and had to have 'the Spirit of the Lord' upon him (Luke 4:18) in order to fulfil his liberating mission, then certainly we cannot manage with less.

Whether, therefore, we see ourselves preaching good news to the poor, releasing the captives, restoring sight to the blind or setting at liberty the oppressed, we need the Holy Spirit in control to ensure that each activity is done in his time and way.

Any method of working for either spiritual or any other kind of freedom which does not go the Spirit's way is therefore to be held in suspicion.

This has to be powerfully stressed, because much so-called Christian action, be it supposedly spiritual or in the socio-political arena, so lacks the style and fruit of Christian grace and spirituality that it becomes a travesty of the gospel and a source of utter confusion to a watching world.

The non-Jesus spirit makes those who might otherwise be willing to change stubbornly resistant to doing so. But to hear the late Festo Kivengere, my Ugandan African Enterprise colleague, talk on a sensitive subject like black and white relationships was to see people changed and freed, because he did it with Calvary love. I remember once when he and I preached at Stellenbosch University together. A huge throng of eleven hundred students turned out. Festo didn't pull any punches, but the effect was electric. One Afrikaans student came up to me and said, 'I am training for the ministry. But I have been full of race prejudice. Today this brother has completely freed me.' And I suspect he spoke for many others. The key was 'the Spirit of the Lord' upon Festo – that made all the difference.

So the people who work for revival and the way of the Spirit do good service to both church and nation, because they set and keep before all of us the priority Jesus himself embraced of moving 'in the power of the Spirit' and with 'the Spirit of the Lord' upon him (Luke 4:14, 18). The Holy Spirit is therefore where it all must start.

Preaching the good news of the kingdom . . .

'The Spirit of the Lord', says Jesus in Luke 4:18, 'is upon me, because he has anointed me to preach good news to the poor.'

No reading of this text can escape the central place given here to evangelism and preaching the gospel as far as any biblical understanding of liberation is concerned.

Jesus was anointed to *preach*. No matter how important political liberation may seem, we dare not down-grade the place of preaching the gospel, the good news of the kingdom.

The good news is that those who submit to the gracious rule of God in their lives now, and who enthrone him as King, can right now know freedom from the present tyranny of evil, freedom from the ultimate and eternal consequences of sin, and freedom from imprisoning attitudes.

I remember once, while in Washington DC, being approached by a man who said he wanted to come out to South Africa to share his testimony. He had been a sort of senior bomber and assassin for the Ku Klux Klan in the southern United States. He had hated blacks so passionately he was willing and ready to commit the most dastardly brutalities against them. He was totally imprisoned by hatred.

One day he shot a black policeman. As this man lay bleeding in a pool of blood, with his life seemingly draining away, he shared the love and gospel of Jesus Christ with his would-be assassin.

'You can imagine the impact on me,' said my acquaintance. 'I couldn't believe what I was hearing from a man I had shot. Such freedom from bitterness or vendetta led me to give my life to Jesus Christ, and he has freed and liberated me too from all hatred. In fact I now love blacks more than they love themselves, and I'd like to come and give my testimony about this in your country.'

The preached message of Jesus' love, forgiveness and death on the cross miraculously freed and liberated this man. Not that we preach the gospel primarily so that people may be liberated from bad racial attitudes, but so that people may be liberated from both the eternal consequences of sin (John 3:16, 18, 36) and from the present power of sin (Rom 6:12–14). As we press on with the truth of the gospel, it should liberate us spiritually, emotionally and psychologically more and more. Said Jesus: 'If you continue in my word, you are truly my disciples, and you will know the truth, and the truth will make you free' (John 8:31–32, RSV; see also John 8:36).

. . . to the poor

It is a fact that Jesus spent much time with the poor peasants of Galilee, the literal poor, and he had a great affinity for all those at the bottom of the heap. Indeed he himself was one of them, and often had 'nowhere to lay his head' (Matt 8:20).

Undoubtedly this affinity with the poor related in part at least to their poignant humility and their moving spiritual openness to the gospel, and to their hope that the coming of the kingdom in their lives would bring new justice. In the smallest and most abandoned people, 'the little ones' who were economically and socially humiliated and marginalised, Jesus found special graciousness and receptivity to the gospel. So that he could one day proclaim: 'Blessed are you who are poor, for yours is the kingdom of God' (Luke 6:20) – and this in contradistinction to the 'rich' mentioned four verses later (vs 24).

I must say that in my own life and ministry some of the most supremely happy moments have come when I have been ministering to or working with poverty-stricken people. I think of the strange ecstasy of preaching in the marginalised communities of Bluefields and Puerto Cabezas in Nicaragua, in the broken-down no-go town of Limon in Costa Rica, in the tatty back streets of Alexandria in Egypt, in the shanty-area of Mathari Valley outside Nairobi, in the sprawling crowdedness of Soweto, or in the rusted tattiness of Monrovia, Liberia. Or I reflect on the sense of God's special presence as I laboured with unaccountable joy among those harassed black teenagers in Kimberley's Galeshewe township in 1980. At that time I almost felt like leaving South Africa. But the perplexing peace of being in that broken place of poverty and hopelessness with kids who were politically helpless and socially demoralised was the experience God used to say to me: 'No, you stay on here. There is a job to be done.'

All this is to receive in one's spirit a genuinely mysterious signal that somehow God is indeed concerned in a very special way for the materially poor.

To be sure, if we want to see healing in South Africa, we will in new ways have to give some of Jesus' special attention to 'the poor'.

The meaning of 'the poor'

Thankfully Jesus did not just say, 'Blessed are you who are poor' (Luke 6:20). He also said, 'Blessed are the poor in spirit, for theirs is the kingdom of heaven' (Matt 5:3).

In the Old Testament the poor were not just the materially needy but the spiritually humble and pious. King David, with all the royal wealth of Israel at his disposal, could not possibly have been alluding to material poverty when he cried out: 'I am poor and needy, and my heart is wounded within me' (Ps 109:22).

We can't imagine that the first beatitude (Matt 5:3) means material poverty is a condition of receiving the kingdom of God. That would be absurd: it would contradict Jesus' attention to the Roman centurion whose slave was ill (Luke 7:1–10), his open-heartedness to upper-crust Nicodemus, who came by night (John 3:1–15), and his insistence on staying with rich, exploitive, and naughty Zacchaeus, who as a government servant was a collaborator with the Roman oppressor, no less (Luke 19:1–10).

No, Jesus loved all and ministered to all.

Perhaps Jesus' quoting in Luke 4:18–19 of the Old Testament (Isa 61:1–2) gives us the clue to the meaning of 'the poor' in our text, because the Old Testament uses five Hebrew words over five hundred times to speak of the poor in three senses – the economically poor (those with little money), the politically poor (those suffering powerlessly as victims of social injustice) and the spiritually poor (those who are humble, meek and spiritually hungering).

Has God a 'bias to the poor'?

This leaves unanswered the question, asked by many, whether God has a bias to the 'poor and oppressed'.

In affluent white South Africa, this kind of question sends blood rushing to the head and makes many a believer divide from his brother or sister, depending on how it is answered.

Personally, I do not much like the vocabulary of 'bias'. Perhaps it is better to ask if there is a ministry priority in God's heart towards the poor and the oppressed. I don't think the answer is too complicated. Obviously God so loved the whole world and everyone in it that he sent his only Son (John 3:16). So he cares about one person as much as about another. But being holy, righteous and just, he is against social injustice and its human consequences, against political oppression and its human consequences, and against greedy financial exploitation and its human consequences.

Because the politically powerful and the financially rich and acquisitive are often, though not always, the perpetrators of social injustice, of political oppression and of financial exploitation, and the poor so often bear the human consequences of all this, God for the very reason that he is unbiased must often be against the powerful and rich while they do this, (though he still loves and calls them) and on the side of the poor and oppressed while they are the victims of exploitation or injustice. God's own moral nature requires this, because one group is doing something which is wrong and the other is suffering in consequence.

Just as truly might God be against the wife-beater and adulterer and biased, if you like, towards the beaten and betrayed wife as the victim of such marital oppression. The Lord goes to the place of weakness and need and stands with the person wronged.

However, even as *not all* powerful and rich are sent away, neither are all poor and oppressed on God's side, as it were. E K Mosothoane, a black South African theologian, writes to blacks saying: 'Do not think that just because you are African, all is well with you. Do not conclude that your black skin automatically puts you on God's side.'[2] The late and great Bishop Alphaeus Zulu once put it in this way: 'The fact that God may be on the side of the poor does not mean that the poor are always on the side of God!'

Thus it is that, on the one hand, blacks working in South Africa for a new day need to exercise caution as to how they use this idea of the bias of God, and, on the other, whites who make prosperity a sign of the blessing of God on their lives need to face with new courage and honesty the important place which Jesus and scripture give to the poor.

Sent for a fourfold purpose

If Jesus was anointed by the Spirit to preach good news to the poor, he also testified in Isaiah's words that he was sent for a further fourfold purpose: 'to proclaim release to the captives and recovering of sight to the blind, to set at liberty those who are oppressed, to proclaim the acceptable year of the Lord' (Luke 4:18–19, RSV).

This astonishing passage now sets before us the heart of the New Testament picture of freedom, liberation and healing. It is important we understand its meaning, because here we see further dimensions of Jesus' model for ministry which he wants us to emulate and copy. After all, he did say: 'As the Father has sent me, even so I send you' (John 20:21, RSV).

The first question we must settle is whether we spiritualise or literalise the captives, the blind and the oppressed.

My own inclination is along these lines.

First of all, if 'the poor' of the first part of verse 18 are indeed to be understood as both the materially poor of Luke 6:20 (in contrast to the materially rich of Luke 6:24) as well as the humble 'poor in spirit' of Matthew 5:3, then this may give a needed clue to interpreting the captives, the blind and the oppressed in our passage also in *both* spiritual and literal terms.

But more important, perhaps, is the clue of the final phrase of the manifesto, which speaks of Jesus proclaiming 'the acceptable year of the Lord' (vs 19, RSV). For within this phrase lie clues calling for both the spiritual and the literal understandings.

Most commentators now concur that this phrase about 'the acceptable year of the Lord' refers to the year of Jubilee spoken about in Leviticus 25.

Every fifty years, during what Isaiah calls 'the year of the Lord's favour' (Isa 61:2), all field labour was to cease, and people were to eat what they had stored up from the previous year. Non-urban property that had been sold could be redeemed, inheritances restored and slaves set free from servitude.

But what is intriguing is that the Jubilee began on the day of atonement or release (Gk., *aphesis* = forgiveness), thereby making clear that the first and basic ingredient of the Lord's 'release' was spiritual release through the forgiveness of sins (see Lev 25:9).

This suggests, then, that there is a primary *spiritual* understanding of Jesus' words in the Nazareth manifesto, with the poor, the captives, the blind and the oppressed all being understood in spiritual terms, and then a secondary sense in which they are to be *literally* understood.

So, then, if the Jubilee principle offered a comprehensive and fivefold freedom or release from moral guilt, financial debt, spiritual lostness, social slavery, and economic exploitation, then from Jesus' allusion to the Jubilee passage to describe his own ministry we can see his loving concern to effect the release of all those anywhere and in any age who are in any sort of captivity – whether moral, social, physical or economic.

In other words, Jesus' ministry had and has clear political implications. This is even more evident if we register, as John Stott has said, that

> The words 'politics' and 'political' may be given either a broad or a narrow definition. Broadly speaking, 'politics' denotes the life of the city (*polis*) and the responsibilities of the citizen (*polites*). It is concerned therefore with the whole of our life in human society. Politics is the art of living together in a community. According to its narrow definition, however, politics is the science of government. It is concerned with the development and adoption of specific policies with a view to their being enshrined in legislation.
>
> Once this distinction is clear, we may ask whether Jesus was involved in politics. In the latter and narrower sense, he clearly was not. He never formed a political party, adopted a political programme or organized a political protest . . . In the other and broader sense of the word, however, his whole ministry was political. For he had himself come into the world, in order to share in the life of the human community, and he sent his followers into the world to do the same. Moreover, the Kingdom of God he proclaimed and inaugurated was a radically new and different social organization whose values and standards challenge those of the old and fallen community. In this way his teaching had 'political' implications.[3]

'BLACK CONSCIOUSNESS' AND 'BLACK THEOLOGY'

As might be imagined, blacks in South Africa have put their own set of questions to the scriptures in general and to this passage in particular.

What has emerged is called 'Black Theology', which is first cousin to so-called Black Consciousness. Some understanding of both is crucial if the present South African church and some of its inner dynamics are to be understood at all.

Obviously South African blacks have been told that they are inferior and are to be set on one side, away from the white man's world. This they have found deeply offensive to their personal dignity, which has in fact been severely wounded by discrimination and enforced servility. So from the South African black world there naturally comes first an affirmation of the black person's dignity and value, based on what he reads from his Old Testament of the creation story and from his New Testament of the universal and affirming love of Jesus. Says Ernest Baartman: 'Black Consciousness is the black man saying "yes" to his blackness and "yes" to who he is in Jesus Christ.'[4]

So there is an understandable reaction away from white theological and ecclesiastical paternalism and lordship. This is hard for many of us whites to handle, but very necessary. I know when I find black Christian friends resisting in some way something I say or do, or a lead I give, I find it emotionally painful; but the pain is healed at the cross, and this is how it has to be.

Inevitably, because South African black Christians have not lived on an island, the black experience elsewhere, especially in North America, with its links with slavery, has affected them considerably.

For example, North American black leaders such as Martin Luther King, James Cone (who in 1969 wrote *Black Theology and Black Power*) and Deotis Roberts emphasised black consciousness, black self-determination and black power, and of course liberation from all forms of white domination and racism. And, of course, there was the Latin American input.

However, a cautionary word is necessary. While North and Latin American influences are not absent from South African Black Theology, nevertheless they do not explain it. In fact it is only really explained in terms of the way the South African situation itself worked on the theological thinking of leading black theologians.

As it happens, the basic drive in South Africa among black theologians was not only to see what the Bible had to say about psychological and political oppression as experienced here by black people, but also to shake off 'the white man's religion and culture' without shaking off the much-embraced and much-loved Christian faith.

The fact is that on the one hand black South African converts found themselves living in an uneasy balance between black and white cultures, and on the other hand they were having extraordinarily painful questions thrust upon them by the unbelievable and paradoxical situation of being oppressed by those very white Christians who brought them the gospel! This, not surprisingly, has made many blacks feel schizophrenic about trying to keep the heart of the gospel while attempting to shake off the white accretions to it.

Steve Biko and Black Consciousness

Of course, one of the key South African figures in the development of Black Consciousness was Steve Biko. In the late 1960s I once met him back-stage in a little church in King William's Town. I was with my friend Maurice Ngakane, who later fled the country. A man of deep personal piety, Maurice was at that time travelling secretary for the black SCM (Student Christian Movement). Maurice and I were in the Eastern Cape to prepare for our evangelistic mission to the University of Fort Hare. In the event, things were so unstable and tense in the university that the rector squashed the mission because he felt the place would 'blow-up' if we had any mass gatherings, even for the purpose of hearing an evangelistic message from Maurice and me!

Anyway, Maurice knew Steve and took me along. He was an impressive man, quiet, restrained, serious – but able suddenly to burst through all that with a radiant, flashing smile.

I remember being perplexed by Steve's Black Consciousness ideas. Here was I, all bright-eyed about integrating blacks and whites and doing things together, while Steve had this other 'keep things black' mind-set. He once put it this way:

> Black Consciousness is in essence the realisation by the black man of the need to rally together with his brothers around the cause of their oppression – the blackness of their skin – and to operate as a group in order to rid themselves of the shackles that bind them to perpetual servitude.[5]

My perplexity resulted, of course, from my not understanding the depth and levels of black frustration with white domination, and specifically with apartheid. What Steve was promoting was a necessary strategy for that time, painful though it might be to whites like me. The strategy was not only to find a way to unite blacks enough to throw off white domination, but also to rebuild the black self-image, to learn to say 'yes' to blackness, and to liberate themselves psychologically so they could deal with whites as equals. Integration was seen as unhelpful for blacks at that time until they could affirm their blackness as something positive – hence separatism as a strategy, with psychological liberation as the goal.

When I met Biko this was totally beyond my understanding, but it has become much more comprehensible to me over the years, even though I do not think it ultimately squares with the scriptures.

South African police action, it seems, has a not uncommon habit of getting things wrong, and to torture Steve Biko to death must rank as one of our greatest follies. While on a visit to Australia, I read Donald Woods' story of Biko (banned in South Africa of course). I cried in my soul over what we had done, because such an act could only accelerate, maybe to an irretrievable degree, the polarisation between black and white. And yet, totally missing historical chain-reactions, we wonder at the stridency and blackness of something like the *Kairos Document*!

On the other hand, there are dangers with the Black Theology movement. One wants different races, cultures and groups to put their distinctive questions to the Bible. But finally there is only biblical theology and the God of the Bible, even if we all rush at him with different agendas we want him to carry out or if we want him to exercise different ministries to fulfil our respective group needs. After all, who would want black separatism to run riot and deteriorate from a very temporary strategy into a permanent point of principle?

All this underlines the difficulties all of us in South Africa experience in trying to break out of our respective captivities into the glorious liberty of the children of God. It also highlights the value of thinking further about the various captivities which enslave us in this very strange society. For not only is the black man held in political and other kinds of bondage, but whites too have their captivities.

SOUTH AFRICAN CAPTIVITIES

If Jesus came to proclaim release to the captives, it is worth considering which South African captivities, beyond the universal captivity to sin and lostness, he would address.

Most of us, because of some strange fascination with the violent struggles between humans, find war films enjoyable. Especially gripping and adventuresome are those which tell of prisoners of war breaking free against impossible odds from some massively fortified fortress.

True stories from the Second World War tell of many valiant but vain efforts by daring escapees who failed because they didn't know quite what they were up against. The ones who really understood the nature and extent of their captivity were the ones who succeeded.

In my quarter of a century of active ministry in South Africa, I have often seen the South African church, both white and black, struggling to free itself from bondage to the South African way of life. But so often the church just couldn't break free. It was like a lion in a net, or a fish well tagged on the end of a line. So often I have seen individuals, groups or congregations struggling like prisoners on a chain, free to run only a few yards before the chain jerked them back to captivity.

In a nutshell, the apartheid and segregationist ideas, born out of fear, are *Christian heresies*, which became a *party policy*, which evolved into a *tribal ideology*, which grew into a *national idol*, and which finally imprisoned all of us in a *demonic stronghold*.

Like the unsuccessful POWs we mentioned above, our problem in breaking free from the cancerous captivity of institutionalised racism is that we have failed to understand the nature and extent of *our* captivity. Ranged against us is the massive combined power of a fourfold bondage to fear, heresy, ideology and spiritual strongholds. Any one of these can hold a nation prisoner, but put all four together and you have a national captivity of such strength that only the Lord who 'proclaims release to the captives' (Luke 4:18, RSV) can deal with it as his people engage in prayer, fasting and spiritual warfare.

Yes, God needs our co-operation in this momentous process of liberating a nation. But prior to that, he needs our understanding.

Let us now look more closely at some of the components of this captivity.

Our captivity to fear

Fear is probably the major captivity which now holds South Africans, both black and white, in its dread grip.

We fear each other. We fear the future. And we fear stepping out of line even with our own group. This is tragic, because in many ways nothing is more to be feared in terms of finding future answers to the South African problem than fear itself.

But if we can break past fear, who knows what a great deliverance could come upon us! Sometimes all it takes for this particular liberation is meaningful contact. The discovery of what and who lies on the other side of the racial divide can be the most remarkable, life-changing experience.

During the height of the first State of Emergency, some colleagues and I, joined by a Dutch Reformed Church theologian, Adrio König, went into New Brighton, a black township near Port Elizabeth, for a preaching engagement. This was part of a series of reconciliation meetings we were holding in the Port Elizabeth area. During our earlier meetings in the white areas we had encouraged Christians to join us for the night we would be in New Brighton. And we waited expectantly to see whether they would turn up.

As we in the team drove into the township that night, two enormous armoured vehicles called Casspirs began to follow us, loaded up with armed soldiers. We parked outside the church, and so did the Casspirs. It became clear as we waited for the congregation to arrive that the presence of the Casspirs was definitely scaring them off, so we asked Adrio to

have a word with the young driver of the front vehicle. Adrio
chatted to this Afrikaans lad, and then asked: 'But why two
Casspirs for a handful of preachers who only have their
Bibles?'

'Dominee,' said the youth, 'we are scared. To go through
here with just one Casspir is not enough!'

Here again was the South African captivity to fear. We
have let the situation become fearful and we are now a people
of fear.

Thankfully the Casspirs finally moved off. As they did so,
the straggling, equally frightened and harassed congregation
began to arrive. And to our joy so too did a handful of whites
who had taken their own fearfulness in hand and braved all
the roadblocks and township unrest to join us.

At the end of my message I asked the twenty or so white
people to come forward and kneel at the altar rail. I then
asked any blacks who were willing to do so to come forward
and pray for them.

The spectacle that followed was profoundly moving. Most
of the black congregation mobbed forward and gathered
around the little group of whites, laid hands on them and
began to pray with loud prayers, tears and, in some cases,
wailings. Several of the whites broke down.

A number of the white group testified later that in this
contact and deep encounter they had been completely liberated of a paralysing fear of blacks. And one black lady
testified that she had lost her hatred and fear of white people
that night when she laid hands on a white man and prayed for
him.

Of course incidents such as this do not address the cold
physical fear of violence which has no easy answer other than
the end of such violence. That we look at in chapter 18.

Our captivity to heresy

J W C Wand, the great church historian, has noted three
marks of a heresy, as identified by the early church fathers.[6]

First of all, it is *novel*.

The idea of separating people on the basis of race, and elevating one group above another in privilege, opportunity, the vote and land possession, not to mention prescribing everything from people's sex and marriage lives to where they might swim, was certainly, *as a Christian doctrine*, something totally new. In reality, sections of the church succumbed to the racial prejudices and fears of society, and legitimised these theologically. The fact that this was not resisted and blocked in time allowed the novel religious idea to develop into a heresy.

Wand's second mark of a heresy is that it is *local*, partial and confined to certain areas only. In other words, it is not embraced or confessed by the universal church.

That the theological support and rationale given by many South African Christians (Afrikaans and English) to the practice of racism and discrimination has been universally condemned by the worldwide church for decades should have long since alerted us to its heretical nature. But most of that opposition has been resisted by characterising it as part of a 'total onslaught' against the country, or as the manipulating work of communists trying to infiltrate and weaken the church. Flat rejection of the universal church was easier than a critical examination of the local heresy into which we had slipped.

Wand's third mark of a heresy, after novelty and partiality, is *stubbornness*: 'Heresy is characterized by an element of stubbornness and disobedience.'[7]

To talk to South African Christians who support racist ways is to have an encounter with stubbornness. It isn't just a case of meeting a person with another idea. It is to meet a person with almost elemental emotion behind their conviction. Every theological conviction can be shared with them, from the inspiration of scripture to the second coming of Jesus, but to differ on the point of race is to become the enemy.

Wand adds to stubbornness the dimension of disobedience, which is also sometimes present – the disobedience not of the person who can't see the error of his viewpoint, but of the one who refuses 'to acknowledge the truth even once it has become clear'.[8]

Another mark of heresy that Wand does not mention, but

which the New Testament affirms, is that distorted truth leads to *division* and *dissension* in the church.

Paul's letters are full of this. So he can remind Timothy that those who do not 'agree with the sound words of our Lord Jesus Christ' (1 Tim 6:3, RSV) will produce 'disputes' and 'dissension' (vs 4). 'Senseless controversies' also 'breed quarrels' (2 Tim 2:23).

Hardly a thing in the South African or worldwide church has produced as much division and alienation between believers as the apartheid system. In my own experience, those who have divided from me have hardly ever done so saying they reject me because of disagreement over a fundamental point of biblical theology. Rejection is based on my view of the apartheid system and stand against it.

In a Christian country, of all countries in the world, we should not, with the knowledge of the power of our reconciling Christ, be the one place in the world where our policy starts out from the principle of *irreconcilability*. In the jaws of heresy is South African Christendom thus held captive, and thereby divided.

Our captivity to strongholds

St Paul says:

> For though we live in the world we are not carrying on a worldly war, for the weapons of our warfare are not worldly but have divine power to destroy strongholds. We destroy arguments and every proud obstacle to the knowledge of God, and take every thought captive to obey Christ. (2 Cor 10:3–5, RSV)

The apostle's reference here to 'arguments', 'knowledge' and 'thoughts' (*e.g.* 'every thought captive to Christ') suggests to me that a stronghold is an area of thinking in our minds which is occupied and controlled not by Christ but by the powers of darkness which set up 'arguments' and 'obstacles' to the 'knowledge of God' and his ways.

One senses these seemingly impenetrable areas of thought, for example, in people gripped by the cultic teaching of sects or the immovable stubbornness of race prejudice. In fact, if there were ever a demonic stronghold it is race prejudice. That is why it never responds to normal human and prayerless argument. It also explains why 'political arguments', so called, are always counter-productive and never actually change anyone, for people are locked in 'strongholds'. But political discussion where there is prayerfulness, openness and a willingness to learn and change is, however, another story.

This 'stronghold' phenomenon also explains why the excellent editorials written by most South African English-language newspapers against apartheid for over forty years have had almost no effect on people's minds in terms of setting them free to forsake race prejudice. Strongholds don't come down that way, as they might in 'a worldly war' (2 Cor 10:3, RSV), they need tackling with weapons which 'are not worldly but have divine power to destroy strongholds' (vs 4). Of these the first and most potent is prayer. Others of course include direct evangelism, true Christian fellowship across the race barriers, social action, and resistance under God to injustice and wrong.

Our captivity to ideology

Once heresy has given way to the grip of spiritual stronghold, our thought processes are now ready to bring forth ideology.

The South African theologian Professor Klaus Nurnberger describes ideology as 'the conscious or unconscious self-justification mechanism of a social group'.[9] He explains it this way:

> Groups do not only have a practical but also an emotional function. They grant a sense of acceptance and belonging to their members. Every person needs the assurance that he has a right to be what he is, to do what he does, to strive for what he cherishes. This right of existence is granted to him by the group to which he belongs. But it is granted only under certain conditions. You have to know and accept the rules of the game if you want to join a football club. Acceptance in any group is conditional.[10]

This being so, it is not surprising that

the group forces its members to conform because it depends on
their continued support for its existence. Therefore groups have
boundaries. There are those inside (the 'ingroup') and those
outside (the 'outgroup'). There is a strong wall in between to
keep those inside in and those outside out. On the other hand
each member feels a strong urge to support and defend the group.
He shares common interests with the other members. They can
be political, economic, social etc. By being and doing the same,
members assure each other that it is 'normal' to be what they are
and to do what they do. The individual is relieved of the necessity
to justify himself. The group justifies him. Therefore he identifies
himself with the group. Any attack on the group he experiences
as an attack on himself. Thus as a whole the group justifies
itself.[11]

So then, it is in this sense that ideology becomes

the conscious or unconscious self-justification mechanism of a
social group. The group will shrug off any blame and try to find
the culprit outside its own fold. We call that *'scape-goating'* (*e.g.*
blaming foreign agitators, or communists for everything). The
group will also see only those aspects of reality which support its
views (*e.g.* seeing the violence of revolutionaries but not of the
system). That is called *'selective perception'*. It will build up a
system of clever arguments with partial truths which seems to
prove its views. We call that *'rationalisation'* (*e.g.* preventing free
flow of information). It may invent or detect indications of
hidden undercurrents and sinister plots and sow suspicions which
harm others and go to its own credit. We call that *'fabrication'*
(*e.g.* all problems are due to external onslaught). It may – in
an advanced stage – claim absolute validity and discredit any
other point of view as both fallacious and vicious. We call that
'fanaticism'.[12]

Nurnberger notes that it is at this stage that group members
put on blinkers, lose their capacity for self-criticism and their
freedom to test new possibilities. Their thinking moves in a
groove. *In most cases people are not aware of their own
ideological enslavements.* They believe they are right and that
they view reality quite objectively, while the other party is
believed to be distorting the picture for its own ends. But then
they also lose their capacity to see and to rectify their own

mistakes and to shoulder their own share of the responsibility. Instead of tackling what is in its own sphere of influence courageously and forcefully, each group blames others and waits for them to act. In this way progress towards a better deal can be paralysed completely. Put differently, this is the way people enter ideological captivity and imprisoned thinking.

The particular imprisoning power of ideological thinking lies

> in the way it works in each of us to make us promote our own vested self-interest. People try to gain or to defend certain privileges, especially political power, social prestige and financial gain. Entrenched or aspiring elites often consciously employ psychological techniques to fabricate and propagate ideologies profitable to their own interests by means of propaganda, through mass media, by withholding information, through name-killing, public ridicule, outcasting and the like. In severe cases there is deliberate indoctrination and brain-washing. At the same time, the victims, the poor, oppressed and exploited, are subject to their own ideological misconceptions as well. In short: an ideology is a spiritual prison, the power of which is derived from the human need for justification, i.e. the need for the confirmation of one's right of existence, especially where it is questioned in one way or another.[13]

Clearly, if Nurnberger is right (and I believe he is), we are all captive, in some degree or other, to this ideological sort of thinking. Clearly apartheid is an ideology. So too are Marxism, socialism and capitalism.

In fact in white South Africa, perhaps especially in English-speaking South Africa, our thinking is strongly captive to capitalist ideology. Not surprisingly, therefore, we never consider ourselves guilty of ideological thinking while we are busy denouncing the ideologies of socialism, Marxism or apartheid. Thus, for example, in a sample survey conducted through the Rand Afrikaans University, white and black South African Christians were asked to react to the statement: 'Peace in South Africa can only be ensured by equal redistribution of wealth among all inhabitants . . .' Sixty-eight per cent of the whites sampled disagreed; thirty-two per cent agreed. On the other hand, eighty-two per cent of the blacks sampled agreed, while eighteen per cent disagreed. The shattering discovery was that the percentages of agreement and disagreement in both groups coincided with whether people in either group were above or below the nation's average incomes.

This sort of finding suggests that most people will read their Bibles from where they stand in the economic structure. Reading and preaching the word from this place of vested self-interest will obviously muzzle the prophetic word as effectively as any political ideology.

We are all living with some measure of self-deception. As Professor Nurnberger has observed, 'the Church has throughout its history tended to excuse and legitimate evil structures and processes rather than transform them'.[14]

The liberation passion as blacks – and especially black Christians – embrace it, can also drift, I believe, without biblical safeguards, into the prison of ideological bondage.

Understandably black Christians in South Africa are building their theology round the desire for liberation. Who can blame them? Says Alan Boesak: 'Black Theology, therefore, because it comes from a situation of oppression and suffering of a people who believe in God and who ask what the Gospel of Jesus Christ has to say about the situation, is also a theology of liberation.'[15]

Says E K Mosothoane: 'Black theology approaches Scripture with a heavy burden of oppression, rejection and suffering, seeking to discover in Scripture God's purpose for humanity in situations of that nature. It understands the divine purpose essentially and fundamentally in terms of liberation.'[16]

This being the case, both Black Theology and Kairos Theology, in my view, partake of some of the strengths and some of the weaknesses of Latin American Liberation Theology (see Appendix 7).

Even so, there is the danger that black Christians might become so totally captive to the liberation passion that other key enterprises of Christian mission such as evangelism will be neglected or even discarded as irrelevant. Or else the work and gifts of the Holy Spirit could be ignored as not bearing on the socio-political priority. Sometimes, even, Christian fellowship between black and white Christians can be rejected as 'not for now' while the political struggle is on. Yet Jesus called both Simon, the revolutionary zealot, and Matthew, the tax-gatherer and system man, into the same fellowship and bade them both seek a higher, better way.

However, while white Christians may lament this preoccupation with liberation, or query it theologically, our mouths must virtually be shut unless we are willing to do whatever is in our power to bring political freedom to blacks and work love into our structures – which is what justice is all about. And of course this is where the South Americans have been so strong. They have anathematised forms of theology and spirituality that stay in the realm of ideas and wordy formulae and which never get down to action as the expression of true Christian love. Their idea of theology as a discipline which starts 'at sundown', after a hard day's practical, Christian action, is powerful indeed.

This action in the political realm could involve many things. As said before, it can and should start with *prayer*, for as Tennyson said, 'more things are wrought by prayer than this world dreams of'.

Then our concern can and should involve *protest*, by whatever legitimate means possible. It has frequently been observed that for evil to triumph it only requires good people to remain silent. I have often thought that I would rather try to do something about this South African tragedy and fail than not try at all. I would also feel dreadful if South Africa came really badly unstuck somewhere down the line, and I had to say to my questioning children that in the 1960s, 1970s and 1980s, when there might have been a chance to turn it all round, I did and said nothing.

Then there can be *active political involvement*, by whatever channel is open, whether by running for public office, or by extra-parliamentary endeavours, or even by writing to and pressuring public servants for appropriate action along Christian lines.

My point here is that whites, and especially white Christians, dare not lament the black captivity to the liberation passion if from our side, where political domination currently lies, we *do nothing* to help blacks with their freedom aspirations.

In South Africa Christians hold the key if only they will first free themselves from their own ideological captivities. The way to do this is to let the body of Christ function – to be truly a body – and for all Christians to begin to relate, work and study the word of God across the imprisoning boundaries of race, class, group, socio-economic levels, culture or whatever. If that happened, we might yet see Jesus Christ bring 'release to the captives and . . . liberty [to] those who are oppressed' (Luke 4:18, RSV).

DOING SOMETHING PRACTICAL

A major challenge, especially from many parts of the Third World, is that we Christians stop theorising and dealing in the coinage of words, and begin to do something practical, each in our own place and space, and in whatever way we can.

It may seem very small. Or it may be or become quite big. But in this way we liberate captives by a combination of spiritual ministry to the inner needs, practical care for the outer needs, and emotional encounter, which releases ourselves and others from excessive captivity to ideological thinking or fear.

Once, in our NIR (National Initiative for Reconciliation) newsletter, I made this plea – 'Let every Christian *do* their bit.' One of the ladies in our church, Mrs Pat Caldwell, read that sentence. She had felt hopelessly captive to paralysis over the magnitude of the South African problem and to frustration at not being able to do anything. Beyond that, she saw many black people in Sweetwaters, the black township near us, who likewise were captive – but to poverty, unemployment, hopelessness and spiritual lostness.

She decided to do her bit: 'My heart responded completely to the message the Lord sent out through that newsletter.' She decided with the Spirit's help and with an act of her own will to be liberated from her own captivity and to help liberate others.

Through Graham Beggs, Betty Bradford and Joyce Krog, also from our church, Pat began to be exposed to the needs of the people of Sweetwaters. With what seemed to be the Spirit's prompting, a soup kitchen was launched to feed children in one of the black schools.

With help from our church, this scheme grew from feeding the forty most needy children in the school to feeding some five hundred children. It also involved hiring a full-time cook and building a little kitchen in the school.

Then Pat and her friends began to pray 'that God would open a door for the message of Jesus, that the mystery of Christ could be proclaimed' (*cf*. Col 4:3). Soon mothers of the children began meeting with Pat and her friends on the grass outside the kitchen twice a week for a time of prayer, praise and teaching. Today between fifty and seventy women of Sweetwaters meet in this way for regular prayer, Bible study and teaching.

Pat observed that many of these women, some with children, were very needy, hopelessly poor, unemployed, and mostly unemployable, and possessed no obvious acquired skill through which income could be generated.

Pat and her friend Sarah Dottridge then began to develop a new vision based on Titus 3:14: 'Our people must learn to devote themselves to doing what is good, in order that they may provide for [their own basic] necessities and not live unproductive lives.'

They began to teach some of these women to make blankets to sell to friends and to shops. Gradually, some of these women began to be delivered from the captivity of helplessness and rock-bottom self-images which made them feel worse than useless. Imagine the excitement and the liberating boost to the morale of them all when a local shop put in an order for R1 500 worth of blankets. Now they work with a regular supply of orders and cannot keep up. In the middle of all of this the liberating gospel of Jesus Christ and the forgiveness of sins continues to be faithfully preached, proclaimed and gloriously received.

There are now about ten other people involved with Pat and Sarah, and hundreds of lives are being positively affected.

A diagram of how it all works appears overleaf.

THE SWEETWATERS CIRCLE OF
LIBERATING CARE

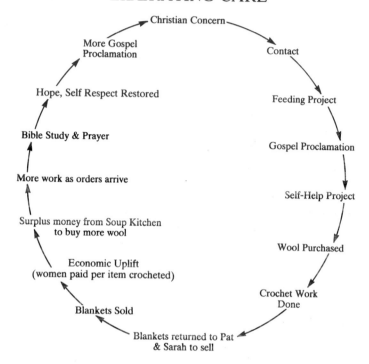

Christian Concern

More Gospel
Proclamation

Contact

Hope, Self Respect Restored

Feeding Project

Bible Study & Prayer

Gospel Proclamation

More work as orders arrive

Self-Help Project

Surplus money from Soup Kitchen
to buy more wool

Wool Purchased

Economic Uplift
(women paid per item crocheted)

Crochet Work
Done

Blankets Sold

Blankets returned to Pat
& Sarah to sell

The late Mavumilusa Makanzu of Zaire, whom I got to know well at PACLA in 1976, used to say: 'The African wants to be liberated at all levels – spiritual, theological, political, economic and cultural.' This is a message from Africa generally, and specifically from South Africa, to the Christian church and to each of us. It is, moreover, a message which plugs us in deeply and poignantly to Jesus' own commitment in the power of the Spirit to preach good news to the poor, to proclaim release to the captives, to help the blind recover their sight, and to set at liberty those who are oppressed in different ways.

It should be clear by now that this is not a challenge in terms of some pretty ideas, but is a call to practical action. In our NIR endeavours we have put out a suggested list of things which people can do and be involved in regardless of who they are and where they are as the Spirit leads them. This list (included in Appendix 6) shows the kind of thing which any Christian anywhere, whether in North America, Australia, the UK, New Zealand or somewhere in the Third World, could pick up on and in a new way become part of the Lord's ongoing and liberating work in the world.

The exciting thing is that not only does it help liberate other captives, it is gloriously liberating for oneself. Indeed, to know Jesus Christ personally and to be active in obedience to him is to enter 'the glorious freedom of the children of God' (Rom 8:21). And that's what life is all about.

But, of course, as far as an unjust society is concerned, this sort of liberating action of which we have spoken is not enough. Its endeavours have to reach the structures of such a society. And so in this direction we must turn in the concluding chapters of this book, beginning with the Christian's relationship to governmental authority, which in large measure determines the sociopolitical structures of any given nation (to be sure, the South African Government determines *ours!*).

18 Rendering to Caesar
(The church's responsibility
to the state)

If there is no final place for civil disobedience, then the government has been made autonomous and as such it has been put in the place of the living God.

Francis Schaeffer

Give to Caesar what is Caesar's, and to God what is God's.

Matthew 22:21

Everyone must submit himself to the governing authorities.

Romans 13:1

It is quite clear, according to the Bible, that the Christian church has a responsibility not only to render to Caesar the things that are Caesar's and to God the things that are God's (Matt 22:21), but to submit to the powers that be (Rom 13:1). However, exactly how all that works out is an issue which the South African situation and people's experiences constantly throw into sharp relief. It can also at times produce massive perplexity.

The cataloguing of a set of experiences and situations illustrates the confusions we face.

SOME REAL-LIFE SITUATIONS

Sweetwaters

Take, for example, the situation down in our black township of Sweetwaters, close to where I live. This, as I said earlier, is where Pat Caldwell, Sarah Dottridge, Graham Beggs and others from our church have been working among the poor.

Now there can be no doubt that the poverty of Sweetwaters and places like it is related at least in part to the apartheid structures and laws and all that goes to make up the South African system. Not that one can blame all poverty and all misfortune on governments. But certainly migratory labour laws, the Group Areas Act, poor wages, inadequate education and, in the past, job reservation have all combined significantly to aggravate the situation for the people of Sweetwaters. In other words, as some would say, their plight is not simply the result of their own misfortune, but is at least in part a result of the sins *of other people* which have been made operative in both political structures of injustice and economic structures of exploitation.

So if the church is genuinely trying to relate appropriately to the state, should it just do ambulance work to pick up the socially and politically wounded, or should it try to resist by whatever legitimate means possible all those structural programmes of the state which contribute to the unhappiness of places such as Sweetwaters?

Some answer those questions by adopting a *laissez-faire* posture and saying: 'The poor are always with us, and the state is doing its best, so let us just get on with the business of life.' Some help with generous and often sacrificial acts of caring and practical assistance.

Others would say that the state which perpetrates, for example, a Group Areas system should be opposed by all parliamentary and extra-parliamentary means at the disposal of the general population. Still others would say that a state which allows Sweetwaters to exist, and on top of that denies a well-to-do person from Sweetwaters the possibility of moving up to the white suburb of Hilton, should be not only opposed but overthrown as expeditiously as possible, preferably by non-violent means, but by violent revolution if necessary.

So what does it mean with regard to Sweetwaters to render to Caesar the things that are Caesar's and to God the things that are God's?

To fight or not to fight?

In the South African context the church/state issue involves trauma for many in terms of whether to fight, either on the black side or the white, for what they believe to be true and important. Thus, for example, my colleague Dennis Bailey had a young white youth come to see him to seek counsel relating to the matter of being a combatant in the South African Defence Force (SADF). This young man was absolutely traumatised at the prospect, as he saw it, of going into the townships against black fellow citizens as part of the Defence Force. His own conscience was in protest. Of course many social and other pressures around him said he should proceed and conform.

While Dennis was trying to help him get to grips with the problem into the room came a young black teenager, also a professing Christian. Leaving the white lad in his office, Dennis asked the young black what he wished to speak about and found that the matter concerned whether he should cross the border to train as a guerrilla-fighter and join the armed wing of the African National Congress (ANC). Dennis told him about the white boy in his office and asked if he would like to join in the discussion so that the two lads could agonise and pray together. The black boy agreed.

It was a poignant encounter. Each struggled with the church/state question, but this time in terms of different aspects of the violence/non-violence issue – one with what it means to be tacitly or actively part of the white forces of the status quo, the other with the issue of revolution.

Gradually the Holy Spirit began to speak to both of them. Finally the two lads fell sobbing into each other's arms, all the while blurting out their prayers to the living God to show them what to do. The upshot was that the white youngster returned to the army, insisting on being a non-combatant, and the young black turned away from his previous plan to go and be a guerrilla-fighter – he would work for change by peaceful means instead.

Tragically the brother of the black lad was killed a few days later when the SADF raided an ANC office in Botswana. The boy's mother was a Christian too, but I can easily imagine her now despairing of the Christian way and saying: 'Last week I did not want my son to cross the border, but now that they've killed my other son, let him go!'

In any event, here were two young South Africans face to face in agonising and internal conflict about what it meant for each of them to render to Caesar what is Caesar's and to God what is God's.

Of course some white youngsters fight in the army with no qualms, while others refuse totally and take their stand as conscientious objectors. Is one of these right and the other wrong? Likewise many young blacks, even some who would definitely profess to be Christians, have opted to go and join the external wing of the ANC. Who is rendering rightly to Caesar and submitting appropriately to the powers that be? How difficult this is! Infallible answers obviously cannot be supplied. But surely we can find at least *some* guiding principles.

Understanding Romans 13 in a South African context

At some point during their deliberations Dennis' two young counsellees would undoubtedly have raised the question how to interpret Romans 13. Both black and white Christians turn to this passage, some to justify and endorse total obedience to the state, others to justify and endorse civil disobedience, and still others to refuse totally to admit the legitimacy of the South African state.

This highlights once again an acute problem of interpretation as we see different Christians, with different backgrounds, at different stages of Christian development and with different preconceptions, all coming to the text and often subconsciously making it support their own previously embraced convictions.

So some go to Romans 13 to support their view that the Nationalist Government is ordained by God and therefore to be fully obeyed. Others, perhaps on the black side, would say that this understanding would make God incomprehensible and there is no way they can accept the present South African Government as ordained by God. Others like to pick and

choose: for example, one prominent former Moderator of the
Dutch Reformed Church said he believed that every Prime
Minister from Hertzog to Verwoerd, with the exception of
General Smuts, had been ordained by God!

In South Africa these issues present both comic and tragic
dimensions. For example, most whites would totally deplore
any form of liberating violence or violent liberation. Yet, I
recollect the delight all over South Africa, and indeed in the
Christian community itself, when President Julius Nyerere
and his army of soldiers and tanks moved in to Uganda to
liberate it from the notorious Idi Amin. There was no problem with violent liberation there. Likewise, we were perfectly
open about supporting UNITA in Southern Angola in its
attempts to overthrow the MPLA Government in Luanda.

So in the light of Romans 13 there arises the awkward
question: Are MPLA 'powers that be' ordained by God and
therefore not to be overthrown by UNITA, South Africa or
anyone else, or are they not? Likewise, with the South
African Government, is it ordained by God or not?

The fact that many of us in South Africa who are Christians
arrive at different conclusions to such questions underlines
the necessity of struggling with these issues. In fact, different
groups and traditions of Christians, both in past church
history and now, have adopted different postures and these
have to be sympathetically understood. But that this is no
simple matter is made clear by the history of church/state
relationships.

THE CHURCH'S RELATIONSHIP
TO THE STATE

Over the centuries the church has embraced three different
stances *vis-a-vis* the state: withdrawal from the state, active
identification with it, and active resistance to it.

Withdrawal

This occurs either because the church is a persecuted minority, as it was in the Roman Empire, or is in the Soviet Union,

China and many Moslem countries today, or because the church by theological conviction stands aloof, with the posture: 'Let preachers preach and politicians govern, and let the twain ne'er meet,' thinking, 'No matter what awful things are being perpetrated by the state, let the church not dirty itself in such matters.' Sadly this happens even in some countries where Christians are numerous and could indeed considerably affect the situation.

Active identification

This developed after the Roman emperor Constantine made Christianity the official religion of the Roman Empire in 313 AD. It finds more modern examples in the Dutch Reformed Church's active support of apartheid (up until recently) and in the Russian Orthodox Church's support of the Soviet Government.

At our PACLA conference (Pan Africa Christian Leadership Assembly) in Nairobi in 1970, I was also astonished at how few black church leaders were prepared to say anything negative about any of their governments, some of which were brutal, dictatorial and totally undemocratic. But they were quite prepared to take 'a courageous stand' on apartheid!

Active resistance

The third option, and perhaps a more obviously twentieth-century one, is when the church takes its stand in active opposition to the state or to some particular state, as in the Philippines. This can even mean, in some situations, sanctioning and being part of a violent revolution. The church, or sections of it, can thus become uncritically allied to a liberation or revolutionary movement, regardless of its methodologies, some of which may be totally unchristian or anti-Christian. As David Bosch has said: 'A theology of the status quo and a theology of revolution are, in fact, merely mirror-images of one another. In both cases the church becomes the lackey of a specific political program.'[1]

So if the previous posture involved the church in a theology and practice of the status quo, then this one involves the church in a theology and praxis of revolution. Either way, the church is basically sanctioning what David Bosch calls 'a specific political blueprint'.

Inevitably South Africa has examples of this on both sides of the racial divide.

In many sections of the black church today there is an uncritical endorsement of liberation movements such as the ANC, PAC (Pan African Congress), SWAPO (South West Africa's People's Organisation), *etc*. While some whites go along with this, most are appalled – especially the Afrikaner.

Yet there is a paradox here. If you remember chapter 6 on patriotism and nationalism, you will recall my story of my grandfather's experience in Heilbron with Deneys Reitz during the Boer Rebellion of 1914. This was an armed uprising against the Government of the day, with its English sympathies, as was evident in South Africa's going into the First World War on the side of Britain.

But what is especially interesting from the perspective of the late 1980s, when issues of civil obedience and disobedience are so alive, especially for black Christians, is that the official position of the Dutch Reformed Church Council following the Boer Rebellion was one of *non-condemnation* of the rebels. In the wrenching furore of post-Rebellion debate, according to a Dutch Reformed theologian, Carel F A Borchardt, the DRC Council, manifestly sympathetic to the rebels, 'allowed that it is only permissible to resist the State should the State act in contradiction to God's laws'.[2]

The resolutions of the DRC Council, which would not condemn the civil disobedience of the rebels, made it clear that Christians should not rebel against the state, or resist it or disobey its laws, 'other than for very weighty and sound reasons which are confirmed by God's Word and by a conscience which has been enlightened by the Word of God'.[3]

The Dutch Reformed Church Council of January 1915 accordingly appealed for a non-partisan inquiry into the 'real motives and purposes of this resistance'.[4] Likewise, in 1988, twenty-five million South African blacks would be more than happy for that principle to be followed once again!

As an Afrikaner, David Bosch makes an intriguing observation on this episode: 'Today the sons and daughters of those same Afrikaner rebels of 1914 denounce any form of Christian support for liberation movements and armed rebellion as anti-Christian and ungodly. Most are solid supporters of a theology of the status quo, whereas their fathers supported a theology of revolution.'[5]

This reality prompts Bosch to 'venture a thesis that the more a Church supports a violent revolution in the pre-revolutionary period, the more that same Church will become a captive of the new regime after the revolution'.[6] What all this shows is that the church/state issue is fraught with difficulty and complication and is not easy to get right: all of us are inconsistent.

The South African situation raises the church/state question so acutely that one is constantly driven back to the scriptures to struggle with it over and over again.

To me the best place to pick up the thread is with Jesus and his famous injunction about rendering to Caesar.

THE 'RENDER TO CAESAR' TEXT

Of all the sayings of Jesus in the Bible this is among the best known to both believer and non-believer alike: 'Render . . . to Caesar the things that are Caesar's, and to God the things that are God's' (Matt 22:21, RSV).

The biblical context

Jesus is here confronting two groups, the Pharisees and the Herodians, the latter being supporters of Herod Antipas. They were normally in bitter opposition to each other. On the question of whether it was lawful to pay the tribute tax to Rome, the Pharisees, being very orthodox, resented paying the tax to a foreign king, seeing it as an infringement of the divine right of God himself. The Herodians, on the other hand, as the party of Herod, the King of Galilee, knew that Herod owed his power to the Romans and that therefore it was wise not to rock the boat but to pay whatever tax was required.

So they put their question to Jesus: 'Tell us, then, what you think. Is it lawful to pay taxes to Caesar, or not?' Their question was so framed that it had to elicit a direct 'yes' or 'no'. If Jesus said it was lawful to pay tribute to the occupying foreign power, his answer would enable the Pharisees to arouse public opinion against him because the ordinary people saw the Romans as their oppressors. But if, on the other hand, he said it was not lawful to pay the tribute tax (evaluated as about one day's wage of a working man) the Herodians would seize on it as providing grounds for a charge of treason, for they knew very well that Herod owed his position to the imperial power and was entrusted by it with the general supervision of taxation.

Although knowing that their intentions were malicious (and hypocritical, vs 18), Jesus responded by asking for one of the tribute coins, which of course bore Caesar's image.

'Whose likeness and inscription is this?' asked Jesus (vs 20). To this there was only one possible answer, which he received: 'Caesar's' (vs 21). Jesus agreed with this and said that, because the coin bore Caesar's image, it belonged to him and could properly be given to him, but that we are to give to God what belongs to God.

The principle of dual citizenship

Jesus' response acknowledged that the two worlds of Caesar and God exist and his followers have dual citizenship. As R V G Tasker has said:

> This all-important pronouncement of Jesus shows that He distinguished without dividing the secular and the sacred, and that He united without unifying the two spheres in which His disciples have to live. They are citizens of two cities, the earthly and the heavenly, and they have duties to discharge in both.[7]

They are indeed citizens of whichever country in the world they happen to live. And to that country they owe much. They owe safety against lawlessness, which only a settled government can give. They owe the public services, which the state brings to its citizens. Light, water, sewerage, upkeep of public facilities, transport services, and so on, they owe to the state. They are thankful for the law courts, education, medical services, provision for unemployment and old age, and for this they must render back to the state what is appropriate in terms of appreciation, tax, and obedience within the limits of conscience. Perhaps if they are civically minded, they will render civic or political service in the public arena. Indeed a Christian should be a good citizen, and failure to be such is a failure in Christian responsibility.

It is a great tragedy for a country or its industry and public life when Christians refuse to take their part in administration and public service, and leave all that to non-Christians, some of whom will be selfish, godless, self-seeking and partisan. So the Christian has a duty to Caesar in return for the privileges which the rule of Caesar brings to him.

At the same time, the Christian is a citizen of the kingdom of God, and we are therefore to give to God what belongs to him.

Which citizenship has priority?

In Jesus' response there are perhaps implied another two questions and answers: 'What do we give to God?' (That which bears *his* image.) And what, in fact, does bear God's image? ('Man', of course, as we know from the creation story in Genesis.)

Peter Hinchcliff, formerly of Rhodes University and now of Oxford, has said that

the implication of this interpretation is that there is no separation of spheres. The whole of a man bears God's image. The whole of himself is owing to God, including his political life. What he owes to Caesar is a small part of what he is worth. God claims the whole and, therefore, God reigns supreme even over the political sphere.[8]

'While you give money to Caesar,' he says, 'you give yourself to God.'[9]

In other words, one's allegiance to God is primary, over-whelming and all-embracing, and all other duties, even to Caesar, are subordinate to that.

It is not that there are two separate, autonomous, water-tight, non-interconnecting spheres – God and Caesar – both of which have equal claim upon the Christian. The point is that we are to render (or more literally *pay back*) what is the proper due to Caesar, and to give back to God *his* proper due, which is the total gift of ourselves. His claim on us is *absolute*. Caesar's is not. We render to Caesar all that is appropriate, so long as it does not compromise what we owe to God. Our first and final loyalty is to *him*.

So the informed Christian conscience, operating in inter-face with the word of God, and perhaps with Christian counsel from others, constitutes part of the check on how we allow Caesar to use his power over us.

Caesar as sinner

The point is that though Caesar has his place in the world, being there to restrain human sin and maintain good law and order, nevertheless Caesar is himself a sinner also, needing both restraining and reminding that he is there under God.

This is why the American Founding Fathers, for example, sought to decentralise power – because they knew that exces-sive power concentrated in the hands of sinful, fallible human beings is a recipe for abuse, then tyranny and finally disaster. As the famous Lord Acton noted: 'Power corrupts and absolute power corrupts absolutely.' He likewise noted that 'when Christ said "Render unto Caesar the things that are Caesar's and unto God the things that are God's," He gave to the State a legitimacy it had never before enjoyed, and set bounds to it that had never yet been acknowledged'.[10] In other words, the church is there to witness to a biblical principle, and especially in a professedly Christian country to act as a conscience to the state.

Ultimate loyalty

So Jesus' utterance on Caesar, God and the believer does not in an absolute sense separate church and state, nor does it lock Christian believers into two separate and disconnected sets of loyalties – but rather it speaks of a dual citizenship with a connected set of relationships with ultimate loyalty to God. In diagram form it would look like this:

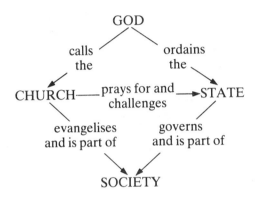

So God both calls the church and ordains the state; the church for its part prays for and challenges the state, and both relate to society as a whole, with the church evangelising it (though obviously being itself part of society) and the state governing it.

Francis Schaeffer's perspective on those relationships is helpful:

When Jesus says in Matthew 22:21 'Give to Caesar what is Caesar's, and to God what is God's', it is not:

GOD and CAESAR

It was, is, and always will be:

GOD
and
CAESAR

The civil government, like all of life, stands *under* the Law of God . . . When *any office* commands that which is contrary to the

Word of God, those who hold that office abrogate their authority and they are not to be obeyed. And that includes the State. God has ordained the State as a *delegated* authority; it is not autonomous. The State is to be an *agent of justice*, to restrain evil by punishing the wrongdoer, and to protect the good in society. *When it does the reverse, it has no proper authority.* It is then a usurped authority and as such it becomes lawless and is tyranny.[11]

THE 'BE SUBJECT TO THE GOVERNING AUTHORITIES' TEXT

Almost every Christian in South Africa from the President to the prisoner has a view on Romans 13. It is not the easiest of passages, and I've had my struggles with it, as have most South Africans. To me Paul in Romans 13:1–7 gives basically the same picture as Jesus in Matthew 22:15–22. In a sense it is a fuller explanation of it. In any event, if we remember the importance of context and the principle of letting scripture interpret scripture, then the interplay of these two passages and others in their contexts is necessary if we are to get closer to their meaning.

The biblical and social context

It seems to be a scholarly consensus that Paul was writing in the first part of Nero's reign, before his persecutions got fully under way. This was a time when the Roman state in considerable measure had served as a protector in the enterprise of the church spreading the gospel to the Gentiles. In fact Paul's experience of the Roman authorities had been reasonably positive, and the *Pax Romana* had enabled him and others to get on with the proclamation of the gospel. Given these factors, it would therefore be very natural and right for Paul to insist that state authority is something given by God, as a God of order rather than chaos, confusion or anarchy.

However, when we come to Revelation 13, which was written nearly forty years later by the apostle John, we have a very different context, in which John presents the Roman state as the Beast. Scholars feel that John's Revelation 13 was probably written during the reign of Domitian, the arch-persecutor of the church, who was possessed of a notorious inferiority complex which finally led him to demand that his subjects worship him as Lord and God. John's witness had already landed him in exile on the Island of Patmos, often used as a place of banishment for political and religious offenders. And it was from there that John wrote his protest about Domitian's state, with its insistence on emperor-worship and its dreadful and deathly devastation of the church. John saw this as a demonic totalitarianism which Christians could not accept and would have to resist.

Although Revelation 13 is full of obscure symbolism, most scholars agree that the apostle here speaks about the Roman state of approximately AD 90–100. By this time the state, in John's view, had thoroughly overstepped the legitimate boundaries ordained for it by God as seen in the rendering to Caesar passage and the Romans 13 passage under consideration. Where it becomes totalitarian and seeks to make demands upon the Christian which compromise duty to God, then the state itself has become demonic. It has broken loose from God's order and limits, and is therefore not to be obeyed.

With this wider perspective and with the importance of context in mind, we now return to Romans 13.

Taking Romans 13 at face value

At face value Romans 13 says that all governments are God-ordained and therefore to be totally obeyed. So whatever the powers that be do is fine. We must simply obey them and leave the whole realm of government and politics alone, though we must pay our taxes!

I have lost count of the number of times this line has been tossed at me in South Africa. And of course Christians everywhere like this interpretation while things are fine for them and they are beneficiaries of a fair government. But if they suddenly get a Hitler, or an Amin, or a Khmer Rouge, or an Ayatollah, what then? I've heard of Rhodesian whites who preached this vigorously under Smith, but who under Mugabe felt they should break his laws relating to currency export because these were 'unfair'. Likewise most Afrikaners preach this now, but they didn't in 1914, when the government of Louis Botha ordered them into Britain's war. In a similar vein, I've met blacks in independent Africa who were insurrectionists while the British ruled them but are now strong proclaimers of Romans 13, even under corrupt military governments who came to power via military coups.

Submission: the whys and wherefores

In the original context of the text Paul does does not countenance revolution or civil disobedience for Christians. Basically Christians are to subject themselves, he says, to the laws of government in order to avoid punishment (vs 3–4), to avoid discipline (vs 2), and because it is the right thing to do (as your conscience allows, vs 5). The Christian is also required to provide the state with the tax money it needs to keep public services going (vs 6–7), and to render a Christian testimony and debt of love to everyone (vs 8). This testimony dimension is likewise picked up by St Peter, who says that we are to submit ourselves to every ordinance of man for the Lord's sake, so that 'by doing good you should silence the ignorant talk of foolish men' (1 Pet 2:15).

Interpreting scripture by scripture

Some further light comes when we let one part of the Bible shed light on another.

As a student of the Old Testament, Paul would obviously have known of Moses' defiance of Pharaoh (Exod 13–15), and of Deborah the prophetess' encouragement of Barak to lead an army in revolt against Jabin, the Canaanite king who had ruled over the Hebrews for twenty years (Judg 4–5). He would also have known of Daniel and his three friends' refusal to worship the golden image set up by King Nebuchadnezzar and their subsequent rescue by the Lord from the consequent penalty (Dan 3), as well as of Daniel's breaking of the law of the Medes and Persians in refusing to address his prayers solely to King Darius. In his own period of history he would have known of Peter's famous statement: 'We must obey God rather than men!' (Acts 5:29).

In the light of all these biblical instances of defiance of the state's power, how are we now to understand Romans 13?

The functions of the state

To prevent social collapse

First of all, God has ordained the phenomenon of government and of the state to keep order and to prevent chaos. This is clear. Whether it obliges us to see every government as God-ordained is less clear. Did he ordain Stalin, Hitler or Amin? Certainly we would have to say he *allowed* them, perhaps even as a judgement whereby both country and church got the government they deserved, though manifestly God could not *approve* them. And most assuredly he could remove them, which he did.

Equally certainly, we cannot see any given government as *indefinitely* ordained of God, otherwise Christians could not participate even in a democratic election, seeking to remove one government and replace it with another.

To be God's servant

The state and its government are jointly 'God's servant' (Rom 13:4), which means that its power is not autonomous but derived from God. It can't do what it likes. It is a servant. And not only that, a servant of the living God who is the Father of our Lord Jesus Christ. So it is meant to function in the Jesus way and operate *under his lordship*. Its power is not absolute, and it is accountable to God. Indeed its obligation to rule is predicated on its higher obligation to obey. And unless we safeguard this biblical principle we have no answer to the ancient question: *Quis custodiet ipsos custodes?* (Who will guard the guardians?)

To function for the good of all

Romans 13 tells us that the state is God's servant, to reward good and punish evil. It is there for our '*good*' (vs 4) – and not just for the good of some under its rule, but for the good of *all*.

This is where the black youths in our South African townships battle so desperately, especially the Christian ones. They know their Bible tells them that the Nationalist Government is God's servant for their good, but nothing in their experience of apartheid suggests much that is explicitly for *their* good. Maybe for the good of whites, but not for theirs. This raises for them a huge question mark as to the legitimacy of such a government.

Their experience has been traumatic and sometimes horrific for so long that even the best reformist intentions of the Government are now irredeemably suspect. So if they are not to embrace the posture of Nationalist illegitimacy, they need a lot of evidence that it really is *their* highest good, and not just that of the whites, which the present order is concerned about. In fact, at times they feel the state is actually punishing good and rewarding evil. What then?

What type of government?

For the state to function for the good of all, what type of government does God require?

The Evangelical Fellowship of South Africa (EFSA) answered this quite succinctly, and also set out its opposite, which produces God's displeasure. Their statement includes the following points:

1. God requires a society ordered in keeping with his righteous character (Lev 19:2).
2. In Israel God was concerned with every area of national life and not simply the religious aspect. Included in the legal

system were laws relating to food and health (Lev 11–13), sanitation (Deut 23:12–14), employment (Deut 24:6), economic policy (Deut 15:1–11) and safety regulations (Deut 22:8).

3. Strikingly, He legislates to protect the under-privileged, the powerless and the foreigners from exploitation (Deut 24:17–22). In fact, this aspect of government is seen as the touchstone to whether a government or individual is honouring God or not (Prov 14:31; Jas 5:1–6).

4. God is angry with a nation when it breaks the laws which flow from His holy and compassionate character. The prophets were messengers from God who warned Israel and surrounding nations that they would be punished if they persisted in breaking God's law. For example, Jonah's warning to Nineveh (Jon 1:2; 3:10), Amos' denunciation of the surrounding nations (Amos 1; 2:1–3).

5. The Church has a God-given responsibility to point out to leaders of a nation when particular laws, policies and practices are contrary to God's standards and to warn of the consequences if they are not changed. The Church should therefore act as the conscience of a nation.[12]

Drawing the threads together from Romans 13 and the rest of scripture, we can say that a state functioning as God's servant and in righteousness will be found serving its citizens (Mark 10:42–43; Rom 13:4), ruling justly (2 Sam 23:3–4; Ps 72:1–2), and impartially (Deut 16:18–20). The state must also create conditions conducive to peaceful living (1 Tim 2:2), as well as encouraging the law-abiding and punishing wrongdoers (Rom 13:4–5; 1 Pet 2:14). Finally, it must collect taxes for state administration (Mark 12:13–17; Rom 13:6–7).

When the government and the state are functioning as God intends, the Christian then has to do his part, which is: to honour the state as having God-given authority and to submit to it (Rom 13:1,5; 1 Pet 2:13,17); to pray for it (1 Tim 2:1–4); to pay taxes (Mark 12:13–17; Rom 13:6) and to live as free men doing good (1 Pet 2:16–17; Rom 12:2; 13:3). The Christian must also bear witness to God's salvation and his standards of righteousness (Mark 13:9). From all this, other caring concerns and actions will flow.

HOW DOES IT ALL WORK OUT IN CONTEMPORARY SOUTH AFRICA?

All of that must obtain in the normal situation. But is South Africa in the 1980s and 1990s a normal situation? And if not, what then?

Romans 13 is still helpful, because, like the rendering to Caesar principle, it sets limits both on the state's use of power and on the citizen's obligation to obey it.

Thus if the state is God's servant for the good of all (unlike the state depicted in Rev 13), it knows it must exercise its power firstly within the moral limits of what is pleasing to God and secondly within the practical and policy imperatives of what is for the greatest good of all. That will certainly curtail brutality and eliminate things like detention without trial, forced removals, discriminatory practices, denying people the vote, legislating where they can live and be educated, and so on. And on the citizen's side his obligations will find their limits in terms of his sincere and prayerful assessment of whether the state is fulfilling its proper functions as already listed.

Two principles of Christian citizenship

In all this the citizen, and especially the Christian citizen, will operate by two principles.

Conscience

The first is his *conscience* (vs 5), which tells him to be subject to the state but which may at some point set a limit to that subjection. That this has to be the case becomes obvious were one to imagine the state ordering us to commit adultery monthly or steal weekly! We today condemn those Nazi officers who meekly yielded to Hitler's order to eliminate Jews. And what of officials who obey orders to knock down shacks and remove defenceless people from Nyanga at 4 a.m. in mid-winter and take them to Transkei?

Love

The second principle the Christian citizen will operate by, even towards Caesar, is the law of love, which is set on either side of the Romans 13:1–7 passage.

Remembering that St Paul had no chapter numbers to make these passages watertight and isolated, we find the 'lead-in' to Romans 13:1–7 is 'Do not be overcome by evil, but overcome evil with good' (Rom 12:21), and the 'lead-away' from it is 'Owe no one anything, except to love one another' (Rom 13:8, RSV). Indeed, says Paul, 'never avenge yourselves, but leave it to the wrath of God' (Rom 12:19, RSV). And remember that 'love does no wrong to a neighbour' (Rom 13:10, RSV) – not even the neighbour who is Caesar.

Love's limits

But what if Caesar seems incorrigibly set on *not* functioning under God as his servant? And what if the state, which is to work for the good of all, seems to three quarters of a country's population not to be doing so? And what if there seems to be no meaningful light on the political horizon of a people? Does the law of love and subjection still operate?

To me there can never be any limit set on the law of love, though sometimes no doubt it has to be worked out in tragic categories – as when young and perhaps Christian RAF pilots who wanted to love and may indeed have loved Germans, were called on by Hitler's folly to fight and kill Germans who wanted to bomb and conquer their country.

Or love may operate from captive to captor, as when Andile Mbete, a black South African pastor, shared Christ and his love with his astonished interrogators who had detained and imprisoned him without charge.

However, though the love principle has no limits, the subjection principle, I believe, does.

All of which raises, especially for South African Christians, three matters with which we must concern ourselves in the remaining sections of this chapter.

1. Civil disobedience

2. Revolutionary violence
3. Whether there is a better way

MATTERS FOR CONCERN

Civil disobedience

Almost any Caesar will in fact always tend irresistibly towards demanding for himself not only that which is rightfully his, but that which is God's. And if he persists in doing so, what is the Christian citizen to do?

Many Christians, and especially those in South Africa, have understood Paul's word on being 'subject' to the powers (Rom 13:1) to mean uncritical, unquestioning and total obedience.

But Paul is not in fact asking that. He is asking for subjection and submission to the authority of the state, even if or when one may have to disobey it. In other words, if you disobey something on the grounds of conscience, you must be ready to submit to the consequences.

So, for example, my friend Paulo Ndala, who once took me into the New Brighton township, disobeyed the letter of the law which said everyone needed a permit to enter, but he and I submitted to the consequences when we were both arrested.

In fact, as the Evangelical Fellowship of South Africa has observed, the words used in the Greek of this and other similar passages are best translated as 'submit'. The Greek word for implicit obedience is not used of government and is used of Christ. The distinction between 'submit' and 'obey' can be seen in Christ's encounter with Pilate. Christ submitted to Pilate's judgement, recognising that his authority came from God; but in refusing to answer, he did not obey and was thus guilty of contempt of court (John 19:9–11).[13]

That this is the preferred understanding of the Greek word seems to be the general scholarly consensus. But does this mean that any disagreement with government policy or practice can be a pretext to catapult Christians into civil disobedience or revolution?

Far from it. In my own struggles with this, I see a staircase of ascendingly forceful steps which many Christians in conscience might take, each one more serious than the previous one, with each successive step to be taken only if the previous one *fails*. Before a Christian can consider civil disobedience or a revolutionary route as a Christian response, all other options have to be exhausted.

Steps of Christian challenge to the state

Private challenge
If a Christian feels in conscience that something is wrong with the way Caesar is functioning, the first step should be either to write privately or better still to go privately to present to the authorities a word of concern or challenge.

Private protest
If this has no effect, the concerned Christian should then take another step. This intensifies the vigour of the private challenge, which now becomes a private protest.

Public challenge and protest
If both private challenge and private protest prove fruitless, the next step surely has to be public challenge and protest.

Thus, back in 1957, when Prime Minister Verwoerd tried to legislate against blacks and whites worshipping together, Archbishop Geoffrey Clayton carried his private protests to Verwoerd into the public arena with a very strong open letter.

In it he said:

> The Church cannot recognize the right of an official secular government to determine whether or where a member of the Church of any race . . . shall discharge his religious duty of participating in public worship . . . We feel bound to state that if the bill were to become law in its present form we should ourselves be unable to obey it or to counsel our clergy and people to do so.[14]

The picture here is of the church in a nation seeking to challenge the conscience of both state and nation so that it might hear the voice and word of God speaking to their soul and addressing their actions.

Questioning of governmental legitimacy

If all this is in vain, an inevitable set of perilous questionings is set in motion – triggered not by irresponsible citizens but by an intransigent state – whereby the very legitimacy of a particular regime begins to be seriously and widely questioned.

In South Africa many feel we are teetering into this territory. South Africa *has* changed in many ways. But the basic system is still in place (Group Areas, Race Classification, Separate Education, and Black Homelands, *etc.*). So, many blacks are beginning to question first of all the moral legitimacy of the South African Government (because it is perceived to be basing its policies on principles contrary to God's laws and the 'common good') and secondly its political legitimacy (because it represents only eighteen per cent of the population).

Withdrawal of popular support and co-operation

A state's real power, not just its nominal authority, is dependent on the consent of the governed. And a nation is not governed which has constantly to be conquered. As G K Chesterton put it, 'a dying monarchy is always one that has too much power, not too little'.

Clearly the more a government has to use force the more evidently has it lost both the capacity and, sometimes, the right to govern.

Some Christians not surprisingly will feel that when Caesar has overstepped certain boundaries of legitimate authority, and remains stubbornly intransigent to all challenge, then the option presents itself of withdrawing popular support.

The American political scientist Gene Sharp has noted that:

> a closer examination of the sources of the ruler's power will indicate that they depend intimately upon the obedience and co-operation of the subjects . . . Authority is necessary for the existence and operation of any regime. No matter how great their means of physical coercion, all rulers require an acceptance of their authority, their right to rule and to command.[15]

The power relationship exists only when completed by the obedience and compliance of the subjects to the ruler's commands and wishes. This fact is now increasingly understood by the black population of South Africa, including many in the church, both black and white.

The loss of South African state authority among many blacks is indeed becoming considerable in South Africa, regardless of appearances. Without rapid and major change, increasing numbers of subjects will begin to withhold their contribution to the system. And once that compliance goes – and it does go when people become hopeless or desperate – the next step in the ladder of ascending resolution is taken.

Civil disobedience
While no one in their right mind wants to see any country, especially one as explosive as South Africa, enter into even casual let alone run-away campaigns of civil disobedience, nevertheless such things can happen and even Christians have become part of them in many places. Where and when they do, it is important to grasp that it is not necessarily perpetrators of such initiatives of civil disobedience who are primarily to blame.

For example, in 1952 there was a campaign of civil disobedience and passive resistance which developed quite widely among South African black people. Mrs Margaret Ballinger, then a Member of Parliament, noted that

> The whole European population would appear not merely to be against it, but to have no sympathy with the legitimate grievances which lie behind it . . . While no responsible citizen would wish to condone law-breaking, I think it behoves all such citizens to consider to what extent they are themselves, as policy makers, responsible for the conditions that lead a whole community to this sort of protest.[16]

The development of this kind of initiative, especially now in the Trade Union movement of South Africa, puts upon everyone, and especially upon the Christian church, a particular challenge with regard to if and when civil disobedience can be justified from a Christian point of view.

When civil disobedience is considered legitimate

Voices from Christian history
Several important Christian figures have thought that civil
disobedience can be sanctioned.

William Tyndale (*c.* 1490–1536) advocated the supreme
authority of the scriptures over against the state, and indeed
over the church. Government authorities harassed him and
sought to capture him, although Tyndale successfully evaded
them for years. He was, however, finally condemned as a
heretic, tried and executed on 6 October 1536.

John Knox, the celebrated Scottish reformer (*c.* 1514–
1572), held the view that while civil government is ordained of
God, nevertheless the state officials also have the duty of
obeying the laws of God, so that he could write: 'Kings have
not an absolute power in their regiment to do what pleases
them; but their power is limited by God's Word.'[17]

Samuel Rutherford (1600–1661) argued in his book *Lex
Rex* that all men, even the king, are *under* the law, and not
above it, a concept that was considered political rebellion and
punishable as treason.

In his *A Christian Manifesto* Francis Schaeffer tells us that

Rutherford argued that Romans 13 indicates that all power is
from God and that government is ordained and instituted by
God. The State, however, is to be administered according to the
principles of God's Law. Acts of State which contradicted God's
Law were illegitimate and acts of tyranny. Tyranny was defined
as ruling without the sanction of God . . . therefore to resist
tyranny is to honour God.[18]

Schaeffer also quotes Charles Finney (1792–1875), one of
the greatest evangelists and revivalists in the history of the
Christian church, who said, especially concerning slavery,
'if a law is wrong, you must disobey it'.[19]

Furthermore, Schaeffer's own posture is totally straightforward: 'The bottom line is that at a certain point there is not
only the right, but the duty to disobey the State.'[20] He adds:

Please read most thoughtfully what I am going to say in the next
sentence: *If there is no final place for civil disobedience, then the*

government has been made autonomous, and as such, it has been put in the place of the Living God, because then you are to obey it even when it tells you, in its own way and time, to worship Caesar. And that point is exactly when the early Christians performed their acts of civil disobedience, even when it cost them their lives.[21]

An even more famous modern voice is that of Martin Luther King, who cried to the heart of the American conscience, saying:

> There comes a time when a moral man can't obey a law which his conscience tells him is unjust. And the important thing is that when he does that, he willingly accepts the penalty – because if he refuses to accept the penalty, then he becomes reckless, he becomes an anarchist.[22]

Controlling principles

None of this ought to make anyone jump lightly into the enterprise of civil disobedience. It is a most serious matter, and God, who is the author of order and of the phenomenon of government, will quickly judge the light-hearted, casual-thinking revolutionary who embarks on such an enterprise lightly, selfishly or irresponsibly.

The action has to be motivated by a sensitively informed and governed Christian conscience. The centrality of the conscience is mentioned in Romans 13, and in Matthew's Gospel it also seems to be implied that Jesus leaves the matter of where we stop rendering to Caesar at the point where it requires us to compromise our rendering to God. Ultimately this is a matter for the individual conscience.

So then, we do not have a hard-and-fast rule as to when we are called upon to cease in our obedience to Caesar. Thus one particular white youth may find his conscience allowing him to join the army and another may find his conscience protesting. Or one black pastor may feel his white colleague should get a permit to enter the black township while another may resist this totally.

Of course, having embraced freedom of conscience, we also have to stress the importance, for a Christian at least, of his or her conscience being captive to Christian truth and principle. After all, our conscience is to some degree socially determined. So the Christian labours for a conscience bound to biblical truth and the inner witness of the Holy Spirit.

Which brings us to the ultimate question: If all valid means of parliamentary and constitutional change have been tried and all instances of controlled civil disobedience have come to naught, is violent revolution ever justifiable?

Violent revolution

In a country like South Africa, where our conditioning pre-disposes us to the view that might is right, every Christian has to reflect afresh on the issue of violence.

Is it ever justifiable?

For whites this discussion may at first seem very academic, because they have behind them all the structures which support and encourage non-violent means of changing things. But many black leaders feel differently. They feel that they are denied the 'space' and the political apparatus to change anything non-violently.

For myself I am totally opposed to both state and revolutionary violence as solutions to the South African problem: given the massive and relatively first-league logistics of white military power versus the vast power of black numbers, violence would only be a recipe for devastating catastrophe, leaving behind a wasteland with no winners.

The statement of the Evangelical Fellowship of South Africa (EFSA) makes some helpful observations on the question whether Christians should ever be involved in the forceful removal of a government:

> How this question is answered is often determined by the stand-point of those involved. Those in power teach submission to their government; those not in power teach 'just revolution' . . . Each Christian needs to grapple with the teaching of Scripture and then, having prayerfully taken a position, needs to seek to apply it consistently. Some Christians having studied the Scriptures believe that they should avoid all use of force. Others believe that

they should serve in the armed forces as their God given responsibility i.e. to become part of the sword by which God punishes evil doers.

In a situation where one group or nation is fighting for its freedom from the rule of another group or nation, the question becomes even more difficult. In this situation the Christian should seek to be consistent. If, as a Christian, he allows for the use of force for the maintenance of his position of superiority, he should also grant that other Christians have the right to remove by force what they perceive as an unjust 'foreign' government. If he condemns the use of force to remove a government from power, he should also condemn the use of force which maintains a government in power against the wishes of the majority of the people.

Those Christians on both sides, who choose to solve such struggles by force, should be aware of the consequences. Christ taught that 'all who draw the sword will perish by the sword' (Matt 26:52)[23]

The state for its part has to face John Kennedy's dictum that 'those who make peaceful revolution impossible make violent revolution inevitable'. The path is paved to violent revolution when non-violent protest or resistance is violently repressed. When valid political protest is met with military power, then protest politics become the militarised politics of violence. It is the extended consequences of what the psalmist calls 'mischief framed by statute' (*cf.* Ps 94:20, RSV).

On the other hand, those opting for the violent way need to realise that they cannot know where that way may end, for once embarked upon it unleashes forces whose nature, duration and end may be totally and tragically unforeseeable. Just ask the people in Northern Ireland and Beirut.

Different types of violence

Clearly, then, there are different types of violence. Thus, for example, Dom Helder Camara, the Roman Catholic Bishop of Recife in Brazil, saw two forms: 'The primary violence of the *injustice* that is everywhere. The reaction of the oppressed is the secondary violence.'

And Professor Klaus Nurnberger, a South African theologian, speaks of *institutional violence*, which is found in the system when people's human rights are removed and in different ways their value, worth and significance are violated. On top of this come specific strong-arm tactics to enforce objectionable legislation, *e.g.* Group Areas Act, Unequal Resource Allocation, Race Classification, Land Acts, Separate Education, no vote in Central Parliament, *etc.*

This, he says, gives rise to *reactive violence* from the grass roots, when people start to protest at the oppressiveness of the system, *e.g.* the ANC's strategically planned violence in the black townships in 1985, *etc.*

Then one gets *repressive violence*, which is the state's response to reactive violence. More police or military force is used to screw the lid down. Not only is the huge South African police force deployed everywhere, but the military is brought in as well.

This in turn produces *destructive violence*, when people in frantic fury and frustration turn their destructive energies against almost anything and everything in sight. It may be against each other (*e.g.* Pietermaritzburg townships in 1987 and 1988) or against a library or a school or a clinic or a municipal bus, or even, as happened in Port Elizabeth a good many years ago, against a nun who had worked among black people in that township for many years.

It is important to distinguish between these different sorts of violence in order to see how it escalates and to get an idea where it starts and why some people can give moral justification to certain forms of reactive violence.

It is also important to understand these different types of violence for strategic reasons, so that in our attempt to stop it we actually go to its root cause. In the case of South Africa, this is not that blacks dislike municipal buses, clinics or libraries, but that they totally hate apartheid and all its works, and deplore the state's response to this loathing, which appears to them to have been more repression rather than significant change. So when and if we condemn the violence of revolutionaries, we must condemn with even greater vigour the first form of violence – the violence of the system. As the EFSA statement makes plain, we need to be consistent in condemnation of all forms of violence.

Just war and just revolution

However, most 'freedom-fighters' would insist that their use of violence is justifiable on the grounds that if you accept the 'just war' theory you also have to accept the 'just revolution' response.

The just war tradition is in fact embraced by the majority of Roman Catholics and Protestants today on the basis of six traditional criteria: 1) that war or revolution be declared by a legitimate authority; 2) that this must be seen to be a last resort; 3) that there is a just cause to fight for; 4) that it is inspired by a right intention; 5) that it is conducted by appropriate means in the light of the end result; and 6) that there is a reasonable hope of success. To this traditional list I would add a seventh criterion, which asks the revolutionary with his supposedly just cause whether his violent struggle will in fact make reconciliation and final solutions to the conflict more likely. If not, and if the later state will be worse than the first, then another way must be sought.

The case against violence

While many black and white Christians in South Africa feel that it has become difficult morally to condemn those who have turned to violence, those who do embrace it need to face its inexorable laws.

First of all, *violence breeds violence*. Once violence is in the system it is very difficult to get out. This came home to me very strongly when I was in the Luweru Triangle in Uganda. There I saw some of the remains – too horrible to detail – of the 200,000 people who had been killed under the rule of Obote, the 'liberator' of Uganda.

The circumstances which took me to the Luweru Triangle were sufficiently strange to make me feel that this was something God wanted me to see. When I prayed, 'Lord, why do you want me exposed to these nightmarish horrors?', I had the sense of this word from the Spirit of God: 'I want you to see and register the full horrors of what happens when tribal violence runs riot.' This word has stuck with me ever since as a devastating warning for South Africa, particularly when one recognises that there are white tribes too!

In some of South Africa's townships today this principle of violence breeding violence and being difficult to curtail once it is in the system is vividly illustrated. The original causes of violence have been almost forgotten, and there has been a spiral of attack and counter attack, with its chain reaction of murder, retaliation and vendetta. How this is to be stopped is a source of perplexity to white and black leaders alike. Yet this is only on the micro-scale of political factionalism, not the larger scale of a full-blown violent racial confrontation.

Second, *violence tends to be uncontrollable.* It is as unrealistic to moralise about violence as it is to legislate against tornadoes – you never know when it might erupt unstoppably.

Third, *violence silences the voice of love.* Che Guevara once said that 'a people without hatred cannot win over a brutal enemy'. To which Martin Luther King replies, 'through violence you may murder the hater, but you do not murder hate'.

Fourth, *violence treats people as things.* Violence dehumanises its victims before it demolishes them. It also dehumanises its agent. Again we balance a quotation of Che Guevara against one from Martin Luther King. Guevara said: 'Hatred transforms a man into an effective, violent, selective and cold mechanism of death.' But as King observed:

> Violence as a way of achieving racial justice is both impractical and immoral. It is impractical because it is a descending spiral ending in destruction for all. The old law of an eye for an eye leaves everybody blind. It is immoral because it seeks to humiliate the opponent rather than win his understanding; it seeks to annihilate rather than to convert; violence is immoral because it thrives on hatred rather than love. It destroys communities and makes brotherhood impossible. It leaves society in monologue rather than dialogue. Violence ends up by defeating itself. It creates bitterness in the survivors and brutality in the destroyers.[24]

Fifth, *revolutionary violence presupposes an improper faith in man's ability to create a new world.* René Padilla of Argentina has noted that 'The Christian's rejection of violence is consistent with his understanding of man and society. The unjust conditions that prevail in the society are not

brought about primarily by causes outside man. They are
rather the result of the inclination to evil that is inherent in
man.'[25] In other words, the violent revolutionary mistakenly
feels that man is good by nature and that evil is not inherent in
man but only in the social structures that condition him. So he
has a totally pessimistic view of those he is overthrowing and a
thoroughly optimistic view of himself and his own exemption
from human sinfulness, power-lust and selfishness.

But, as Padilla points out:

> Revolution does not change man; it does not touch the root of
> social evils. For this reason, as soon as the revolutionary regime is
> established, the injustices of the old order reappear and the
> revolutionary class becomes a new oligarchy. The revolutionary
> becomes the defender of the status quo . . . Man has power over
> many things, and today more than ever, but he does not have
> power over his own power.[26]

Is there a better way?

All of this leads us to ask whether there is not a better way or
even a best way. We naturally find ourselves turning again
towards Jesus Christ, his way and his gospel.

If Christians do find themselves in a situation where Caesar
is demanding what belongs to God, there is indeed a better
way, which is different from violent revolution and also from
that type of non-violence which is simply acquiescence in an
unjust status quo. It is what is called by many today 'non-
violent active resistance'. This is the sort of thing in which
Martin Luther King involved himself. He was passionately
committed to the way of love, forgiveness and non-violence.
But he also felt that he could not sit back and do nothing. He
had to engage the situation. He would not flee, fight or freeze,
these being our usual reactions, but engaged and resisted evil
– only in a non-violent way.

The American theologian Walter Wink finds special biblical justification for this stance in Jesus' famous words:

> You have heard that it was said, 'An eye for an eye and a tooth for
> a tooth.' But I say to you, Do not resist one who is evil. But if any
> one strikes you on the right cheek, turn to him the other also; and

if any one would sue you and take your coat, let him have your cloak as well; and if any one forces you to go one mile, go with him two miles. (Matt 5:38–41, RSV)

Wink observes that *antistenai*, the Greek word translated here as 'resist', is made up of two parts: *anti*, a word still used in English for 'against', and *histemi*, a verb which in its noun form, *stasis*, means violent rebellion, armed revolt, sharp dissension. So in Wink's judgement, the proper translation of Jesus' teaching here would be, 'Do not strike back at evil (or one who has done you evil) in kind. Do not give blow for blow. Do not retaliate against violence with violence.'

'Jesus', says Wink, 'was no less committed to opposing evil than the anti-Roman resistance fighters. The only difference was over the means to be used; how one should fight evil.' Wink presents three general responses to evil: passivity, violent opposition and the 'third way' of militant non-violence articulated by Jesus.

So what, in Wink's view, is Jesus speaking of in Matthew 5: 38–39, where a victim is urged to offer his left cheek after a blow on the right? In a right-handed world, this can only mean that Jesus is speaking of someone hit on the right cheek by a back-handed clout, signifying insult, scorn and humiliation. It is the act of a superior dealing roughly and dehumanisingly with an inferior. The relationship is unequal, and retaliation here from the underling to the so-called superior would be totally precarious.

But in offering the other (*i.e.* the left) cheek, the humiliated person is saying that he is refusing to be dehumanised by the back-hander, with its implications of inequality, and he is inviting the striker to hit the left cheek also. This forces the striker's acknowledgement that he is inflicting a blow not on an inferior, dehumanised person, but on a peer who is lovingly sure of his own dignity, yet unwilling to hate or retaliate in kind to the striker. The striker thus has to recognise that in his violent behaviour he has in fact dehumanised *himself*, not the one he struck. In this he is challenged to new understandings of human dignity, both his own and that of other people.

Then we might think of Matthew 5:40 and the offering of

the cloak (an outer garment) to the one suing you (almost certainly here in exploitation or mercilessness) for your tunic or shirt (the inner garment). This act would effectively leave the debtor naked before the merciless creditor, who would not only be embarrassed by precipitating this situation of taboo, but also forced to evaluate the exploitive system which could reduce his debtor to such destitution. The action is therefore not retaliatory or injurious to the creditor, but remains morally educational and instructive to him. Likewise, when a robber steals your cloak or outer garment (Luke 6:29), you are to give him your shirt or tunic (inner garment) as well. Again the naked plight of the victim challenges the behaviour of the aggressor.

And what about the matter of 'going the extra mile'? Apparently a Roman soldier could constrain a civilian to carry his pack one mile only. To force the civilian to go further carried with it severe penalties under Roman military law. In this way, observes Wink,

> Rome attempted to limit the anger of the occupied people and still keep its armies on the move. Nevertheless, this levy was a bitter reminder to the Jews that they were a subject people even in the Promised Land . . . But why walk the second mile? Is this not to rebound to the opposite extreme; aiding and abetting the enemy? Not at all. The question here, as in the two previous instances, is how the oppressed can recover the initiative; how they can assert their human dignity in a situation that cannot for the time being be changed.[27]

The point is that in going the second mile, you have thrown off your servility and seized the moral initiative and the power of choice. If the soldier has previously 'enjoyed feeling superior to the vanquished, he will not enjoy it today'. And you may have forced him to ask himself some real questions about the whole situation which allows him to force you to carry his goods even one mile!

There is then here, in Wink's understanding, a certain 'loving confrontation' which frees both the oppressed person from his servile and docile spirit, as well as the oppressor from his heavy-handed action. Both are positively changed in the process.

Wink, Martin Luther King and many others believe that this kind of 'third way' bears at its heart the whole challenge from Jesus to love our enemies and thereby to change them in the process. Being non-violent, it also terminates and avoids the spiral of violence. More than that, it requires walking the way of Calvary and the cross, and this demands an ever-deepening spirituality.

It was this sort of philosophy which controlled Martin Luther King's campaigns for change in the Southern States of America. He saw it as the only force which would really work when the normal channels of political protest seemed ineffective. His strategies and his refusal to go along with segregationist ways had to be carried out under a spiritual and Christian self-discipline which showed not only a basic respect for the order of society but also a moral concern to change the heart of his opponent and oppressor.

Despite all of the above, it remains a fact that all of this presumes recalcitrance and stubbornness in a Caesar who perpetrates injustice and will not change. But does it have to be that way?

Is there a best way?

Quite obviously everything I have written about in the last few sections tells in every instance of something less than the best.

The best way of all is for both those who govern and those who are governed to live in mutual respect and under the control of the living God, and that when there are problems – even serious ones such as we currently have in South Africa – to bring them together under Christ to the negotiating table and to find a gracious and accommodating way through in Christian grace and under the Holy Spirit's guidance.

This way forward will involve a commitment to winning in the struggle for peace and justice in a spirit of togetherness and by working out together all the implications of the politics of love.

To this we now turn in the penultimate section of this volume.

Part Six

THE POLITICS OF LOVE
(The outworking of love as a valid political principle)

19 Winning in the World's Workshop

The debate about the future of South Africa is in many ways a debate about the future of our life together in this small earth.

                                        Richard Neuhaus

You have deeply ventured: but all must do so who would greatly win.

                                        Lord Byron

If a thing is possible and proper to man, deem it attainable by thee.

                                        Marcus Aurelius

Are you not the result of my work in the Lord?
                                        1 Corinthians 9:1

One of the things about children is that they know how to catch you by surprise!

A couple of months ago, out of the blue, my twelve-year-old son Marty asked me, just before going to sleep, about the reasons for the American Civil War!

The question took me completely aback. It also made me realise that even very young South African children, both white and black, are suddenly conscious that our society may be drifting slowly but surely into a low-intensity civil war. And it appals them. After all, what else can they conclude with everyone seemingly fighting everyone else, either verbally or literally?

I tried to give an explanation – telling him also of the

awfulness of solving problems the war way, because there are no real winners in wars.

'In fact, son,' I told him, 'America lost more lives in the Civil War, over a hundred years ago, than in the First World War, the Second World War, the Korean War and the Vietnam War combined.'

There was a long silence, then another bomb-shell question.

'Daddy,' he asked slowly, 'was it worth it?'

In a sense Marty was asking 'Who, or what, won?'

How do you answer that, especially in the context of South Africa, the context within which he raised the question?

I suppose one would have to say that at one level the American Civil War *was* worth it, because the Union was saved and a truly great nation reborn for a mighty destiny. But did it really *have* to necessitate such a titanic struggle and such dreadful, tragic cost? Was it worth all that loss? Did it really have to be? Could not the politics of love and mutual respect and negotiation and common sense have won? Or maybe while the politics of love lost in the pre-Civil War context, perhaps some other ultimate values like justice and equality came out final winners in the long run of the post-Civil War context.

All of this prompts another key question: What does it really mean, in Christian terms, to 'win' in a situation like South Africa? At one level such language sounds triumphal-istic and contrary to the cross and to the non-utopian realism of scripture's view (*e.g.* Matt 24) as to where unaided man will finally take the planet in the home-straight of history.

Yet Charles Wesley could sing out his exhortation:

> From strength to strength go on,
> Wrestle and fight and pray,
> Tread all the Powers of darkness down,
> And *win* the well-fought day!

Here then is our clue. Ultimate winning is where the way of Christ remains active and alive in a situation in which good-ness, honesty, purity, integrity and self sacrifice do not suc-cumb to all the dark demons of division and human folly. It is a case of the light shining in darkness and the darkness not overcoming it.

That is why it *is* possible, both politically and humanly, to lose in a situation, yet know that there is victory regardless, because eternal Calvary qualities have not been obliterated amidst the temporal struggles and failures.

Yet in the South African context, those great and primary truths notwithstanding, I dare not resign myself or capitulate to the tempting mechanisms of defeat and despair. I can live and cope only when I hold on to the fact that working for the kingdom of God, both in individual people's hearts and on earth, commits me to thinking 'solution'. I refuse to believe that there is some final and inevitable historical necessity that we be defeated by all these grim Goliaths.

Beyond this, I find that for myself the moral imperative of trying to think 'solution' impels me also to find other categories for thinking of South Africa than as the ultimate write-off place which houses the ultimate lost cause.

Emotionally I cannot bear to think that way. That is why I warm so much to the idea of South Africa, not as the impossibly wicked pole-cat and pariah of the world, but as in fact the workshop of the world. Viewed that way, it is an incredibly exciting place, where winning over all the odds presents as glorious a challenge as any which has ever landed in the laps of anyone anywhere.

So in this chapter I want unashamedly, though admittedly from within my own limiting and constricting history and stage of spiritual pilgrimage, to try and think what would be involved for us and the wider world, not only in seeing ultimate spiritual things triumph here, but also in seeing the politics of love prevail in this workshop of the world. For if such a thing could come to pass, I believe God's name would be glorified and an epic tragedy as great as the American Civil War averted.

I think I first began to think of South Africa as the workshop of the world in 1973, when (at the South African Congress on Mission and Evangelism) Hans-Ruedi Weber from Switzerland referred to South Africa as the laboratory of the world.

The main reason for this metaphor was that we were the

one nation in the world which approximately reflected the planet's racial composition. South Africa's people not classified as white outnumbered the whites by about five to one. That is roughly the proportion of other races to whites in the rest of the world.

Understanding this interplay of various factors and forces, the American theologian Richard Neuhaus writes:

> The debate about the future of South Africa is in many ways a debate about the future of our life together on this small earth – about relations between rich and poor, between races and ideologies, indeed about the meaning of freedom, peace, and justice in a deeply disordered world. Much of the debate is about oddities, wrongs, and fears peculiar to South African society. But those who have ears to hear should be left with no doubt that South Africans talking about themselves are in fact talking about all of us, the kind of people we think we are and the kind of people we sometimes hope and sometimes fear we may really be.[1]

If this is indeed the case, what a challenge if we in South Africa could work out our problems and show the world it can be done! Would it not inspire, encourage and bless the world if this were to happen? But that places a great responsibility on South African Christians. For scripture's word is that it is we who are to prepare the way of the Lord, and it is we who are to 'make straight in the wilderness a highway for our God' (Isa 40:3). God works and acts as his people by repentance, prayer, faith, humility and obedience do their part to prepare a situation.

This preparatory work could be done by pursuing the following set of expedients, as required by both Christian love and common sense.

1. ACTING WHILE THERE IS STILL POLITICAL ROOM FOR MANOEUVRE

Some years ago the Rockefeller Foundation published a report on South Africa entitled *Time Running Out.* It was a stirring and urgent document. Time can actually run out for nations. As Martin Luther King once said: 'It is indeed possible to be too late in history with the right answers.' He added: 'Life often leaves us standing bare, naked and dejected with a lost opportunity.'[2]

For example, it is instructive to note that nearly 150 years before the American Civil War, a far-sighted and deeply spiritual American prophet called John Woolman spoke of the dire consequences of racism and oppression: 'I saw a dark gloominess hanging over the land,' he wrote. If people were not willing to 'break the yoke of oppression,' he said, 'the consequence [would] be grievous to posterity.'[3] If the American nation had truly listened, it would have averted the epic catastrophe of that war, plus a hundred years of unimaginable trauma before the modern Civil Rights legislation of the United States was passed in the early 1960s.

Early in 1987, in Denver, Colorado, I asked Dr Vincent Harding, a major historian of the Black Civil Rights Movement, and himself an American black, how this was possible: 'Well,' he said pensively, 'you see, you can't wait until after a war to get things sorted out. If you have not sorted them out before such a conflict, you will run into very serious difficulty after the conflict. The problem is that all kinds of new dynamics and forces are released and developed during the war itself. And beyond that, war by its very nature builds irrationality rather than rationality.'

As Dr Harding said this I couldn't help reflecting specifically on South Africa, where it is increasingly true that our politics are controlled more by heat and emotion than by light and rationality. Indeed it often seems to me that reason has gone clear out the window and we seem bent on every kind of irrational folly.

'There was also the problem', Harding went on, 'that the whole American nation after the Civil War was so totally exhausted that they were unable to take the matter further. So the main issue got buried again and not properly dealt with, and segregationist practices were allowed to continue. Beyond that, there was the priority of developing the South economically and industrially, and they did not want to have sticky social problems on their hands when economic development was their major concern.'[4]

Harding's line and application of all this was as follows. An economically preoccupied South Africa is going to have to face the human and justice issue right now, because there is a great temptation to try and subsume the human issues and problems beneath white questions such as: 'How can we keep this economy going? How can we continue to gain significant benefits from it? How can we be sure it stays out of the hands of socialists and communists?', *etc*. But that kind of economic agenda quickly buries the real human agenda with which the blacks are concerned. And what will then happen is that their issues will arise again and again and again, until they are really addressed and finally dealt with.

'That is what happened with us in the Southern States,' said the Professor. In his mind the delaying, 'put-it-off' factor before the Civil War, and then for decades afterwards, was what contributed so powerfully to the major tragedy of war. After that the country was so out of kilter and politically exhausted that it took a hundred years to sort the matter out. 'And during that time,' said Dr Harding, 'of course the pressures for violence built up out of frustration. You see,' he went on, 'blacks here became convinced that it was only through armed pressure that whites would do anything even approximating to what was right. So armed pressure got built up in people's minds as a kind of god. But it is a terrible god. It is a god which eventually eats us all up.'

I went to bed that night in my Denver hotel determined more than ever before to grasp the importance of acting in a situation while there is still political manoeuvrability and flexibility, and before hostilities become irreversibly set in concrete, because I knew that days of political negotiation and flexibility are by then tragically lost.

A thousand John Woolmans in South Africa have given their words for nearly half a century and had their say. Will the nation heed? Or will it wait for an epic tragedy which will so exhaust it that a century will pass before things come even remotely right?

I remember a conversation I once had with an overseas visitor who was leaving South Africa. During it he said to me,

'Your country is the hidden jewel of the world. It's worth doing everything possible to save it.' And it is. Not just for its physical beauty, but most especially for its human resources, its planetary importance and its social significance in the world.

2. SEEING IT STRAIGHT AND FROM ALL SIDES

One of the real minefields facing those who seek solutions for South Africa is that different perceptions lead to different solutions. Each individual sees the problem from where he or she is and then bases a solution on that limited perception, and on what seems to be in his or her highest personal or group interest.

In part, this variety stems from the hugeness of the problem and from the *enforced* separation we all live under constantly. This makes it very difficult to see the whole picture or to fulfil Augustine's famous dictum: 'audi alteram partem' ('Hear the other side').

Imagine if South Africans of all races broke out of the dual bondage of legal and social apartheid and not only heard the other side but also 'felt' it. Of whites this would require them not only to listen to blacks speak of their pain but also to enter right into it. To be with blacks when they are discriminated against or humiliated by the system is both an eye-opening and sometimes a heart-stopping experience. It also results in 'feeling' black frustrations and understanding more fully the cry for the end of apartheid.

To hear the other side also means to perceive that the time has come when blacks have finally announced their refusal to have white ears turned to them in deafness any longer. And if in frantic frustration blacks shout radical slogans and preach a 'winner-takes-all' political philosophy for a 'black' future, it behoves the sincere white South African to understand how and why that cry was born. For to miss the valid notes amidst all the discord of that cry is to step back into darkness and go one step nearer the abyss.

But of course a black future, in more ways than one, is what

South Africa will get unless blacks also enter into the 'inner-place' of white hearts. No workable answers will come for this land until blacks recognise and take account of certain rational white fears. These include anxiety about a drop in educational, living and medical standards, and about the loss of white, Western identity.

Another major fear among whites is of ongoing and escalating factional black violence in a post-apartheid society under black majority rule. The spectre, whether valid or not, of an ANC-Inkatha-PAC-UDF or even tribal slug out has certainly intensified white despair that black majority rule would not bring an even remotely peaceful dispensation.

Further underlining the apparent validity of these fears is the political record of black Africa. Speaking in Kenya in December 1987, Archbishop Desmond Tutu said: 'South Africa is noted, and rightly noted, for its vicious violation of human rights. But sadly for a black African, integrity requires me to say that very many times there is now *less freedom* in independent African countries than there was under the much maligned Colonial System.'

Having travelled the length and breadth of Africa, the author David Lamb writes:

> Calamity waits within arms' reach, oblivious of Africa's potential strength. Across the whole continent, economies are collapsing, cities are deteriorating, food production is declining, populations are growing like weed-seeds turned loose in a garden. Governments fall at the whim of illiterate sergeants and disgruntled despots, prisons are as overcrowded as the farmlands are empty, and at the last count the number of foreign refugees in Africa had reached the incredible figure of five million – people driven from their homelands by wars, tyrants and poverty.[5]

On such things are white fears based. But can blacks see this?

Seeing the *whole* problem, straight and from all sides, is a key ingredient in winning through. It also helps us in the process of seeing and embracing a bigger vision.

3.   EMBRACING A BIGGER VISION

Every time I travel outside South Africa (and I do so two or three times a year) I return horrified at the insularity of this nation.

We need to shake ourselves vigorously out of past parochialisms and seek a wider vision.

Phillips Brooks, the great American pastor (1835–1893) who wrote the hymn 'O little town of Bethlehem', once said:

> Bad will be the day for every man . . . when he becomes absolutely contented with the life that he is living, with the thoughts that he is thinking, with the deeds that he is doing . . . when there is not forever beating at the doors of his soul some great desire to do something larger which he knows he was meant and made to do.[6]

Quite so. And if it is bad for every man or woman anywhere, then it is most assuredly bad for every South African. That is why the hour is upon us to 'dream the impossible dream' of what a post-apartheid society might look like, and then to begin working to make it happen.

It is a case of seeing the bigger vision and then getting involved in making it come to fruition. The imperative is to hear beating at the doors of our soul, as Phillips Brooks would say, 'some great desire to do something larger'.

One man at whose door that desire has beaten is Professor Es'kia Mpahlele, Head of African Literature in the University of the Witwatersrand. Of a future South Africa, he says: 'We visualise citizens living together wherever they choose, enjoying freedom of mobility and association, equality of opportunity, equal choice of educational institutions, careers and employment, freedom to establish independent schools, and so on . . .'[7]

Another person with a vision of a different South Africa is Clem Sunter, a scenario specialist at Anglo-American. The South Africa that he wants to see is a 'winning nation' with a high level of education, an absence of over-government, a sound system of family life, an effective industrial and commercial relationship between the corporate giants and small business, a harmonious political balance, and a competitive national capability in the global market-place.[8]

Both are noble and splendid visions, and no doubt others have similar visions of their own.

My own vision for South Africa is of a genuinely *Christian* nation (which is after all what we already claim to be) – a nation where what we profess and what we actually *are* will begin to synchronise, an apartheid-free nation where the courts will be free to uphold the rule of law with truly impartial justice, a South Africa where the politics and economics of love will seek to promote the good of all groups.

Would that be suicide for whites and result in the declension and death of the nation? Not at all – not if God is alive. For the Bible says that 'righteousness *exalts* a nation' (Prov 14:34) – it doesn't make it collapse, it exalts it.

My vision for the country also includes equality of educational opportunity and voting rights for all.

I realise, of course, that educational standards might drop if there was a unified system. Yet we have massive financial and human resources that can be used to make the reformed educational system recover. And I would rather our children sat in a modest classroom and made slightly slower educational progress together than that they fought Beirut-style street battles and got no education at all.

As to the Government, in a Christian nation, where responsibility, justice, human dignity and hard work were flourishing, it could be white or black or both – it wouldn't matter to me. What I do know is that I would rather be justly governed by blacks, assuming they can defeat the odds against them responding that way, than be unjustly governed by whites and every day have my conscience seared by guilt. Of course I would prefer to have both whites and blacks govern me, with the skills of each working together in harmonious interplay.

But surely, someone is bound to argue, this is incredibly naive and is a practical impossibility?

I don't agree – not if we shake off the clutching ghost of the past, with all its myths and mistakes. Professor Sampie Terreblanche of Stellenbosch University has rightly said that 'the key to the future may lie in the death of the myths of the past'.[9] When the past is as fraught with mistakes as ours is in South Africa, then to glorify it in the present is to ensure that we miss the bigger vision and lose the future.

How then are we to rescue this future? Only by negotiating the way forward together. And if we doubt that this is the correct way, a brief reflection on the alternative scenarios should lay such doubts to their deserved rest.

4.   CHOOSING THE ONLY SCENARIO WHICH CAN SAVE US

Like every other South African, I think a lot about the future. As we do this it is clear that at present South Africa is at a crossroads of choices.

The question for all of us right now is how we will exercise our choices at this time, whether we are white or black. This is where a consideration of future scenarios is important, because scenarios provide glimpses of how the future might work out if one particular set of choices is made rather than another.

I see seven possible scenarios.

Scenario 1: Semi-indefinite white rule, by screwing the lid down

It is not impossible that whites might make choices which send them down this path, but note that I do not say 'indefinite' white rule, but rather 'semi-indefinite'. In other words, white rule must have its limits and its terminal point, for an ever-increasing majority of blacks cannot be forever suppressed by an ever-diminishing minority (in percentage terms) of whites. Sheer arithmetic tells me that. Indeed, not only are numbers against this scenario, even with its semi-indefinite categories, but time is against it, history is against it, and the moral law will not allow it, especially from a people professing to be Christian. God will pull the rug on us if we try.

So the choice for South Africans at this point is this: Do we want to live this way, with the lid screwed down more and more, so that we become an ever more endemically violent and unhappy society? Or do we want to seek another way?

Scenario 2: A short, sharp, successful revolution, leading to black power overnight

Some blacks make choices which would attempt to realise this scenario. To be sure, such things have happened before in history, so no one can say that it could never happen in South Africa, for history is full of inscrutables and unpredictable occurrences.

But overnight revolutions have usually happened only when the ruling elite was weak and lacking in resolve to govern. That is certainly not true of the South African Government. Secondly, such overnight revolutions generally depend for their success upon the military of the state becoming disloyal and abandoning the ruling elite. (This is of course what happened to President Marcos in the Philippines.) But the chances of that happening in South Africa are no greater than the proverbial snowball's hope in hell. If blacks chose to pursue this way, they might stand history's one chance in a million; but it is much more likely that they would bump their heads against some terrible white military realities.

Scenario 3: An endless, low-intensity civil war of attrition, revolution and counter-revolution

This nightmarish scenario, lasting over who knows how many dreadful decades, would finally lead to totalitarian black power – perhaps preceded by horrific black versus black struggles (following black/white civil war) – and then finally to a chaotic and broken country of ashes, social mayhem, economic ruin and ongoing tragedy. And at the end of it all there would probably be legions of white terrorists making the nation as ungovernable under black rule as black terrorists would have finally made it under white rule.

In the medium term there would be a stalemate, but in the

long term the whole thing would gather momentum in a rising tide of violence.

This scenario would make South Africa a combination of Lebanon, Northern Ireland and Uganda at its worst, and all set in the economy of Moçambique! This is, in former Prime Minister John Vorster's celebrated dictum, 'too ghastly to contemplate'. Not to contemplate it, however, risks leaving us on the road to that ghastliness. Sadly, in many ways this looks, in human terms, the most likely South African scenario at this time – not because we have *chosen* it, but because we have not definitely chosen against it and steered away from it.

Scenario 4: Hundred per cent white surrender to blacks

By this scenario, whites suddenly see the light: they recognise that they have been wrong and that they must now hand over to blacks the government, the economy, the industry, the military and security apparatus, plus all agricultural land, which will now be nationalised by a black government and socialistically reapportioned to the masses on an egalitarian and nationalised basis.

Of course whites could choose that, but South African whites are not yet either in heaven or in Utopia – it is therefore somewhat of a 'fairyland' scenario! Even so, a crossroads choice still stands before South Africans: If we won't surrender everything now, will we surrender *enough* now so that we won't have to surrender *everything* later?

Scenario 5: Partition

This scenario totally despairs of whites and blacks ever living peaceably, amicably and with authentic power-sharing within the same body politic. It calls for a radical partitioning of the country, pointing to places like Cyprus, where even Turks and Cypriots can barely coexist without some kind of partition.

The underlying presupposition here is that no two major

ethnic groups can share political power in the same body politic.

In South African terms this is a clinging to the old classical apartheid of Dr Verwoerd, with his macro-vision of Bantustans where everybody would have their political rights in their own designated area.

In fact some in the ultra-right wing of South African politics have now pressed this most strongly, so as to demand in effect two separate countries. The Afrikaners would have what they see as their traditional homeland of the Transvaal, the Orange Free State and Northern Natal, and the blacks perhaps could have the rest.

There is only one technical hitch here: the homeland wanted by many Afrikaners as a 'Boerestaat' (a Boer state) is the same land most Africans would see as their traditional fatherland!

This option becomes, therefore, another version not only of the fairyland scenario but also of the wasteland scenario, for that, to be sure, via indefinite conflict, is where it would finally lead.

Scenario 6: Constitutional reform by consultation

Under this proposal, and as a result of both internal and external pressures, a half-hearted, stop-start reform would continue on the basis of a series of consultations between whites and so-called 'moderate blacks', leading to some sort of political *modus vivendi* which would then be imposed on everybody. However, any such 'agreed solution' would be totally rejected by the more militant black political movements and trade unions. Such a solution, like the present tricameral (three-chambered) parliament, would also be totally unacceptable to the world as a whole.

The major flaw within this scenario, which is one that whites are currently tempted to follow, is that it is based on the type of consultation where whites canvass the views of moderate blacks but then in effect go away and do their own thing. They remain the top dogs and retain the right and power to have the final say. This sort of consultation is the easy kind, because the top dog basically controls the process and keeps the final decision in his hands; but in the end it satisfies no one, because it has not won true majority support.

It is to be remembered here that a constitution is only a piece of paper with ink on it, so it is only as strong as the commitment of a nation to it. The American Constitution is very strong because the American nation is deeply committed to it; by contrast, P W Botha's Tricameral Constitution is precariously weak because most South Africans are not committed to it.

As I see it, the most likely outcome of this scenario would be another version of the civil conflict scenario. Blacks would never be satisfied with the plan, because they would always feel that they should be getting more; beyond that, they would reject such a solution because it would have to be an imposed one. Whites, for their part, would become totally weary and disillusioned with the seemingly endless new and unsatisfactory constitutions, and would finally settle for a military dictatorship under the guise of parliamentary rule.

The crossroads choice posed by this scenario is obvious: Do we want real reform, leading to a real democracy, or do we want a tragic travesty of both?

Scenario 7: A properly negotiated future, worked out by all together

In this scenario all participants in the South African drama would choose to sit down together and talk. Furthermore, they would resolve to work out a plan while sitting down at the negotiating table as equals.

Though the exact shape this scenario would take is not clear – simply because no one quite knows how everything would turn out, nevertheless common sense says this must be the safest way to a just solution to the South African situation: it is risky, but it is right. Moreover, it is congruent with the moral law of the universe – after all, did not even God himself say, 'Come now, let us reason together' (Isa 1:18)?

Herein lies our only hope as a nation. As such, our reflections on this scenario require a section to themselves.

5.   WALKING THE PATH OF REAL NEGOTIATION

It is clear, I would have thought, that if you don't fight out an answer you have to talk one out. Recent events surely bear this out.

The hitherto modest degree of fighting has got us nowhere. Early in the day the counter-productive nature of black violence has become evident. Attempts at change by black violence, while perhaps initially precipitating *some* white reform (which may have deluded its practitioners into a false estimate of its efficiency), have also succeeded in bringing effective reform to a halt.

Additionally, the black factional violence of some townships has, rightly or wrongly, confirmed many white fears that 'these people are certainly not ready to govern us'. The very idea that as a result of black acts of violence the whites would suddenly be intimidated or encouraged into becoming the epitome of sweet reasonableness is a dangerous delusion. Such actions can only serve to make whites *more* obtuse and stubborn, for their perception is that if the matter is to be resolved by violence it is a battle that they *can* win.

White attempts to contain the present political unrest by means of force are not a means to a resolution of the situation either. White political muscle, both institutional and physical, currently has half the country's key black leadership either imprisoned or exiled, and (as from March 1988) most black opposition groups severely restricted or banned. But no sane person can imagine that this will work indefinitely. For, as I have already said, a country is not being governed which constantly has to be conquered. Nor can we live indefinitely into the future under a State of Emergency. All the Emergency can do is temporarily stem escalating chaos – it doesn't actually solve anything.

These things being so, and to keep everyone from trying to operate in the realms of reaction, prejudice or fantasy, the cry from the belly of both history and common sense is that all South African groupings should get to the table fast, to talk out and negotiate a future in which all can have a part.

Of one thing I am sure: the relative balance of power –
whites with their political dominance and massive military-
cum-police apparatus, and blacks with their vast numbers –
means that compromise, if we are going to stay in 'the real
world', will at the end of the day have to be the name of the
game.

If we do not find room for compromise, we will in fact make
the best, the ideal and perhaps the impossible the enemy of
the good, the realistic and the workable. For both sides the
alternatives are either an amicably acceptable compromise,
which has meaning, or an out-and-out conflict, which has
none: the choice is ours.

What is negotiation?

But when we talk about negotiation, what do we mean?
Surely, as Clem Sunter noted in an interview, we are talking
about a *process* requiring at least four things:

i.   That there be give and take on both sides. This costs
     everyone some sacrifice, but it also creates the potential
     for a better settlement than anybody thought possible.
ii. That no one person or group has control over the agenda
     or can decide who participates (or cannot participate).
iii. That there is a willingness to face risk, since the outcome
     is bound to be uncertain.
iv. That all sides to the negotiating process possess strength.
     This is because 'when you have struck a settlement, you
     want everybody to go back to the people they represent
     in order to make the deal stick'.[10]

Of course in South African terms true negotiation would
mean that whites couldn't unilaterally determine the precon-
ditions (*e.g.* 'You must first stop your violence'), nor could
blacks unilaterally determine the agenda (*e.g.* 'The only thing
to talk about is the transfer of power'). Far better would it be
to negotiate an initial truce, during which both sides would
refrain from violent acts while the pre-negotiation processes
are set in motion and the open agenda agreed on.

Another precondition, if negotiation is to work, is that all

sides stop demonising their political adversaries. If the liberation movements are all demonised into being just a bunch
of violent Moscow-controlled terrorists, and if the South
African Government is cast as an irretrievably illegitimate
bunch of lost-cause, racist brigands who can somehow be
wished away, we won't get very far. Indeed, for as long as all
the different South African groupings decline to accept the
true legitimacy of the other groups, true negotiation is
forestalled.

Inevitably this raises the question when negotiations in
South Africa can start. I know many who would not argue that
it is too late for negotiation, but that it is too early. They say
this because conditions for negotiation don't truly exist while
each side thinks it can win on its own terms and is busy
demonising the other. But with the situation sliding away
towards who knows what, and with the country 'picnicking
on Vesuvius', as one observer put it, it is folly to think of it
being too early. The fact is, the longer we wait to take the first
steps and at least make a start in the process, the greater will
be the level of alienation and mistrust when finally negotiation begins, and the greater the consequent likelihood of
failure; for generous give and take, which is so necessary, is
vastly harder with a sworn enemy than with an incipient
friend.

One other point: while we may not all like each other much,
the fact is that in sincere encounter, interface and dialogue a
godly chemistry is released which changes people and not
only brings them closer to each other but develops in them
new and untapped resources of flexibility and understanding
not previously much in evidence. And, marvel of marvels,
they start liking each other!

Many who participated in the Natal Kwa-Zulu Indaba,
whose chief value perhaps lay in just this discovery, and also
in the Dakar talks (between the ANC and Van Zyl Slabbert's
group of avant-garde Afrikaners), testified that they themselves were changed in the process.

This gives great grounds for hope.

The Christian belief in the equality of all before God must
commit us, professing Christian country as we are, to the
inclusion of *everyone* in negotiations.

This surely means that the Government cannot exclude the ANC or PAC, nor can the liberation movements exclude major Afrikaner political groupings. This is not to pronounce on whether the liberation movements or the Afrikaner groupings are 'goodies' or 'baddies', but only to recognise that they are major parties to this dispute, all of whom profess strong claims to the land.

By way of an analogy, in a marriage counselling situation with an alienated couple, a pastor can't say to the husband, 'Because you're an adulterer and a wife-beater I won't talk to you, but only to your sister, cousin or aunt!' If he is a major party to the situation he must be addressed, and the pastor will facilitate (not prevent or complicate) the man's communication and reconciliation with his wife.

The inclusion of the South African liberation movements in negotiations would in my judgement not only make political sense, but would also be a means of demythologising ordinary groups of intelligent black politicians, who are neither gods nor demons but are key figures who cannot be ignored. Moreover, in open debate and interface in the country their fallibilities and humanness would be as evident as their positive contributions and undoubted abilities, which are currently being wasted on frustrated acts of protest and destabilisation.

It is my strong conviction that the same applies to Nelson Mandela, who also needs demythologising. At the time of writing he is still in prison after twenty-five years. And with each passing day the myth becomes greater than the man, to the point where one trembles at the consequences of what would happen were he to die in jail. Languishing there, his influence is restricted. But let him die there and the real reign of the martyr will begin.

Mmutlanyane Mogoba, President of the Methodist Church, told me recently of going to Pollsmore prison to minister the sacrament to Nelson Mandela a couple of months ago. He feels he is a believer, a negotiator and a man of balance. 'In fact,' said Mogoba, 'we have no other black leaders out there with his balance and authority. He is the one person who could help us all come through.'

'When the little threesome gathered for the Communion,'

Mogoba told me, 'the police Brigadier was by the door. "Please join us," the group asked. At which the Brigadier drew to the outer edge of the little circle. "No, come closer," they said. At which the Brigadier joined the circle and completed it.'

This image greatly moved me. Imagine if we all asked each other to 'Come closer', as Joseph urged his brothers (see Gen 45:4).

Many feel that, if released, Mandela could be the man to save this situation. Clearly he would need to come out as a real statesman, somewhat in the way Jomo Kenyatta emerged from prison and acted to calm irate blacks and nervous whites.

Mandela would need to come out activating the Christian faith he apparently professes. The EPG people said they found in him 'no trace of bitterness', and this suggests he could be a real force for reconciliation.

He would, moreover, need to come out as a true patriot rather than as the communist some have portrayed him to be. If he was such twenty-five years ago, he apparently no longer embraces that philosophy.

A great service to the situation would also be rendered if as a key leader he would constrain some of his constituency to hold out the olive branch to Chief Mangusuthu Buthelezi of KwaZulu, who is also a significant figure in the situation, as President Kaunda said to me back in 1986. (This is also held to be self-evident by many thousands of blacks and whites, the detractors of Chief Buthelezi notwithstanding.) Chief Buthelezi himself has repeatedly called for the release of Nelson Mandela, and I have personally heard him say that he would be prepared to serve under a democratically elected Mandela.

Of course in such things as the release of Mandela and the unbanning of liberation movements there is a risk. But there is no course open to us in this land without risk, and nothing is riskier than the course on which we are presently embarked.

Real negotiation between *all* the actors in this drama remains the safest way.

Of course I also know that even breathing this sort of thing lays one open to a peculiar South African peril – being labelled a communist or communistic! This is because postures which favour unbanning the liberation movements or releasing Mandela are equated in the popular white mind with being either soft on communism or naive about it. But the two ideas should not be simplistically linked. In fact I believe it is very important for South Africa to keep communism at bay: even more than apartheid, it has naught for our comfort.

6.   KEEPING COMMUNISM AT BAY

To my mind a communist take-over in South Africa, by whatever means, would be a tragedy. Such an eventuality should be resisted with all vigour.

The ANC's embrace of the South African Communist Party (likened in ANC minds to the Allies linking up with Russia to defeat Germany in the Second World War) does indeed constitute a massive stumbling-block to the legitimising and unbanning of that body by any Afrikaner Government. This is because communism is the ultimate bogeyman to most white South Africans, and with some justification.

All of this raises the question of the nature of communism.

What is communism?

I've often thought it would be instructive in a gathering of South African whites, all passionately opposed to communism, to ask them to write out what they understand a communist to be. I guess few would really know!

One evening, when he was in our home, I asked my friend Bishop Philip le Feuvre, who is a student of Marxism, to explain in layman's language exactly what a communist is. Here's a summary of his reply.

A communist is someone who self-consciously believes something. He believes that ever since the entering into human society of the institution of private ownership, society has been divided into those who own and possess and those who are dependent for their livelihood on the owners for whom they have to work. The Marxist believes this has introduced into human society a measure of alienation or antagonism.

Because one group has to work for the other, the working group are alienated from their work. Instead of enjoying it, it becomes drudgery that they have to do for others. So people have become alienated from the context of the world where they have to live.

The Marxist also believes that there is a movement taking place in history, and that history is controlled by something called the 'dialectic', the name for the opposing forces which are always confronting one another in the course of history. He also believes that these forces are leading onwards eventually to a society which will be classless (*i.e.* no higher or lower class) with everybody equal, and everybody 'a worker'.[11]

Philip went on to underline that these beliefs 'committed' the Marxist or communist to certain action.

First of all, he must align himself with this movement of history and become actively committed to bringing about this classless worker society.

Second, the communist believes that this can be done through the revolutionary overthrow of regimes, whether capitalist, colonial or feudal.

The third plan of action is the 'socialist' restructuring of the economic system. This means that the old system has to be destroyed and replaced by a system of state ownership of all business and industry, with equal distribution of both products and profits.

'When all that is achieved,' said Philip, 'and the classless worker's society emerges, then history will have reached that goal to which it has always been moving and there will emerge a new world of peace and perfect justice.'[12]

Of course, speaking in broad terms, the appeal of all that is enormous, and is something that should not be missed.

What is wrong with communism?

However, having conceded that, we must ask what is wrong with communism and why it would be a tragedy if it were allowed to take hold in South Africa.

Space forbids any lengthy statement, but I will note several points which from a Christian perspective are totally unacceptable.

Communism is atheistic

Lenin said, 'Atheism is a natural and inseparable portion of Marxism.' Marx said, 'Religion is the opium of the people.' Nikita Kruschev reiterated the cry from *Notebook for An Agitator*, which says: 'National enlightenment . . . leaves no room for faith in God . . .'[13]

This atheistic stance results in the abolition of moral absolutes, it sanctions a 'might is right' philosophy, it devalues human life, it reduces life to accidental absurdity, it demolishes ultimate meaning, it leaves the state free to declare its own supremacy over the individual and it destroys any eternal hope beyond the grave.

A Russian wag has put it this way: 'Thank God that God does not exist! But what if, may God forbid, God does exist?'

Communism is materialistic

This is not the Western idea of materialism, where people are obsessed by things and acquisitiveness. It is a philosophical idea which says, in the words of Mao Tse Tung, 'There is nothing in the world except matter in motion.'[14]

It is not Absolute Spirit that leads us forward in history but *Absolute Matter*. This of course robs a person of spiritual essence and makes him totally material and fully explicable in terms of the natural processes at work in physics and chemistry. It opens the door to the devaluation of human life, along with incredible programmes of human and social engineering, regardless of the cost in human life or suffering – and if that means liquidation, so be it: 'Eliminate the bourgeoisie,' said the *Peking Review* of 14 February 1975.

Such eliminations have indeed been attempted, with staggering cost to human life. An estimate of lives lost on such exercises in this century has been set at 33–45 million in the Soviet Union and 34–63 million in China.[15]

This evaluation and treatment of human life is anathema to

the Christian. And in South Africa we have a difficult enough time respecting human life without philosophical materialism lowering our view even more.

Communism does not make for happiness, nor does it work

I remember walking along the West Berlin side of the Berlin Wall with Francis Schaeffer in 1966. As we saw these armed East German guards at countless points along the wall and the mined no-man's-land between East and West Berlin, Schaeffer reflected: 'What kind of advertisement is this for a system when you have to have a wall like that to keep your citizens in and stop them fleeing!' And the little memorial crosses at many points along the way revealed how many had tried vainly to escape and paid the supreme price.

Given the nature and oppressiveness of communist dictatorships, observes Dr Fred Schwarz, an authority on communism,

> is it surprising that every chink in the Iron Curtain is clogged with a constant stream of refugees now totalling many millions despite extensive border barriers? They leave all, cross concrete walls, cut through barbed wire barricades, often under a hail of bullets, all to end up in a refugee camp with usually only the bare essentials of life, yet they are more satisfied and thankful because at last they are free. It is this constant stream of fleeing humanity which most ably exposes the lie that Communism is a haven of peace and progress.[16]

Ultimately, it would seem, the promised Marxist Utopia is largely illusory.

Joseph Ton, a Rumanian exile whom I met in the UK, writes in an article entitled 'The Failure of Communism':

> The communist system has now been tested for 70 years in the Soviet Union, for 40 years in 10 Eastern European countries and in three countries in Asia. Yet more than 80 percent of the refugees in the world today come from communist countries . . . This is long enough to test any system . . . But what in fact is revealed is that communist promises have not been kept and

practically everyone in the communist countries now knows it and is saying so. We are at the end of an era![17]

Interestingly enough, even Mikhail Gorbachev, in his new book *Perestroika*, confesses that the Soviet system does not work – though he tries to rescue it by blaming all its failures on Stalin. The fact is that worldwide most strict socialisms are in retreat.

Communism's glorification of revolution is dangerous

It is particularly dangerous when it goes hand in glove with an acceptance, if not a glorification, of *violent* revolution. If one makes matter and the state absolute, if the classless society is the desired end, then means of any sort, however horrific, become sanctified. The modern experience of Afghanistan serves notice as to how menacing this could be for South Africa.

Though inevitably sketchy, this view of communism does, I think, indicate that a philosophy with these tenets will never bring an answer to South Africa's problems. If we are to find an answer, we certainly dare not look in that direction.

But, paradoxically, some of the ways we South Africans seek to protect ourselves from communism actually promote it.

First, *we play into communist hands by calling everyone who is against apartheid a communist or communistic*. This is disastrous because it gives appeal to the communist system. After all, if every person fighting apartheid is labelled a 'communist' or 'communistic', it should not surprise us if many blacks, especially young ones, say 'Well, we don't quite know what this thing is. But if all the people trying to help us out of apartheid are communists, then this unknown thing must be OK and worth trying!'

Second, this ploy makes it very difficult for either the authorities, the general population, the trade union movements or even the church to spot the real thing. Genuine communists can now swim and flow almost anywhere, unde-tected and undetectable. Beyond that, as Fred Schwarz once wrote to me, 'The inescapable truth is that if every communist in the world disappeared tomorrow, the problems and many of the conflicts which trouble South Africa would continue unabated.' In other words, one can blame communists for some things, but not for everything.

Another South African way of inadvertently promoting communism is to *see that all who are most rabidly or even irrationally anti-communist are basically silent when it comes to apartheid*.

To thunder about the evils of communism and then be feeble or passive when it comes to the evils of apartheid is to ensure in the minds of all oppressed blacks that the anti-communist voices are totally discredited and their posture robbed of all credibility. This is why so many young blacks become immediately sceptical of anyone, especially a white, who warns that Marxism or communism is not the way for this land. They've heard that *ad nauseam*. But who from? From those who support apartheid! And we still wonder that huge numbers of young blacks now wish seriously to explore this option.

But that is not all. Our whole system, by its very nature, promotes communism. For *the maintenance of an unjust society is the classic way to open the door for a classical Marxist revolution*. Communists are masterly exploiters of such situations, and they do it with a tried and tested strategy: *i.e. 'find out what people want, promise it to them, go to work to get it for them so you can come to power over them'*. [18]

When people, especially the rank-and-file masses, have little or no say in the way their lives are politically and economically controlled, they are ready recipients for Marxist promises of a new day and a new order. Thus the communists harness social forces which they do not create, as a sailor harnesses the wind.

Furthermore, in South Africa *we compound the problem and weaken our resistance to communism by being weak on individual human worth*. The communist also has a low view of man which allows him to move people around at will, detain them indefinitely and persecute them if they oppose or protest.

To use the very methods or worse of one's opponent is hardly to make a case for the strength of one's own philosophy, especially if all the oppressive practices are accompanied by Christian profession. As Fred Schwarz has said, 'While communists are certainly not to blame for all the problems of South Africa, it will be tragic if they are the major beneficiaries of those problems.'

Quite so. Therefore, if we would take the wind out of the communists' sails we need to usher in a new and just social order in South Africa with all haste.

It is also noteworthy for South Africans that communism and Marxism make such a strong appeal to the future as compared with our national style. After all, what in South Africa do we offer blacks in terms of the future other than thirteen per cent of the land, a vote in the homelands, some say in a white dominated parliament and semi-permanent economic subservience? Clearly this won't do. It is a recipe to advance the cause of communism.

Lastly, if Christians in South Africa stand aside from the issues of justice and righteousness in the land and leave all things 'secular' to the political authorities, then we become nothing other than unwitting allies of the Kremlin and all its works.

Speaking at SACLA (South African Christian Leadership Assembly) in Pretoria in 1979, Dr Andrew Kirk of the UK, who has spent many years in Latin America and studied Marxist programmes and philosophy deeply, said to South African Christians: 'Go on supporting the present system here as it is, or perhaps even worse, suggest a few minor insignificant changes which leave the balance of power basically where it was before, and Marxism, I can assure you, will spread like a prairie fire.'

The trouble is, I don't think anyone 'heard' him.

What all this says is that if we in South Africa were actively to work against these ways of promoting communism then it could have little appeal here. In fact a theistic Africa and a just South Africa are not natural candidates for communism. But if we in this land want to keep it at bay we need to move quickly to a different kind of society, with justice and equality, plus political participation and economic involvement, for all.

7.   WINNING IN THE WIDER WORLD

There is one other area where South Africans are currently losing badly: the wider world. And that is something we can't afford to allow to continue. If we are to win through in this South African workshop of the world, we must, I believe, win through also with the wider world. Yet, sad to say, we stand almost totally friendless and isolated in the wider world. It is almost as if both history and perhaps God himself had said: 'The judgement on your desire to be separated and apart is that separated and apart you shall be!'

It has been my privilege over the last twenty-five years to travel abroad two or three times a year. In meeting people overseas I have recognised that there are many aspects of South Africa which are not understood and which need explaining. But there are many others which are understood only too well.

In mid-1985 in London, I was invited to give a briefing, from a Christian perspective, to a room full of Christian members from the British House of Commons and House of Lords. Afterwards, I asked one of the honourable members why he felt South Africa was so much on the world agenda. 'Rightly or wrongly,' he said, 'the wider world feels that South Africa and apartheid are facing it with the clearest moral issue since Germany in the 1930s.'

In the United States a few days later I conducted a similar briefing for a number of members of the American State Department, some of whom were Christians. Again I felt that many of them were most anxious and desperately eager to see South Africa come through and find a way out. 'But,' they said, 'you people are your own worst enemies. You make it very difficult for us to help you through.'

That same day a senior member of President Reagan's bi-partisan think-tank on South Africa said to me: 'We are profoundly concerned for your situation, not only for its own sake, but even for our own. The South African issue and how we handle it has a potential to set hundreds of American cities into racial flames according to the way this or future governments handle it. But please know also that we are praying for you.'

The huge numbers of concerned people overseas speak endlessly to my spirit, saying that the majority of people in the wider world, and especially in the church, desperately desire to see us come through in South Africa. The standpoint is increasingly one of deep human and humanitarian concern. In the case of multiplied thousands in the church, they view South Africa from the place of intercession upon their knees.

All of which brings us to two questions: What is our word to the wider world? And what should be the wider world's response to us?

A word to the wider world

Of course different South Africans, be they Afrikaners, blacks or English-speakers, will have different words to the wider world, and I cannot at this point speak for anyone other than myself. So I share the line I have taken in my travels abroad during the last couple of years. Whether this is right or wrong, history alone will have to judge. I am also the first to admit that the wisdom of hindsight may be greater than that of foresight.

In a nutshell, it is: 'Humbly, sincerely, lovingly, sensitively, wisely, prayerfully, you should work a combination of pressure and of positive encouragement. In other words, work a combination of the small stick and the big carrot.'

I would spell it out in the following terms.

1.   Whatever you do, do it humbly
Even South Africans can spot moral humbug at a thousand yards. So to whites in Australia, New Zealand, North America or the UK, I would ask whether their moral indignation would be at the same level if the black populations of their respective countries outnumbered them five to one. Would their elevated political morality triumph over their fear of being swamped and their instinct for political self-preservation?

To blacks in Africa or beyond, I would also put the question already raised in a different form in these pages: 'How are things looking in your own back yard?'

In other words, all overseas or outside people have to beware that their idealism on the South African subject is not in inverse proportion to their distance from the problem. This calls for humility from our outside critics.

2. *Whatever you do, do it sincerely, wisely and with love*
On sanctions, for example, the real questions are: 'What is in your heart? Is it a desire to punish a naughty, distant and stubborn people? Or is it a desire to precipitate and spectate a massive and epic political drama from the safety of a grandstand seat – when it is not *your* life, *your* family or *your* nation that is involved? Or, are you, if a politician, desiring to make domestic political capital out of someone else's tragedy?

'Or, on the other hand, are you sincerely, humbly and with love and tears trying to save a potentially great and actually very important nation from itself by exerting political, economic and moral pressure upon it?'

The fact is that South Africans will read outsiders like a book. South Africans know what is in the hearts of others. And their own reaction, whether positive or negative, depends on what they discern. If what is being done to us is purely punitive, then the effect will be counter-productive.

For example, before sanctions become a knee-jerk response of emotional politics, outsiders need to think through the implications of what they propose. They need to think of what will actually work to bring about the scenario they desire. And they have to realise afresh that they are grappling with one of the most intractable and complex situations in the world, and any simplistic solutions will get laughed out of court here.

The wider world's response to South Africa

First of all, I want to look at overseas Christians and what they can do, and then I want to reflect on the responses of secular agencies and governments, especially in terms of the sanctions issue.

Let it be registered right away that Christians in the wider world *have to be* concerned about South Africa, because, whether they like it or not, know it or not, believe it or not, they are part of the church's life and responsibility in this place.

As I see it, the primary responsibility of Christians overseas and everywhere is to pray – not just to say they will, but actually to do it. This is the greatest single contribution which Christians anywhere can make.

The second responsibility is to give financially towards those agencies, organisations, churches and groups which are really doing something positive to bring about non-violent and substantial change.

With the South African economy in recession it is often difficult for South African Christians to finance programmes and support all the worthy agencies which are working for a new day in South Africa. In addition to specifically religious organisations needing this kind of help, there are several very worthy educational projects which are multiracial in nature and working to put in place a new breed of black and white young South African which is equipped to face the future.[19]

Third, overseas Christians can also take the initiative of coming out here to see what the situation is like for themselves, not just looking at the negative things, but at the positive as well. Many are already doing this and this is creative and helpful.

Fourth, overseas Christians need to pastor and succour South African Christian leaders who from time to time need to get away from South Africa for retreat, renewal and emotional restoration. To make it possible for a Christian leader, his wife and perhaps family to be away from South Africa for a few weeks or months for this kind of recuperation is a worthy contribution indeed. This can be part of a whole process of forming friendships, building up and encouraging all who are at the emotionally costly forefront of the processes of change.

Fifth, where overseas Christians have access to the levers of power in their own countries, they should also encourage help and financial support for any and every type of initiative in this land which is positive, especially with reference to any kind of training and leadership programmes for blacks.

Sixth, Christian academics overseas, plus Christian doctors, nurses and physicians, can also come out here on short-term volunteer assignments to render their services in colleges or hospitals on a *gratis* basis, financed by their sending churches or agencies.

That said, what now should be the responses to South Africa of overseas governments, secular agencies and lobbies?

Several thoughts occur to me.

First, *support and invest positively in internal movements for change and in black education*. This is positive directed investment. Of course those internal movements working for peaceful change vary in nature from the political to the educational and the religious.

Second, *don't despair of ongoing initiatives such as the Eminent Person's Group*. The EPG report is to me a superb piece of work, and I was never more frustrated than when this group gave up after a mere three months' effort to solve a problem that has been generations in the making. (Did they honestly think they would get a breakthrough in a mere ninety days?) Yet what their report makes clear is that they made incredible progress on the basis of an amazing set of cards put in their hands which allowed them to meet not only the whole South African cabinet, all the internal political and business leaders in South Africa, but also the external leaders in Lusaka and on top of that have three encounters with Nelson Mandela. No one ever had a hand like that dealt them. And after three months they threw it away. But in spite of that, an instinct tells me there is still room for really serious 'honest broker' initiatives from leadership in the wider world. The Methodist leader Mmutlanyane Mogoba concurs, and urges the formation of a new international mediating team to help polarised South African groups to find a way through.

Should sanctions be imposed?

What then of sanctions? I do not profess 20:20 vision in this, and my perceptions may be wrong. But for better or worse this is my line overseas.

First of all, *we in South Africa deserve sanctions*. We have brought them on our heads by unbelievable obtuseness and political perversity over a very long time. And perhaps in the final economy of things they will be seen to have been part of God's divine judgement upon us. Yet I pray not.

Second, let us be clear amidst all the other confusions that the blame for sanctions cannot be laid at the door of the American Congress, Jesse Jackson, the OAU or the Archbishop of Cape Town. The blame must be laid fairly and squarely where it belongs – at the door of apartheid and its authors. But for apartheid, even the thought of sanctions would never have arisen.

Third, it is *understandable, emotionally speaking*, why the world, driven mad with frustration and anger over South African intransigence, should want to pull out the biggest stick possible and impose full, mandatory and punitive sanctions.

When I myself am emotionally down, frustrated and angry at the set-up, I sometimes feel: 'Let sanctions come, we deserve them. We have brought them on our own heads.' But when my emotions have calmed and my mind has re-engaged, I say: 'No, this is not the way.' So while my heart says yes, my head says no, even though I do recognise that many people of integrity are advocating sanctions to avoid the worse fate of violent explosion. It is just that I'm not sure whether sanctions do not increase that possibility rather than diminish it.

Not that some measure of ongoing pressure is inappropriate if it is very carefully modulated and targeted. This is just so that we white South Africans do not slip back into the illusion that all is well and we can go it alone and in our global village ignore the rest of the planet.

As I see it, there is a place for certain forms of pressure to be kept on us so that we face the inevitability and necessity of far more radical, rapid and courageous change than we have seen thus far. But I cannot find it in myself to go with any pressures which inflict deep and permanent damage on the South African economy. After all, if comprehensive sanctions and massive disinvestment developed so that the economy was finally smashed, who would put the economic humpty-dumpty together again? And having seen countries in Africa where the economies are irrevocably and irreparably damaged I know we are talking about an economic and human nightmare whose proportions cannot be measured.

It is important to remember that sanctions are not an end in themselves but are a means to an end. The end in view, presumably, is a more just and responsible society in South Africa. Sanctions are intended to be a means to that end and therefore need to be judged in terms of how effective they will in fact be.

This raises for me a number of factors to consider.

1.   Full sanctions will drive the Afrikaner back to the laager, just when he is coming out of it

When in Australia in 1986, I predicted to Australians and their law-makers in Canberra and elsewhere that sanctions would push the whole South African electorate to the right. The election of May 1987 has admirably demonstrated the accuracy of at least that prediction.

In that election the Nationalist Government was returned to power with huge numbers of English-speakers now moving politically to the right and supporting the Government. Beyond that, the 'liberal' opposition (Progressives) were severely mauled and the Conservative Party, a far right group, became the official opposition. In March 1988 they also won two by-elections with increased majorities. They talk of taking power by 1994, and no one is laughing. Greatly intensified overseas pressure on South Africa might put this latter group into power even sooner. That is, unless the present Government officially called up the generals and finally laid to rest the vestiges of democracy in South Africa – and where would that put us?

2.   The sanction drive involves a miscalculation of the Afrikaner psyche

I said in 1986 in Australia, the UK and the USA (and again the course of events since then has confirmed it) that sanctions would stiffen the white resolve in general and the Afrikaner resolve in particular. For the Afrikaner is not a sort of Dutch-speaking version of Ian Smith; rather he is a creature far more akin to the Israeli, with a 'do or die' survival instinct on the Masada model. The Afrikaner is not prone to intimidation, frustrating as this may be. Alan Paton has put it this way: 'I have a word to those who think they can bring the South African Government to its knees. They will not succeed. Afrikaner Nationalists may at times behave like fools, *but they do not behave like cowards.*'

3.   *Full sanctions will force an unnatural Dunkirk-type political unity on South African whites*

Another of my big fears is that heightened overseas pressure will only serve to drive those who are not natural political bed-fellows of the present Government into their arms. As a result all white South Africans will end up fighting the world instead of trying to remove apartheid. Reform will thereby become not merely a lost cause but a forgotten one.

4.   *Even South Africans strongly opposed to the apartheid system are divided on the sanctions question*

Various surveys conducted by different groups reveal different statistics pro and con, especially among the blacks. It is true to say that probably the majority of black intellectuals and trade unionists do in fact favour sanctions. Yet John Kane-Burman, Director of the South African Institute for Race Relations, said in London in November 1987 that

> the number of blacks who thought sanctions would work to end apartheid has dropped from 57% to 41% in the last two years, and the number who supported sanctions at any cost has dropped from 26% to 14%, while the number who would not support sanctions if this meant any job losses has increased from 48% to 60%.[20]

Even so, the number of key blacks supporting sanctions is considerable and powerful, and courageous spokesmen of integrity such as Desmond Tutu are well known for their pleas along this line. History may prove the Archbishop right, but in the meantime I take friendly issue with him at this point, knowing that history may likewise prove me wrong.

5.   *Full sanctions and comprehensive disinvestment will seriously aggravate unemployment, which even without sanctions is already very serious*

It is calculated that by the year 2000, even without sanctions, on the basis of the exploding population and political troubles alone, thirty-six per cent of the black workforce of South Africa will be unemployed. The consequence of this, says the Director of the Production Management Institute of South Africa, will be 'inconceivable hardship'. How accelerating such hardship will help us find answers I don't know. (The Unemployment Research Unit of Vista University in Port Elizabeth calculates unemployment in the black townships around Port Elizabeth at fifty-seven per cent in July 1988 (up ten per cent from July 1987). The unofficial figure for Walmer Township is seventy-five per cent.) Beyond that, severe unemployment greatly diminishes black economic leverage through the Trade Unions.

6.   *Full sanctions will therefore very seriously affect South Africa's ability to feed itself*

And this is against the backdrop of a continent where already thirty per cent of the population is threatened with famine. It is said that for South Africa just to feed itself over the next couple of decades, the economy needs to generate a thousand jobs per day for the thousand workers per day who are entering the job market. To provide jobs for these people and feed them, the South African economy needs a five per cent annual growth rate. Only three per cent will be possible without overseas trade and investment, and in all likelihood the growth will go even lower than that if the pressures build up much more. Some say sanctions have already cost South Africa between sixty and a hundred thousand jobs. Even as soon as by 1990, according to Dr Chris van Wyk, Director of the Trust Bank, the foreign reserves of South Africa will have suffered a net loss of R30 billion, resulting from sanctions and disinvestment. This will result, he says, in South Africa being unable to generate new employment.

It is also worth noting in passing that on present trends South Africa's population will be a hundred million in the year 2020, only about eight or nine million of whom will be white. Senior environmentalist Lynn Hurry feels that, given present agricultural conditions and maximally using all agricultural, mineral and industrial resources, South Africa can carry, sustain and properly feed only *fifty million* people. The consequences, therefore, of intentionally damaging or destroying those resources are clearly both devastating and dangerous, especially when the population is set to be twice that figure.

7. *As hunger and unemployment increase, the propensity*
    for violence among those affected, both black and white,
    increases

As reaction and retaliation set in, chaos is bred and violence, often unreasoning and undirected, becomes endemic. It is already evident that where unemployment is at its highest violence tends to be at its highest as well. Such violence makes political solutions even more difficult and remote.

8. *Sanctions may easily drive the South African authorities*
    to retaliate against the countries round about us, and so
    finally destabilise the whole region economically

A black economist in Zimbabwe said to me: 'If South Africa closes all its borders to our trade we will be in economic collapse within three weeks.' The hard fact is that this whole subcontinent is economically interdependent. For example, Zaire has fifty-seven per cent of its imports coming through South Africa, Malawi sixty per cent, Zimbabwe sixty-eight per cent and Zambia seventy per cent. As for exports, forty-five per cent of Zaire's go through South Africa, fifty per cent of Malawi's, sixty-five per cent of Zimbabwe's and forty per cent of Zambia's. A trade war in the region will get no one anywhere.

9. *Capital disinvested from South Africa at this time is not,*
    in my mind, likely at the end of a thirty-year
    revolutionary struggle to be reinvested in a highly
    socialist Azania

In other words, the likelihood of a permanent flight of capital from South Africa, if present trends continue, is very real. And the new nation, which will need extensive overseas investment, will not have it. This will make the problem of a black Government rising from the economic ashes of a white Government that much more difficult.

*10.   The enforceability and effectiveness of sanctions are by
no means assured*

One of the problems with sanctions is the difficulty of enforc-
ing them. This makes them ultimately very damaging, but not
decisive. Related to this is the potential development here of
a certain type of white bravado and heroics as sanctions are
'busted' and by-passed. It is also a fact that hitherto the record
of sanctions being truly effective anywhere is totally uncon-
vincing. Not that white South Africans can take comfort in the
notion that sanctions have hitherto not brought us to our
knees; in the long run, unless we turn things around politically, they and many other factors will take us spiralling down
into the abyss.

Conclusion

A young South African economist who deplores apartheid
but also has an emotional feel for those wishing to impose
sanctions has written:

> Sanctions will indeed punish, but will punish more those groups
> who do not merit the punishment. Sanctions do express the
> justifiable outrage of the world, even though tarnished by indi-
> vidual interests, but the costs of expressing outrage in this way
> need to be realistically considered. Sanctions furthermore show
> no evidence of deterring government plans or of speeding them
> up. The riling effect witnessed suggests the opposite. Lastly,
> sanctions do not offer the possibility of rehabilitating the
> economy but rather of exacerbating already severe economic
> problems for any future government.[21]

All that has been said above has driven me, at least, to the
irresistible conclusion that there has to be another way. And
while the world follows its convictions and does what it feels it
has to do, we in South Africa have got to work that other way.

I have called it 'the politics of love'. To make such politics
work, we must see love as a political virtue and reflect further
on how it works. To that we now turn.

20   Love as a Political Virtue

I want love in South Africa, dear God.

Title of children's book

Love is a political virtue . . . The world languishes because love is being tried so little. It is imperative that it should be admitted into the field of political thought.

Edgar Brookes

Do to us what you will and we will still love You.

Martin Luther King

Christ's love compels us.

2 Corinthians 5:14

In 1987 many sayings by South African children, both black and white, were collected and published. Thousands of South African children helped. The book's title, drawn from a quote by one of these children was: 'I Want Love in South Africa, Dear God.' And who, dear God, doesn't?

But maybe we ask that question too glibly and quickly. Maybe our problem is exactly there. Maybe we *don't* want love in South Africa. Certainly there is evidence to suggest that we don't.

Yet deep down, on reflection, every South African knows that the child's strong inner longing reflects our own – we want love in South Africa. Love, St Paul says, is the greatest thing in the universe – a force which 'never fails' (1 Cor 13:8).

But, we ask, isn't all that something rather sentimental, impractical, 'airy-fairy', something beautiful and moving in rhetoric but not really suited to the rough and gritty world of politics, which deals with power clashes, group strife, racial confrontation, parliamentary argument, constitutional planning, *etc*? Surely some other principle must apply in politics – anything but love.

No. That is just where we are so dreadfully wrong. Love is the most neglected yet the most necessary political virtue, especially in South Africa, where every other form of politics has been tried and found wanting. In fact to labour for such love in the social arena is to labour for the kingdom of God.

My deepest conviction is that on this path and along this way lies the answer for South Africa. Fortunately South Africa is one of the best equipped nations in the world to walk this way. And for four reasons.

Constitutionally, South Africa is honour-bound to the politics of love by the declaration in its own constitution that it is a self-confessedly and self-consciously Christian nation.

Statistically, the fact that seventy-eight per cent of South Africans have in broad terms a Christian profession means that South Africa, more than any other nation, cannot escape a commitment to the politics of love without declaring itself a blatant hypocrite – nationally content with the despicable expedient of professing one thing and doing another.

Inspirationally, the politics of love also makes good sense, because it sets before us as a nation the challenge that a nation can actually live out its faith and confession, thereby both saving itself and inspiring the planet with new visions of hope.

Practically, the politics of love also makes sense because every Christian, from the far right to the extreme left, could unite around the way of love and agree that the golden rule is finally what life is all about.

Maybe most people would say something like this: 'It's beautiful in theory. But as practical politics it's a non-starter.' Presumably meaning that Jesus Christ was impractical – with pretty words and ideas for sermons on hillsides but not for the hurly-burly of life. But that is nonsense! He meant love to be the way in every area of life, including the political, because it is the best way – and the only way which works.

Let me share how I see it working. There are ten steps which I will examine in turn in the next two chapters.

In many ways the politics of love means that as Christians we begin our political reasoning from the cross. Pictorially it might look like this:

		The 'politics of love' means		
1 Dealing with one's own heart	2 Abandoning the negative because love is positive	3 Working out what we profess as a Christian nation	4 Rising to the demands of enemy love and forgiveness	5 Accepting love as a political virtue
		6 Working for structural reconciliation		
		7 Putting love into a constitutional framework		
		8 Working love into economic structures		
		9 Prayerfully thinking and acting ourselves into a new order and a new way		
		10 Taking the long view		

The politics of love

For these principles to work, it requires every person of good will, from the lowest to the highest, to say: 'I want to be part of this. I want to be part of the solution where I am, not part of the problem. I'm not leaving everything to the "high-ups".'

What the ordinary person does is critical. For change will

assuredly come from the grass-roots when enough people
want it and are prepared to be part of the process and press
their leaders to bring in a new day. As Martin Luther King
said:

> When evil men plot, good men must plan. When evil men burn
> and bomb, good men must build and bind. When evil men shout
> ugly words of hatred, good men must commit themselves to the
> glories of love. Where evil men would seek to perpetrate an
> unjust status quo, good men must seek to bring into being a real
> order of justice.[1]

THE POLITICS OF LOVE MEANS DEALING WITH ONE'S OWN HEART

The answer for South Africa lies in the politics of love. But the
first step is a difficult one. It involves dealing with one's own
heart. This is where the primary battlefield lies.

What is allowed to conquer each heart will conquer the
country. If hatred conquers my heart, I must not be surprised
if it conquers South Africa. If bigotry and prejudice conquer
your heart, they will conquer in your country, wherever you
are. If despair and defeatism rule in your heart and mine, they
will rule in the citadels of the land and prevail in its policies,
and we will reap the bitter fruit in full measure.

However, if love and forgiveness conquer in individual
hearts, then love and forgiveness will conquer the country. If
largeness of heart can vanquish shrunken narrowness of mind
and spirit in you and me as individuals, if love can banish fear,
if hope can overwhelm despair, if the positive can swamp the
negative, then the nation can be born again.

But it has to start in the individual human heart. That is the
battleground. If enough people win there, the nation wins.
And if enough lose there, not only does the nation lose, but
the nation is lost.

This is not simply a matter of generating some warm
feelings of benevolence on the macro-level towards broad
groupings of people, such as 'the blacks', or 'Zulus' or
'Afrikaners' or 'the English'. To profess love for humanity is a

futile profession unless you can love Mr Sam Dingleton, the individual specimen of humanity who works in the corner drug store and whom you dislike.

In South Africa, then, the first test, the real one, is at the level of that one problematic black man or Englishman or Afrikaner who is either in your own circle or who, though a distant public figure, nevertheless straddles the emotional horizon of your own political soul like a colossus, obstructing your pathway to the politics of love. By God's grace conquer, there – there in the microcosm of one person – and you are home and dry.

How can that be? It is because if you conquer in the microcosm of your attitude to one problem individual, you are then freed to deal with the macrocosm of one's problem group. If you come to Jesus in love (not necessarily in agreement) for that problem individual, be it Tutu, P W Botha, Buthelezi, Boesak, Mandela or Treurnicht, the highway then opens up to the politics of love. Deal with your heart-attitude to your political problem person, and a new world of political possibilities opens – because love has won.

To some friends of mine the late Bishop Alphaeus Zulu once said, 'You must never allow hatred in your heart ever for anyone.' To someone else he said, 'You may hate the sin, but never the sinner.'

If we get to the point where love has conquered in our relationship with our problem figure we can then move on. Not that this means arriving at a place of agreement or even affection with the problem figure, for one can love someone one does not like. Love simply means desiring the highest and the best for the other person, respecting his dignity and viewing him with compassion and forgiveness. I don't think it requires affection, but it will often lead to it.

This I have personally experienced in my own heart-attitude to President P W Botha. After our difficult and tense encounter in 1985 I found hard attitudes in my heart towards him. While working on my earlier chapter on reconciliation I felt the Spirit of God convict me on this. The Spirit seemed to say, 'How can you write on reconciliation when your heart-attitudes to the President are wrong?'

So I dictated a letter to Mr Botha. When I finally read it it contained more blame, condemnation and judgement than apology and forgiveness. I took out all the blame, condemnation and judgement and left just the apology and forgiveness.

I am not suggesting, of course, that such letters or initiatives work magic in either one's own heart or that of the recipient, but I do know that I have felt freer in spirit since sending that communication, and more able to view the President's plight with compassion, though in no way surrendering my antipathy to his policies.

The important point is that I had first to deal with my own heart, which is an ongoing project. It is part of the new spiritual Great Trek upon which all South Africans must embark – the trek from intransigence to a change of heart. As the Dutch Reformed Moderator Johan Heyns says, 'Unless a complete change of heart takes place in South Africa, there will be no political solution.'[2] And if I don't let it start in my own heart, I cannot expect it to start at all.

Dealing with one's own heart also involves repenting of that most delicious of South African pastimes, 'scapegoating'. This is the process of laying *all* the blame at the door of the Government or the communists or the blacks, but always exonerating oneself.

The trouble with scape-goating is that it is dangerously self-deceiving and enslaving. It absolves us of facing our own political and social sins and their consequences.

The great devotional mystic Thomas Merton notes how

we tend unconsciously to ease ourselves . . . of the burden of guilt that is in us by passing it on to somebody else . . . The temptation is, then, to account for my fault by seeing an equivalent amount of evil in someone else, hence (I) minimize my own sins and compensate for doing so by exaggerating the faults of others.[3]

This mechanism of shifting blame on to others is one which we all use. Husbands do it with wives, and bosses with staff. An angry child kicks the dog. South African whites blame all problems on the ANC and the communists. Blacks blame 'the system'. If you fail or are incompetent at some point you can blame whites, capitalists, the system, the West or neocolonialists. It is the same mechanism of shifting blame and responsibility, whoever your target is.

None of this is to say that the scapegoat you choose, whether communist, capitalist or nationalist (white or black), may not be up to some of the mischief of which you accuse him. But if you want to know if you are projecting and scapegoating, there is a clue that may help: if you are fixated on unpleasant actions or strategies in others, without humbly and repentantly acknowledging blame in yourself, then you are scapegoating. Many of us in South Africa have got this down to a fine art.

THE POLITICS OF LOVE MEANS ABANDONING THE NEGATIVE, BECAUSE LOVE IS POSITIVE

I have already mentioned in chapter 2 how I met a wonderful black pastor in the Eastern Cape at the height of the crisis that precipitated the introduction of the State of Emergency. When I asked him how he was, despite the fact that everything in his world was in a shambles, he replied, 'Positive!' – and beamed at me. I found that amazing and instructive, because South Africa is a place where it is very hard to stay positive. As Alan Paton once said, 'This is a country where you hope on Monday and despair on Tuesday!'

For many years I have found it relatively easy to keep hope alive and to stay positive. But since 1985 I have found this increasingly difficult. Finally, last year, I was shocked when a dear friend said to me, 'You are becoming negative.' That was when I realised I needed to take this to the Lord and ask for his healing. Nor has it been easy to start getting it right, especially when so much awfulness continues.

Inevitably the situation gets to people. Why else would 2 600 professionals leave the country in 1986? At one point it was over forty a day. (According to the South Africa Institute for Race Relations, the average emigration loss to South Africa from October to December 1987 was 624 per month. In April 1988, taking immigration into account, the net loss was 206 per month, many of them professionals or semiprofessionals.) A December 1987 survey at Rhodes University in Grahamstown revealed that fifty-three per cent of recent Rhodes graduates were contemplating emigration. Each of these young adults is a once positive person who has begun to be overwhelmed by the negative.

Recently I spoke to the wife of a local school headmaster; we were commenting on how many young people were leaving the country when she said, 'Yes, but where in the world is there such a positive challenge for young people as here?'

'That is the attitude we need,' I thought.

I am persuaded that we should not capitulate to the negative, for is not the cross a minus sign crossed out and made into God's great positive plus sign over the world? In fact he took the single most negative thing which had ever happened in the world, namely the judicial murder of his own Son, Jesus Christ, on a criminal's gallows, and made it into the most positive thing in our planet's history, namely the means by which sinful, negative human beings might come to eternal salvation.

The trouble with South Africa is that it is in fact a nation whose whole foundation is negative. It is a nation built on a series of negatives: that humans of different sorts *cannot* get along together, *cannot* live harmoniously side by side, are *not* equal and are *not* reconcilable. To attack that with the positive affirmation that they are and then to meet with denunciation, opposition, social pressure, or even banning or imprisonment is to have an odyssey into the negative.

Yet Calvary, and especially Calvary love, keeps calling us back to the positive. The cross says, 'Do not see only what is dying. See what is being born. For these death throes of the one thing are the birth pangs of another.'

Translating that into the South African context, perhaps South Africa is a place where finally a new type of civilisation will be born. We need to see South Africa entering and enduring this trauma so that it may emerge finally under God as a nation which will not only bless the continent of Africa but the whole world.

The trouble is that too many of us in this land have built

prisons for ourselves and have occupied them for so long and become so accustomed to their walls that we have accepted the notion that we must be incarcerated for life. This makes us abandon any hope of ever getting the place right or seeing our dreams of better things fulfilled.

I believe the Lord says: 'Away with such thoughts. And consign the words "irreconcilability" and "impossible" to the verbal wastebasket. For with me *all things are possible* – even a new and just South Africa. Believe it and work for it' (*cf.* Matt 19:26; Mark 9:23; 10:27; Luke 18:27).

The thing is that we are made or unmade by how we think. If a nation's thought patterns are at heart negative it forges and fashions the weapons by which it destroys itself. And that is true of you and me too.

I'm told the computer people have an acronym GIGO – standing for 'Garbage In, Garbage Out'. Put faulty, garbaged information into the computer and out comes garbage. To programme our national or individual soul with negative garbage about not being able to live together as whites and blacks, and therefore being in perpetual despair and hopelessness about the future, is to promote the outflow of political garbage and national depression which overwhelms us now.

The cure is to replace the negative by the positive. As St Paul said: 'be transformed by the renewing of your mind' (Rom 12:2). Part of that at least means 'be positive'. And the key to getting there is by embracing, often painfully, God's great plus sign, the cross.

THE POLITICS OF LOVE MEANS FACING THE ULTIMATE NATIONAL CHALLENGE OF WORKING OUT WHAT WE PROFESS AS A CHRISTIAN NATION

In 1960 whites constituted twenty per cent of the South African population. Today some fifteen per cent of all South Africans are white. By the end of the century, only eleven years from the date of publication of this book, the percentage will be down to seven or eight per cent. This says something. It says first that major transformation of the political structure is totally inevitable. For a diminishing minority with an ever-diminishing power base means an ever-diminishing ability to govern, even unjustly, let alone justly.

Add to this the fact that in May 1987 only slightly more than a million people (out of over thirty million) voted the Government back into power, and one realises the precarious arithmetic of white South African politics.

In other words, South Africa is in a transitional phase from what is, to something new. That new thing may be unimaginably dreadful or unexpectedly splendid. The choice is ours. We can choose the cesspool of endless strife and chaotic tragedy, or perhaps the dull grey and sometimes brutal monotony of Marxist authoritarianism. Or we can choose the demanding but splendid destiny of becoming a truly Christian nation working out what we profess. The key to which path we take rests very specially with the Afrikaner. But it's no easy way for him. It is the way of the cross. Yet he, maybe more than most, is equipped via his deep Christian convictions to set out on it.

Whether or not this happens will depend on whether the Afrikaner people and churches can forgo the old identity of yesterday to find the new identity of tomorrow, and on whether they can 'let go and let God'.

Some years ago, the late Dr Edgar Brookes also saw the difficulty and yet the possibility of acts of national self-abrogation which work for the inner healing of nations:

> To save the undoubted achievement and national identity of the Afrikaner people seems to most Afrikaners the right and indeed the only course. To ask for a different outlook is to ask for a higher standard than has been general among other nations in past history. Yet undoubtedly, the Afrikaner people, if willing to lose themselves, would for the first time fully find themselves, would earn the respect of all humanity and would break free from restricting fears and life-destroying narrowness.[4]

Brookes went on: 'Since the Afrikaner people claim to be *par excellence* a Christian people, the appeal must be to their

Christian faith . . . God is love, and on God's self-giving rests the only ultimate hope of humanity.'[5]

And imagine if in South Africa the spirit of love began to take hold upon our national soul so that groups began to think of the other before themselves and to embrace the love imperative, to 'do to others what you would have them do to you' (Matt 7:12).

If we could rise to this, we could realise the vision of producing at the tip of Africa a truly Christian nation, not the travesty of one.

But if we choose to stay sectional, if as Jesus said we love only those who love us and are part of our own in-group or our own sub-culture, then 'what reward will you get? Are not even the tax collectors doing that?' (Matt 5:46).

Put politically and nationally, we might ask ourselves: If in South Africa we don't show real love and mutual respect and justice to individuals and groupings which are not our own, and which are different or difficult, why bother to hold on to our profession as a Christian country? For how then are we different from other pagan or communist countries? And if we aren't different from them, why not cut our Christian profession and officially declare ourselves a secular, pagan state? Then what we do will be consistent with what we profess.

However, if by contrast we rise to the glorious and epic challenge to be and to work out what we profess, then I believe we will know God's protective care and blessing as enshrined in the psalmist's word: 'Trust in the Lord and *do good*; dwell in the land and enjoy safe pasture' (Ps 37:3).

What a splendid national challenge! To trust God, do the right thing, and leave the outcome to him! Why not? For goodness sake, why not?

Perhaps the real reason why we can't or don't rise to this challenge is that we are trapped in enmity or hostility. Which brings us to the Christian demands of rising to enemy love and forgiveness.

THE POLITICS OF LOVE MEANS RISING TO THE DEMANDS OF ENEMY LOVE AND FORGIVENESS

Enemy love

In South Africa the key lies in blacks surrendering the black position and whites surrendering the white position and both coming to God's position. The mechanism of this lies in rising by God's supernatural and available grace to a great resolution to love and forgive the one who was or is perceived as the enemy. After all, both countries and people that go ahead are those which have not wasted time getting even. Said Abraham Lincoln: 'The only way to destroy your enemy is to make him your friend.' To get even with your enemy is to set his enmity in concrete and keep you for ever apart. Enemy love, however, embraces the principle that you so resist your enemy in love that you not only change the situation, but you transform your enemy. So the goal of enemy love includes not only transforming the bad situation but the enemy responsible for it. If we don't do it this way we actually don't change the situation at all.

In our land so many have become enemies to each other that what the New Testament has to say about enemy love presents itself to us as marvellously relevant.

In 1948, when Dr D F Malan came to power, my grandmother, Molly Craufurd, sent him an excerpt of the speech by the British Boer War nurse Emily Hobhouse, when she unveiled a national monument in honour of the Boer women and children who died in the concentration camps. I don't know how Malan received it, but the text encapsulated Miss Hobhouse's spirit and my grandmother's spirit and the Christian spirit. It is the spirit needed today more than ever:

> Alongside the honour we pay the Sainted Dead forgiveness must find a place. I have read that when Christ said 'Forgive your enemies', it is not only for the sake of the enemy He says so, but for one's own sake, 'because love is more beautiful than hate'. Surely your dead, with the wisdom that now is theirs, know this. To harbour hate is fatal to your own self-development. It makes a

flaw, for hatred, like rust, eats into the soul of a nation, as of an individual.

As your tribute to the dead, bury unforgiveness and bitterness at the foot of this monument forever. Instead, forgive, for you can afford it. Forgive the rich who were greedy of more riches, the statesmen who could not guide affairs, the bad generalship that warred on weaklings and babes – forgive – for so only can you rise to full nobility of character and a broad and noble national life.

Be merciful towards the weak, the down-trodden, the stranger. Do not open your gates to those worst foes of freedom – tyranny and selfishness. Are not these the withholding from others in your control the very liberties and rights which you have valued and won for yourselves? So will the monument speak to you.[6]

The relevance of these great and simple truths struck me afresh in mid 1985, not long before the State of Emergency was declared.

I was invited to participate in a huge gathering in the Dan Qeqe Stadium of New Brighton, one of Port Elizabeth's black townships. The scene was incredible – about forty thousand chanting blacks laced with about twenty overwhelmed whites, had set up an electric mix of spiritual zeal and political protest. Rhythmic shouting, wild hand waving and antiphonal shouts from both audience and speakers charged the meeting with emotion and passion.

I was thankful as a white to feel not only void of fear but exhilarated by the atmosphere.

As I sat near the speakers' rostrum I began to realise that the black political aspirations represented in this sort of gathering could not be held in check indefinitely. Such monumental and massive political emotion could easily run amok and burst its banks in wild destructiveness unless channelled and controlled by godly principles.

The speeches of the day made much of the Exodus story. Passionate parallels were drawn between the Israelites and black South Africans, between Pharaoh and President Botha. The cries from the crowd edged closer to frenzy as the story neared the part where Pharaoh and the Egyptians are destroyed in the waters of the Red Sea.

When it came to my turn to speak, I said I wished to say

something about the spirit of the cross. I spoke of what the cross would mean for whites. They must repent (personally and politically), ask for forgiveness, end the system of exclusive power and privilege, and face the challenges of redress and restitution. This means land reform and restoring detained leaders.

For blacks the cross means forgiveness of whites, no matter how hard and costly. With that must go repentance for the spirit of vengeance, vendetta, hatred and retaliatory violence. I noted that even a hardened politician like Jomo Kenyatta at Kenya's independence had said, 'Unless we build our nation on forgiveness, we will lose the day.'

From what took place in that heady meeting two issues emerged for me. The first is the nature and consequences of enemy love; the second is the basic ingredient here, even for political life, of forgiveness.

Two scriptural passages immediately come to mind. The first is from the lips of Jesus: 'You have heard that it was said, "Love your neighbour and hate your enemy." But I tell you: Love your enemies and pray for those who persecute you, that you may be sons of your Father in heaven' (Matt 5:43–45).

The second passage comes from St Paul:

> Bless those who persecute you; bless and do not curse . . . Live in harmony with one another . . . Do not repay anyone evil for evil. Be careful to do what is right in the eyes of everybody . . . Do not take revenge, my friends, but leave room for God's wrath . . . On the contrary:
> 'If your enemy is hungry, feed him;
> if he is thirsty, give him something to drink.
> In doing this, you will heap burning coals on his head.'
> Do not be overcome by evil, but overcome evil with good.
>
> (Rom 12:14–21)

Clearly we are learning here of the Christian way of dealing with one's enemy. It is to love and forgive him. Most would accept that this is the right thing personally and privately. But I am proposing that is also the right thing politically. Sometimes it is the only thing, and surely never more truly so than in South Africa.

But isn't this unrealistic, romantic naivety?

I don't believe so. For I believe that 'enemy love' needs to become part of a new vision, part of a new style of thinking, and part of a moral 'about-face' which so many of the world's societies desperately need.

After all, we are not talking here about a journey into political sentimentality where we feel good about our political enemies. Rather we are thinking of a purposeful, decided resolution to respect our enemies as human beings, to be prepared to leave the past and its hurts behind and to enter into the hard negotiating work of resolving our differences and, with God's help, hammering out a future together for the good of all. In fact enemy love and forgiveness present themselves as the only dynamic, demanding though it is, which can bring antagonists together to become co-operators in working out a common and better future for the good of all.

And if enemy love isn't the way, can you think of another? I can't – other than political and military exhaustion at the tragic end of a prolonged and titanic civil war. Then people collapse around the conference table to talk about the ashes around them which they now want to share. What folly to wait till then! Why not now rise to the moral challenge of enemy love and forgiveness? After all, it worked for Gandhi in India, for Martin Luther King in America and, in a different way, for Kenya under Kenyatta. Perhaps even now it may be starting to work between Ndebele and Shona in Zimbabwe, and between black and white.

Interestingly enough, Michael Borodin, the man who was largely responsible for the communisation of China, said the greatest enemy of the advance of communism was the Christian doctrine of forgiveness. So he at least saw enemy love and Christian forgiveness as a highly influential political force, where it could be harnessed.

Not only that, but enemy love and the politics of forgiveness will do everything in their power to see the real humanity and plight of the enemy. They will work against keeping our enemies faceless, so that we can continue to assure ourselves that they are nothing like us as human beings. Enemy love will prevent us saying that the enemy is all-bad and we are all-good, that our cause is noble, and theirs is evil. Enemy love will stop us saying that only *we* are to be trusted while *they* are totally untrustworthy. Enemy love will prevent us saying that the enemy knows neither reason nor love, but only irrationality and hate.

Enemy love and the politics of forgiveness require us to hate conditions, situations and policies, not individuals, who are never as evil as the social and political situations in which they are involved, and which they symbolise.

Forgiveness

I want to make one or two other observations about the politics of forgiveness. First of all, I believe in it because I believe that forgiveness is the Jesus way and that Jesus is the cosmic Lord and the author of all creation. His ways are therefore stamped into the way the universe and all within it, including all on planet Earth, are to function and work. And if the way of forgiveness is morally and spiritually valid for individuals, I see no reason why it should not be so for groups, tribes or nations.

Second, I interpret the state – its laws and history and politics – in the light of the cosmic centrality of Christ, in whom all men and women find their humanity and their best way of relating to God and to one another. (See also chapter 12.)

In other words just as there is no individual and personal Christian faith that is not focused in Jesus Christ, there cannot be any Christian message in the socio-political context that is not grounded in him and in his way. In him we see matchlessly displayed an eternal, all-forgiving love, which must be the way for us, his creatures.

As I believe that in the personal realm we are called on to forgive those who have injured us (whether they have repented or not), so also I believe that in the socio-political realm it is valid to call for the attitude of forgiveness to those who have socially or politically wounded us, even before they have repented and ushered in the mechanisms of justice. While true reconciliation cannot happen (as we shall see in the next section) until justice is in place and the two sides have really found each other, nevertheless forgiveness is something which we send out to our enemy unilaterally and unconditionally. It will often be the signal and the means by which the enemy is freed to move towards us in repentance and restitution which usher in a new day of justice and equity for all.

Alan Torrance, the Scottish theologian, puts it this way: 'It is because this [the attitude of acceptance] is a character of forgiveness, that forgiveness is logically prior to repentance on a proper understanding of grace . . . and never conditional upon repentance.'[7]

The point is that, as the ethicist and social thinker David Atkinson has said,

> forgiveness is a dynamic concept of change. It refuses to be trapped into fatalistic determinism. It acknowledges the reality of evil, wrong and injustice, and it seeks to respond to wrong in a way that is creative of new possibilities. Forgiveness signals an approach to wrong in terms, not of peace at any price, nor of a destructive intention to destroy the wrong-doer, but of a willingness to seek to reshape the future in the light of the wrong, in the most creative way possible.[8]

In a nutshell, the difficulty of it all does not excuse us from the obligation of it all.

Said Martin Luther King at the height of the Civil Rights struggle:

> We must develop and maintain the capacity to forgive. He who is devoid of the power to forgive is devoid of the power to love. There is some good in the worst of us and some evil in the best of us. When we discover this, we are less prone to hate our enemies . . . Forgiveness is not just an occasional act; it is a permanent attitude.[9]

In the light of all this, it is perhaps worth noting the power of the symbolic, and asking whether certain pilgrimages of repentance and forgiveness are not in order if the South African trauma is to be resolved and a South African tragedy to be averted.

For example, what if a delegation of British church and

political leaders were to come to South Africa to ask of their counterparts here forgiveness for the British part in this nation's history in generating that fierce Afrikaner national-ism that finally produced the policy of apartheid? And might not certain influential Afrikaner political and church leaders make similar pilgrimages to the blacks, in order to ask forgiveness for what they have done to blacks over the centuries, and most particularly in the last fifty years? And might not some South African English leaders go both to the Afrikaners and to the blacks in pilgrimages of repentance and forgiveness? (From the Afrikaners forgiveness is needed for example, for the imperialism of the past; and from blacks forgiveness is needed for economic exploitation and political apathy.) And might not an Inkatha delegation and a United Democratic Front delegation thus face each other in repent-ance and forgiveness in order to end the mutual massacres and devastation to one another which is currently taking place in some of Natal's townships?

Far-fetched? I don't think so. Not if the Holy Spirit works.

The parties themselves may not be able to get to this place alone. So then, maybe the church of Jesus Christ in South Africa and beyond should rise to the glorious destiny of being facilitators and mediators in this process.

But the church will never rise to such an assignment unless it can indeed accept the validity of love as a political virtue.

THE POLITICS OF LOVE MEANS ACCEPTING LOVE AS A POLITICAL VIRTUE

In this connection a brief historical reflection is instructive.

The political history of the eighteenth and nineteenth centuries was profoundly affected by two men who came to a love of Christ and, thereby, of their fellow men. One was William Wilberforce (1759–1833); the other was Lord Anthony Ashley, better known as the seventh Earl of Shaftes-bury (1801–1885). Both men demonstrated that love, far from being too sentimental to affect the tough political world, is in fact the greatest political virtue of all.

For Wilberforce, his love of Christ and his love of people

drove him to labour relentlessly for some fifty years in the British parliament to secure the abolition of slavery. Love of Christ and of people bred in him a profound sense of human dignity and value, and this was the primary motivation in his epic crusade.

Beyond that, says one of his biographers, 'Wilberforce believed that England's destiny lay safest in the hands of men of clear Christian principle and that submission to Christ was a man's most important *political* as well as religious decision.'[10]

Indeed, for Wilberforce and others who were caught up in the eighteenth-century Wesleyan revival, Christian love led naturally into a sense of *responsibility* to care politically for the poor, the broken and the defenceless. While not all were guilty, all were responsible. Christian love gave birth to 'a moral sentiment that permanently changed England's attitude to distant and defenceless peoples and to her own brutal and degraded masses at home'.[11] Love was no sloppy irrelevance: it was the engine of change.

In Shaftesbury's case the well-springs of Christian love were profoundly moved by the plight of children (as young as six years old) who were forced to work more than ten hours a day, sometimes almost naked, down mines in unimaginably awful conditions.

Shaftesbury said he took up the issue 'as a matter of *conscience*, and as such I am determined to carry it through . . . I cannot feel by halves . . . I take it I suffer very often much more than the people do themselves.'[12]

The horrors and misery of these and many other social and political abuses overwhelmed him and drove him on to ever-more untiring efforts to change the political structures which produced these aberrations.

In consequence Shaftesbury got this whole situation not only before the British parliament, but before the conscience of the nation.

With the consequences of the politics of love historically evident, we dare not deny that love is a relevant virtue for public and political office – it is the highest and noblest.

Edgar Brookes once wrote:

Love is a political virtue – shall we call it the unfound political virtue? And one to which we must strive to approximate. If justice is a political virtue, then so is love. Justice, too, can never be more than an approximation in states as we know them, but that does not mean that it must not be tried. The world languishes because love is being tried so little. It is imperative that it must be admitted into the field of political thought: only so will at least an attempt at an approximation be made.[13]

As far as the modern philosophy of politics goes, Brookes asks: 'But has the exclusion of love been so wise? Have fear and suspicion and commonsense brought us very far? Can we not [therefore] apply love in public life?'[14]

What we are really doing here is committing ourselves to putting love into structures – which is what justice is all about. It is also the Hebrew concept of *shalom* which we mentioned in chapter 16. As Jim Punton says:

For the individual, Shalom is soundness of being in every way; between persons it means relationships of trust, openness and caring that enable wholeness; in groups and society it involves social justice so that no sectional interest oppresses or exploits another; for nature it means living interdependently and responsibly, without pollution or destruction.[15]

The implications of love as a political virtue

The implications of this are several. First of all, the politics of love and shalom, which obviously involves a desire for the well-being of each person, *leads to the idea of basic rights for each person.*

Professor Stephen Mott of Gordon Conwell Seminary has noted that the concept of human rights reflects three aspects of love – 'love as equality, in that rights are possessed by all: love as respect, in that rights help preserve human dignity: love as perception of common needs, in that rights work to protect the minimal conditions for life together'.[16]

Second, the politics of love also *involves caring for the needs of the other man in his infinite possibilities as a human being.* We saw this vividly illustrated in Wilberforce and Shaftesbury. In South Africa the sight of the horrendous effects of apartheid should arouse in every white's heart an uncompromising passion to see it ended fully, uncompromisingly and with no half-measures. The politics of love requires it.

Third, the politics of love *involves redress*. Again, Professor Stephen Mott says:

> The goal of redress is to return people to a normal level of advantage and satisfaction in the community, particularly with respect to the capacity to earn a living and to have a reasonably happy life . . . When the number of sufferers becomes too large, private charity cannot cope with the ills of society; love then requires structural measures to achieve social justice.[17]

All this requires us to grasp that racism and discrimination, which violate the politics of love, are not just a matter of attitudes but a matter of structures. If a political system makes one group dominate, the politics of love will protest. More than that, the politics of love will declare it a heresy when something other than love is set at the heart of a nation's political life – and especially when that is defended in the name of scripture. Then the politics of love are twisted into ideology, which is the moral and theological justification of vested interest rather than the well-being of the other person or group.

Love and the law-maker

In his book *An Interpretation of Christian Ethics*, Reinhold Niebuhr recognises that it is very difficult for the law-maker to build love into his laws in an ideal way.

Niebuhr emphasises that perhaps the best way forward for Christians is to define their political ideals in terms of *freedom* and *equality*. Our highest good, therefore, will consist in *freedom* to develop the essential potentialities of our natures without hindrance. This is what law-makers who embrace the Christian ideal must recognise. Summarising Niebuhr, I have elsewhere written and commented in these terms:

Since people live in social contexts where other human beings are also competing with them for the opportunity of a fuller life, the other highest good is *equality*. Otherwise we have no means of deciding between conflicting human interests except that which equates the worth of all the different competing individuals. Of course we will never achieve perfect equality in our societies, but Christians at least should never rest in an acceptance of inequalities.

On the other hand, both the governing and the governed need to recognise that the principles of equality and of justice are in fact only approximations of the law of love in the kind of imperfect world we have. That insight should slow us down a bit in terms of facile and crude judgements on everything our political leaders do. Perhaps that is why Paul so strongly urged Christians to pray for political leaders (1 Tim. 2:1–2). I have found it a challenge and a blessing, as I have said before, to seek to pray regularly and sometimes daily for six or seven South African political leaders, including the President – men who span the total spectrum from status quo to revolutionary extremist. My prayer is that each may find 'the mind of Christ'. If all seven converged on that 'mind', we'd have a solution for South Africa.[18]

Mutual care, concern, unselfishness, conscience, worth, political vigilance and insight into structural injustice are all part of the politics of love.

But what does this all mean practically, especially for the Christian who wants to see his society reconciled and healed?

To that we must now turn.

21   Love in Structures

No one can think clearly or sensibly about the vast and
burning topic of the value of a constitution without in the
first instance making up his mind upon the fundamental
issue. Does he value the State above the citizen or the
citizen above the State?

Winston Churchill

Cheap reconciliation means tearing faith and justice asunder, driving a wedge between the vertical and the horizontal. It suggests that we can have peace with God without
having justice in our mutual relationships.

David J Bosch

At the present time your plenty will supply what they need,
so that in turn their plenty will supply what you need. Then
there will be equality.

2 Corinthians 8:14

One cannot in these times go to any meeting where black
South African intellectuals are present without hearing the
word 'structures' mentioned. Nothing irritates these blacks
more than Christian talk of love, reconciliation or reform
which does not connect meaningfully and substantially to the
structural issue. For they feel held down, restricted and
oppressed not just by white individuals but most especially by
white political, social and economic *structures*. They are only
too aware that Nationalist Afrikaners worked their theology
into the structures which currently dominate the South
African political landscape.

Thoughts, ideas and philosophies can indeed be enshrined
in structures. This emboldens me to believe that the demands

446 THE PASSING SUMMER

of Christian love can also be enshrined in a set of structures which will enable South Africans of all backgrounds to live peaceably together.

In the last chapter we looked at five principles required by the politics of love. I now want to look at five further principles related to structural issues. In so doing, I note that the ordinary Christian cannot offer to the professional politician anything more than Christian principles to guide him. It is beyond both our expertise and our province to tell him how to work these out in practical politics. In that sense, Christian laypeople must leave politics to the politicians.

THE POLITICS OF LOVE MEANS WORKING FOR STRUCTURAL RECONCILIATION

In chapter 15, I talked about reconciliation in personal terms. But if South Africa is to be healed by the politics of love we have to grasp that true reconciliation must also have strong structural components.

Many who see reconciliation as the answer to South Africa perceive it as just a matter of being nice to one another, or of securing peace at any price, or of negotiating some sort of truce when the stronger party dominates the weaker party and extracts their compliance. It is especially seen as something which must arrive inevitably without conflict. But once we understand some of the structural dynamics of reconciliation it becomes evident that conflict and violence can indeed end up being the tragic way to ultimate reconciliation, simply because the absence of political concession has given the underdog no other way of getting to the conference table as an equal.

Far better is to accord one another full equality now, and then choose together to take the non-violent but costly way through to changing current political structures. Only in this way can social reconciliation in this country finally become both possible and real.

The point is that there can be no genuine reconciliation if the cause of the conflict in South Africa is not tackled. This means distinguishing between alienation on a personal level between individuals and alienation on a socio-political level between groups. In individual alienation, an offending party may apologise and then receive the forgiveness of the offended and a happy relationship be restored. But on the level of socio-political structures, a conflict is not just the result of a lack of love between individuals, but of a clash between large groups of people due to different kinds of structural imbalance and social maladjustment inherent in the social order. So we see that reconciliation here depends not only on repentance and forgiveness of individuals, but also on structural adjustments which restore social and political balance.

In the simplest of terms this means that the top dog in the social situation has to climb down and give others a chance to compete and participate in society on an equal and dignified footing.

The South African theologian Klaus Nurnberger loves to point to 2 Corinthians 8:9, where the apostle Paul writes: 'For you know the grace of our Lord Jesus Christ, that though he was rich, yet for your sakes he became poor, so that you through his poverty might become rich.' Thus in his humility Jesus came down that we might come up. Nurnberger adds:

> Christ thus let us into the secret of horizontalising our relationships. We can easily substitute 'powerful' for 'rich' and 'weak' for 'poor' and the sentence still applies: he who is at the top moves down to enable others to move up. The idea is that the latter move up so that they too can move down with Christ so that others can move up. Only when you have, can you give; only when you are up can you move down. Those who can afford to carry the burden at any point in time, are invited to do so. God himself set the example.

Nurnberger also notes that apartheid appears to divide the population in a horizontal fashion, so that the system can be rationalised into 'separate but equal'. This slogan overlooks what happens in the power base at the centre. There one finds that the division is not horizontal but is actually vertical. Whites are *above* and blacks are *below* the barrier. So:

> Being in an elitist position, it is in the interest of Whites to close the door underneath themselves, both to keep challengers to

their position at bay and to keep weaker members of their own group from dropping out. Racial segregation constitutes, for them, a platform for further advance. It is an opportunity too good to miss. But Blacks want to advance as well. However, because they find themselves below the line, they hit their heads against the ceiling of racial segregation. So the latter is against their vital interests – whether political, economic, structural or whatever. It is interesting to note that the Afrikaners, in their day, put up a violent fight against the ceiling created by the British rule. All of us tend to believe in barriers underneath ourselves, not above ourselves.[1]

Pictorially this insight looks like this:

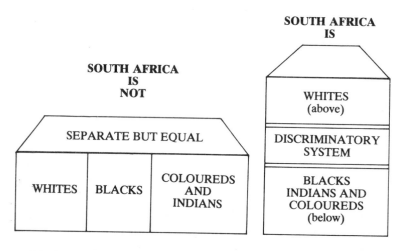

Obviously, for this ceiling over the blacks to be removed, it will take a change of heart on the part of whites to remove it. This implies an adjustment of the political structures. In fact, what reconciliation really means and involves is a change in both parties which leads to a change in the relationship between them. This requires from all concerned for reconciliation a confrontation with the evil or wrong which is preventing it. It also necessitates an embracing, both personally and politically, of those processes of change which will bring this about.

What this underlines is that peacemaking, reconciliation and establishing justice can never really be separated. Jesus explains peacemaking by saying: 'If your brother sins against you, go and show him his fault' (Matt 18:15). There is no real peace between the brothers until the fault is dealt with. Likewise socially and politically there is no peace until justice is restored.

For this to happen, bold initiatives will have to come from people of goodwill both among the oppressed and among the privileged. Those who see themselves as oppressed and on the receiving end of unjust structures obviously have to put pressure on these structures to change, and they have to look at the best ways of applying this pressure.

The privileged, for their part, have to do everything in their power to begin working on the dismantling of unjust structures. This will mean not only work at the top level politically but also serious attempts to fight the basic attitudes underlying these structures.

The point is that we have to realise that sin is not just a personal and individual thing, but it can become a social attitude which becomes imbedded in a culture and in its political and economic structures. So just having goodwill towards alienated people on either side of a political struggle is not enough. If car accidents keep happening at a crossroads the need is not for more hospitals and ambulances but for civic leaders to authorise a good set of working traffic lights: structural change is required.

Unless this concern for structural change is present, the call for reconciliation, as Klaus Nurnberger has noted,

> can only be construed by the weaker section (the victim of the injustice) as an attempt to make the weaker section acquiesce so that the stronger section can continue to exploit its power at the expense of the weaker – as a clever trick to legitimate the continuation of the injustices.
>
> Under such circumstances even the word reconciliation is suspect in the weaker section although its members may be longing for fellowship and peace.

Since the chain, as Nurnberger shows, goes from injustice to conflict to rage and violence, it is useless to try and overcome the hatred with reconciliation unless its mainspring is tackled.

Graphically the problem looks like this:

INJUSTICE   ----------   CONFLICT   ----------   RAGE & VIOLENCE

And the solution in the sociopolitical realm looks like this:

JUSTICE   ----------------   PEACE   ----------------   RECONCILIATION

In spite of the huge difficulties of achieving the solution depicted above, everyone in a land like South Africa, and especially its Christians, must labour now to keep the spirit of reconciliation alive by persistently seeking to build bridges across the chasms of personal and social life.

Such efforts constitute the basic building-blocks in the process of finally achieving reconciliation and justice in the nation's structures.

In elaborating on the implications of this sort of thinking the National Initiative for Reconciliation has stated:

> Rejection of injustices and repression does not mean rejection of those who are regarded as part of the unjust and oppressive system . . . The way to wean them from an unacceptable order is to assure them of their place in a restructured society. The NIR therefore tries to explore ways of (a) visibly standing with the victims of a sinful system, (b) overcoming this unacceptable system and (c) reassuring those who find themselves entangled in this system of their future in the new community.

Viewed in these terms it is clear that we are a very long way from structural reconciliation in South Africa. The white ruling class and the leaders of the black majority are miles apart. The present status quo is contained only by military force, legal restrictions and general exhaustion. Perceptions of what the struggle is all about vary on all sides. Yet neither South African Christians nor Christians in the wider world community dare give up on the situation or allow the social impasse to be seen as a match for the power of God's love as it is worked out in this confusing cauldron in terms of the politics of love and forgiveness.

We must not allow our dreams of harmony and ultimate reconciliation to die, nor must we become dispirited and irresolute in tackling the real difficulties which have created the alienations.

Part of the problem is that most of us whites are really reluctant to acknowledge the awfulness of the apartheid system and the desperate pain which it has inflicted on blacks. So we are slow to face our guilt in creating the system and sustaining it. Blacks for their part find it difficult to concede that white fears and apprehensions about black rule have any validity.

But if, in God's name, by Christ's grace and by the power of the Holy Spirit, even a moderate percentage of South African Christians could rise to the moral demands of the politics of love with their great cost in terms of structural reconciliation, we could yet find a way through for the glory of God, the blessing of the continent of Africa and the inspiration of the world.

THE POLITICS OF LOVE MEANS PUTTING LOVE INTO A CONSTITUTIONAL FRAMEWORK

Any reflection on the politics of love obviously requires that sooner or later the great challenge has to be faced of putting love into a constitutional framework. This is to ensure that the principles of love are worked out structurally in society. For what is justice other than power implementing love? And how is justice to be secured on the widest basis for the greatest number other than by entrenching it within the structural framework of a constitution which controls and governs a nation's life?

In the first instance, a constitution is nothing more than a piece of paper with some ideas on it about how a society should be structured and run.

Clearly, as we have already noted elsewhere, the strength of a constitution lies in the commitment to those words written on that piece of paper. We observed that the American constitution is strong because the American nation as a whole is committed to what is written on that piece of paper. The South African constitution, by contrast, is very weak because the majority of the nation is not committed to it or willing to live under its ideas.

However, a constitution needs to be more than strong: it needs to have goodness and love enshrined within it. It needs to entrench and safeguard the highest and best standards of justice, dignity, human value and equity which man can bring forth.

A good constitution also has to take seriously and realistically the sinfulness and fallenness of man. This means regulating with checks and balances the perennial inclination of people in power to drift into the abuse of power. A good constitution will work to promote that higher reason in us which helps subdue the savage and ignorant regions of our make-up.

When the American Founding Fathers developed a constitution which involved considerable transfer of power away from the centre and into individual states, it was because of a theological presupposition which recognised the sinfulness and fallenness of man, and therefore his inclination to abuse power. The greater his power, the greater the likelihood of his abuse of it; beyond that, the greater the likelihood of his corruption, until finally comes absolute corruption stemming from absolute power.

Positively, the American Founding Fathers wanted to enshrine godly values in their constitutional framework. Negatively, they wished to express a healthy biblical fear of the autocratic domination by any one man or group of men. Hence their strong restraints on any use of arbitrary power.

If in our South African situation we were to think of some of the godly principles which need to be enshrined in a constitution in terms of the dictates of the politics of love, we might consider some of the following.

First of all, there are those principles which flow from the nature of God himself as we see this in the Bible. Pride of place must go to where the Bible starts, with *God as creator*. Having created human beings in his image, all are equally valuable, and their value should be reflected in the way a constitution is set up. There will be no structural abuse of human dignity and value. Nor will individuals or groups of individuals be treated preferentially in a way which offends or violates their equality of value. A godly constitution will therefore avoid all discrimination.

The scriptures depict *God as fatherly and loving*, which means that the spirit of mercy, care and protection for his children is integral to his make-up. In constitutional terms, this clearly implies the merciful protection and care of those least able to protect and care for themselves.

The scriptures also present us with a *God of justice*. This is clear in both the Old Testament and in the New. This would speak constitutionally of equality of protection for all before the law. Such concerns involve protecting the rule of law, namely the right to stand innocent until proven guilty; the right to confront one's accuser; the right of all to representation in the courts; and the possibility of winning one's case even if it is against the state.

The Bible as a whole and the politics of love as a concept call for us to protect the rights of the individual and to set him above the state in importance and value. Winston Churchill once wrote:

> No one can think clearly or sensibly about the vast and burning topic of the value of a constitution without in the first instance making up his mind upon the fundamental issue. Does he value the State above the citizen or the citizen above the State? Does the Government exist for the individual, or do the individuals exist for the Government?[2]

He adds:

> The question is whether a fixed constitution is a bulwark or a fetter. I incline to the side of those who would regard it as a bulwark, and that I rank the citizen higher than the State and regard the State as useful only insofar as it preserves his inherent rights.[3]

Laurie Ackermann, Professor of Human Rights Law at the University of Stellenbosch, has stressed that the rights of people to enjoy their own culture or practice or use their own language should be protected as *individual* rights. Group rights, he says, should simply be the aggregate of a particular group's individual rights. In this sense, and only in this sense, does the idea of group rights have a validity not open to abuse.

Professor Ackermann comments: 'If, however, the protection of group rights means the entrenchment of existing privileges and restrictions such as, for example, superior residential areas, superior government schools, superior hospitals and so forth, such a concept would be wholly at variance with universal, international, human rights norms.'[4]

Of course in South Africa we are polarised by group rights, and perhaps a great breakthrough would come if we were able to move away from this in a new constitution. After all, in a heterogeneous society, individuals can and will associate themselves freely in groupings to protect their individual rights on a collective basis. But the focus should be kept more on the individual than the group, thereby minimising the mindset of group confrontation and group conflict.

St Paul's great words have relevance here: 'If it is possible, as far as it depends on you, live at peace with everyone' (Rom 12:18).

The search for peace *must* finally find consummation in the working out of a constitution which will enshrine and protect the peace we all long for. Obviously none of the principles mentioned in this section dictate a particular form of government or constitution, and we all know that nothing utopian will ever arrive, but by aiming for a constitutional framework which has the concerns of love and justice at its heart we are certainly embarking on the right track.

Of course both the processes and the final result are fragile in the extreme, and can be jeopardised by bad, power-hungry or selfish people. But if in the democratic spirit which lets everyone into the process, we are able to achieve finally in South Africa a constitution which protects human rights and which is based on universal adult suffrage and strong independent law courts, then we will in our generation have achieved something for which our children and our children's children will rise to bless us.

At first blush we might seem to have more than adequate grounds for profound discouragement, given the huge polarisations and anguished history of South Africa. But let us take heart from the fact that even George Washington – when he went to the Constitutional Convention of 1787 – lamented as he did so: 'I almost despair of seeing a favourable issue to the proceedings of the Convention.'[5] But they won through. In

South Africa we can do the same. And we must enshrine it in a constitutional framework.

THE POLITICS OF LOVE MEANS WORKING LOVE INTO ECONOMIC STRUCTURES

The Bible, as I understand it, has no specific economic system to promote, any more than it has a constitutional system to present as God's only way. But there are some principles to guide us especially here in South Africa as we look to the economic future of this land.

To me it is very crucial that our economy stays strong, so that not only may our expanding population be satisfactorily fed, housed, clothed and educated, but also so that political change and its complex processes may be adequately financed.

To let the economy of this land be shattered, to allow all foreign investment to flee, to diminish employment prospects for the thousand people a day coming into the job market and to tear ourselves to pieces by violence, political convulsion and economic slow down, and then finally to imagine that a socio-economic phoenix will rise magically from the ashes to bless the new South Africa – all that is to me just political and economic fantasy. All that would happen is that the new political and constitutional dispensation would before long collapse under the economic stresses, strains and eventual chaos around it.

The economy must keep developing. But what we can't have is a situation here where the rich keep getting richer and the poor keep getting poorer.

So then, what scriptural principles can serve as guidelines for an economic order relevant to this context, especially when we bear in mind that the ultimate and basic purpose of economic life is to 'liberate us from being dominated by scarcity and to provide us with the conditions necessary to a fully human existence'?[6]

Christian criteria for economic systems

There are perhaps six Christian criteria which are particularly noteworthy.

1. *Does the system take material adequacy and absence of scarcity seriously as a basic ingredient in human well-being?*

This does not mean 'Does the system make people wealthy?' but 'Does it labour for financial adequacy and the elimination of poverty?' In South Africa, which is located on a Third World continent, this has to be the posture of economic planners.

2. *Does the economic system fit God's intentions for man's good?*

God is always concerned for the good of *all*. Does the economic system of a nation share that concern in its onward rush for economic progress? Does it remember the poor and the economically weak?

3. *Is the system committed to the basic unity of the human family?*

Does the system for example work against divisive tendencies between people or groups of people? And does it support and strengthen the basic unit of the family?

4. *Does the system include belief in the value of each individual human being?*

Is it committed to individual freedom and opportunity for individual creative development and expression? Fulfilled individuals produce a fulfilled society.

5. *Does it consider human beings to be equal? And if so, does this guide the formulation of economic objectives and policies?*

This is admittedly difficult to work out practically, but at the very least it means management seeing workers not just as impersonal cogs in a *money-orientated* production process but as valued participants in a *people-orientated* production process.

6. *Does it take the universality of human sinfulness*
   seriously and does it make realistic provision for the
   effects of self-centredness in its proposed policies?

This is not to eliminate economic incentive but to curtail greed.

If these six criteria are taken into account two major challenges face South African economic thinkers – how to share the cake more fairly, and how to expand it.

In the first case the challenge relates to bringing about a fairer distribution of wealth, land, resources and the means of production. If the New Testament is taken at all seriously, it is evident that the economics of the converted involved a greater degree of fellowship, sharing and mutual caring than they had ever known in the days before their Christian commitment.

The early Christians shared their lives both spiritually and economically (see Acts 2:42–47). Though this was very difficult to maintain, nevertheless their attempts show that the accumulation of huge wealth among some while others languished in abject poverty was very much contrary to the generous principles they sought to follow. Paul spells out some of these principles in 2 Corinthians 8 – his famous chapter on financial giving. For example: 'At the present time your plenty will supply what they need, so that in turn their plenty will supply what you need. Then there will be equality' (vs 14).

However, the apostle is not concerned here to see everyone equal in poverty, but rather everyone equal in financial adequacy. This militates against some becoming laden with luxuries while others live crushed without basic necessities. In South Africa a top five per cent of whites own eighty-eight per cent of personally owned wealth. In the United States a top five per cent owns only forty-four per cent of personally owned wealth. So the South African top five per cent are streets 'ahead' of even their American counterparts.

Economic reform must go hand in glove with political reform. So must land reform. No longer may eighty-four per cent of the people own only thirteen per cent of the land while sixteen per cent own eighty-seven per cent! Massive land reform and redistribution, such as took place in Japan after the war and on which in many ways its economic miracle is built, will be necessary in South Africa before final solutions are reached. (Incidentally, the Japanese programme, carried out under pressure from General MacArthur and the occupation authorities, resulted in the transfer of ownership of thirty-five per cent of the total cultivated area of Japan. It involved the purchase of over thirty million different pieces of land from two million families and their resale to over five million families. So it can be done. South Africa must face this.)

Such realities have led *Leadership South Africa*'s editor, Hugh Murray, to say: 'Whites must take a leap of faith and accept that their lot in the immediate future involves considerable sacrifice.'[7] The road ahead is not easy.

So equal job opportunities, equal access to the labour market, equal pay for equal work, equal access to land and resource acquisition – all this should be provided for in an economic system reflecting the politics of love. Incidentally, all this was called for in the momentous Dutch Reformed Synod of 1986.

This brings us to the second challenge – to expand the cake.

To avoid a sharing of abject economic poverty and misery, as is found in many African countries where so called 'African Socialism' is the economic way, it is necessary for economic thinkers to grapple as much with the processes of wealth creation as of wealth distribution – though this must not involve raping the earth or denuding it of its God-given resources as we seek to progress economically.

In a 1986 interview, the South African industrialist Anton Rupert said:

Many countries in Africa are beginning to realise that the creation of wealth should get preference to the distribution of wealth as a first step towards meaningful economic and social development . . . The process of wealth creation, therefore, will have to be increased and a prerequisite for this to materialise is the removal of all unnecessary regulations and controls in order to free our people economically and to allow them to bring about innovations and to offer their labour wherever the demand is greatest. The moment opportunities are diminished and people are deprived of the responsibility of their destiny, the way is paved for inefficiency and stagnation and for a dull, unimaginative form of survival.[8]

Faced with the twin challenges of sharing the cake and expanding it, one has to ask which economic system best accomplishes both these goals.

First of all, for the Christian in South Africa a pure, unrestrained, rampant capitalism – in other words an economic freedom to operate without any central control – is immediately problematic. For this feeds rampant acquisitiveness, selfishness and greed, and often furthers gross exploitation of others. One cannot embrace the unrestrained sovereignty of the market and the conviction that the market, and the market alone, determines how resources should be allocated. There has to be a sense of the individual existing within the society and moved by a sense of economic responsibility towards others in that society.

Second, at the other end of the spectrum, a Marxist economic system where there is full control at the centre and no freedom for people to develop economic incentive, show economic initiative or enterprise, or even to take issue and to criticise, is also unacceptable.

The exclusion of both an unrestrained capitalism and a centralised Marxist economic system would suggest that some form of mixed economy must emerge for South Africa. This is confirmed by Professor James Leatt, a South African economist, who stresses the need (rightly I believe) to avoid blind allegiance to either a capitalist creed or to a socialist one.[9] This well reflects the kind of economic concerns which both the scriptures and the politics of love would set before us as we look to the economic future of this nation.

THE POLITICS OF LOVE MEANS PRAYERFULLY THINKING OUR WAY INTO A NEW ORDER

For the politics of love to be worked into economic structures and into a constitutional framework, and for it to effect structural reconciliation, requires a new brand of thinking and acting.

Right now South Africa risks destroying itself by wrong thinking and by its reluctance to thrust itself into a truly national meeting of minds out of which a change of direction and a real renewal of structures could come.

The politics of love, however, requires us to love God, our land and each other with our *minds* as well as our other faculties. God's way to both our personal and our national salvation is still: 'Come now, let us *reason* together' (Isa 1:18). A prayerful, calm national reasoning together under God is an urgent necessity if a new order and a new day are to arrive in this perplexing place.

Grasp the importance of thinking

What people do, as we have noted previously, is profoundly affected by what they think. What is happening in our heads determines our whole behaviour – morally, practically and politically. Conviction determines action. Right thinking is therefore of paramount importance: not only right thinking in you and me as individuals, but in all of us corporately. The need in South Africa most especially is for a meeting not only of forgiving hearts but of creative minds – minds resolved to work out *together*, prayerfully, and under God, the best way forward.

This means avoiding knee-jerk reactions which are controlled more by emotional heat than rational, reflective light. There is no national salvation for us in South Africa save in finding the *mind of Christ* for this nation. And that will involve attuning our minds to his by a creative and Christian interplay of thousands of minds in intellectual encounter.

Thomas Edison's wry observation, well illustrated in this land, is that 'there is no expedient to which men will not go to avoid the real labour of thinking'. This view was shared by Bertrand Russell when he bewailed that 'men fear thought as they fear nothing else on earth and more than ruin, more even than death'.

But we must think: it is imperative. Sir Frederick Catherwood, a member of the European Parliament, has written: 'There are times when a movement of Christian opinion is all that stands between a country and moral disaster.'[10] Movements of opinion, of thinking, of reflecting, of struggling intellectually for the best answer, can save a nation from moral or political disaster. Such a movement now could save South Africa, if South Africans take on a new readiness to think.

Be willing to change your mind

To grow intellectually, but more importantly, to find answers to complex problems, also means being willing to change one's mind and adjust one's thinking and embrace new and previously 'unthinkable' solutions.

An old Scottish prayer says: 'Grant, O God, that we may always be right, for Thou knowest we will never change our minds!' That mindset, currently prevalent among many South Africans, will lose us the day if we persist in it.

Be willing to reflect open-mindedly with others of contrary opinion

No chance of change, or of a rescuing movement of genuine Christian opinion, is even remotely possible unless people are willing – genuinely and open-mindedly – to struggle with others who hold contrary views so as to attempt to spawn new answers for a new day.

Edward J Perkins, an American black and the current USA ambassador to South Africa, has expressed his astonishment at being asked again and again by whites what blacks are thinking, and vice versa. 'Some day,' he says, 'I will just answer that question with a question of my own: "Why don't you ask each other?"'[11]

It is a good question, because that would inevitably involve blacks and whites in a genuine face-to-face encounter from which they could each learn much.

One good reason why it is crucial to meet and think things through with others who hold contrary opinions is that it breaks us out of the logjam, on both black and white sides, of prescriptive thinking about the future which tends to take the form: 'This is the answer I've worked out, and you can take it or leave it.'

Inevitably, when such an ultimatum is given, the other side 'leaves it', and so the two uncompromising and mutually incompatible prescriptive answers float off across the still-unbridged chasm into the political limbo.

Become part of a think-tank movement

How marvellous it would be if the willingness to think prayer-fully together could issue in a great think-tank movement across South Africa! In this thousands of people could begin to meet in groups to reflect and pray together about a way forward.

We noted early in this story (see chapter 7) that the South African Broederbond, which brought forth the apartheid policy as a consciously worked out system, was in effect a gigantic think-tank, comprising hundreds of cells whose thoughts and decisions were filtered back to a central controlling body.

If that was how the apartheid system was born, then perhaps therein lies the clue to the way it can be dismantled and a better system put in place which is more reflective of an agreed national consensus of all races.

Many in the Broederbond, I know, are rethinking matters, and from that much reform has come. But the debate has to widen to every nook and cranny of South African life, and to every race sector working in concert with the other.

If hundreds of heterogeneous cells, bringing together English and Afrikaner, black and white, young and old, could begin to meet, the first heart-beats of a saving movement of Christian political opinion and solution could begin to resonate in the chest of this nation.

These cells should meet first at the grass-roots level, feed-ing their thoughts and conclusions to their leadership net-work, whether in the church or at work or in some political grouping.

The process of think-tank encounter should also go on at a second-tier level (*i.e.* where senior leaders can feed their thinking to the very top, to which they would have access). And at the top the process would, one hopes, finally achieve consummation.

But one also needs to bear in mind some unfortunate human realities. For example, many at the top these days seem to be politically paralysed, while the grass-roots people in their turn seem stuck at the level of the passion of prejudice or the despair of helplessness. Many other ordinary people are also trapped in an unthinking fatalism which is enshrined in the popular South African heresy that 'Alles sal regkom' ('Everything will come right') – as if some indeterminate force will work magic on our behalf, without our concerted effort.

We must grasp that human progress is neither automatic nor inevitable. Social advance in history, as Martin Luther King once observed, does not 'roll on the wheels of inevitability'. In fact, he said, 'every step towards the goal of justice requires . . . tireless exertions . . . Without persistent effort, time itself becomes an ally of the insurgent and primitive forces of irrational emotionalism and social destruction. This is no time for apathy or complacency. This is a time for vigorous and positive action.'[12]

This could not be more true. But the vigorous and positive action has to be based on resolute, vigorous and positive reflection. The framework for this could be a think-tank movement at every level, where the chemistry of personal encounter and discussion finally brings the breakthrough we need.

Many in South Africa at this time feel hugely indebted to Hugh Murray, the editor of the distinguished magazine *Leadership*. The genius of this magazine is that it is the nearest thing to a national convention which we have going at this time! But its problem is that it is on paper! One reads the ideas and viewpoints of an extraordinary range of people. And this is most valuable. But the final elements of the change we need will come when all the people who meet in the pages of South Africa's *Leadership* magazine actually meet each other in the transforming and hugely creative intellectual encounter of personal meeting and exchange.

If Hugh Murray and his *Leadership* magazine have shown anything over the last few years, it is that South Africa certainly does not lack the human, intellectual, political, moral and spiritual resources to find a way through. The only problem is that these resources are currently operating independently of each other. Once they are put together, as part of a mighty think-tank movement in our nation, operating at top level, at second-tier level and at grass-roots level, the way will be opened for God to do and bring about a brand new thing.

The point is to make a fresh start. First steps are always the hardest. But once our feet are on the path and once the current paralysis of helplessness is overcome, we will be away. All that is required is resolution, some organisational steps to get going, Christian goodwill and a determination to forget and forgive the past, to unlock the present and to save the future.

Let shared reflection and prayer generate new relational building-blocks

If South Africans of conscience and concern were to begin to meet together in cells, think-tanks, brainstorming groups, *etc.*, they would not only find that they are moving to a new place which was intellectually more likely to bring forth productive answers, but they would start forging new relationships which are critical to the post-apartheid society. These need to be put in place at the grass-roots level, where people live and work. All kinds of paralysis would end if this happened widely.

Without such endeavours and without such relationships there can be no solid foundation for whatever new society finally replaces apartheid. Every time a church or organisation or local community takes steps to develop models of more just and participatory relationships some new building-blocks are put in place. These can constitute the foundation upon which the new South Africa will finally rise. So the small, informal, dialogue group, or think-tank or brainstorming cell or prayer group, is a mini-workshop bringing forth the relationships of tomorrow. On this principle also is built the vital Koinonia movement led by Professor Nico

Smith. This seeks to get whites and blacks together over meals and in one another's homes.

The key thing to ensure is that a network of relationships is established across all barriers. In this the Christian church is uniquely placed to play a critically important role, given that its membership spans the entire political spectrum from extreme left to far right. Imagine if we allowed the Holy Spirit to activate that network for the sake of the kingdom of God and the good of South Africa!

All of which brings us to one aspect of the church's contribution which should not be overlooked.

Every local church should make itself an agent of change

In all this the local South African church congregation has a great role to play in making itself a creative, godly and peaceful agent of change in the place where it is. Beyond that, every congregation could produce a mini think-tank which would struggle with some of the issues around us, including the structural – for people need to be prepared both intellectually and spiritually for structural change.

More significant still would be the result if every church study or fellowship group also made itself an *action group*, so that it met not only to pray, study or think, but to carry out certain practical initiatives of action (see Appendix 6). These groups could become *PRAC* groups, where PRAC stands for:

> *P*rayer
> *R*eflection
> *A*ction
> *C*onsolidation.

In any event, a great need in the South African church is for all clergy and Christian leaders to help their people intellectually, spiritually and practically to understand what it means to face the challenges of the society around them. This will often have to be preceded by helping people into an analysis of the social factors in our current situation which inhibit solution.

If this sort of thing caught on across South Africa,

especially on a non-racial basis, there would be no telling the creative and saving good which might come forth.

In any event, I remain convinced that at the end of the day it will be seen that the Christian church in South Africa had all the trump cards. Whether history will say that we played them aright – or in time – remains to be seen.

THE POLITICS OF LOVE MEANS TAKING THE LONG VIEW

Many times as my children have been growing up I have gone into their bedrooms at night while they were asleep and reflected: 'O God, what kind of world are these young people going to inherit here in South Africa unless we can turn this thing round?' And I have then prayed: 'O, Lord, help me at least for their sakes to do my bit, so that whatever comes down the line I can know I tried to bequeath them a place of happiness and stability and goodness and hope.' In this way I have prayed myself afresh into taking the long view.

This is really what the politics of love requires. It is in a sense an investment in Christian political principle which affirms that nothing which is morally right can ever in the long term be politically wrong. And this applies as much to political structures as to anything else. It affirms, moreover, that loving God and our neighbour is a risk we can and must take and whose consequences we can by faith leave with God.

As I wrote to a Cabinet Minister some years ago, the politics of love embraces as a central article of faith the principle that it is better to lose in the short term with that which must ultimately win, than to win in the short term with that which must ultimately lose.

The politics of selfishness, though perhaps winning in the short term, must finally lose. The universe, God, life, scripture and history ultimately side with the right and sanction it and bless it. It is right which finally works: wrong doesn't.

Doing the right thing, as I have already said, takes courage. But much more fearful is the prospect of letting the politics of selfishness run their dreadful course towards the abyss. We would be wise if we saw that the function of fear is to warn us of the consequences of wrong, rather than to make us afraid of the challenges of doing right.

So the politics of love calls us to take the long view. While politicians look to the next election, let us pray for statesmen who will look to the next generation – and the next, and the next.

In taking the long view, the *politics of love* therefore calls us away from political paralysis to the adventure of doing right in the political arena and seeing God work it all out. The politics of love pulls us in hope to the future and prises us loose from both the false optimism that we can do wrong and get away with it and from the futile fatalism which says that nothing we do can avert the advent of a South African armageddon.

The politics of love affirms that, God helping us, we can indeed not only burst free from the clutches of human folly, political logjam and historical inevitability, but in doing so we can actually await with excitement the surprises of God in history on our behalf. These will arrive as we embrace and demonstrate that the kingdom of God transcends all earthly kingdoms; the identity of 'Christian' transcends all earthly identities; the power of Christ and his gospel transcends all earthly powers; and his way transcends all earthly ways – it is the better way, and it is the way to a new society.

But in South Africa we will not get to even a remote approximation of that new society without *national repentance* and *a new social vision*. These are requirements now for the long view. New perspectives involving political details are not enough; a whole new social vision built round the politics of love and faith in the God of love is called for, along with a clear decisive turning from our former ways: history calls for it, God calls for it, common sense calls for it, the long view calls for it, South Africa calls for it.

It is in many ways a call to Christian obedience. South Africa stands at a crisis-point in its history as a Christian nation. And this crisis relates to the very heart of its self-understanding as a Christian nation. In a nutshell, the challenge is whether we will obey God or prepare for the national, long-term consequences of disobedience. In this we will remember that history is littered with the debris of nations which knew his way and then turned from it to their own.

For such nations the clocks of history and of opportunity run down. And their predictable lament goes forth to the world: 'The harvest is past, the summer has ended, and we are not saved' (Jer 8:20).

That need not be our fate if we would act in time. But it means acting now, with the long view in mind, before it is too late.

If we act in time, we will embrace the unprecedented moral and political opportunity of this place at this time. We will not despair, but will thank God, who has matched us with this hour and called us to the moral demands of the long view.

And if at any time on the journey we find the tempter pressing us to surrender hope or faith or love or forgiveness, then let the words of the sage get our feet again upon the path:

> Nothing that is worth doing can be achieved in a lifetime; therefore we must be saved by *hope*. Nothing which is true or beautiful or good makes complete sense in any immediate context of history; therefore we must be saved by *faith*. Nothing we do, however virtuous, can be accomplished alone. Therefore we must be saved by *love*. And nothing is as virtuous from our friend's or enemy's standpoint as it is from our own. Therefore we must be saved by the final form of love, which is *forgiveness*.[13]

Faith, hope, love and forgiveness stand as beacons – showing the long view for South Africa. But they also mark the pathway of forward movement for the here and now.

And yes, they are, I confess it, the signposts to a dream: the dream of a nation saved, the dream of the Beloved Country rising from the ashes and tears of lostness and ascending to the laughter of serving with honour once again in both the family of nations and the family of God.

But in case you are one of those who make little of dreams, let me petition you with the poet's words: 'I have spread my dreams under your feet. Tread softly, for you tread upon my dreams.'[14] And not only tread softly, but ask inwardly: 'Why should I look at what is, and only ask why, when I could dream of what is not yet, and ask *why not*?'

God said to Habakkuk: 'Write the vision . . . so he may run who reads it' (Hab 2:2, RSV). I have sought to do just that. May you who have read the vision be helped to run: and Godspeed.

Part Seven

POSTLUDE
(Maintaining eternal perspectives)

22   No Continuing City
(Maintaining eternal perspectives)

The only ultimate disaster that can befall us is to feel ourselves at home in this world.

Malcolm Muggeridge

The Church was created by the Resurrection and though it exists as the servant of God's world, its centre of gravity is not in this world.

F R Barry

For here have we no continuing city, but we seek one to come.

Hebrews 13:14, AV

Within about seventy years every reader of these pages (and their author!) will have kept that final appointment with the last enemy. We will all be in eternity – with Christ or without him, according to whether or not we took him as our Saviour upon this earth.

Then all our works, of whatever sort, will come before his eyes to see whether they are 'gold, silver, costly stones, wood, hay or straw' (1 Cor 3:12). 'The Day will bring it to light' and 'fire will test the quality of each man's work' (vs 13).

This lays upon us the weight of a wise man's words:

> Only one life,
> T'will soon be past.
> Only what's done for Christ
> Will last.

It also lays upon us right now, amidst all our best endeavours upon earth and on the earth's behalf, the imperative to keep our eyes tirelessly on heaven and endlessly on heaven's Lord. For if we do not live under the aspect of eternity we will be corrupted into thinking that earth is our home, and we will be seduced into false reactions and into mistaken modes of going about things.

THE PRECARIOUS EQUILIBRIUM

In these pages I have sought to bear in mind that we have been taught to pray and work so that God's kingdom will come and his purpose will be done here on earth as it is in heaven. Consequently, earth and what is done on earth have rightly occupied the content and thought of this book.

But we must never forget our Saviour's other word: 'My kingdom is not of this world' (John 18:36).

In his great high priestly prayer to his heavenly Father he acknowledged of his early disciples, as of all others since, that 'they are not of the world any more than I am of the world' (John 17:14). That said, though, he could not, would not and did not pray that we should be taken *out of* the world, but only that we would be protected from 'the evil one' (John 17:15) while we do the Father's business in the world into which he sends us (John 17:18).

To be sure, our Saviour knew that being *in* the world but not *of it* would require ceaseless and prayerful precision in keeping that precarious equilibrium – otherwise we would fall into the chasm of catastrophe whereby the church, in refusing to be kept from the evil one, does earth's business in earth's way and is loved by the earth for it.

Jesus was clear that if we were in the world but not of it, we would be 'hated' (John 17:14) by the world. From where, then, comes this earthly favour in which the church is often held by worldly people? Have we lost our balance and fallen fatally to the ground, so that the world, though pleased to praise us when we do its bidding, is left without the vision of God's eternal realm beyond?

KEEPING THE ETERNAL PERSPECTIVE

It has been said that 'if men indeed exist for the glory of God, then their final end and their destiny as persons is not to be found in this passing world . . .'[1] It lies at the heart of the Christian worldview that we have been given 'new birth into a living hope through the resurrection of Jesus Christ from the dead, and into an inheritance that can never perish, spoil or fade – kept in heaven for [us]' (1 Pet 1:3–4). This perception is pivotal, for it alerts us to the fact that, though created by the resurrection to exist as God's servant in and for the world, the church nevertheless has its centre of gravity outside this world.

Several things follow from this.

First, *we are citizens of two cities*. Our earthly citizenship is temporary, for here indeed we are only 'aliens and strangers' (Heb 11:13) who are obliged to live 'making it clear' (Heb 11:14, RSV) – and how little we actually make it clear! – that we are seeking and desiring 'a better country – a heavenly one, whose architect and builder is God' (Heb 11:14–15, 10).

Indeed without a vision of eternity we cannot get a true hold on time, and without seeing the heavenly country we miss even the earthly one. So we have no right to accustom ourselves to this world as if it were a destination rather than part of a journey. We are in two cities and are not permitted to abandon either. Though involved in the material history of this world and in caring for it, we do so as representatives of another order. We become an outcrop of the kingdom of God on earth, and we not only serve notice on the world that there is more to reality than meets the eye, but we show the truth that 'because we love something else more than this world, we love even this world better than those who know no other'.[2]

This puts a prayer upon my heart for every reader of these pages, and for myself too, that

> . . . in a season of calm weather,
>   Though inland far we be,
> Our souls have sight of that immortal sea
>   Which brought us hither.[3]

Second, having our centre of gravity in eternity, we must know as Christians that in those proper though precarious labours related to the political, *all professed solutions to the woes of the world will be but temporary.* They will also be spoilt by the sin and short-sightedness which affect both the world and us.

Apartheid and all its works will pass away. So will every answer which replaces it, whether better and nobler or yet more sinful and worse.

Such an eternal perspective will make us avoid both the folly of putting second things first and the arrogance of professing 20:20 vision on what should or should not be done on earth. This will end all imaginings that our funny little obsessions and proposals have the automatic sanction of the One whose thoughts are as high above ours as the heavens are high above the earth. Many undoubtedly will not avoid these mistakes. Even so, we will take joy in knowing that to seek on earth the greatest happiness and the fullest freedom of the greatest number, and to urge Caesar to do the same, is good and right in the sight of God. To have aimed for this and failed will surely be judged less harshly than not to have aimed at all.

Third, our heavenly centre of gravity and our knowledge that 'here we have no continuing city' will alert us to the fact that *man is meant to be the great link between nature and supernature.*

We move between these worlds, and we serve them both under the lordship of the one who is Lord over both. Indeed he places us at the point of contact between two currents – the will of the world and the will of the Lord. And while the will of the world is always a will to death and destruction, because it pursues life the wrong way, the will of the Lord, coming through the believer to the world, is God's current from on high, empowering true connection to the source of life.

This is why preaching is so important, because here the Christian stands at the point of man's most suicidal impulse (which is to reject his eternal Lord and to settle for temporal trivialities) and calls out: 'No, don't settle down! Don't make the penultimate ultimate! Come this way – the way to the One who is the way, the truth and the life!' For as the poet has it:

He is a path, if any be misled;
He is a robe, if any naked be;
If any chance to hunger, He is bread;
If any be a bondman, He is free;
If any be but weak, how strong is He!
To dead men, life is He;
    to sick men, health;
To blind men, sight;
    and to the needy, wealth;
A pleasure without loss;
    a treasure without stealth.[4]

In all this we are saying to governors and to governed, to high and low, young and old, that our place upon this planet cannot find true explanation – nor the end of contradiction, nor the best arrangements of personal, political and economic life – unless in reference to that world beyond, on which all earth depends and by which it is transcended.

This is why, whatever happens, whether in the Beloved Country or in any other, *we remain and must remain a worshipping people*. For our God reigns. Finally, at the end of the day, when the curtain comes down on all we have sought to be and do during our brief pilgrimage upon the planet, we will know that it was good and right to worship God regardless, and to say with the prophet of old:

Though the fig-tree does not bud
    and there are no grapes on the vines,
though the olive crop fails
    and the fields produce no food,
though there are no sheep in the pen
    and no cattle in the stalls,
yet I will rejoice in the Lord,
    I will be joyful in God my Saviour.

(Hab 3:17–18)

And, worshipping, we will work for that city and that day when the dwelling of God is with his own, when 'the dwelling of God is with men, and he will live with them . . . He will wipe every tear from their eyes. There will be no more death or mourning or crying or pain, for the old order of things has passed away' (Rev 21:3–4).

And with that number of the redeemed that cannot be numbered, a thousand times ten thousand and thousands of thousands, we will gather round the throne to sing: 'Worthy is the Lamb, who was slain, to receive power and wealth and wisdom and strength and honour and glory and praise!' (Rev 5:12). For by then, *Deo gloria*, all summers of every sort will have passed, save only the summer of our Saviour's love.

Appendix 1

MAJOR EVENTS IN THE HISTORY OF SOUTH AFRICA

200–300	Bantu-speaking people move into the eastern part of South Africa (possible migration of farmers).
900	Emergence of the first large African state-systems in North and Western Transvaal and Southern Botswana.
1200	Colonisation of the highveld (Southern Transvaal and the Orange Free State). Movement from Northern Transvaal and Natal. These groups are ancestral to modern-day Sotho-Tswana culture which emerged locally, not through migration.
1488	Bartholomew Dias discovers the Cape.
1552	First historical contact between blacks and whites. Portuguese shipwreck survivors meet Zulu and Xhosa-speaking peoples in present-day Ciskei and Natal.
1652	Van Riebeeck establishes first white settlement at the Cape.
1657	First Free-burghers begin independent farming.
1658	First slaves imported.
1688	Arrival of the first Huguenot settlers.
1750	Recorded emergence of the large African state (Pedi) in the Eastern Transvaal. African state formation in Natal and Zululand.

1760	Coetzee crosses the Orange River.
1779	First of the eight Frontier Wars erupts along Cape settlement's eastern boundary.
1795–1803	First British occupation of the Cape.
1803–1806	Resumption of Dutch rule.
1806	Second British occupation.
1820 (approx.)	Emergence of the Zulu nation.
1820	Four thousand British settlers arrive at Algoa Bay.
1828	Zulu king Shaka murdered; succeeded by half-brother Dingane. Coloured people granted equal political rights in Cape Colony.
1834	Slavery abolished.
1835	Durban founded.
1836	Start of the Great Trek.
1838	Retief's trekker party massacred on Dingane's instructions. Battle of Blood River. Republic of Natalia founded.
1843	British proclaim Natal a colony. Natal trekkers move north.
1848	Proclamation of Orange River sovereignty. Battle of Boomplaats.
1852	Sand River Convention. Transvaal's independence recognised.
1854	Bloemfontein Convention. Orange Free State's independence recognised.
1860	First indentured Indian labour arrives in Natal.
1869	Diamonds discovered near Kimberley.
1870	Diamond fields annexed by Britain.
1872	Cape Colony granted Responsible Government.
1877	Transvaal annexed by Britain.
1879	Zulu empire crushed at Battle of Ulundi.
1880	Transvaal war of independence begins.
1881	British defeated at Majuba Hill. Transvaal (the South African Republic) regains independence.

1883	Paul Kruger becomes President of the South African Republic.
1886	Gold discovered on the Witwatersrand.
1897	Dr L S Jameson raids the Transvaal and is defeated at Krugersdorp.
1899	South African (Boer) War breaks out.
1902	Peace of Vereeniging. Transvaal and Orange Free State become British colonies.
1910	South Africa united by Act of Union.
1912	African National Congress founded.
1913	Miners strikes and riots on the Witwatersrand.
1914	Outbreak of First World War. Boer rebellion crushed by Prime Minister Louis Botha, who goes on to defeat the German forces in South West Africa. J M Hertzog founds the National Party.
1919	South West Africa mandated to South Africa.
1920	South African Indian Congress founded.
1922	Outbreak and suppression of the white 'Rand Revolt'.
1925	Afrikaans recognised as second official language.
1930	White women get the vote.
1931	Statute of Westminster. South Africa granted full legislative powers.
1936	Blacks removed from Cape common roll.
1939–1945	Second World War. South Africans fight with imperial forces in East Africa, North Africa and Italy.
1947	British royal family visits South Africa.
1948	National Party comes to power.
1950	Suppression of Communism Act passed.
1951	Group Areas Act passed.
1953	Bantu (Black) Education Act passed.
1955	First oil-from-coal plant (Sasol) comes into operation.
1956	Coloured people removed from Cape

common roll. Freedom Charter signed at Kliptown.

1959   Promotion of Black Self-Government Act passed. Pan-Africanist movement formed.

1960   Demonstration at Sharpeville against pass laws – sixty-nine blacks killed. British Prime Minister Harold Macmillan delivers his 'Winds of Change' speech to joint sitting of South African Parliament.

1961   South Africa withdraws from Commonwealth. South Africa becomes a republic.

1963   Transkei granted internal self-government.

1966   Prime Minister Verwoerd assassinated.

1970   South African scientists develop new uranium enrichment process.

1971   Black Homelands Constitution Act passed.

1976   Transkei gains 'independence'.

1977   Bophuthatswana granted 'independence'. Steve Biko dies in custody.

1978   P W Botha becomes Prime Minister.

1979   Wiehahn and Riekert commissions' recommendations on labour submitted – most are accepted. Venda granted 'independence'. Azanian Peoples Organisation founded.

1980   President's Council replaces Senate.

1981   Ciskei granted 'independence'.

1982   United States President Ronald Reagan announces policy of constructive engagement. President's Council recommends new constitution. Dissident MPs break away from National Party to form Conservative Party. Black Local Authorities Act passed.

1983   United Democratic Front formed. Tricameral constitution adopted.

1985   P W Botha announces reform of some

aspects of the apartheid system. State of Emergency declared. Economic recession deepens.

1986   Eminent Persons Group visits South Africa. South African forces raid neighbouring states. Eminent Persons Group mission fails.

1987   General Election for (white) House of Assembly. National Party wins comfortably, but right-wing Conservative Party improves its parliamentary position to become the official opposition.

1988   P W Botha opens up African Diplomatic Initiative. Nationwide municipal elections for newly constituted municipal councils.

(Information taken from Peter Joyce, *The South African Pocket Yearbook, 1987–88* (Cape Town: C Struik, 1987), pp. 154–156, augmented by material from Prof. John Wright, University of Natal, Pietermaritzburg, given in interview)

Appendix 2

THE FREEDOM CHARTER

The Freedom Charter was unanimously adopted by the largest gathering of black leadership in South African history, the 'Congress of the People', in 1955. It remains the clearest statement of black aspirations for the future of their country.

We, the people of South Africa, declare for all our country and the world to know:

– that South Africa belongs to all who live in it, black and white, and that no government can justly claim authority unless it is based on the will of all the people;
– that our people have been robbed of their birthright to land, liberty and peace by a form of government founded on injustice and inequality;
– that our country will never be prosperous or free until all our people live in brotherhood, enjoying equal rights and opportunities;
– that only a democratic state, based on the will of all the people, can secure to all their birthright without distinction of colour, race, sex or belief;
And therefore, we the people of South Africa, black and white together – equals, countrymen and brothers – adopt this Freedom Charter. And we pledge ourselves to strive together, sparing neither strength nor courage, until the democratic changes set out here have been won.

The people shall govern!

Every man and woman shall have the right to vote for and to stand as a candidate for all bodies which make laws;

All people shall be entitled to take part in the administration of the country;

The rights of the people shall be the same, regardless of race, colour or sex;

All bodies of minority-rule, advisory boards, councils and authorities shall be replaced by democratic organs of self-government.

All national groups shall have equal rights!

There shall be equal status in the bodies of state, in the courts and in the schools for all national groups and races;

All people shall have equal right to use their own languages, and to develop their own folk culture and customs;

All national groups shall be protected by law against insults to their race and national pride;

The preaching and practice of national, race or colour discrimination and contempt shall be a punishable crime;

All apartheid laws and practices shall be set aside.

The people shall share in the country's wealth!

The national wealth of our country, the heritage of all South Africans, shall be restored to the people;

The mineral wealth beneath the soil, the banks and monopoly industry shall be transferred to the ownership of the people as a whole;

All other industry and trade shall be controlled to assist the well-being of the people;

All people shall have equal rights to trade where they choose, to manufacture and to enter all trades, crafts and professions.

The land shall be shared among those who work it!

Restriction of land ownership on a racial basis shall be ended, and all the land redivided amongst those who work it, to banish famine and land hunger;

The state shall help the peasants with implements, seed, tractors and dams to save the soil and assist the tillers.

Freedom of movement shall be guaranteed to all who work on the land;

All shall have the right to occupy land wherever they choose;

People shall not be robbed of their cattle, and forced labour and farm prisons shall be abolished.

All shall be equal before the law!

No one shall be imprisoned, deported or restricted without a fair trial;

No one shall be condemned by the order of any government official;

The courts shall be representative of all people;

Imprisonment shall be only for serious crimes against the people, and shall aim at re-education, not vengeance;

The police force and army shall be open to all on an equal basis and shall be the helpers and protectors of the people;

All laws which discriminate on grounds of races, colour or belief shall be repealed.

All shall enjoy human rights!

The law shall guarantee to all their rights to speak, to organise, to meet together, to punish, to preach, to worship and to educate their children;

The privacy of the house from police raids shall be protected by law;

All shall be free to travel without restriction from countryside to town, from province to province and from South Africa abroad;

Pass Laws, permits, and all other laws restricting these freedoms, shall be abolished.

There shall be work and security!

All who work shall be free to form unions, to elect their officers and to make wage agreements with their employers;

The state shall recognise the right and duty of all to work, and to draw full unemployment benefits;

Men and women of all races shall receive equal pay for equal work;

There shall be a forty-hour working week, a national minimum wage, paid annual leave, and sick leave for all workers, and maternity leave on full pay for all working mothers;

Miners, domestic workers, farm workers, and civil servants shall have the same rights as all others who work;

Child labour, compound labour, the tot system and contract labour shall be abolished.

The doors of learning and of culture shall be opened!

The government shall discover, develop and encourage national talent for the enhancement of our cultural life;

All the cultural treasures of mankind shall be open to all, by free exchange of books, ideas and contact with other lands;

The aim of education shall be to teach the youth to love their people and their culture, to honour human brotherhood, liberty and peace;

Education shall be free, compulsory, universal and equal for all children;

Higher education and technical training shall be opened to all by means of state allowances and scholarships awarded on the basis of merit;

Adult illiteracy shall be ended by a mass state education plan;

Teachers shall have all the rights of other citizens;

The colour bar in cultural life, in sports and in education shall be abolished.

There shall be houses, security and comfort!

All people shall have the rights to live where they choose, to be decently housed, and to bring up their families in comfort, and security;

Unused housing space shall be made available to the people;

Rent and prices shall be lowered, food plentiful and no one shall go hungry;

A preventive health scheme shall be run by the state;

Free medical care and hospitalisation shall be provided for all, with special care for mothers and young children;

Slums shall be demolished, and new suburbs built where all have transport, roads, lighting, playing fields, crèches and social centres;

The aged, the orphans, the disabled and the sick shall be cared for by the state;

Rest, leisure and recreation shall be the right of all;

Fenced locations and ghettoes shall be abolished, and laws which break up families shall be repealed;

South Africa shall be a fully independent state, which respects the rights and sovereignty of nations.

There shall be peace and friendship!

South Africa shall strive to maintain world peace and the settlement of all international disputes by negotiation – not war.

Peace and friendship amongst all our people shall be secured by upholding the equal rights, opportunities and status of all;

The people of the protectorates – Basutoland (Lesotho), Bechuanaland (Botswana) and Swaziland – shall be free to decide for themselves their own future;

The rights of all the people of Africa to independence and

self-government shall be recognised, and shall be the basis of close co-operation;

Let all who love their people and their country now say, as we say here:

'These freedoms we will fight for, side by side, throughout our lives, until we have won our liberty.'

Taken from G. D. Aeschliman, *Apartheid: Tragedy in Black and White* (Ventura: Regal Books, 1986), pp. 161–167.

Appendix 3

A BIBLICAL PICTURE OF HUMAN RIGHTS

1 *Legal processes* (*cf.* European Convention, Articles 5, 6, 7)

Impartiality of tribunal	Mal 2:9; 1 Tim 5:21
Fair hearing	Exod 22:9
Speedy trial	Ezra 7:26
Confrontation of witnesses	Isa 43:9
No double jeopardy	Nah 1:9

2 *No discrimination* (*cf.* European Convention, Article 14)

Versus unjust discrimination in general	Acts 10:34; Deut 16:19; Prov 24:23.
The just and the unjust stand equally before the law	Matt 5:45
Likewise all races and both sexes; condition or servitude irrelevant (versus slavery)	Gal 3:28; Amos 9:7; Exod 21:2
Likewise rich and poor	James 2:1–7; Amos 5:12; Isa 1:16–17
Likewise citizens and foreigners	Exod 12:49; Lev 23:22; 24:22; Num 9:14; 15:15–16
Even the sovereign is under the law	2 Sam 11–12

3 *Miscellaneous basic rights*

Right to life (*cf.* American Convention)	Exod 20:13; Ps 51:5; Matt 5:21–22; Luke 1:15, 41

Right to family life	1 Tim 5:8
Versus inhuman or degrading treatment/punishment and torture	Luke 6:45 (*cf.* Publications of Action des Chretiens pour l'Abolition de la Torture, 252 rue St-Jacques, Paris)
Freedom of thought, conscience, religion, expression, assembly, association, movement	John 7:17
Social and economic rights in general	1 Cor 6:19–20
Right to universal education	Deut 6:7; 11:19
Right to work, to a fair remuneration, and to good working conditions (protection of labour)	Luke 10:7; 1 Tim 5:18; Deut 23:24–25; 24:6,10,12–13,15
Right to protection of honour and personal reputation	Exod 20:16
Right to leisure time	Exod 20:8–11
Right to asylum	Exod 21:13; Josh 20; 1 Chron 6:67; et al. (cities of refuge)
Right to equitable distribution of land	Num 33:54; Lev 25:14–18, 25–34
Environmental rights	Scripture expresses horror over murder, for example, by personifying matrix earth being forced to drink the blood of her offspring. In the biblical imagery, crimes *pollute* the soil and the land will vomit its polluting population into exile. The modern concern with preventing the extinction of various species of animal life is in resonance with the biblical prescription not to collect the dam with her chicks but to release her to hatch another generation. Cruelty to animals is proscribed in such prescriptions as not to yoke animals of different strengths (ox and ass) to the plough or

not to muzzle the ox which treads the grain. Ecological considerations are exemplified in the prohibition of sowing the vineyard's aisles with a second crop or the destruction of defenseless fruit trees while waging war in enemy territory. Such concerns must be perceived for what they are – a sensitivity to the human capacities for greed, rapaciousness, wanton cruelty, and ingratitude, capacities which cross over from the human realm into the non-human.

Taken from John Warwick Montgomery, *Human Rights and Human Dignity* (Grand Rapids: Zondervan Publications, 1986), pp. 168–169.[1]

Appendix 4

EVANGELISM AND SOCIAL RESPONSIBILITY STATEMENTS FROM THE LAUSANNE COVENANT

Clause 4   The nature of evangelism

To evangelize is to spread the good news that Jesus Christ died for our sins and was raised from the dead according to the Scriptures, and that as the reigning Lord he now offers the forgiveness of sins and the liberating gift of the Spirit to all who repent and believe. Our Christian presence in the world is indispensable to evangelism, and so is that kind of dialogue whose purpose is to listen sensitively in order to understand. But evangelism itself is the proclamation of the historical, biblical Christ as Savior and Lord, with a view to persuading people to come to him personally and so be reconciled to God. In issuing the Gospel invitation we have no liberty to conceal the cost of discipleship. Jesus still calls all who would follow him to deny themselves, take up their cross, and identify themselves with his new community. The results of evangelism include obedience to Christ, incorporation into his church and responsible service in the world.

(1 Cor 15:3,4; Acts 2:32–39; John 20:21; 1 Cor 1:23; 2 Cor 4:5; 5:11,20; Luke 14:25–33; Mark 8:34; Acts 2:40,47; Mark 10:43–45)

Clause 5 Christian Social Responsibility

We affirm that God is both the Creator and the Judge of all men. We therefore should share his concern for justice and reconciliation throughout human society and for the liberation of men from every kind of oppression. Because mankind is made in the image of God, every person, regardless of race, religion, color, culture, class, sex or age, has an intrinsic dignity because of which he should be respected and served, not exploited. Here too we express penitence both for our neglect and for having sometimes regarded evangelism and social concern as mutually exclusive. Although reconciliation with man is not reconciliation with God, nor is social action evangelism, nor is political liberation salvation, nevertheless we affirm that evangelism and socio-political involvement are both part of our Christian duty. For both are necessary expressions of our doctrines of God and man, our love for our neighbor and our obedience to Jesus Christ. The message of salvation implies also a message of judgment upon every form of alienation, oppression and discrimination, and we should not be afraid to denounce evil and injustice wherever they exist. When people receive Christ they are born again into his kingdom and must seek not only to exhibit but also to spread its righteousness in the midst of an unrighteous world. The salvation we claim should be transforming us in the totality of our personal and social responsibilities. Faith without works is dead.

(Acts 17:26,31; Gen 18:25; Isa 1:17; Psa 45:7; Gen 1:26,27; Jas 3:9; Lev 19:18; Luke 6:27,35; Jas 2:14–26; John 3:3,5; Matt 5:20; 6:33; 2 Cor 3:18; Jas 2:20)

Taken from *The Lausanne Covenant: An Exposition and Commentary*, Lausanne Occasional Paper No. 3 (The Lausanne Committee for World Evangelization, 1975), pp. 12, 15.

Appendix 5

NATIONAL INITIATIVE FOR RECONCILIATION

STATEMENT OF AFFIRMATION
12 September 1985

Preamble

This message comes to you from a very wide cross-section of Christian leadership, spanning many denominations, drawn from every part of the nation, representative of every racial group, meeting in Pietermaritzburg from 10th–12th September 1985 for the launching of the National Initiative for Reconciliation. It is to be noted that this is not a single event but the initiating of an ongoing process. This gathering of church unity in our present context of polarization is, we believe, in itself a sign of hope for our nation at this time.

We have come together in humility and deep repentance for our sin and guilt in order to listen to God and to discover one another in new ways. We give thankful testimony to God that a deep thing has happened to us in this process as we have struggled under God with many hard and complex issues and found an astonishing measure of unity where formerly we knew little but division. The spirit of compassion and forgiveness, as well as resolution to move forward together, has laid hold upon us all and is impelling us towards extending God's Kingdom together and building a new South Africa along with all its peoples.

Past experience with statements or resolutions of racial church bodies demonstrate that too often they emphasize divisions rather than an encouragement for action. Therefore, this assembly of Christian leadership does not issue a statement of words but issues a commitment to action.

We believe the Spirit of God is urging us and the whole South African Church in new and more determined ways.

1. To seek every opportunity, corporately, congregationally and individually to proclaim and witness to the good news of Jesus Christ, crucified and risen, persuading all that in Him alone is to be found forgiveness and that newness of life that is eternal.
2. To continue in prayer and fasting for renewal in the Holy Spirit and re-awakening of the Church of Jesus Christ and for peace and justice in our land.
3. To create concrete opportunities for meaningful worship, fellowship and discussion with people of differing racial and cultural groups.
4. To help remove ignorance of events in South Africa and prepare people for living in a changed and totally non-racial land.
5. To share the South African reality of suffering by extending and accepting invitations to experience the life of fellow Christians in the townships.
6. To plan and mount regional gatherings of Christian leadership to continue this process of reconciliation and to initiate concrete changes in South African society.

Furthermore:

We feel compelled as witnesses of Jesus Christ to share with the nation the hope that we have experienced together. For those who suffer under the pain and despair of the South African reality we feel bound by God to visible and obedient actions of hope. While not every participant in the conference could agree on the details of these actions, the clear majority of the Christian leaders gathered here in such remarkable denominational diversity resolved:

A. That on Wednesday October 9th, 1985 Christians, rather than attending the places of their usual employment (except so far as essential services are concerned), should give the day to repentance, mourning and prayer for those sinful aspects of our national life which have led us to the present crisis. Congregational leadership should further enable this process by bringing greater awareness to members regarding those aspects of our national life. Moreover, Christian employers should encourage their employees to observe such a day and observe it themselves by suspending their normal commercial and professional activities.

B. That a delegation representing this Assembly will visit the State President immediately to present the following positive initiatives:

1. End the state of emergency.
2. Remove the SADF and the emergency Police forces from the townships.
3. Release all detainees and political prisoners, withdraw charges against the treason trialists and allow exiles to return home.
4. Begin talks immediately with authentic leadership of the various population groups with a view toward equitable power sharing in South Africa.
5. Begin the process of introducing a common system of education.
6. Take the necessary steps towards the elimination of all forms of legislated discrimination.

Appendix 6

NIR POSSIBLE OPTIONS OF INITIATIVE, ACTION AND RESPONSE

Relevant prayer, worship and Bible study

1 Mount an interchurch or local church evangelistic campaign with a strong interracial component.

2 Start a prayer cell for revival, healing and justice in South Africa.

3 Organise effective monthly days of prayer and fasting on the first Wednesday, Thursday or Friday of each month in your area/church.

4 Plan an evangelistic outreach to business and professional leadership in your area. Also alert them to cross-cultural dialogue and action.

5 Plan a series of renewal meetings or Bible studies to explore the work of the Holy Spirit. Also investigate the history of the social change wrought through spiritual awakening.

6 Plan a public event of united Christian witness or prayer in your local town hall or city hall.

7 Plan a study series on past revivals in scripture and in history (*e.g.* Wesleyan, Welsh, East African or Indonesian revivals). Examine what acts of obedience the church was called to by the Spirit to demonstrate the love and righteousness of Jesus.

Interracial church activities for awareness

1 Organise interracial dialogue and/or Bible study group. Discover one another's real concerns and needs. Work out solutions together. You may want to use denominational relationships to make initial contact with Christians of another racial group.

2 Plan an exchange of pulpits between black and white ministers. Discuss the concept with your minister and offer to help make arrangements.

3 Plan non-racial 'coming together' services of worship as South Africans. Contact a church in town or in the township and plan for a shared service.

4 Mount symposia, debates or study evenings on key South African issues. Invite interracial input. Encourage your church to provide a platform to help our separated society to hear, understand and interact with perceived needs and issues.

5 Mount a series of interracial morning-fellowship gatherings for clergy wives. What about evening youth gatherings in your area? Have the black and white youth in your denomination met together in your area?

6 Plan dialogue evenings between different race-language groups in your region of South Africa.

7 Organise to spend a night with a Christian family in the township to ask them to show you the problems and conditions in their area. Share your experience with your local fellowship and write a joint letter to the authorities about what you discovered.

8 Organise a discussion on the Group Areas Act with your congregation and a congregation from another racial group. Write a joint letter to the State President and your local newspaper about what you determined together.

9 Work up a study and counselling project to help young people work through the issues relating to call up, military service *etc*.

10 Develop awareness of problem areas in the country.

Projects in education

1 Plan an educational project (*e.g.* school or pre-school) in a township where children are out of school or at a loose end.
2 Organise a lobby or raise funds for the upgrading of black teacher-training colleges. Organise supplementary education for teachers with Christian educators, computer experts, and science instructors.
3 Raise funds for improving black education. Funds are needed for building more schools, employing more teachers and purchasing laboratory equipment and technical education. Bursaries, school books, and uniforms are also needed.
4 Contact organisations which are struggling for a new and more equitable education system for all (*e.g.* Student Parent Teacher Association, Parents Crisis Committee, *etc.*). Whether white or black, learn about the problems and possible solutions in black education.

Ministries of mercy

1 Initiate a school feeding scheme.
2 Be involved in an Aid and Development Project to assist the poor or destitute.
3 Develop a sensitive and compassionate ministry with local domestic workers.
4 Work out how to challenge any labour management practices in your work-place which do not conform to Christ's law of love.

Crisis aid

1 Develop emergency counselling or help service for the unemployed, for families of people detained, for those released from detention, for the elderly, the bereaved, alcoholics, *etc.* Begin by seeking out service agencies in

your area which may already be involved with these concerns. Volunteer your service.

2 Set up a committee of caring people to look after the health and welfare of those detained without trial. Housewives, lawyers, businessmen, teachers, *etc.* – every member of the body could help speak for and care for detainees.

3 Assist in meeting the needs of victims of faction-fighting, those left homeless and bereaved.

4 Organise a panel of lawyers in your area who would be willing to educate black community leaders of their rights and provide legal counsel to any who feel themselves victims of any forms of violence.

5 Start an Action/Aid Group to assist people with Workmen's Compensation Act, taxation, unemployment, pension, legal aid.

Leadership dialogue

1 Set up a delegation of concern for a private visit to a local MP or township power groups to stimulate dialogue and negotiations.

2 Write a letter to the State President, your local MP or the local newspaper editor encouraging negotiations between Government authorities and black South African leaders both internal and external.

Economic assistance

1 Mount a job-creation scheme with churches in your area on an interracial basis.

2 Check with the Department of Manpower via your local Town or City Council about how to take advantage of the Government's Unemployment Project, whereby the private citizen provides the work for the unemployed and the Government pays.

Appendix 7

LATIN AMERICAN LIBERATION THEOLOGY
(a personal view by Michael Cassidy)

INTRODUCTION

Although South African Black Theology, out of which the Kairos Document was born, has drawn more on North American black theologians like James Cone, nevertheless the liberation theology of Latin America is what is tossed around the South African white Christian circuit and media scene (SATV *etc.*) as the main villain of the piece because it does have many points of similarity or identity with Kairos theology and therefore the plusses and minuses of liberation theology are not unrelated to Kairos theology.

An appendix forbids a lengthy discussion, but a few comments may be in order for other laymen like me who are trying to explore and find their way through that part of the church's biblical responsibility which we describe as liberating the captives.

Right process

The easy thing for white evangelical Christians like me is to denounce liberation theology (because it comes from a different theological stable), thereby avoiding its challenge. The other danger is to embrace it uncritically. In my judgement the right process, surely, is for each person (in integrity and being true to themselves and to their Lord) to look at it, draw on its insights, be challenged by its posture, and discard what cannot be accepted. The same thing should be done with charismatic, Pentecostal, ecumenical or evangelical theologies. We draw on what God has given different sections or groupings in the body of Christ and let the other man's strengths and insights correct our own heresies and imbalances and challenge our incomplete Christian responses to the global task of mission. And the other person must let my stance and strengths do the same for him or her. It is really a matter of allowing the body of Christ to work.

WHAT LIBERATION THEOLOGY SAYS

Context and reaction

Before assessing liberation theology's strengths and weaknesses let us see what it says.

Liberation theology comes in the first instance out of Latin America, which is a context of massive poverty, economic exploitation and political oppression. Having been there and moved among many victims of this, I know this is true. It is also a place where there is a huge disparity between rich and poor, and where the rich get richer and the poor get poorer.

Second, liberation theology arose as a reaction to much Western theology which was cognitive and cerebral. It was seen as primarily idea- and concept-orientated, and found finally in the 1960s in Latin America to bear little relevance to the real life and practical problems of ordinary people. Imported Western theology began with the Bible, Greek philosophy and Western debates about fine points of doctrinal statements, and never seemed to these Latin leaders to effect anything practically at grass-roots; it was too abstract, not concrete enough.

Action and method

The desperate cry arose for a theology in the church which required action. Theology, they felt, should be a reflection more on what is *done* and *to be done* than on what is believed or to be believed. Everything had to have a practical intention in view. Many gravitated to Marx's idea that 'the time has come to stop reflecting on the world. The time has come to transform the world.'

If theology does not work truly to effect the lives of people, it does not fulfil its task. So, instead of starting with the Bible, liberation theologians developed a new way of 'doing theology' by beginning with a commitment to action, which they called 'praxis'. The point was to steer away from knowledge and reflection for its own sake and get people committed to trying to do something to change the situation. It is more important to do than to know.

Theology, they said, was the second step *after* loving acts of service. Theology 'rises at sundown', at the end of a day which has been committed to action. Active Christian obedience comes first. Historical praxis, they would say, takes precedence over theologising. One must respond to God who expects his people to co-operate with him in the task of changing the world.

If, by contrast, the church is not interested in changing the world, it reveals its own hypocrisy and sham.

Historical situation as starting point

If, then, theology is basically an exercise of reflection on action, then clearly the actual historical situation in which people must 'act out that action' is where you must begin. The 'text', they say, is your situation. Here lies the radical difference from traditional theology.

Now if your historical situation where you live and work is the Latin American context of overwhelming poverty, then where you start is with the poor. So the 'poor' become your bias, your option, your preferred point of departure. You commit yourself in solidarity to the poor and you read and interpret your Bible from there. (In the South African context it would mean starting from the givens of an apartheid context with its unique realities.)

The insistence is that not just the local pastor do this but also the theologian and the intellectual. He too must think and reflect from that posture of commitment, loving action and solidarity with the poor. All of which may mean, says the liberationist, that he must identify with them in a liberating or even revolutionary struggle. The theologian cannot indulge in knowledge for its own sake. The situations Christians are in are too urgent and desperate for that. The theologian must not theologise 'from an armchair' – but via 'sinking roots into where the pulse of history is beating at this moment' (Guttiérez).

Use of social sciences

It is not difficult from here to see why liberationists would find a deep sympathy with Karl Marx, because he started from the poor, the underdog and the downtrodden.

This predisposition to Marx by virtue of a common commitment to the poor meant that liberationists were ready to let Marx tell them how to analyse and understand the social situation they were in. So they self-consciously embraced Marx's social analysis, whereby society is basically viewed as a liberation struggle between the poor oppressed and the rich oppressor, leading hopefully to a just society, even if it has to come through revolution.

The point was that Marx was seen as the thinker who best explained the causes of poverty and not just the phenomenon of it. The poor are seen not just as the victims of fate but of political injustice or economic exploitation. To Marx a new social order, not economic development, was the answer. Nothing capitalism could produce would solve these imbalances. Only a socialist system would do it.

New way to interact

All this of course must lead, says liberation theology, to a new way of interpreting the Bible. The way it is supposed to work is that you begin with the present context, understood by the tools of social analysis which show you what action is needed. Then you go to the Bible which gives the past revelation of God and you see where and how the two intersect and relate. The movement from one to the other is seen as a circle where there is an interplay between the one and the other, supposedly leading to both right acting and right thinking.

This, say the liberationists, will involve consciously reading the Bible from the standpoint of the poor. This is necessary apart from anything else as a corrective of sorts to prevent us reading the Bible (which we all do) from our own socio-economic place and space and therefore making the text simply support and legitimate our own posture and prejudices.

For Marx, of course, the praxis or action required was liberating action by the oppressed themselves to end their oppression. This would lead to a new man in a new society, resulting from the proletarian revolution and the overthrow of capitalism. Praxis is the effort to transform social structures. Theologians who went this far became exponents of what is known as 'the theology of revolution'.

CRITIQUE AND CONFESSION

The quick and easy critique of all this, and inevitably the one in vogue in South Africa, says it is all Marxist, it espouses violence, it reduces the gospel to sociology, economics and politics, it is too conditioned by its context, and it uses the Bible selectively and arbitrarily. Then we walk away from its challenge without asking how *we* are articulating and working out our faith, for example in South Africa, in a context of poverty, political trauma and hopelessness.

It is far better in a context like South Africa's – where three quarters of the population are clamouring for liberation and many black Christians are exploring this theology – to look at liberation theology's strengths and weaknesses and at least understand what is going on. Such understanding may even serve to break some of the current paralysis.

At this point, however, I need to make a confession. Bearing in mind that this volume is admittedly and self-consciously the story of a personal pilgrimage through issues thrown up by trying to be a Christian in South Africa, I need to confess that my own theological background, personal mindset and white privilege, *etc.*, predispose me to view liberation theology and all its works negatively. But a struggling honesty before this and other issues has required me to try and be open.

Without therefore professing to have it all right, this is my confession of where right now I see strengths in liberation theology and where I am forced to have very serious reservations.

STRENGTHS

Because space is tight, let me list the features that have impressed me about liberation theology.

1   It calls us to move from the *discussion* of faith to the *obedience* of faith.
2   It says faith is not primarily a way of thinking, but a way of living.
3   It constitutes a massive challenge to every Christian to be concerned about action, deeds and service, not just ideas, talk, rhetoric and ivory-tower theologising or pamphleteering. Springing not from the ivory tower but from the dungeon beneath the tower, liberation theology requires us to practise truth and do it.
4   Moving not from privilege but from pain, liberation theology challenges each of us to be involved in changing situations for the better rather than copping out and resting in resigned contentment with the *status quo*.
5   It asks every Christian to understand deeply the historical situation they are in and the *causes* of the underlying ills in that situation.
6   It requires that we look not just at our personal sin but at sin in structures – *i.e.* social and political sin.

7   It asks us not to look just at other people's sin but at the *consequences* down the line of other people's sin. In South African terms that would mean, for example, not just lamenting apartheid but drawing attention to the effects of it on those it controls.

8   It challenges traditional evangelical Christianity to repent of having presented a disembodied Christ for disembodied souls.

9   It challenges evangelical Christians to reflect on how Jesus would live and act in our current situation and context. (Liberation theologians would call this the challenge to rethink Christology contextually.) We cannot leave him confined to heavenly heights and require that he remain uninvolved and uninterested in the problems of broken humanity. In this way we risk robbing Jesus of his humanity.[1]

10 It rightly presses on every Christian the challenge to be suspicious of certain distortions in the way he or she may have interpreted the Bible based on the background or pre-understanding which we bring to the text, especially if our socio-political instincts are all conservative.

11 It challenges the church to be more prophetic in the wrong it addresses in society and not to keep Jesus simply as the focus of purely private devotion.

Who can deny that liberation theology profoundly challenges any Christian who is willing to be open to what other believers in other parts of the world have found? Hence it is not surprising that many South African blacks see their own plight reflected in that of many poor Latin Americans, though the issue there is class while here it is race.

WEAKNESSES AND CONSEQUENT RESERVATIONS

All the above points are well and good; but I have to say that I could never be a card-carrying liberationist, much as I am challenged by many of their commitments. My reservations would be along these lines:

1 Liberation theology's insistence on starting with the context bothers me. For those of us who seek to make the Bible our final authority in all matters of faith and morals, there is a problem in starting with the context and then moving to the Bible rather than vice versa. As far as I can see, without the finally authoritative word of the Bible there is little possibility of evaluating so-called 'praxis' on the basis of a norm outside the praxis itself. The way can surely easily open for the justification of any praxis as long as it works. The danger is of the end justifying the means.

2 Liberation theology seems to me to forget that there has to be a truth in place before there can be a doing of it. In other words, God's revelation in scripture precedes man's obedience to it. This must make the Bible precede any 'praxis' of it. In other words, while doing the truth is vitally important, there must first be a truth to be done! Doing the truth doesn't make it. The truth in fact is given in scripture by God's revelation in Jesus. As the Lord who identifies with human need and suffering he gives us his truth and *then* sends us to work it out in the world. The fact, as liberation theology says, that Western Christians have so often failed to do so should not make us overreact and forsake the primary authority of God's word – because if we do, where is the authoritative norm to judge whether what is being done is acceptable to God or not?

In other words, if the context is self-consciously over-exalted to be normative it becomes very hard for scripture to be normative. Therefore, instead of insisting that the circle of interpretation go from the context to the biblical text and back to the context, it would seem to this writer far safer to start the circle with the Bible (and taking a high view of it) and then move in integrity, earnestness and relevance to the context (as the Bible itself urges) and then back to the scriptures and then back to the context. My concern would be to see the circle and everything else beginning from scripture as master over all. The scriptures ask questions of the context before the context provides questions for scripture.

3 Liberation theology surely overstates the case when it insists on the primacy of so-called Christian praxis as the basis of spiritual knowledge, so that theology has to become the

'second act' following on action. I can accordingly identify with Emilio Núñez of El Salvador when he comments on Jesus' words: 'If anyone chooses to do God's will, he will find out whether my teaching comes from God or whether I speak on my own' (John 7:17). Says Núñez:

> Unless the hearers of Jesus were prepared to submit themselves to the divine will, they would not come to know whether the teaching was coming from Himself or from the Father. Jesus had already spoken to them. It was not a matter of producing revelation, but of believing it. To us revelation has already been given in the Scriptures. The existence of that revelation does not depend on our response to it. At the same time we realize that we cannot grow as we should in our knowledge of the written revelation if we are not prepared to obey it. But in any case our responsibility is to submit praxis to the Word, instead of giving supremacy to praxis.[2]

4 I question liberation theology's insistence that liberation is the central theme of scripture. From the New Testament perspective Jesus, it seems to me, gives pride of place to the kingdom of God. And the authority of that kingship over all areas of life should surely send us relevantly into the context. The more shame on us when it hasn't.

5 This leads me to another concern – namely that liberation theology *does* indeed seem to use scripture selectively. Almost everything is reduced to the socio-political struggle. But where is evangelism and the new birth, and the gifts of the Spirit and healing and spiritual warfare and so on? Rene Padilla, an Argentinian Christian leader very sympathetic to many aspects of liberation theology, writes:

> The concentration of liberation theology hermeneutics [hermeneutics = the science of interpreting the Bible] on ethics and politics results in a theology which does an injustice to the totality of biblical revelation. Whatever is not in keeping with the interests of praxis is set aside as irrelevant. It is not by accident that liberation theology is extremely inadequate when it comes to questions which have no immediate bearing on politics or point to the supra-historical and personal dimensions of the gospel. It has nothing to say, for instance, on the question of the ultimate meaning of a person's life. The fact is that if the life of the

individual person has meaning only in relation to the world of public, historical events, then it has no meaning beyond death. According to biblical teaching, however, the meaning of human existence is not exclusively found in relation to the historical process, but also in the ultimate destiny of the individual.[3]

6 Liberation theology ignores the supernatural forces (the so-called principalities and powers of Ephesians 6:12) which are at work behind humanly oppressive structures *etc*. Ignoring these demonic forces at work in the world can easily lead liberation theologians to utopian and romantic notions of the 'just society' which liberation struggles are supposedly meant to usher in. Liberation theology accordingly seems to me over-optimistic on man's ability to liberate himself and transform his fundamental social relationships.

7 All of which raises a related issue – namely whether liberation theology underplays human sin and depravity. To be sure, sin is certainly evident in many oppressive people and structures. But is it not just as present and pervasive in the 'poor and oppressed'? Again and again today's revolutionary is tomorrow's oppressor and today's overthrower of the status quo is tomorrow's forceful preserver of it. Witness Obote's liberation of Uganda from Amin. Man seems basically 'unfree' and unable on his own to change things in such a way as to secure not just his own freedom but freedom for all.

8 Blindness at this point may surely also take us perilously close to sanctifying violence. I have great difficulty reconciling the universal love of God with a violent struggle against oppressors whom we supposedly love while fighting them with violence.

9 Liberation theology's use of social analysis is helpful, but the exclusive embrace of Marxist analysis is problematic. After all, the Bible does not make its basic division of the world into 'oppressor and oppressed' – but rather into believers and unbelievers, the saved and the lost, the sheep and the goats, the many (on the broad road to destruction) and the few (on the narrow road to life), and so on. Beyond that, a situation such as South Africa can be viewed, as Derek Morphew has noted, from any one of the following perspectives:

i)   A *race* conflict, between black and white.

ii) A *tribal* conflict, between Afrikaner and Zulu, Zulu and Xhosa, *etc.*

iii) A *colonial*, *de-colonial conflict*, between the forces of post-colonial Africa (the Organisation of African Unity), and the neo-colonial South African system.

iv) A *First World*, *Third World conflict*, where tensions that are elsewhere reflected between peoples on different continents are reflected in South Africa in the same country.

v)   A *class struggle*, between affluent state-capitalist and underprivileged working-class interests, and therefore an economic struggle between capitalism and African socialism and/or Marxism-Leninism.

vi) *An ideological struggle between East and West*, with South Africa as the frontline state between two international power structures.

vii) *An ideological struggle between neo-Fascist and Marxist forces*, the one waning and the other emerging, and therefore between apartheid and reactionary power structures.

viii) *A religious struggle*, between various forces, Christian, humanist, Islamic, African tribalism, and Marxist 'religion'.[4]

Morphew feels, and I think he's right, that

> The moment anyone confidently informs us that South Africa can be understood in terms of one or two of these, then one can be sure that an ideological, political analysis is being offered. One can also be sure that the motive behind such a simplistic analysis is to justify one of the worldly value systems.[5]

10   Liberation theology risks pressing on us a revolutionary, left-wing language which biblically is as foreign to Jesus Christ as the right-wing jargon and ideology which dresses him up as the ultimate sponsor of all conservative politics. We cannot reduce the gospel to any ideology or let it fall into any ideological captivity. Jesus will not be neatly dragooned either way. For myself, I cannot be at peace with a view which identifies the church as God's basic agent in either a class or a

race struggle (though the God of all life would obviously be concerned about both), nor can I bind him to a preconceived pattern of social witness.

11   Liberation theology risks reinterpreting key biblical truths to fit its liberating passions. Thus *salvation* can be made to be potential liberation, the church can become not those redeemed by the blood of Christ and born again of the Spirit of God, but the liberated community and the agents of change (*i.e.* those working to change the structures of society), and especially the poor themselves. Not only could this exclude many real believers, but it can also cut the nerve of the evangelistic imperative by allowing us to say God will save all, regardless (= universalism). Furthermore, in liberation theology's Christology Jesus himself can be made from below to ascend by his obedience to the status of Son of God instead of being the pre-existent, eternal Word who came down from the Father to become man in order to bring us to God by his death, resurrection, offer of eternal life and bestowal of his Holy Spirit.

CONCLUSION: LATIN AMERICA AND SOUTH AFRICA

The liberation theology of Latin America clearly has much which speaks to South Africa, and this should not be missed. The positive aspects of this system of Christian thinking should be heeded, and those elements which are less satisfactory should be set on one side. The challenge to all Christians to terminate social escapism cannot be evaded. However, the counter-challenge to liberation theology in all its forms is to avoid the utopian illusion that in a fallen world full liberation can be achieved and to avoid reducing the total Christian message and preoccupation to one of liberation.

That said, one must also note that because Latin America and South Africa have quite a bit in common, it will not be surprising if we face more and more influence from that quarter. Hence my modest reflections at this point.

Also to be reiterated is that there are important clues in

terms of Latin American liberation theology which can guide us in assessing both 'black' and 'white' theologies (plus their strengths and weaknesses) as they unfold in South Africa and in the future.

Appendix 8

DEFINING THE DIALECTIC
(Derek Morphew)

1 Dialectical progress

Our analysis of Fascism showed the development through pantheism, Boehme, Spinoza, and the German idealists. Hegel represents the high mark of idealism. Marx studied in Berlin and mixed with a group who called themselves the 'young Hegelians'. Hegel's ideas were a major influence. Hegel taught that 'spirit' or 'mind' develops progressively in history through a *dialectic* of thesis, antithesis and synthesis. Marx's whole system assumes this dialectic. Hegel, along with all post-enlightenment thinkers, believed in *historical progress*, that man's history is developing upwards, from bad to good, by this inner thrust of 'spirit'. This was also Marx's assumption. Human nature will eventually come through into selflessness, community, *etc.*, because it is always improving.

2 Dialectical materialism

Ludwig Feuerbach followed Hegel in Berlin as a major thinker. He accepted Hegel's belief in dialectical progress, but 'turned it on its head'. Instead of 'absolute spirit' being the 'thing' that progresses in history, he held that it was 'matter', and nothing else. Absolute matter progresses in history through a dialectical process. Instead of 'absolute spirit' becoming self-conscious in human beings, 'absolute matter' becomes conscious in human beings. Human beings are, in fact, absolute matter in development. This means that '*The divine being is nothing else than the human being . . .*' and that '*theology is nothing else than anthropology – the knowledge of God nothing else than a knowledge of man*'. Marx believed that Feuerbach's views were supported by Darwin, who taught that man is the product of purely material evolution. He believed that he [Marx] had now discovered the 'laws' of evolution in society, or history.

3   Dialectical economics

What Marx added to these beliefs was that the key factor in the dialectical advance of nature/man through thesis, antithesis and synthesis, is that man is fundamentally an economic creature, or more specifically, that the essence of human nature is to work, to *produce* so as to live and survive. The whole history of man must be understood from the perspective of this key factor.

4   The division of labour, surplus value, and capitalism

The dialectic progresses in history from one form of human production to another, from primitive communism (before the fall) to slave society, from slavery to feudalism, from feudalism to bourgeois Capitalism, from Capitalism to socialism, and from socialism to the classless society. The dialectic must involve a certain amount of violence, or revolution, as one form of production overcomes the previous one.

The value of a commodity (*e.g.* a chair) is the value of the labour used to make it (to change it from wood to chair). The Capitalist factory owner however, does not pay the labourer what the chair is worth (what it sells for), but far less. The difference between what he pays the labourer and what it is worth is *surplus value*. This the Capitalist robs (exploits) from the labourer and uses to build up more capital (machines, wealth *etc.*) so as to produce more commodities (*i.e.* chairs). This evil state of affairs is only possible because in Capitalist society there is a *division of labour*, *i.e.* the person who makes a commodity is not the same person who therefore sells it. As the Capitalist robs more and more surplus value he has to manufacture more and more commodities to feed his Capitalist monster of production and to do this he pushes the labourers' wages as low as possible and accumulates more and more capital (machines, property *etc.*). This produces a surplus of supply over demand, which leads to unemployment. Eventually society is polarised into fewer and fewer owners of capital (small businesses bought out by bigger ones, and bigger ones *etc.*) and more and more poor, miserable members of the working class (proletariat).

5 Class struggle and colonialism

This polarisation produces two opposing classes in society, the Capitalist bourgeoise (land and business owners), and the working class. The thesis and antithesis which develops will be kept from breaking point by colonialisation, because new lands become markets for the surplus of production and the exploitation process. Colonialisation therefore means exploitation. Rich countries get wealthier and poor countries get poorer. However, eventually even this release will not save the system, and a class struggle must emerge, where the working class have nothing to lose and everything to gain, and the middle class have everything to lose.

6 Revolution

This thesis/antithesis develops to a point of ripeness, where the workers revolt and overthrow the state. All the land, industry, and state corporations are taken over by the workers, who form communes, where decisions are made by the people. This is the *'dictatorship of the proletariat' which should not have to last long. It has to last as long as it takes to root out all vestiges of private ownership and Capitalism.*

7   The classless society

When the process is complete, the antithesis between Capitalism and the dictatorship of the proletariat will eventually produce a new synthesis, the classless society.

Taken from Derek Morphew, *Principalities and Ideologies in South Africa Today* (Tygerpark: Cape Fellowship Ministries, 1986), pp. 36–38.

Notes

Chapter 1

1   Editorial, *Business Day* (Johannesburg), Wednesday 4 June 1986.
2   *Cape Argus* (Cape Town), Friday 6 June 1986.

Chapter 2

1   *Cape Argus* (Cape Town), Monday 9 June 1986.
2   *ibid.*
3   The facts are taken from a pamphlet entitled *Diakonia* (Durban, 1987) and have been endorsed by the following individuals: The Rt Rev. Michael Nuttall (Diocese of Natal), Rev. E Dlamini (Chairman, Natal Regional Council UCCSA), The Rt Rev. P T Mngoma (Roman Catholic Diocese of Marianhill), The Rev. Dr J Borman (Chairman, Natal Coastal District, MCSA), The Rev. S Khumalo (Moderator, Natal and KwaZulu Presbytery of the PCA).
4   *Natal Witness*, Saturday 13 June 1987.
5   *ibid.*
6   *Government Gazette* (Pretoria), Thursday 12 June 1986, p. 2.

Chapter 3

1   'Volk' is the Afrikaans word for a nation, though in Afrikaner minds it takes on almost religious overtones (*cf.* the prewar German idea of the *Herrenvolk*, or chosen nation).
2   John Fisher, *The Afrikaners* (London: Cassell, 1969), p. 6.
3   The Prince of Orange (ruler of the Netherlands) had been driven out of Holland by forces in sympathy with the French Revolution, and fled to Britain. In the Palace of Kew he was induced to sign a paper authorising the British to seize the Cape on his behalf, in order to ensure that it remained royalist rather than Republican, and Dutch rather than French.
    But while the British expedition was still on the high seas the 'Batavian Republic' (as the Netherlands became in 1795) signed a

Treaty of Alliance with the Revolutionary Government of France, then already at war again with Britain. Consequently the British landed not as trustees for an exiled Dutch Prince but as enemies of the French, of the Dutch Republic and also of those Cape Dutch who had become infected with French Republican ideals. The invaders received instructions from London to annex the Cape territory as belligerents and were thus able to occupy it in the name of King George III. So the Afrikaners of today are strictly correct when they talk of 1795 as the year of the first British occupation.

(Fisher, *The Afrikaners*, p. 31)

4   I have lifted this section pretty much *holus-bolus* from my book on the 1973 Congress on Mission and Evangelism, *Prisoners of Hope* (Pietermaritzburg: Africa Enterprise, 1974), pp. 7–9.

5   Eric Pringle, Mark E Pringle and John A Pringle, *Pringles of the Valley*, published by Eric Pringle of Glen Thorn, Adelaide, Cape Province, 1957, p. 26.

6   *ibid.*, pp. 29–30.

7   During the struggle for Dutch independence and union leading to 'The United Dutch Netherlands' (1609), the Dutch Reformed Church was taking shape. Successive synods, some of them held at Dort (Dordrecht) helped to give it form. The synod of 1618–1619 was particularly important in affirming the Calvinist faith which the South African Dutch Reformed Church embraced.

8   Eric Walker, *A History of South Africa* (London: Longman, 1962), p. 197.

9   See note 4 above; the same applies here.

10   Taken from my *Prisoners of Hope*, p. 13.

11   W A de Klerk, *The Puritans in Africa* (Harmondsworth: Penguin Books, 1975), p. 81.

12   Taken from the unpublished Boer War diary of Captain Edward Reading (1900).

13   Thomas Pakenham, *The Boer War* (London: Macdonald & Co., 1982), p. 330.

14   *ibid.*, p. 378.

15   Taken from the privately published diary of Ada (Molly) Craufurd, *A Nurse's Diary in Besieged Mafeking*, p. 245.

16   *ibid.*, p. 290.

17   J Emerson Neilly, *Besieged with Baden Powell* (London: Arthur Pearson Ltd, 1900), pp. 262–263.

18   *Daily Telegraph* date unknown.

19   Ada (Molly) Craufurd, *A Nurse's Diary in Besieged Mafeking*, cited in Ellen Thornycroft-Fowler, *Concerning Isabel Carnaby* (London: Hodder & Stoughton), p. 291.

20   Lilli Hillcourt, *Baden Powell, Two Lives of a Hero* (London: Heinemann, 1964), p. 201.

21   Dee Cassidy, in an interview with the author, April 1987.

22   Deneys Reitz, *Commando: A Boer Journal of the Boer War* (London: Faber & Faber, 1939), p. 296.

23 *ibid.*
24 *ibid.*
25 Taken from the *Westminster Gazette* and quoted in John Fisher, *The Afrikaners*, p. 196.
26 L March Phillipps, *With Rimington* (London: Edward Arnold, 1901), p. 188.
27 *ibid.*, pp. 208–209.
28 Pakenham, *The Boer War*, p. 571.
29 Source unknown.

Chapter 4

1 Michael Cassidy, *Bursting the Wineskins* (London: Hodder & Stoughton, 1983), pp. 195–196.
2 Alan Paton, *Cry the Beloved Country* (London: Jonathan Cape, 1948), p. 262.
3 John Pollock, *The Cambridge Seven* (Basingstoke: Marshall, Morgan & Scott, second edition 1985).
4 Trevor Huddleston, *Naught for Your Comfort* (London: Collins, 1956), p. 25.
5 *ibid.*, p. 36.
6 *ibid.*, p. 60.
7 *ibid.*, p. 78.
8 *ibid.*, p. 232.
9 *ibid.*, pp. 238–239.
10 *ibid.*, p. 247.
11 Alexander Steward, *You are Wrong Father Huddleston* (Cape Town: Culemborg Publishers, 1956), p. 56.
12 *ibid.*, p. 99.
13 *ibid.*, p. 109.
14 *The Times* (London), May 1956 (exact date not known).
15 *Cape Times* (Cape Town), Friday 18 May 1956.

Chapter 5

1 Universalism is the theological view which says that ultimately God will save all people regardless.
2 Clayborne Carson, David J Garrow, Vincent Harding, Darlene Clark Hine, *Eyes on the Prize: America's Civil Rights Years* (New York: Penguin Books, 1987), pp. 68–69.
3 *ibid.*, p. 44.
4 *ibid.*, p. 45.
5 Norman Grubb, *Modern Viking* (Grand Rapids: Zondervan Publishing, 1961), p. 53.
6 *ibid.*, p. 52.
7 *ibid.*, p. 109.

8   Edgar Brookes, *A South African Pilgrimage* (Johannesburg: Ravan Press, 1977), pp. 54–55.
9   Michael Attwell, *South Africa, Background to the Crisis* (London: Sidgwick & Jackson, 1986), p. 99.
10 *ibid*.
11 Albert Luthuli, *Let My People Go* (London: Collins Fontana, 1963), p. 200.

Chapter 6

1   Quoted in David Lamb, *The Africans: Encounters from the Sudan to the Cape* (London: The Bodley Head, 1982), p. 313.
2   Quoted in Richard J Neuhaus, *Dispensations: The Future of South Africa as South Africans see it* (Grand Rapids: Wm B Eerdmans, 1986), p. 63.
3   *ibid*., p. 9.
4   Quoted in Tony Castle (ed.), *The Hodder Book of Christian Quotations* (London: Hodder & Stoughton, 1982), p. 179.
5   *ibid*.
6   Deneys Reitz, *Trekking On* (London: Faber & Faber, 1933), p. 13.
7   *ibid*., p. 59.
8   *ibid*., p. 61.
9   Dee Cassidy, in an interview with the author, April 1987.
10 Reitz, *Trekking On*, p. 85.
11 *The Parys Post and Vredefort Advertiser*, Tuesday 6 February 1917.
12 Sir Frederick Catherwood, *A Better Way* (Leicester: IVP, 1975), p. 94.
13 The text of my paper is reproduced in Carl F H Henry and W Stanley Mooneyham (eds), *One Race, One Gospel, One Task* (Minneapolis: Worldwide Publications, 1967), pp. 313–316.

Chapter 7

1   J D Kestell, *Met de Boeren-Commando's* (Amsterdam, 1903), p. 276, quoted in W A de Klerk, *The Puritans in Africa* (Harmondsworth: Penguin Books, 1975), p. 89.
2   de Klerk, *Puritans in Africa*, p. 91.
3   Andries Treurnicht is leader of the right-wing Conservative Party in the South African Parliament. The Northern Transvaal area in question was in his constituency.
4   David Bosch, 'Afrikaner Civil Religion and the Current South African Crisis', *Transformation* 3/2 (April/June 1986), p. 24.
5   *ibid*., p. 25.
6   de Klerk, *Puritans in Africa*, p. 91.
7   Helen de Waal in *Sunday Times Magazine* (Johannesburg), 11 June 1972.

8   Quoted in Winston Churchill, *My Early Life* (London: Collins Fontana, 1930), pp. 262–263.

9   Quoted in Ivor Wilkins and Hans Strydom, *The Super Afrikaners* (Johannesburg: Jonathan Ball Publishers, 1978), p. 141.

10 *ibid.*, p. 89.

11 *ibid.*, p. 89.

12 *ibid.*, p. 342.

13 *ibid.*, p. 343.

14 Abraham Kuyper, *Calvinism: Six Stone Lectures* (Grand Rapids: Wm B Eerdmans, 1943), p. 81.

15 Bosch, 'Afrikaner Civil Religion and the Current South African Crisis', p. 26.

16 *ibid.*, p. 26.

17 Those considered to be members of 'the coffee party' were: Dr Nico Diederichs, Dr Piet Meyer, Dr H F Verwoerd, Dr Geoff Cronjé, Dr J de W Keyter, Dr Albert Hertzog, Dr T J Hugo.

18 Adapted from Derek Morphew, *Principalities and Ideologies in South Africa Today* (Tygerpark: Cape Fellowship Ministries, 1986), pp. 26–29.

19 Cronjé, *'n Tuiste vir die Nageslag (A Home for Posterity)* (Cape Town, 1945), p. 24, quoted in de Klerk, *Puritans in Africa*, pp. 215–216.

20 Cronjé, *'n Tuiste vir die Nageslag*, pp. 110, 149.

21 *ibid.*, p. 202.

22 *ibid.*, pp. 37, 41.

23 *ibid.*, p. 79.

24 Quoted in Jaap Durant, 'Afrikaner Piety and Descent', in Charles Villa-Vicencio and John de Gruchy (eds), *Resistance and Hope: South African essays in honour of Beyers Naudé* (Grand Rapids: Wm B Eerdmans, 1985), p. 44.

25 Quoted in David Bosch, 'The Fragmentation of Afrikanerdom', in Villa-Vicencio and de Gruchy, *Resistance and Hope*, p. 66.

26 G Cronjé, *Regverdige Rasse-apartheid* (Stellenbosch, 1947), p. 41, quoted in de Klerk, *Puritans in Africa*, p. 220.

Chapter 8

1   Harry Oppenheimer, in an interview with the author, April 1987.

2   Nico Smith, in an interview with the author, April 1987.

3   W A de Klerk, *The Puritans in Africa* (Harmondsworth: Penguin Books, 1975), p. 223.

4   Peter Townsend, *Time and Chance* (London: Collins, 1978), p. 171.

5   *ibid.*, p. 172.

6   *ibid.*, pp. 173–4.

7   *ibid.*, p. 176.

8   Edgar Brookes, *A South African Pilgrimage* (Johannesburg: Ravan Press, 1977), p. 85.

9   *ibid.*, p. 85.

10   Wentzel du Plessis in an interview on Granada Television, 1986.
11   de Klerk, *Puritans in Africa*, p. 250.
12   'Die Filosofiese Grondslag van die Beleid van Afsonderlike Ontwik-keling', *Journal of Racial Affairs* (October 1971), p. 150. See also de Klerk, *Puritans in Africa*, p. 249.
13   'Die Filosofiese Grondslag van die Beleid van Afsonderlike Ontwik-keling', p. 152.
14   *ibid.*, pp. 148–149.
15   *ibid.*, p. 152.
16   de Klerk, *Puritans in Africa*, p. 24.
17   *ibid.*, p. 241.
18   *ibid.*, p. 241.
19   *ibid.*, p. 247.
20   Ivor Wilkins and Hans Strydom, *The Super Afrikaners* (Johannes-burg: Jonathan Ball Publishers, 1978), p. 345.
21   *ibid.*, pp. 345–346.
22   John de Gruchy, *The Church Struggle in South Africa* (Cape Town: David Philip, 1979), p. 63.
23   Leslie A Hewson, *Cottesloe Constitution: The Report of the Consul-tation* (Johannesburg, 1961), p. 74.
24   de Gruchy, *Church Struggle in South Africa*, pp. 66–67.
25   de Klerk, *Puritans in Africa*, p. 254.
26   *ibid.*, p. 255.
27   *ibid.*, p. 267.
28   Nico Smith, in an interview with the author, April 1987.
29   David Bosch, 'Afrikaner Civil Religion and the Current South African Crisis', *Transformation* 3/2 (April/June 1986), p. 29.
30   'Johan Heyns and the NGK Change of Heart', *Leadership* 5/5 (1986), p. 46.

Chapter 9

1   Letter from the author to Dr F Hartzenberg, Minister of Education and Training, 3 December 1980.

Chapter 10

1   Don Foster, *Detention and Torture in South Africa* (Cape Town and Johannesburg: David Philip, 1987), p. iv. Don Foster is Associate Professor in the Department of Psychology, University of Cape Town; the book also contains contributions from Dennis Davis, Associate Professor in the Faculty of Law, and Diane Sandler, who was formerly attached to the Institute of Criminology, University of Cape Town, as a researcher.
2   *ibid.*, p. 1.
3   Report in *Natal Witness*, Saturday 13 February 1988.

4 Foster, *Detention and Torture in South Africa*, p. 29.
5 *ibid.*, pp. 4–5.
6 *ibid.*, p. 5.
7 See the South African Catholic Bishops' Conference report, *The Last Affidavits* (Pretoria, 1987), p. 6.
8 *University of Cape Town News Magazine*, Alumni Edition 14/4 (June 1987), p. 17.
9 Foster, *Detention and Torture in South Africa*, pp. 217–218.
10 Detainees Parents' Support Committee. (The figures quoted include deaths in detention and police custody.)
11 *Sunday Tribune*, 2 November 1986.
12 *Natal Witness*, Thursday 18 September 1986.

Chapter 11

1 Colin Bundy, *The Rise and Fall of the South African Peasantry* (London: Heinemann, 1979), p. 33.
2 *ibid.*, p. 71.
3 Leon Louw and Frances Kendall, *South Africa, The Solution* (Norwood: Amagi Publications, 1987), p. 10. For fuller discussion of this issue see Louw and Kendall, pp. 3–17.
4 *ibid.*, pp. 10–11.
5 *ibid.*, pp. 12–13.
6 *ibid.*, p. 11.
7 *ibid.*, pp. 11–12.
8 *ibid.*, p. 16.
9 John L Comaroff (ed.), *The Boer War Diary of Sol T Plaatje* (Johannesburg: Macmillan, 1973), pp. xix–xx.
10 *ibid.*, pp. xx.
11 South African Catholic Bishops' Conference, *Working Paper on Pastoral Planning* (Pretoria, 1984), p. 21.
12 Cited in Louw and Kendall, *South Africa, The Solution*, p. 39.
13 SA Catholic Bishops' Conference, *Working Paper on Pastoral Planning*, p. 21.
14 *PACSA Fact Sheet* 9 (December 1981).
15 Black Sash Document, July 1963.
16 2.2 million = 1.2 million squatters and 1 million farm workers who face evictions. A further one million people may be affected by so-called 'political removals' which happen when an area or a region is declared part of a homeland, and all its people lose their South African citizenship (*e.g.* the OFS township of Botsabello, with seven hundred thousand people, which is now about to be incorporated in QuaQua homeland).
17 Mr M C Botha, *The Star*, Friday 21 November 1969.
18 Mr G F van L Froneman, MP, in an address to the Institute of Citizenship (CT), Thursday 30 May 1968. Though stated twenty years ago, this remains a Government perception.
19 South African Institute of Race Relations, *Race Relations Survey*,

1984 (Johannesburg, 1985), p. 439. Statement by Dr George Morrison, deputy Minister of Co-operation.

20   *Rand Daily Mail* (Johannesburg), Saturday 22 August 1981.
21   *Race Relations Survey, 1984*, p. 470.
22   *PACSA News Sheet*, August 1982.
23   Desmond Tutu, 'Christianity and Apartheid' in John de Gruchy and Charles Villa-Vicencio (eds), *Apartheid is a Heresy* (Cape Town: David Philip, 1983), p. 45.

Chapter 12

1   John Stott, *Issues Facing Christians Today* (Basingstoke: Marshall, Morgan & Scott, 1984), pp. 143–144.
2   R C Sproul, *In Search of Dignity* (Ventura, California: Regal Books, 1983), pp. 98–99.
3   Stephen Charles Mott, *Biblical Ethics and Social Change* (Oxford: Oxford University Press, 1982), p. 52.
4   René Cassin, 'From the Ten Commandments to the Rights of Man' in *Of Law and Man: Essays in Honour of Haim H Cohn* (New York and Tel Aviv: Sabra Books, 1971), pp. 13–25.
5   Mott, *Biblical Ethics and Social Change*, p. 52.
6   Quoted in Eric Walker, *A History of South Africa* (London: Longman, 1962), p. 677.
7   Letter to the author, June 1987.
8   Quoted in Lebamang J Sebidi, 'Towards an Understanding of the Current Unrest in South Africa', in B Tlhagale and I Mosala (eds), *Hammering Swords into Ploughshares: Essays in Honour of Archbishop Mpilo Desmond Tutu* (Braamfontain: Skotaville Publishers, 1986), p. 254.
9   Stott, *Issues Facing Christians Today*, p. 147.
10   Ernest Marshall Howse, *Saints in Politics: The 'Clapham Sect' and the growth of freedom* (London: George Allen & Unwin, 1953), p. 7.
11   Letter to the author, Wednesday 29 July 1987.
12   Simon Maimela, 'An Anthropological Heresy' in Tlhagale and Mosala, *Hammering Swords into Ploughshares*, p. 55.
13   Prof. George Ayittey, 'Why Single out South Africa?', *Wall Street Journal*, reprinted in *The Times* (London), Thursday 1 August 1985.
14   *ibid.*
15   Mott, *Biblical Ethics and Social Change*, p. 14.
16   Letter from the author to Dr Piet Koornhof, 24 June 1980.
17   Coretta Scott King (ed.), *Words of Martin Luther King* (London: Collins Fount, 1985), p. 42.

Chapter 13

1   Michael Cassidy, *Prisoners of Hope* (Pietermaritzburg: Africa Enterprise, 1974).

2 *ibid.*, p. 60.
3 Michael Cassidy (ed.), *I Will Heal Their Land* (Maseru, Lesotho: Africa Enterprise, 1974), p. 269.
4 Beyers Naudé, quoted in *ibid.*, p. 278.
5 For what follows, I am much indebted to a series of lectures delivered in Australia in 1986 by John Walsh, and to insights from his book *Evangelization and Justice* (Maryknoll, NY: Orbis Books, 1984).

Chapter 14

1 Jim Wallis, *Call to Conversion* (Tring: Lion Publishing, 1981), p. 127.
2 Edgar Brookes, 'Evangelism and Civic Affairs' in Michael Cassidy (ed.), *I Will Heal Their Land* (Maseru, Lesotho: Africa Enterprise, 1974), p. 174.
3 Michael Cassidy, *Prisoners of Hope* (Pietermaritzburg: Africa Enterprise, 1974), p. 116.
4 Wallis, *Call to Conversion*, pp. 6–7.
5 *ibid.*, p. 9.
6 David O Moberg, *The Great Reversal* (Philadelphia and New York: J Lippincott Co., 1972), p. 28.
7 *ibid.*
8 Carl F H Henry, 'Evangelicals in the Social Struggle' in Donald E Hanstock (ed.), *Contemporary Religious Issues* (Belmont, CA: Wadsworth Publishing Co., 1968), pp. 284–299.
9 Moberg, *Great Reversal*, p. 36.
10 The Concerned Evangelicals, *Evangelical Witness in South Africa* (Dobsonville, 1986), p. 35.
11 William Barclay, *The Gospel of Matthew*, Daily Study Bible (Edinburgh: St Andrew Press, 1968), p. 212.
12 Alfred Edersheim, *The Life and Times of Jesus the Messiah* (New York: E R Herrick & Co., 1884), vol. 1, p. 270.

Chapter 15

1 A paper entitled 'The Ministry of Reconciliation', which was read at the South African Renewal Conference, Milner Park, Wednesday 2 January 1980, by Justus Du Plessis.
2 Roy Hession, *Calvary Road* (London: Christian Literature Crusade, 1950), p. 22.
3 *ibid.*, p. 23.
4 *ibid.* p. 22.
5 Michael Cassidy, *Together in One Place* (Kisumu: Evangel Press, 1978), p. 51.
6 *ibid.*, p. 119.
7 *ibid.*, p. 46.

8   *ibid.*, p. 47.
9   *ibid.*, p. 129.
10 *ibid.*
11 *ibid.*, p. 132.
12 Coretta Scott King (ed.), *The Words of Martin Luther King* (London: Collins Fount, 1985), p. 23.
13 Sister Margaret Magdalen, CSMV, *Jesus Man of Prayer* (London: Hodder & Stoughton, 1987), pp. 132–133.
14 *ibid.*, p. 133.
15 *ibid.*, p. 134.
16 Andrew Elphinstone, *Freedom, Suffering and Love* (London: SCM Press, 1976), pp. 137–138.
17 Magdalen, *Jesus Man of Prayer*, p. 140.
18 Reprinted in David Bosch, 'Reconciliation – An Afrikaner Speaks', *Leadership* 4/4 (1985), p. 62.
19 *ibid.*
20 *ibid.*
21 Bonganjalo Goba, paper produced for NIR National Strategy and Theology Group, 1985.
22 Klaus Nurnberger, paper produced for NIR National Strategy and Theology Group, 1985.
23 *ibid.*

Chapter 16

1   Elton Trueblood, *Abraham Lincoln, Theologian of American Anguish* (New York and London: Harper & Row, 1973), p. 86.
2   *ibid.*, p. 88.
3   *ibid.*, p. 89.
4   Carl F Ellis, Jr, *Beyond Liberation, The Gospel in the Black American Experience* (Downers Grove: IVP, 1983), p. 29.
5   *ibid.*, pp. 174–175.
6   Letter from Derek Crumpton to the author, Wednesday 29 July 1987.
7   Michael Green, *I Believe in Satan's Downfall* (London: Hodder & Stoughton, 1981), p. 84. Green (p. 85) says:
    the use of these terms [principalities and powers, *etc.*] to refer to both human and spiritual rulers is exegetically demonstrable. For example: Luke 12:11 clearly refers to man when it says, 'When they bring you before the synagogues and the rulers and authorities'. Acts 4:26 equally obviously indicates men, 'The kings of the earth set themselves in array and the rulers were gathered together, against the Lord and against his anointed'. On the other hand, it is perfectly manifest that the powers and thrones and authorities in Col. 1:16, 2:15, Rom. 8:38, Eph. 6:12 are superhuman powers. There are some passages which could be taken either way, notably 1 Cor. 2:8, Titus 3:1, Romans 13:1. Probably the ambiguity is deliberate.

8 Richard J Foster, *Money, Sex & Power* (London: Hodder &
   Stoughton, 1985), p. 181. See also Walter Wink's comments on
   Colossians 1:16, in his *Naming the Powers* (Basingstoke: Marshall,
   Morgan & Scott, 1988), vol. 1, p. 11:

   These Powers are both heavenly and earthly, divine and human,
   spiritual and political, invisible and structural. The clearest statement of this is Col. 1:16, which should have been made the standard
   for all discussions of the Powers: 'For in him [the Son] all things were
   created, in heaven and on earth, visible and invisible, whether
   thrones (*thronoi*) or dominions (*kyriotetes*) or principalities (*archai*)
   or authorities (*exousiai*) – all things were created through him and
   for him.' The parallelism of the Greek, ably rendered here by the
   RSV, indicates that these Powers are themselves both earthly *and*
   heavenly, visible *and* invisible. We should expect them to include
   human agents, social structures and systems, and also divine powers. The reiteration of 'whether on earth or in heaven' in v. 20
   connects back to v. 16 and suggests that the cosmic reconciliation
   which God is bringing about through Christ will specifically include
   these powers, human and divine, and that no reconciliation would
   be complete without them.

9 Foster, *Money, Sex & Power*, p. 182.
10 J Edwin Orr, quoted in Winkie Pratney, *Revival* (Springdale, PA:
   Whitaker House, 1983), p. 17.
11 Orr, *Eager Feet*, p. viii.
12 James Burns, *Revivals, Their Laws and Leaders* (Grand Rapids:
   Baker Book House, 1960), p. 67.
13 *ibid.*, p. 34.
14 *ibid.*, p. 35.
15 *ibid.*, p. 36.
16 Francis Schaeffer, source unknown.
17 John Stott, *Issues Facing Christians Today* (Basingstoke: Marshall,
   Morgan & Scott, 1984), p. 5.
18 Garth Lean, *John Wesley, Anglican* (London: Blandford Press, 1964),
   p. 110.
19 Ernest Marshall Howse, *Saints in Politics: The 'Clapham Sect' and the
   growth of freedom* (London: George Allen & Unwin, 1953), p. 7.

Chapter 17

1 *Challenge to the Church, The Kairos Document* (Braamfontein: The
   Kairos Theologians, 1985), p. 1.
2 E K Mosothoane, 'The Message of the New Testament Seen in African
   Perspective' in H J Becken (ed.), *Relevant Theology for Africa* (Durban: Lutheran Publishing House, 1973), p. 67.
3 John Stott, *Issues Facing Christians Today* (Basingstoke: Marshall,
   Morgan & Scott, 1984), pp. 10–11.
4 Ernest Baartman, 'The Significance of the Development of Black

Consciousness for the Church', *Journal of Theology for Southern Africa* 2 (March 1973), pp. 18–19.

5   Steve Biko, *I Write What I Like* (London: Heinemann, 1978), p. 49.

6   J W C Wand, *The Four Great Heresies* (London: Mowbray, 1955). See also G C Berkouwer, *The Church* (Grand Rapids: Wm B Eerdmans, 1976), p. 377.

7   Wand, *Four Great Heresies*, p. 16.

8   *ibid.*, p. 383.

9   Klaus Nurnberger, *Capitalism, Socialism and Marxism* (Mapumulo: Lutheran Publishing House, 1979), p. 5.

10 *ibid.*, p. 5.

11 *ibid.*, pp. 5–6.

12 *ibid.*, p. 6.

13 *ibid.*, pp. 6–7.

14 K Nurnberger, 'How Does the Church Address the Structure-Related Convictions of its Members?' *Journal of Theology for Southern Africa* 53 (1985), p. 29.

15 Alan Boesak, 'Liberation Theology in South Africa', in K Appicah-Kubi and S Torres (eds), *African Theology en Route* (Maryknoll, NY: Orbis Books, 1979), p. 173.

16 E K Mosothoane, 'The Use of Scripture in Black Theology' in W S Vorster (ed.), *Scripture and the Use of Scripture* (Pretoria: University of South Africa, 1979), p. 32.

Chapter 18

1   David Bosch, 'Church, State and Power', an unpublished paper read at the Rhodesian Christian Leaders' Consultation, Salisbury, Wednesday 23 November 1977, p. 4.

2   Carel F A Borchardt, 'Die Afrikaner Kerke en die Rebellie', in I Eybers, A Konig and C Borchardt (eds), *Teologie en Vernuwing* (Pretoria: University of South Africa, 1975), p. 113.

3   'Handelingen van eene Buitengewone vergardering van den Raad van der Ned. Geref. Kerken', 27 January 1915.

4   *ibid.*

5   Bosch, 'Church, State and Power', p. 4.

6   *ibid.*, p. 5.

7   R V G Tasker, *The Gospel According to St Matthew*, Tyndale New Testament Commentaries (London: Tyndale Press, 1961), p. 210.

8   Peter Hinchcliff, *Holiness and Politics* (London: Darton, Longman & Todd, 1982), p. 4.

9   *ibid.*

10 Quoted in John Eidsmoe, *God and Caesar: Christian Faith and Political Action* (Westchester, Il: Crossway Books, 1984), p. 12.

11 Francis Schaeffer, *A Christian Manifesto* (Westchester, Il: Crossway Books, 1981), p. 90.

12 *The Bible and Socio-Political Action* (Pietermaritzburg: The Evangelical Fellowship of South Africa, 1988), clauses 4 and 5.
13 *ibid.*, clause 8.
14 Alan Paton, *Apartheid and the Archbishop: The Life and Times of Geoffrey Clayton* (Cape Town: David Philip, 1973), pp. 279–280.
15 Gene Sharp, *Power and Struggle, The Politics of Non Violent Action* (Boston: Porter Sargent Publishers, 1973), pp. 12–13.
16 Quoted in Bob Clarke, *Church and State*, unpublished PhD thesis, University of Natal, Pietermaritzburg, 1983, p. 390.
17 John Knox, *Works* (New York: AMS Press, 1968), vol. 6, pp. 236–238.
18 Schaeffer, *A Christian Manifesto*, pp. 99–100.
19 *ibid.*, p. 66.
20 *ibid.*, p. 93.
21 *ibid.*, p. 130.
22 Coretta Scott King (ed.), *The Words of Martin Luther King* (London: Collins Fount, 1985), p. 42.
23 *Evangelicals and Socio-Political Action, A Biblical Understanding*, clause 11.
24 King (ed.), *Words of Martin Luther King*, p. 73.
25 Rene Padilla, 'Revolution and Revelation' in Brian Griffiths (ed.), *Is Revolution Change?* (Leicester: IVP, 1972), p. 75.
26 *ibid.*, pp. 75–76.
27 Walter Wink, *Jesus' Third Way* (Philadelphia: New Society Publishers, 1987), p. 21.

Chapter 19

1   Richard J Neuhaus, *Dispensations: The Future of South Africa as South Africans see it* (Grand Rapids: Wm B Eerdmans, 1986), p. xi.
2   Coretta Scott King (ed.), *The Words of Martin Luther King* (London: Collins Fount, 1985), p. 90.
3   John Woolman, *The Journals and Essays of John Woolman* (New York: Macmillan, 1922), p. 167.
4   Dr Vincent Harding in interview with the author, March 1987.
5   David Lamb, *The Africans: Encounters from the Sudan to the Cape* (London: The Bodley Head, 1982), p. xv.
6   Source unknown.
7   Es'kia Mpahlele, 'Dark Gods and Hope' in *Leadership*, 'The High Road' issue (1987), p. 7.
8   Clem Sunter, *The World and South Africa in the 1990s* (Cape Town: Human & Rousseau, 1987). See also Paul Bell, 'Win or Lose' in *Leadership*, 'The High Road' issue (April 1988), p. 4.
9   Sampie Terreblanche, *Sunday Times*, 22 November 1987.
10 Sunter, *Leadership* 6/3 (1987), p. 38.
11 The following statement on the origin of the dialectic comes from the

pen of a seminary friend, David Benson, who has given his life to getting the Christian gospel into Russia. David V Benson, *Christianity, Communism and Survival* (Glendale, Ca.: Regal Books, 1967), pp. 47–49:

What does this word, so much used by the communists, *dialectic*, mean?

Its origin goes back to classical Greece. In the *Dialogues* of Plato we find discussions between philosophers, primarily those of Socrates and his opponents. Socrates was seeking truth, and his method of investigation was to debate with those of opposing views until, in the course of discussing conflicting ideas, some conclusion could be reached. Thus he would challenge one idea (thesis) with an opposing idea (antithesis) until a conclusion would be evolved (synthesis). This method of conversation and debate was called the dialectic method. In the course of the development of philosophy the art of dialectical debate grew in importance, especially in the study of logic. But it is important for us to remember its original idea: one idea, challenged by another, issuing into a third.

The famous German philosopher Hegel (died 1831) was much attracted to this dialectical process. As German philosophers are wont to do, he made a mountain out of a molehill. The dialectical method is more than a mere procedure for debate or logic; it is indeed the way the whole universe works. Hegel was a pantheist (all is God) in that he made no distinction between God (the Universal Mind) and the universe. God's Spirit, he said, is the thinking process of the universe. History is therefore but the unfolding of God's mind. All that is and happens is the outworking of God's thoughts, a reflection of his will. This theory was called idealism because it made Idea (God) the essence of all that is.

And how does God think? That is, how does the Universal Spirit operate in history? Of course through the dialectical method: idea (thesis), conflicting idea (antithesis), resolution of the conflict (synthesis). And the synthesis of the old conflict becomes the basic idea (thesis) for a new conflict, and the process starts all over again.

We see three basic ideas in Hegel's philosophy: (1) All that is, is God, or 'Absolute Spirit'. (2) This Spirit is the action of history developing, or evolving, to a higher order. (3) This developing process moves through the pattern of the dialectic (thesis, antithesis and synthesis), and is thus characterised by conflict.

The reader will already see many ideas in Hegel similar to what we have discovered in communism: history moving towards higher stages by conflict, the evolutionary process in history, opposition of ideas or movements (revolution) resulting in a higher order (synthesis, communism).

Derek Morphew gives a more technical explanation of the dialectic in his very helpful little book, *Principalities and Ideologies in South Africa Today* (Tygerpark: Cape Fellowship Ministries, 1986), pp. 36–38, which is reproduced in Appendix 8 at the end of this book.

12 Philip le Feuvre in interview with the author, Monday 7 December 1987.

13 *Isvestia*, Wednesday 24 April 1929, quoted in Paul Miliukov, 'Religion and the Church in Russia', p. 198 and in Anonymous, *Notebook for an Agitator* (1959), pp. 5–13 and Benson, *Christianity, Communism and Survival*, p. 13.

14 Quoted in Fred Schwartz, *Why I am Against Communism* (Long Beach, Ca.: Christian Anti-Communism Crusade, n.d.), p. 9.

15 *Time*, Monday 21 February 1977, p. 13.

16 Schwarz, *Why I am Against Communism*, p. 20.

17 Joseph P Ton, 'The Failure of Marxism', *Eternity* (November 1987), pp. 14–15.

18 Fred Schwarz, in a letter to the author, 1987.

19 Two such educational projects come to mind.
   First, the proposed chain of new multiracial schools initiated by Richard Todd and operating under the name of Leadership Education and Advancement Foundation. (Address: Box 534, Cape Town, 8 000 South Africa.) The first three of these are in place and others are on the drawing board.
   Second, the NEST (New Era Schools Trust) schools, launched by Mr Deane Yates. (Address: 60 Killarney Mall, Killarney 2193 South Africa.)
   These educational projects need huge funding, and if they receive it they could be destined to play a great part in paving the way for the future.

20 John Kane-Burman, quoted in *Natal Witness*, Tuesday 10 November 1987.

21 David Porteous, 'Towards a Christian Approach to Sanctions Against South Africa' (unpublished paper, November 1987), p. 7.

Chapter 20

1 Coretta Scott King (ed.), *The Words of Martin Luther King* (London: Collins Fount, 1985), p. 51.

2 Johan Heyns, 'Change of Heart', *Leadership* 5/5 (1986), p. 46.

3 Thomas Merton, 'The Root of War is Fear', from *New Seeds of Contemplation* (Norfolk, CO: New Directions, 1961), p. 113.

4 Edgar Brookes, *Power, Law, Right and Love* (Durham, NC: Duke University Press, 1963), pp. 78–79.

5 *ibid.*, p. 79.

6 Emily Hobhouse. The full text occurs in a document in my grandmother's possession; partial reference is made to it in John Fisher, *The Afrikaners* (London: Cassell, 1969), p. 197.

7 Alan Torrance, 'Forgiveness? The essential Socio-political Structure of Personal Being', *Journal of Theology for Southern Africa* 56 (September 1986), p. 47.

8 David Atkinson, *Peace in Our Time?* (Leicester: IVP, 1985), p. 167,

quoted in John Stott, *The Cross of Christ* (Leicester: IVP, 1986), p. 310.

9   King (ed.), *Words of Martin Luther King*, p. 23.
10   John Pollock, *Wilberforce* (Tring: Lion Publishing 1977), p. 66.
11   Ernest Marshall Howse, *Saints in Politics: The 'Clapham Sect' and the growth of freedom* (London: George Allen & Unwin, 1953), p. 7.
12   John Pollock, *Shaftesbury, The Poor Man's Earl* (London: Hodder & Stoughton, 1986), p. 62.
13   Brookes, *Power, Law, Right and Love*, p. 14.
14   *ibid.*, p. 80.
15   Jim Punton, 'Shalom', in Robin Keeley (ed.), *The Lion Handbook of Christian Belief* (Tring: Lion Publishing 1982), p. 314.
16   Stephen Charles Mott, *Biblical Ethics and Social Change* (Oxford: Oxford University Press, 1982), p. 51.
17   *ibid.*, p. 67.
18   US edition of Michael Cassidy, *Bursting the Wineskins* (Wheaton, IL: Harold Shaw, 1983), pp. 198–199. See Reinhold Niebuhr, *An Interpretation of Christian Ethics* (New York: Meridian Books, 1956), chs 4 and 5.

Chapter 21

1   Klaus Nurnberger, 'Costly Reconciliation', an unpublished message to the clergy of Port Elizabeth, Thursday 19 June 1986, p. 4.
2   Winston Churchill, *If I Had My Life Over Again*, comp. and ed. Jack Fishman (London: W H Allen, 1974), p. 169.
3   *ibid.*, p. 172.
4   Laurie Ackermann, 'New Benchmarks', *Leadership* 6/6 (1987), p. 77.
5   'The Ark of America', *Time*, 6 July 1987, p. 49.
6   J Philip Wogaman, *The Great Economic Debate* (Philadelphia: Westminster Press, 1977), p. 155, and pp. 51–53.
7   Hugh Murray, 'A Leap of Faith', *Leadership*, 'The High Road' issue (November 1987), p. 3.
8   Anton Rupert in interview with Hugh Murray, *Leadership* 5/4 (1986), p. 12.
9   James Leatt, *Leadership*, 'The High Road' issue (November 1987), p. 44.
10   Sir Frederick Catherwood, *A Better Way* (Leicester: IVP, 1975), p. 24.
11   Edward J Perkins, 'In Your Hands', *Leadership* 6/5 (1987), p. 55.
12   Coretta Scott King (ed.), *The Words of Martin Luther King* (London: Collins Fount, 1985), p. 59.
13   Source unknown.
14   From W B Yeats, 'He Wishes for the Cloths of Heaven'.

Chapter 22

1 F R Barry, *Christian Ethics, Secular Society* (London: Hodder & Stoughton, 1966), pp. 278–279.
2 C S Lewis, *God in the Dock* (Grand Rapids: Wm B Eerdmans, 1970), p. 150.
3 William Wordsworth, 'Intimations of Immortality'.
4 Giles Fletcher, *Christ's Victory and Triumph*.

Appendix 3

1 See also Francis Schaeffer, *Pollution and the Death of Man: The Christian View of Ecology* (Wheaton: Tyndale Press, 1970), reprinted in his *Complete Works: A Christian Worldview* (Westchester, Il.: Crossway Books, 1982), vol. 5, pp. 1–76, and John Stott, 'Our Human Environment', chapter 6 of his *Issues Facing Christians Today* (Basingstoke: Marshall, Morgan & Scott, 1984), pp. 109–121.

Appendix 7

1 Emilio Antonio Núñez C., an evangelical leader in El Salvador, comments in his book *Liberation Theology*, tr. P E Sywulka (Chicago: Moody Press, 1985), pp. 236–237, on the way both Roman Catholics and evangelicals have removed Christ from everyday life and issues:

In a sense, this new emphasis on the humanity of Christ is a reaction to the lack of balance in a Christology that magnifies the deity of the Word incarnate at the expense of His humanity. Many of us Latin American evangelicals are the heirs of an Anglo-Saxon Christology formulated in answer to Protestant liberalism, which questioned or openly denied the deity of Jesus Christ. Thus what was emphasised in evangelical conservative Christology was necessarily the deity of the Logos, without denying His humanity. We were presented with a divine-human Christ in the theological formula; but in practice He was far removed from the stage of this world, aloof to our social problems.

For Roman Catholics, He was the Christ nailed to the cross or shut up in His funerary casket; He was the Christ exalted to glory on the altars, but silent and immobile before the painful drama of injustice that millions of Latin Americans were living. He was not the man Christ, powerful in word and deed, who identified Himself fully with the people, who experienced their anguish and heartaches as one of them, among them and on their behalf, announcing the kingdom of God and its liberating power.

The Christ proclaimed to many of us evangelical Christians gave the impression of being confined to the heavenly heights, from which He dealt with each of us as individuals, preparing us for our journey to glory and promising us that He would come back to the world to solve all the problems of humanity. For the present He had nothing to say about social problems; nor should we become interested in them, because our mission was only to rescue the greatest possible number of souls from the sinking boat of the world. That may seem like a caricature, but it is not. At least it is the way in which many of us who came to the evangelical church in the years of the Second World War perceived Christ. Unfortunately, even today there are those who claim that we should continue to perceive Him that way. A great number of evangelical Christians hold to a Christ who remained immobile and silent before the painful social panorama of Latin America.

Sociologically speaking, the great difference between the evangelical Christ and the Christ of popular Catholic religiosity was that the former was seen resurrected and exalted at the right hand of the Father in the heavenly heights, not nailed to the cross or shut up, lying still, in a crystal casket. But He was still far removed from social conflicts. He was the Christ whom His followers guarded diligently so that He might not be identified with liberal preachers such as Harry Emerson Fosdick or with Walter Rauschenbusch, champion of 'the social gospel'. The purpose was noble and the effort was necessary in a time of great doctrinal controversies; but at some point the balance was lost, and in practice, evangelical Christology has run the risk of becoming docetic.

2   *ibid.*, p. 151.
3   See C. Rene Padilla, 'Liberation Theology', in L Verlinden and M̄. Cassidy (eds), *Facing the New Challenges* (Kisumu: Evangel Publishing House, 1978), pp. 425–431.
4   Derek Morphew, *Principalities and Ideologies in South Africa Today* (Tygerpark: Cape Fellowship Ministries, 1986), p. 100.
5   *ibid.*